Where To Begin

**Be Equipped To Share The Gospel
With People From 50 Other Religions And
Answer 53 Of The Toughest Questions**

Howard Goldthwaite
Author of *Quiet Time Well Spent* and *Great Excuses of the Bible*

ISBN 978-0615609874

Dedicated to believers everywhere
who care enough about other people to share
the good news of God's salvation.

———— ⚬ ————

What This Book Is For

People come to God through Christ, and they tend to come to Christ through Christians. If you're a Christian today, it's because people just like you throughout the centuries have been faithful in sharing their faith. Telling others about Christ is one of the most exciting things you can do, and it almost always takes you out of your comfort zone. But that's good, because when we're comfortable we tend to trust in ourselves instead of trusting in God.

When it comes to sharing your faith, it's all about connecting with people. Paul admonished us in Colossians 4:6, "Let your speech always be with grace, seasoned as it were with salt, so that you may know how to respond to each person." This book will help equip you to respond to – and connect with – people with many different backgrounds, belief systems, and questions.

When Paul was in Athens, he was walking among the temples and noticed an altar dedicated to "an unknown God." He used this altar, which was familiar to the Athenians, as a unique connecting point and springboard to proclaim the gospel to them. He also quoted one of their local poets during his message. This book does much the same thing by helping you start at a point which is familiar to the person being shared with, and then from that starting point focusing on how the gospel relates specifically to that person's way of thinking, values, and pre-existing belief system.

There is usually a small amount of truth mingled in with every false religion; just enough truth to make people accept what is false. But at the foundation of every false religion there is a lie. If a person cannot see through that lie and believes that lie to be true, then it makes the Christian faith appear to be based on a lie. This book does not address every single unbiblical doctrine of those you will share with, nor does it provide an exhaustive explanation of every false religion. It focuses on the areas most critical to seeing that person come to Christ.

On the other hand, many of the people we meet aren't hindered by years of misguided teachings, and may have no religious background or affiliation whatsoever; they simply have honest questions. Scripture has answers for many of those tough questions, but it's not easy to remember where to find all those verses in the middle of a lively discussion, or to present them in a logical progression.

This book relies on quotes from God's Word to provide the answers because it just makes sense to let God speak for Himself. And it's always good for unbelievers to hear how much wisdom and insight the Bible has to offer. Hebrews 4:12 tells us, "The Word of God is living and active, and sharper than any two edged sword." We can also envision God's Word as being His sacred scalpel that He uses to heal our spiritual wounds. Even though someone may not quickly respond when you present these truths, the process of spiritual surgery by God's Word has begun. Sometimes a blade can be so sharp we never even feel it cut.

You will find this book contains three sections. Section One is designed to reach people who are already followers of specific religions or philosophies. Section Two provides answers to people whose beliefs are less firm, but who are seeking the truth about specific issues or questions regarding the Christian faith. You'll quickly notice that the presentations in these first two sections each lead to focusing on Christ and how to become a believer. Section Three is simply a topical file of Scriptures commonly used when sharing the faith.

Trust in God – not in your wisdom or in this book – to change the hearts of those with whom you share. Be sure to always pray for the person you are sharing with, and pray for yourself that God will speak through you. You can do the talking, but rely on the Holy Spirit to do the convincing.

Never underestimate the importance of forming caring relationships that pave the way for sharing the gospel to bring others to Christ. As you invest in the time to get to know a person, you'll have a better understanding of their needs, and you'll be sensitive to the best time to share the gospel as a way to demonstrate your love. The best way to earn the right to be heard is to first be a sincere listener. A well-prepared gospel presentation is never a substitute for loving someone. As the saying goes, people don't care how much you know until they know how much you care.

This book has been written and designed so you can "always be ready to make a defense to everyone who asks you to give an account for the hope that is in you, yet with gentleness and reverence." (1 Peter 3:15) Ideally, the presentations and answers in this book are intended to be read out loud and discussed with the unbeliever. Obviously, this is not the only way they can be used, and won't fit every situation or person. So feel free to use them in the way that best fits your style, personality, or situation. You might even loan them the book, then set a definite time to get back together to discuss their views. This book may not offer all the answers, but it offers THE answer: Jesus Christ. And once we have THE answer, He gives us the patience to wait until we have answers to all our other questions.

As you share these truths with unbelievers, you're likely to encounter the same three types of responses Paul received when he finished his message to the Athenians in Acts 17: "Some began to sneer, but others said, 'We shall hear you again concerning this.' But some men joined him and believed."

Of course, sharing your faith is also a type of spiritual warfare against evil, unseen forces. So you can also expect some opposition from Satan. After all, you'll never meet the devil head on if you're going the same way as him. Remember that unsaved people have been held captive by the snare of sin and false beliefs. And like an animal caught in a snare that tries to bite the person setting it free, a person may lash out at you even though you're sincerely trying to help. The decision to turn to Christ can often be a slow and difficult process, so trust in God's strength to be patient, bold, and faithful to say what needs to be said; and always say it in love.

"For as the rain and the snow come down from heaven, and do not return there without watering the earth, and making it bear and sprout, and furnishing seed to the sower and bread to the eater; so shall My word be which goes forth from My mouth; it shall not return to Me empty, without accomplishing what I desire, and without succeeding in the matter for which I sent it." *Isaiah 55:10,11*

"And the Lord's bondservant must not be quarrelsome, but be kind to all, able to teach, patient when wronged, with gentleness correcting those who are in opposition, if perhaps God may grant them repentance leading to the knowledge of the truth, and they may come to their senses and escape from the snare of the devil, having been held captive by him to do his will." *2 Timothy 2:24-26*

"My brethren, if any among you strays from the truth, and one turns him back, let him know that he who turns a sinner from the error of his way will save his soul from death, and will cover a multitude of sins." *James 5:19,20*

"Finally, be strong in the Lord and in the strength of His might. Put on the full armor of God, so that you will be able to stand firm against the schemes of the devil. For our struggle is not against flesh and blood, but against the rulers, against the powers, against the world forces of this darkness, against the spiritual forces of wickedness in the heavenly places. Therefore, take up the full armor of God, so that you will be able to resist in the evil day, and having done everything, to stand firm. Stand firm therefore, having girded your loins with truth, and having put on the breastplate of righteousness, and having shod your feet with the preparation of the gospel of peace; in addition to all, taking up the shield of faith with which you will be able to extinguish all the flaming arrows of the evil one. And take the helmet of salvation, and the sword of the Spirit, which is the word of God. With all prayer and petition pray at all times in the Spirit, and with this in view, be on the alert with all perseverance and petition for all the saints." *Ephesians 6:10-18*

"Be on the alert, stand firm in the faith, act like men, be strong. Let all that you do be done in love." *1 Corinthians 16:13,14*

"Go therefore and make disciples of all the nations, baptizing them in the name of the Father and the Son and the Holy Spirit, teaching them to observe all that I commanded you; and lo, I am with you always, even to the end of the age." *Matthew 28:19,20*

Table of Contents

Section One

How is Christianity Unique From Other Faiths And Philosophies?

Table of Contents

Section Two

Biblical Answers to Tough Questions

Table of Contents

Section Two Continued

Section Three

Topical Scripture File

Section One

⌘

How is Christianity Unique from Other Faiths and Philosophies?

1 Agnosticism

Some agnostics feel that God might exist and that He might be knowable. Other agnostics believe it is impossible to know whether God exists or is knowable.

But regardless of what type of agnostic you are, the Bible teaches that God certainly does exist, and we can know God on a very personal basis. The Bible also teaches that God loves us and wants us to know Him.

1. How can we believe in the existence of a God we can't see or touch? The Bible starts off by telling us that everything we can see or touch has been created by God. The most indisputable evidence that God exists is that His creation exists. How many things have you ever seen spring into existence out of nothing?

"In the beginning, God created the heavens and the earth." *Genesis 1:1*

"The heavens are telling of the glory of God; and the firmament is declaring the work of His hands. Day to day pours forth speech, and night to night reveals knowledge... Their line has gone out through all the earth, and their utterances to the end of the world." *Psalm 19:1,2,4*

"For since the creation of the world His invisible attributes, His eternal power and divine nature, have been clearly seen, being understood through what has been made, so that they are without excuse." *Romans 1:20*

2. God is also knowable. He has promised in the Bible that if we sincerely seek Him, He will let us find Him.

"The God who made the world and all things in it made from one, every nation of mankind to live on all the face of the earth... that they should seek God, if perhaps they might grope for Him and find Him, though He is not far from each one of us." *Acts 17: 24,26,27*

"And you will seek Me and find Me, when you search for Me with all your heart." *Jeremiah 29:13*

"If you seek Him, He will let you find Him; but if you forsake Him, He will reject you forever." *1 Chronicles 28:9*

3. God is also seeking those who truly want to know Him.

"Draw near to God and He will draw near to you." *James 4:8*

"For the eyes of the Lord move to and fro throughout the earth that He may strongly support those whose heart is completely His." *2 Chronicles 16:9*

"True worshipers shall worship the Father in spirit and truth; for such people the Father seeks to be His worshipers." *John 4:23*

4. If it feels like mankind is separated from God, that's because we are. We are separated from God because He is holy and we are sinful.

"But your iniquities have made a separation between you and your God, and your sins have hid His face from you, so that He does not hear." *Isaiah 59:2*

"For all have sinned and fall short of the glory of God." *Romans 3:23*

5. God sent His Son Jesus to earth. By learning from Jesus, we can learn about the Father.

"And He (Jesus) is the image of the invisible of God..." *Colossians 1:15*

"God... has spoken to us in His Son, whom He appointed heir of all things, through whom also He made the world. And He is the radiance of His glory and the exact representation of His nature, and upholds all things by the word of His power. When He had made purification of sins, He sat down at the right hand of the Majesty on high." *Hebrews 1:1-3*

Jesus said: "He who has seen Me has seen the Father." *John 14:9*

6. Jesus not only taught us about God, He gave His life so that we can be forgiven and made holy. We are given the same level of holiness as Jesus so we can be reconciled with God who is holy.

"For God so loved the world that He gave His only begotten Son, that whoever believes in Him shall not perish but have everlasting life." *John 3:16*

"But God demonstrates His own love for us in that while we were yet sinners, Christ died for us." *Romans 5:8*

"Though your sins are as scarlet, they shall be white as snow." *Isaiah 64:6*

7. Because Jesus was fully God and fully man, He is uniquely qualified to give us access to God. He gave His life to take the penalty for all the sins of mankind.

"Jesus said to him, 'I am the way, and the truth, and the life; no one comes to the Father, but through Me.'" *John 14:6*

"For there is salvation in no one else; for there is no other name under heaven that has been given among men, by which we must be saved." *Acts 4:12*

"For there is one God, and one mediator also between God and men, the man Christ Jesus, who gave Himself as a ransom for all." *1 Timothy 2:5,6a*

8. Even though the creation itself tells us that God exists, no amount of scientific evidence will completely prove everything we are told in the Bilbe. That's why the Christian faith is called the Christian faith.

"And without faith it is impossible to please Him, for he who comes to God must believe that He is, and that He is a rewarder of those who seek Him." *Hebrews 11:6*

"Faith is the assurance of things hoped for, the conviction of things not seen." *Hebrews 11:1*

9. It doesn't take a great amount of faith to first become a Christian. As we grow closer to God and learn to walk in His ways, our faith grows also.

"He (Jesus) presented another parable to them: 'The Kingdom of heaven is like a mustard seed, which a man took and sowed in his field; and this is smaller than all other seeds; but when it is full grown, it is larger than the garden plants, and becomes a tree, so that the birds of the air come and nest in its branches.'" *Matthew 13:31*

10. As we obey and apply the truths and commands God has given us in Scripture, it has a way of inviting God closer to us, and bringing clarity to spiritual issues.

"He who has my commandments and keeps them is the one who loves Me; and he who loves Me will be loved by My Father, and I will love him and will disclose Myself to him." *John 14:21*

"Jesus said to the people who believed in him, 'You are truly my disciples if you keep obeying my teachings. And you will know the truth, and the truth will set you free." *John 8:31,32 (NLT)*

11. Sometimes our reluctance to believe is not an issue of the intellect, but of the will.

Jesus once told those who doubted His teaching: "If any man is willing to do His will, he shall know of the teaching, whether it is of God, or whether I speak from Myself." *John 7:17*

12. To begin to get to know God, ask Jesus into your heart. Then your new relationship with your Heavenly Father will begin.

"But as many as received Him, to them He gave the right to become children of God, even to those who believe in His name." *John 1:12*

"Behold, I stand at the door and knock; if any one hears My voice and opens the door, I will come into him, and dine with him, and he with Me." *Revelation 3:20*

2 Animism

Animism has no formalized belief system, and no unified holy writings on which to base its beliefs. Nor does it have one main, historical, prophet figure who founded it. However, as a belief system it is extremely widespread, and there are common beliefs held by animists all over the world.

For example, animists believe that everything that exists in the world – whether animal, vegetable, or mineral – shares in the same type of spiritual power. This power in itself is neither good nor bad, but is simply a neutral force. This power can be used to give a person good luck, or to cause harm. It can be called upon with sacrifices or offerings for healing, or to receive a blessing or send a curse.

Animists also believe in spirit beings who are involved in all aspects of life on Earth. These many spirits may be good or evil, strong or weak. They can be attached or associated with an animal, an object, a holy place, or with living people such as shamans or witch doctors, or associated with dead ancestors. Many animists seek a personal "spirit guide" to lead them through life.

The Bible also presents the concept of how the physical world and the spiritual world are related. But how is the biblical description of these two realms different from that of animism?

1. God created the physical realm and the spiritual realm, and rules over both.

"For in Him all things were created, both in the heavens and on earth, visible and invisible, whether thrones or dominions or rulers or authorities – all things have been created through Him and for Him. And He is before all things, and in Him all things hold together." *Colossians 1:16,17*

2. God created man in His image. Even though we are still lower than God Himself, He has placed us on earth as the highest members of His creation.

"When I consider Your heavens, the work of Your fingers, the moon and the stars, which You have ordained; what is man, that You take thought of him? Yet You have made him a little lower than God, and crown him with glory and majesty! You make him to rule over the works of Your hands." *Psalm 8:3-6*

3. As we observe God's creation, it leads us to worship God as the divine creator. Even though we view God's creation with great respect, we are not to worship it.

"For since the creation of the world His divine attributes, His eternal power and divine nature, have been clearly seen, being understood through what has been made, so that they are without excuse.... Professing to be wise, they became fools.... For they exchanged the truth of God for a lie, and worshiped and served the creature rather than the Creator, who is blessed forever. Amen." *Romans 1:20,22,25*

4. The Bible tells us that at some point in the distant past, there was a rebellion in the spiritual realm, led by an angel God created named Lucifer.

"You were the anointed cherub who covers; and I placed you there. You were on the holy mountain of God; you walked in the midst of the stones of fire. You were blameless in your ways from the day you were created, until unrighteousness was found in you. By the abundance of your trade you were internally filled with violence, therefore I have cast you as profane from the Mountain of God." *Ezekiel 28:14-16*

5. Lucifer (also called Satan, the devil, and the "god of this world") convinced the first humans to rebel against God much like he did. And he continues to deceive us.

"And the great dragon was thrown down, the serpent of old who is called the devil and Satan, who deceives the whole world; he was thrown down to the earth, and his angels were thrown down with him." *Revelation 12:9*

"The god of this world has blinded the minds of the unbelieving, that they might not see the light of the glory of Christ, who is the image of God." *2 Corinthians 4:4*

6. God is holy, and He cannot tolerate sin. Ever since mankind sinned, the physical realm where man lives has been separated from the spiritual realm where God lives.

"But your iniquities have made a separation between you and your God, and your sins have hid His face from you, so that He does not hear." *Isaiah 59:2*

"For all have sinned and fall short of the glory of God." *Romans 3:23*

7. God sent His only Son Jesus Christ, who was fully God and fully man, to reunite humans back with God. Jesus did this by giving His own life as payment for our sins.

"For in Him (Jesus) all the fulness of Deity dwells in bodily form." *Colossians 2:9*

"God demonstrates His own love for us in that while we were yet sinners Christ died for us." *Romans 5:8*

8. Why was Jesus qualified to be the payment for the sins of mankind? Because He was the only person who ever lived a completely sinless life.

"And you know that He appeared in order to take away sins; and in Him there is no sin." *1 John 3:5*

9. Someday all people who have ever lived, and all spirit beings, will give Jesus the worship He deserves.

"Therefore also God highly exalted Him (Jesus), and bestowed on Him the name which is above every name, that at the name of Jesus every knee should bow, of those who are in heaven, and on earth, and under the earth, and that every tongue should confess that Jesus Christ is Lord, to the glory of God the Father." *Philippians 2:9-11*

10. People often seek guidance from a spirit guide as a mediator between the physical world and the spiritual world. However, spirits can be deceptive. But when we become Christians, God Himself comes to dwell within us and becomes our guide.

"Jesus answered and said to him, 'If anyone loves Me, he will keep My word; and My Father will love him, and We will come to him, and make our abode with him.... But the Helper, the Holy Spirit, whom the Father will send in My name, He will teach you all things.'" *John 14:23,26*

"But when He, the Spirit of truth, comes, He will guide you into all the truth." *John 16:13*

11. We cannot be reunited with God by doing good deeds, or by our offerings, or by trying to pay the price for our own sins. Forgiveness can come only through trusting in what Christ did for us.

"Then they asked Him, 'What must we do to do the works God requires?' Jesus answered, 'The work of God is this: to believe in the One He has sent.'" *John 6:28,29*

"Jesus said to him, 'I am the way, and the truth, and the life; no one comes to the Father, but through Me.'" *John 14:6*

"For there is salvation in no one else; for there is no other name under heaven that has been given among men, by which we must be saved." *Acts 4:12*

"For there is one God, and one mediator also between God and men, the man Christ Jesus, who gave Himself as a ransom for all." *1 Timothy 2:5,6a*

12. You can be reunited with God by having your sins paid for by the death of Jesus Christ. Simply confess your sins to God and trust Him to forgive you.

"The wages of sin is death, but the free gift of God is eternal life in Christ Jesus our Lord." *Romans 6:23*

"For God so loved the world, that He gave His only begotten Son, that whoever believes in Him shall not perish, but have everlasting life." *John 3:16*

"Behold, I stand at the door and knock; if any one hears My voice and opens the door, I will come in to him, and will dine with him and he with me." *Revelation 3:20*

3 Atheism

The atheist believes that no supreme being of any kind exists. But the atheist and the Christian have one thing in common; the atheist's beliefs and the Christian's beliefs are both based on faith.

Atheists are quick to remind us that science cannot prove God exists. On the other hand, science has yet to prove God does not exist, or prove how the physical matter of the universe, with all the amazing complexities from galaxies to atoms, came into existence without having been created. If this universe came into existence after a previous universe collapsed into itself and exploded into this one, or if this universe is a result of other universes colliding, then where did those previous universes come from? Atheists try to explain such issues with great confidence, but how could it have all happened by chance with no intelligent designer guiding the process, yet resulted in a universe with the precision of a gigantic clock? And until science finds a way to fully explore every corner and dimension of the entire, infinite universe, then how can one confidently declare that God does not exist?

Does it take more faith to believe the evidence that God exists, or to believe, in spite of the evidence of creation, that God does not exist? And if God does exist, has He made it possible for us to know Him?

1. **How can we believe in the existence of a God we can't see or touch? The Bible starts off by telling us that everything we can see or touch has been created by God. The most indisputable evidence that God exists is that His creation exists. How many things have you ever seen spring into existence out of nothing?**

    "In the beginning, God created the heavens and the earth." *Genesis 1:1*

    "The heavens are telling of the glory of God; and the firmament is declaring the work of His hands. Day to day pours forth speech, and night to night reveals knowledge.... Their line has gone out through all the earth, and their utterances to the end of the world." *Psalm 19:1,2,4*

    "For since the creation of the world His invisible attributes, His eternal power and divine nature, have been clearly seen, being understood through what has been made, so that they are without excuse." *Romans 1:20*

    According to Christian author Gregory Koukl: "Believing in leprechauns is irrational. Believing in God, by contrast, is like believing in atoms. The process is exactly the same. You follow the evidence of what you can see to conclude the existence of something you cannot see. The effect needs a cause adequate to explain it."

2. **Often, the reason a person does not believe in God is simply because that person has never made a serious effort to know God. Perhaps there's a concern that if God turns out to be real, then He will require significant lifestyle changes. As Dosteovsky wrote in his novel *The Brothers Karamazov*: "If God does not exist, everything is permitted."**

    "The wicked, in the haughtiness of his countenance, does not seek Him. All his thoughts are, 'There is no God.'" *Psalm 10:4*

    "The fool has said in his heart, 'There is no God.' They are corrupt, they have committed abominable deeds; there is no one who does good. The Lord has looked down from heaven upon the sons of men, to see if there are any who understand, who seek after God. they have all turned aside, together they have become corrupt; there is no one who does good, not even one." *Psalm 14:1-3*

3. **The Bible promises that those who seriously seek God will find Him.**

    "The God who made the world and all things in it made from one, every nation of mankind to live on all the face of the earth... that they should seek God, if perhaps they might grope for Him and find Him, though He is not far from each one of us." *Acts 17:24,26,27*

    "And you will seek Me and find Me, when you search for Me with all your heart." *Jeremiah 29:13*

    "If you seek Him, He will let you find Him; but if you forsake Him, He will reject you forever." *1 Chronicles 28:9*

4. Not only are we to seek God, but God is also seeking those who truly want to know Him!

"Draw near to God and He will draw near to you." *James 4:8*

"For the eyes of the Lord move to and fro throughout the earth that He may strongly support those whose heart is completely His." *2 Chronicles 16:9*

"True worshipers shall worship the Father in spirit and truth; for such people the Father seeks to be His worshipers." *John 4:23*

5. If God feels distant, that is because mankind has become separated from God. We are sinful and God is holy.

"But your iniquities have made a separation between you and your God, and your sins have hid His face from you, so that He does not hear." *Isaiah 59:2*

"For all have sinned and fall short of the glory of God." *Romans 3:23*

6. God sent His Son Jesus to the earth. By learning from Him, we learn about the Father.

"God...has spoken to us in His Son, whom He appointed heir of all things, through whom also He made the world. And He is the radiance of His glory and the exact representation of His nature, and upholds all things by the word of His power. When He had made purification of sins, He sat down at the right hand of the Majesty on high." *Hebrews 1:1-3*

Jesus said: "He who has seen Me has seen the Father." *John 14:9*

7. Jesus not only taught us about God, He gave His life so that we can be forgiven and made holy. This is what makes it possible for us to be reconciled with God who is holy. Jesus is uniquely qualified to pay the price for all the sins of mankind because He lived a sinless life, and He was fully God and fully man.

"For there is one God, and one mediator also between God and man, the man Christ Jesus, who gave Himself as a ransom for all." *1 Timothy 2:5,6a*

"For in Him (Jesus) all the fulness of deity dwells in bodily form." *Colossians 2:9*

"For God so loved the world that He gave His only begotten Son, that whoever believes in Him shall not perish but have everlasting life." *John 3:16*

"But God demonstrates His own love for us in that while we were yet sinners, Christ died for us." *Romans 5:8*

8. Even though the creation itself tells us that God exists, no amount of scientific evidence will completely prove everything we are told in the Bible. That's why the Christian faith is called the Christian faith.

"And without faith it is impossible to please Him, for he who comes to God must believe that He is, and that He is a rewarder of those who seek Him." *Hebrews 11:6*

9. It doesn't take a great amount of faith to first become a Christian. As we grow closer to God, our faith grows also.

"The Kingdom of heaven is like a mustard seed, which a man took and sowed in his field; and this is smaller than all other seeds; but when it is full grown, it is larger than the garden plants, and becomes a tree, so that the birds of the air come and nest in its branches." *Matthew 13:31*

10. Sometimes our unwillingness to believe is not an issue of the intellect, but of the will.

Jesus once told those who doubted His teaching: "If any man is willing to do His will, he shall know of the teaching, whether it is of God, or whether I speak from Myself." *John 7:17*

11. To start a relationship with God, confess your sins and ask Christ into your heart.

"But as many as received Him, to them He gave the right to become children of God, even to those who believe in His name." *John 1:12*

4 Baha'i

Baha'is believe that God has revealed Himself to mankind throughout the ages by sending various "Divine Messengers," such as Moses, Krishna, Buddha, Zoroaster, Jesus, and Muhammed. Baha'is believe that Baha'u'llah, born in Iran in 1817, is the most recent in this line of messengers. Speaking of these messengers from God, Baha'u'llah wrote: "As a token of His mercy... He hath manifested unto men the Day Stars of His divine guidance, the Symbols of His divine unity, and hath ordained the knowledge of these sanctified Beings to be identical with the knowledge of His own Self." (Gleanings from the Writings of the Baha'u'llah, 49)

Every Baha'i temple, such as the one in Wilmette, Illinois, is designed to illustrate their beliefs. The temples have nine sides with a door in each side to symbolize that no matter which of the nine major world religions you choose, each will lead you to the same truth. All the "Divine Messengers" stressed the importance of love, as well as faith in God. But if God really did send these men to tell us about Himself, then why did they give conflicting accounts about God Himself? Krishna taught that there are many gods. Moses, Jesus, and Muhammed taught that there is one God. Zoroaster taught that there are two primary gods; one good, one evil. Jesus taught that He was God in the flesh and would rise from the dead. Muhammed taught that Jesus was not God and did not rise from the dead.

By accepting the teachings of all these men, one can only assume that God is contradictory and deceptive regarding how He reveals Himself to mankind.

Although Baha'is are not overly concerned with these differences, Jesus taught in no uncertain terms that He is unique from the others. How does Jesus stand apart from other religious leaders?

---

1. First of all, Jesus did not claim to be simply a messenger from God, He claimed to be God.

- Jesus claimed to be God's Son, making Himself equal with God. *John 5:18, 10:33*
- Jesus claimed to be the Messiah. *John 4:25,26*
- Jesus claimed to be the Christ. *Mark 14:61-62*

"For in Him (Christ) all the fulness of Deity dwells in bodily form." *Colossians 2:9*

2. Through Jesus the world was made.

"And He is the image of the invisible God, the firstborn of all creation. For in Him all things were created, both in the heavens and on earth, visible and invisible... all things have been created through Him and for Him." *Colossians 1:15,16*

"All things came into being through Him: and apart from Him nothing came into being that has come into being."

3. Even though the combined teachings of all the other "Divine Messengers" might lead one to believe that God changes, or that His message changes, the Bible teaches that God does not change.

"Jesus Christ is the same yesterday, today, yes and forever." *Hebrews 13:8*

"For I, the Lord, do not change..." *Malachi 3:6*

"...God...cannot lie." *Titus 1:2*

4. Unlike the other "Divine Messengers," Jesus lived a perfect, sinless life.

"For we do not have a high priest who cannot sympathize with our weaknesses, but one who has been tempted in all things as we are, yet without sin." *Hebrews 4:15*

5. Jesus willingly gave His life as the only perfect, sinless sacrifice to pay the penalty for our sins and make us holy.

"For this reason the Father loves me, because I lay down my life that I may take it up again. No one has taken it from Me, for I lay it down on my own initiative." *John 10:17,18*

"God demonstrates His own love toward us in that while we were yet sinners, Christ died for us." *Romans 5:8*

"He made Him who knew no sin to be sin on our behalf, that we might become the righteousness of God in Him." *2 Corinthians 5:21*

6. Because Christ led the only sinless life, His payment for our sin is the only way to obtain forgiveness so that we can be allowed into God's presence.

"Jesus said to him, 'I am the way, and the truth, and the life; no one comes to the Father but through Me.'" *John 14:6*

"For there is salvation in no one else; for there is no other name under heaven that has been given among men, by which we must be saved." *Acts 4:12*

"For there is one God, and one mediator also between God and men, the man Christ Jesus, who gave Himself as a ransom for all." *1 Timothy 2:5*

7. After Jesus died, He rose from the dead to verify that He was indeed God's only begotten Son.

"Christ died for our sins... He was buried... He was raised on the third day according to the Scriptures... He appeared to Cephas, then to the twelve. After that He appeared to more than five hundred...." *1 Corinthians 15:3-6*

Jesus was, "declared with power to be the Son of God by the resurrection from the dead." *Romans 1:4*

"If Christ has not been raised, your faith is worthless; you are still in your sins." *1 Corinthians 15:17*

8. For further proof of the supernatural uniqueness of Christ, consider the many predictions concerning His life which were written centuries before His birth!

- He would be born from the tribe of Judah. *Genesis 49:10, Matthew 1:2, Revelation 5:5*
- He would be born in Bethlehem. *Micah 5:2, Matthew 2:1*
- He would be born of a virgin. *Isaiah 7:14, Matthew 1:18-25*
- He would work miracles. *Isaiah 61:1, Matthew 11:1-5, Luke 4:16-21*
- He would be betrayed for exactly thirty pieces of silver. *Zechariah 11:12, Matthew 26:14-16*
- His hands and feet would be pierced. *Psalm 22:16, John 19:35,37, John 20:24-28*
- People would gamble for His clothing by casting lots. *Psalm 22:18, John 19:23,24*
- He would be executed along with criminals. *Isaiah 53:9,12, Luke 23:32,33*
- He would be buried in a rich man's tomb. *Isaiah 53:9, Matthew 27:57-60*
- His body would not decay, but be resurrected. *Psalm 16:8-11, Luke 24:1-43, Romans 1:4*

9. Christ predicted that false messiahs would come after Him, and warned us not to be misled.

"See to it that no one mislead you. For many will come in My name, saying, 'I am the Christ,' and will mislead many.... Many false prophets will arise, and will mislead many.... Then if any one says to you, 'Behold, here is the Christ,' or 'There He is,' do not believe him. For false Christs and false prophets will arise and will show great signs and wonders, so as to mislead, if possible, even the elect. Behold, I have told you in advance." *Matthew 24:4,5,11,23-25.*

10. To know God personally and experience His love and forgiveness for you, simply receive Christ into your life as your only Savior and Lord.

"But as many as received Him, to them He gave the right to become children of God, even to those who believe in His name." *John 1:12*

"If you confess with your mouth Jesus as Lord, and believe in your heart that God raised Him from the dead, you shall be saved." *Romans 10:9*

"I am the door; if anyone enters through Me, he shall be saved, and shall go in and out, and find pasture." *John 10:9*

5 Buddhism

Siddhartha Guatama was born a wealthy prince in India about 560 years before Christ. He grew up living a very sheltered life, and then as a young man he rejected his pampered lifestyle and spent years seeking enlightenment. Finally, at the age of 35, after spending seven days meditating under a fig tree, he emerged from his meditation as the "Buddha" or "Enlightened One." He began to teach others how to achieve the level of wisdom and enlightenment that he had attained.

Today's buddhists believe that the truths he taught have also been taught in other periods of world history by other illuminated beings called buddhas – the name "buddha" meaning simply "enlightened one."

But was Jesus Christ just one of many "enlightened ones" who have achieved "Buddhahood," or was Jesus someone far greater, possibly even the creator of the universe, and God in the flesh?

1. **Christianity, like Buddhism, encourages people to do good deeds and gain wisdom. Of course, almost all major religions encourage people to do good deeds and gain wisdom. So how was Jesus different? Jesus taught that our good deeds and spiritual wisdom are not what make us worthy to be allowed into heaven. Buddhism and other religions basically teach ways for us to improve ourselves, but Jesus taught that we can never make ourselves perfect enough or holy enough to be allowed into God's presence.**

    "For all have sinned and fall short of the glory of God." *Romans 3:23*

2. **Buddha was the son of a wealthy king in India, but Jesus claimed to be the Son of God.**

    • Jesus claimed to be God's Son, making Himself equal with God. *John 5:18*

    • Jesus claimed to be the Messiah. *John 4:25,26*

    • Jesus claimed to be the Christ. *Mark 14:61-62*

    "For in Him all the fulness of Deity dwells in bodily form." *Colossians 2:9*

3. **The Bible teaches that it was through Jesus the world was made.**

    "And He is the image of the invisible God, the firstborn of all creation. For in Him all things were created, both in the heavens and on earth, visible and invisible… all things have been created through Him and for Him." *Colossians 1:15,16*

    "All things came into being through Him: and apart from Him nothing came into being that has come into being." *John 1:3*

4. **If the founders of all the major world religions really were enlightened, then one would assume they would all be in agreement on important points about God. But they were not in agreement, and there's no way they can all be right.**

    • Krishna. Buddha, and Confucius taught that there are many gods.
    • Moses, Jesus, and Muhammed taught that there is one God.
    • Zoroaster taught that there are two gods; one good, one evil.
    • Jesus taught that He would rise from the dead, yet Muhammed taught that Jesus did not rise from the dead.

5. **If one tries to accept all the contradictory teachings of other religions, it would lead one to believe that God is very contradictory, or even deceptive. But the Bible tells us otherwise.**

    "Jesus Christ is the same yesterday, today, yes and forever." *Hebrews 13:8*

    "For I, the Lord, do not change..." *Malachi 3:6*

    "God...cannot lie." *Titus 1:2*

6. Unlike Buddha, other religious founders, and all other people, Jesus lived a perfect, sinless life.

"For we do not have a high priest who cannot sympathize with our weaknesses, but one who has been tempted in all things as we are, yet without sin." *Hebrews 4:15*

7. Jesus willingly gave His life as the only perfect, sinless sacrifice to pay the penalty for our sins and make us holy.

"For this reason the Father loves me, because I lay down my life that I may take it up again. No one has taken it from Me, for I lay it down on my own initiative." *John 10:17,18*

"God demonstrates His own love toward us in that while we were yet sinners, Christ died for us." *Romans 5:8*

"He (God) made Him (Jesus) who knew no sin to be sin on our behalf, that we might become the righteousness of God in Him." *2 Corinthians 5:21*

8. Because Christ led the only sinless life, His payment for our sin is the only way to obtain forgiveness so that we can be allowed into God's kingdom.

"Jesus said to him, 'I am the way, and the truth, and the life; no one comes to the Father but through Me.'" *John 14:6*

"I am the door; if anyone enters through Me, he shall be saved, and shall go in and out, and find pasture." *John 10:9*

"For there is salvation in no one else; for there is no other name under heaven that has been given among men, by which we must be saved." *Acts 4:12*

"For there is one God, and one mediator also between God and men, the man Christ Jesus, who gave Himself as a ransom for all." *1 Timothy 2:5,6a*

9. After Jesus died, He rose from the dead to verify that He was indeed God's Son.

"Christ died for our sins... He was buried... He was raised on the third day according to the Scriptures... He appeared to Peter, then to the twelve. After that He appeared to more than five hundred..." *1 Corinthians 15:3-6*

Jesus Christ was, "declared with power to be the Son of God by the resurrection from the dead." *Romans 1:4*

"If Christ has not been raised, your faith is worthless; you are still in your sins." *1 Corinthians 15:17*

10. To experience God's love and forgiveness for you, simply receive Christ into your life as your only Savior and Lord.

"For God so loved the world that He gave His only begotten Son, that whoever believes in Him will not perish, but have everlasting life." *John 3:16*

"Behold I stand at the door and knock; if any one hears My voice and opens the door, I will come in to him, and dine with him, and he with Me." *Revelation 3:20*

"But as many as received Him, to them He gave the right to become children of God, even to those who believe in His name." *John 1:12*

11. Buddhists seek freedom through meditation and purity of mind. Jesus also knew the importance of freedom, and He taught that we can only be free by knowing Him.

"If you abide in My word, then you are truly disciples of Mine, and you shall know the truth and the truth shall make you free.... If therefore the Son shall make you free, you shall be free indeed." *John 8:31,32,36*

"Come to Me all who are weary and heavy-laden, and I will give you rest. Take My yoke upon you and learn from Me, for I am gentle and humble in heart, and you will find rest for your souls. For My yoke is easy and My burden is light." *Matthew 11:28-30*

6 Children of God (Family of Love)

David Berg started the Children of God (or Family of Love) in Huntington Beach, California in 1968. He soon began calling himself Moses David and started writing his famous MO letters to his followers, which he said have the full authority of Scripture. And because his revelations are more recent than those in the Bible, he feels his writings are more appropriate to today's culture.

He started out as part of the 1960's "Jesus Movement." But has Moses David stayed true to the teachings of Jesus, as well as the teachings of the entire Bible? After all, if his writings are truly as reliable as Scripture, then they would have to be compatible with other teachings of Scripture. In regard to his teachings, he wrote, "If they agree that I'm wrong about one thing, then they believe that I could be wrong about it all. That's why in court if a witness lies about one thing, they throw his whole testimony out, all of it." (Moses David, Grace vs. Law, Rome: Children of God, Nov. 1977, DFO no 635, p 5)

If his teachings are true, then they should be heeded. 1 Thessalonians 5:20 tells us, "Do not despise prophetic utterances." But the very next two verses also warn us, "But examine everything carefully, hold fast to that which is good; abstain from every form (or appearance) of evil."

Christ also commanded us to be on guard against false teaching. "See to it that no one misleads you... And many false prophets will arise, and will mislead many." (Matthew 24:4,11) "Beware of the false prophets, who come to you in sheep's clothing, but inwardly they are ravenous wolves. You will know them by their fruits." (Matthew 7:15)

Let's take a look at some of the teachings of Moses David and see how they compare with what is already taught in the Bible.

---

1. Christ taught that our love for one another would tell people that we are His disciples.

"By this all men will know that you are my disciples, if you have love for one another." *John 13:35*

2. But Moses David teaches that sexual activity of the flesh is more effective than love to attract others to the faith.

"Now you and your flesh and your spirit and your love and real affection are the bait. But particularly your flesh is the bait." (Moses David, *FFers' Handbook, Condensed Selected Quotes from More than 50 FFer's Letters,* Justus Ashtree, ed., Children of God, Rome, January 1977, p.3).

"Help her, O God, to catch men. Help her to catch men, be bold, unashamed and brazen, to use anything she has, O God, to catch men for Thee! Even if it be through the flesh, the attractive lure, delicious flesh on a steel hook of Thy reality, the steel of Thy Spirit." (Moses David, *The Flirty Little Fish,* in *The Basic Mo Letters*, op, cit., p 528)

3. The teachings of Moses David regarding sex are very different from what is taught in the Bible.

"Let marriage be held in honor among all, and let the marriage bed be undefiled; for fornicators and adulterers God will judge." *Hebrews 13:4*

"Do you not know that your bodies are members of Christ? Shall I then take away the members of Christ and make them members of a harlot? May it never be! Flee immorality. Every other sin that a man commits is outside the body, but the immoral man sins against his own body." *1 Corinthians 6:15,18*

4. The Bible teaches that a life of fleshly indulgence as taught by Moses David, is harmful to our spiritual development and displeasing to God.

"For those who are according to the flesh set their minds on the things of the flesh, but those who are according to the Spirit, the things of the Spirit. For the mind set on the flesh is death, but the mind set on the Spirit is life and peace; because the mind set on the flesh is hostile toward God; for it does not subject itself to the Law of God, for it is not even able to do so; and those who are in the flesh cannot please God." *Romans 8:5-8*

5. **Regarding salvation, Moses David teaches that almost everyone who goes to hell will eventually get out and go to heaven. But Christ taught differently.**

"I'm looking forward to the day when – this may be another shocking thing for some people – when everybody or almost everybody will be saved – at least there won't be many left in Hell, if any." (Moses David, *Revolutionary New Life!* London: Children of God, June 1974, p. 1)

"And these will go away to eternal punishment, but the righteous into eternal life." *Matthew 25:46*

6. **The Bible gives stern warnings to those who claim to be teaching God's truths, but are really teaching falsehood.**

"But even though we, or an angel from heaven should preach to you a gospel contrary to that which we have preached to you, let him be accursed." *Galatians 1:8*

7. **Moses David claims that his own writings must take precedence over the Bible. In his own words:**

"God forced me to write what needed to be written and to show me the Bible was not enough... He feels it's more important to know what God says today than 2000 years ago." *(Mo Letter #175:19, Vol.2)*

8. **But God promises that His words are timeless, and their meanings will not fade.**

"For the word of God is living and active and sharper than any two-edged sword, and piercing as far as the division of soul and spirit, of both joints and marrow, and able to judge the thoughts and intentions of the heart." *Hebrews 4:12*

"Heaven and earth will pass away, but My words will not pass away." *Matthew 24:35*

"For as the rain and snow come down from heaven, and do not return there without watering the earth, and making it bear and sprout, and furnishing seed to the sower and bread to the eater; so shall My word be which goes forth from My mouth; it shall not return to Me empty, without accomplishing what I desire, and without succeeding in the matter for which I sent it." *Isaiah 55:10,11*

9. **Because of so many inconsistencies with the Bible, Moses David cannot be considered a true prophet of God and his teachings should not be followed. But God will forgive you for following his false teachings if you will confess your sin to God.**

"If we say that we have fellowship with Him and yet walk in the darkness, we lie and do not pracrtive the truth; but if we walk in the Light as He Himself is in the Light, we have fellowship with one another, and the blood of Jesus His Son cleanses us from all sin. If we say that we have no sin, we are deceiving ourselves and the truth is not in us. If we confess our sins, He is faithful and righteous to forgive us our sins and to cleanse us from all unrighteousness. If we say that we have not sinned, we make Him a liar and His word is not in us." *1 John 1:6-10*

10. **The best thing to do to stay close to God and avoid false teaching is to study the true Scriptures for yourself.**

"For they received the word with great eagerness, examining the Scriptures daily, to see whether these things were so." *Acts 17:11*

"All Scripture is inspired by God, and is profitable for teaching, for reproof, for correction, for training in righteousness; that the man of God may be adequate, equipped for every good work." *1 Timothy 3:16,17*

11. **Christ will forgive every sin and make us a true child of God, if we simply place our trust in Him.**

"But as many as received Him, to them He gave the right to become children of God, even to those who believe in His name." *John 1:12*

"I am the door; if anyone enters through Me, he will be saved, and will go in and out and find pasture. The thief comes only to steal and kill and destroy; I came that they may have life, and have it abundantly." *John 10:9,10*

7 Christian Science

Mary Baker Eddy (1821-1910) is the founder of Christian Science and author of "Science and Health With Key to the Scriptures." She was quite an innovative thinker when it came to matters of religion, and broke from traditional mainstream Christian doctrines in many areas.

She taught that sin, disease, and death are only illusions. For example: "Disease is an experience of a so-called mortal mind. It is fear made manifest in the body." And again: "Health is not a condition of matter, but of Mind."

But are sin, disease, and death mere illusions?

She also taught that Christ's sacrificial death on the cross did nothing to pay the penalty for the sins of mankind. After all, if sin is an illusion, then why should we be concerned about it? In Science and Health 25:6-8 she wrote, "The material blood of Jesus was no more efficacious to cleanse from sin when it was shed upon 'the accursed tree' than when it was flowing in his veins as he went about his Father's business."

If Jesus agreed with Mary Baker Eddy that sin and death were only illusions, then why did He willingly endure such terrible pain and suffering by dying on the cross to overcome them?

---

1. Mary Baker Eddy taught that Jesus was a very good man, but still just a man.

"Jesus is the name of the man who, more than all other men, has presented Christ, the true idea of God. Jesus is the human man, and Christ is the divine idea; hence the duality of Jesus the Christ." (*Science and Health 473:9-16*)

2. But the Bible makes it clear in no uncertain terms that Jesus was not merely a "divine idea," He was both fully God and fully man.

"For in Him all the fulness of Deity dwells in bodily form." *Colossians 2:9*

"For this cause therefore the Jews were seeking all the more to kill Him, because He... was calling God His own Father, making Himself equal with God." *John 5:18*

"The Jews answered Him, 'For a good work we do not stone You, but for blasphemy; and because You, being a man, make Yourself out to be God.'" *John 10:33*

"For there is one God, and one mediator also between God and men, the man Christ Jesus, who gave Himself as a ransom for all." *1 Timothy 2:5*

3. If Jesus was just a man, He certainly could not have made the world. But the Bible teaches that the world was made through Jesus.

"And He is the image of the invisible God, the firstborn of all creation. For in Him all things were created, both in the heavens and on earth, visible and invisible... all things have been created through Him and for Him." *Colossians 1:15,16*

"All things came into being through Him: and apart from Him nothing came into being that has come into being." *John 1:3*

4. The Bible teaches that sin and death are very real, and that all of us are sinners. Our sin separates us from God.

"But your iniquities have made a separation between you and your God, and your sins have hid His face from you, so that He does not hear." *Isaiah 59:2*

"For all have sinned and fall short of the glory of God." *Romans 3:23*

"The wages of sin is death, but the free gift of God is eternal life in Christ Jesus our Lord." *Romans 6:23*

5. The Scriptures tell us when Adam and Eve committed the very first sin, the entire human race became separated from God from then on.

"So then as through one transgression there resulted condemnation to all men, even so through one act of righteousness there resulted justification of life to all men. For as through the one man's disobedience the many were made sinners, even so through the obedience of the One the many will be made righteous." *Romans 5:18,19*

6. Christ paid the penalty for our sins by dying on the cross in order to reconcile us with God.

"But He was pierced for our transgressions, He was crushed for our iniquities; the punishment that brought us peace was upon Him, and by His wounds we are healed. We all, like sheep, have gone astray, each of us has turned to his own way; and the Lord has laid on Him the iniquity of us all." *Isaiah 53:5,6*

"God demonstrates His own love for us in that while we were yet sinners, Christ died for us. Much more then, having now been justified by His blood, we shall be saved from the wrath of God through Him. For if while we were enemies, we were reconciled to God through the death of His Son, much more having been reconciled, we shall be saved by His life." *Romans 5:8-10*

"Do not be afraid; I am the first and the last, and the living One; and I was dead, and behold, I am alive forevermore, and I have the keys of death and of Hades." *Revelation 1:17,18*

7. The only illusion the Bible presents regarding sin is pretending it is an illusion.

"If we say that we have no sin, we are deceiving ourselves, and the truth is not in us. If we confess our sins, He is faithful and righteous to forgive us our sins and to cleanse us from all unrighteousness. If we say that we have not sinned, we make Him a liar, and His word is not in us." *1 John 1:8-10*

8. As for Ms. Eddy's *Key to the Scriptures,* a key basically has two purposes: It can either be used to unlock something to make it accessible, or a key can be used to lock something away so that no one can get at it. Jesus Himself once denounced some of His critics for this very reason:

"For you have taken away the key of knowledge; you did not enter in yourselves, and those who were entering in you hindered." *Luke 11:52*

Has Mary Baker Eddy really unlocked the true meaning of the Scriptures, or has she locked away the true meaning so that her followers are not being exposed to what the Scriptures really teach?

9. In *Science and Health*, Ms. Eddy diminished the ability of Christ's sacrifice to pay the penalty for our sins.

"One sacrifice, however great, is insufficient to pay the debt of sin. The atonemenet requires constant self-immolation on the sinner's part. That God's wrath should be vented upon His beloved Son, is divinely unnatural. Such a theory is man-made." (*Science and Health 23:3-7*)

10. But the Bible teaches that Christ is the only way that sinful man can have access to God.

"Jesus said to him, 'I am the way, and the truth, and the life; no one comes to the Father except through Me.'" *John 14:6*

"I am the door; if anyone enters through Me, he shall be saved, and shall go in and out, and find pasture." *John 10:9*

"John saw Jesus coming toward him and said, 'Look, the Lamb of God who takes away the sin of the world!'" *John 1:29*

"For God so loved the world, that He gave His only begotten Son, that whoever believes in Him shall not perish, but have everlasting life." *John 3:16*

"For there is salvation in no one else; for there is no other name under heaven that has been given among men, by which we must be saved." *Acts 4:12*

11. To obtain forgiveness and salvation, confess your sinful nature to God and ask Christ into your heart.

"Behold, I stand at the door and knock; if any one hears My voice and opens the door, I will come in to him." *Revelation 3:20*

"But as many as received Him, to them He gave the right to become children of God, even to those who believe in His name." *John 1:12*

8 Confucianism

In his "Book of Analects," Confucius (550 B.C to 479 B.C.) said: "When you know a thing, maintain you know it; when you do not, acknowledge it. This is the characteristic of knowledge." He stayed true to this philosophy when he was asked a question about life after death. His answer was, "We know so little about life, how can we then know about death?"

The teachings of Confucius deal mainly with life here on earth, with little emphasis on the next life. Confucius himself was more concerned with matters of philosophy than with matters of religion. Though basically polytheistic, he willingly acknowledged that he did not have a full understanding of spiritual matters.

The goal of his teaching was peace and harmony between men. He gave much less emphasis on how to have peace and harmony between men and God.

Jesus was different. The teachings of Confucius focused mainly on our dealings in this life, but Jesus taught about this life as well as the next. While Confucius taught how men could have peace and harmony with each other, Jesus taught how men could have peace and harmony with each other, and with God. So who was Jesus, and how did He know so much about this world and the next?

1. Jesus did not claim to be just a teacher, He claimed to be the Son of God. He was both fully God and fully man.

- Jesus claimed to be God's Son, making Himself equal with God. *John 5:18*

- Jesus claimed to be the Messiah. *John 4: 25,26*

- Jesus claimed to be the Christ. *Mark 14:61-62*

2. Through Jesus the world was made.

"And He is the image of the invisible God, the firstborn of all creation. For in Him all things were created, both in the heavens and on earth, visible and invisible,...all things have been created through Him and for Him." *Colossians 1:15,16*

"All things came into being through Him: and apart from Him nothing came into being that has come into being." *John 1:3*

"God, after He spoke long ago to the fathers in the prophets in many portions and in many ways, in these last days has spoken to us in His Son, whom He appointed heir of all things, through whom also He made the world. And He is the radiance of His glory and the exact representation of His nature, and upholds all things by the word of His power. When He had made purification of sins, He sat down at the right hand of the Majesty of high." *Hebrews 1:1-3*

3. Even though Mencius, an early teacher of Confucianism, taught that man was basically good, the Bible tells us that after the human race was created, man rebelled against God. Because of our sin we have become separated from God and need a savior to pay for our sins.

"For all have sinned and fall short of the glory of God." *Romans 3:23*

"But your iniquities have made a separation between you and your God, and your sins have hid His face from you, so that He does not hear." *Isaiah 59:2*

"If we say that we have no sin, we are deceiving ourselves, and the truth is not in us. If we confess our sins, He is faithful and righteous to forgive us our sins and to cleanse us from all unrighteousness. If we say that we have not sinned, we make Him a liar, and His word is not in us." *1 John 1:8-10*

4. Unlike Confucius and all other people, Jesus lived a perfect, sinless life.

"And you know that He appeared in order to take away sins; and in Him there is no sin." 1 John 3:5

"For we do not have a high priest who cannot sympathize with our weaknesses, but one who has been tempted in all things as we are, yet without sin." Hebrews 4:15

5. Jesus willingly gave His life as the only perfect, sinless sacrifice to pay the penalty for our sins and make us holy. He took our sins onto Himself and gives us His righteousness.

"God demonstrates His own love toward us in that while we were yet sinners, Christ died for us." *Romans 5:8*

"Therefore we are ambassadors for Christ, as though God were making an appeal through us; we beg you on behalf of Christ, be reconciled to God. He made Him who knew no sin to be sin on our behalf, that we might become the righteousness of God in Him." *2 Corinthians 5:20,21*

"All of us like sheep have gone astray, each of us has turned to his own way; but the Lord has caused the iniquity of us all to fall on Him." *Isaiah 53:6*

"John saw Jesus coming toward him and said, 'Look, the Lamb of God who takes away the sin of the world!'" *John 1:29*

6. Because Christ lived the only sinless life, He is uniquely qualified to be the payment for our sin. He is the only way to obtain forgiveness so that we can be allowed into God's holy presence.

"Jesus said to him, 'I am the way, and the truth, and the life; no one comes to the Father but through Me.'" *John 14:6*

"I am the door; if anyone enters through Me, he shall be saved, and shall go in and out, and find pasture. The thief comes only to steal and kill and destroy; I came that they might have life, and have it abundantly." *John 10:9,10*

"For there is salvation in no one else; for there is no other name under heaven that has been given among men, by which we must be saved." *Acts 4:12*

"For there is one God, and one mediator also between God and men, the man Christ Jesus, who gave Himself as a ransom for all." *1 Timothy 2:5,6a*

7. The Bible encourages us to gain wisdom, but also warns us that sometimes philosophy can be used to distract us from focusing on Christ.

"See to it that no one takes you captive through philosophy and empty deception, according to the tradition of men, according to the elementary principles of the world, rather than according to Christ. For in Him all the fulness of deity dwells in bodily form." *Colossians 2:8,9*

8. After Jesus died, He rose from the dead to verify that He was indeed God's Son.

Jesus Christ was, "declared with power to be the Son of God by the resurrection from the dead." *Romans 1:4*

"Christ died for our sins... He was buried... He was raised on the third day according to the Scriptures... He appeared to Cephas, then to the twelve. After that He appeared to more than five hundred..." *1 Corinthians 15:3-6*

"If Christ has not been raised, your faith is worthless; you are still in your sins." *1 Corinthians 15:17*

9. To experience God's love and forgiveness for yourself, simply receive Christ into your life as your Savior and Lord.

"For God so loved the world, that He gave His only begotten Son, that whoever believes in Him shall not perish, but have everlasting life." *John 3:16*

"If you confess with your mouth Jesus as Lord, and believe in your heart that God raised Him from the dead, you shall be saved." *Romans 10:9*

"Behold I stand at the door and knock; if any one hears My voice and opens the door, I will come in to him, and will dine with him, and he with Me." *Revelation 3:20*

"But as many as received Him, to them He gave the right to become children of God, even to those who believe in His name." *John 1:12*

9 Deism

Deism became popular in the seventeenth century as a school of thought intended to bring unity from the chaos of trying to resolve discussions regarding theology and philosophy.

But like many movements, those who call themselves deists don't necessarily agree with each other on every view or doctrine. For instance, some deists, such as Voltaire, were hostile to Christianity, while others, like John Locke, were not.

Some of the basic points of deism are embraced by all sides. Deism believes in the existence of God, but there is great debate as to whether God intervenes with human affairs. Deists agree that much can be learned about God by observing nature. Prior to the advance of deism, the Scriptures were regarded as having the final authority on matters of the divine. The deists however, shifted the final authority away from the Scriptures to human reason.

The Bible tells us it is important to use our minds. For example, Christ said in Luke 10:27, "You shall love the Lord your God with all your heart, and with all your soul, and with all your strength, and with all your mind." But even though the Bible encourages us to use our minds, it also warns us not to suppose that our minds are all we need. "Trust in the Lord with all your heart, and do not lean on your own understanding." (Proverbs 3:5)

Even though deists don't see the Bible as having final authority on divine matters, it does address many of the issues which deists debate among themselves.

---

1. God has indeed revealed Himself through His creation.

"The heavens are telling of the glory of God; and their expanse is declaring the work of His hands. Day to day pours forth speech, and night to night reveals knowledge. There is no speech, nor are there words; their voice is not heard. Their line has gone out through all the earth, and their utterances to the end of the world." *Psalm 19:1-4*

"For since the creation of the world His invisible attributes, His eternal power and divine nature, have been clearly seen, being understood through what has been made, so that they are without excuse." *Romans 1:20*

2. God has also revealed Himself through the Scriptures. Christians view the Bible as the final authority on divine matters because it is inspired by God. Many people have disputed the Bible, but have never disproven any of it!

"All Scripture is inspired by God and profitable for teaching, for reproof, for correction, for training in righteousness; that the man of God may be adequate, equipped for every good work." *2 Timothy 3:16,17*

"Heaven and earth will pass away, but My words will not pass away." *Matthew 24:35*

"The Word of God is living and active and sharper than any two-edged sword." *Hebrews 4:12*

"But know this first of all, that no prophecy of Scripture is a matter of one's own interpretation, for no prophecy was ever made by an act of human will, but men moved by the Holy Spirit spoke from God." *2 Peter 1:20,21*

3. We can try to rely on reason to understand God, but our capacity to reason will never be enough to fully understand God, because He is infinite and we are finite.

"He counts the number of the stars; He gives names to all of them. Great is our Lord, and abundant in strength; His understanding is infinite." *Psalm 147:4,5*

4. God has also revealed Himself in the person of Jesus Christ.

"God...has spoken to us in His Son, whom He appointed heir of all things, through whom also He made the world. And He is the radiance of His glory and the exact representation of His nature." *Hebrews 1:1-3*

"And He (Jesus) is the image of the invisible of God." *Colossians 1:15*

5. **The deist would agree with the Bible in saying that mankind is separated from God, although the deist is really not sure why we are separated. The Bible tells us the reason we are separated is because man is sinful and God is holy.**

"But your iniquities have made a separation between you and your God, and your sins have hid His face from you, so that He does not hear." *Isaiah 59:2*

6. **Even though deists think it is impossible to know God, the Bible tells us that God is indeed knowable. God has promised in the Bible that if we seek Him, He will let us find Him.**

"The God who made the world and all things in it made from one, every nation of mankind to live on all the face of the earth... that they should seek God, if perhaps they might grope for Him and find Him, though He is not far from each one of us." *Acts 17:24,26,27*

"And you will seek Me and find Me, when you search for Me with all your heart." *Jeremiah 29:13*

"If you seek Him, He will let you find Him; but if you forsake Him, He will reject you forever." *1 Chronicles 28:9*

"Draw near to God and He will draw near to you." *James 4:8*

7. **Deists see the current state of the world as not being fallen or abnormal, but simply the way it is. However, the Bible tells us the current world has fallen far from the perfect state it was in before sin entered into the world.**

"For all have sinned and fall short of the glory of God." *Romans 3:23*

"The Lord has looked down from heaven upon the sons of men to see if there are any who understand, who seek after God. They have all turned aside, together they have become corrupt; there is no one who does good, not even one." *Psalm 14:2,3*

8. **Even though mankind is separated from God, He does care for us and loves us very much. God has provided a way for us to have our sins forgiven so that we can be reunited with Him and begin a personal relationship with Him. He sent His sinless Son to give His life as the payment for our sins.**

"For Christ also died for sins once for all, the just for the unjust, in order that He might bring us to God." *1 Peter 3:18*

"God demonstrates His own love toward us in that while we were yet sinners, Christ died for us." *Romans 5:8*

9. **Why is Jesus Christ the link between God and man? Because Jesus was both fully God and fully man, and was the only sinless man to ever live. This is why only Jesus is qualified to pay the penalty for our sin.**

"For in Him all the fullness of Deity dwells in bodily form." *Colossians 2:9*

"Jesus said to him, 'I am the way, and the truth, and the life; no one comes to the Father, but through Me.'" *John 14:6*

"For there is one God, and one mediator also between God and men, the man Christ Jesus, who gave Himself as a ransom for all." *1 Timothy 2:5,6a*

10. **We can't know everything God is doing because He is infinite and our understanding is limited. That's why we should defer to His wisdom and not make our own wisdom the ultimate standard for making decisions.**

"Trust in the Lord with all your heart and do not lean on your own understanding. In all your ways acknowledge Him, and He will make your paths straight." *Proverbs 3:5,6*

11. **To experience God's love and forgiveness for yourself, receive Christ as your Savior. You will deepen your relationship with God when you allow Christ to be Lord of your life by submitting every area to His control.**

"For God so loved the world, that He gave His only begotten Son, that whoever believes in Him shall not perish, but have everlasting life." *John 3:16*

"But as many as received Him, to them He gave the right to become children of God, even to those who believe in His name." *John 1:12*

10 Eckankar

Eckankar is a religious movement founded in the United States in 1965. Eckankar means "co-worker with God." One of the basic teachings is the Soul, or true self, can leave the body in full consciousness and visit other places and realms. Prior to 1985, Eckankar was known as, "The Ancient Science of Soul Travel." They consider soul travel to be one of the spiritual experiences that helps us find a natural way back to God. Every member has a card which states: "The aim and purpose of Eckankar has always been to take Soul by Its own path back to Its divine source."

Followers of Eckankar, known as "chelas," view the late Paul Twitchell as the "Mahanta, God made flesh on earth," or living Eck Master, the full incarnation of the "Sugmad" (God). After the death of Paul Twitchell in 1971, his successor Darwin Gross was viewed as the Mahanta. In 1981, Gross gave the title to Harold Klemp who maintains the title as of this writing. The current view of the Mahanta is one who is "given respect but not worship."

Throughout the ages and today as well, other people have claimed to be God in the flesh. One of the most famous to have made this claim was Jesus Christ. However, there are some important differences that separate Jesus from all the others who have claimed to be God in the flesh.

---

1. First of all Jesus claimed to be not just a messenger from God, Jesus claimed to be God.

- Jesus claimed to be God's Son, making Himself equal with God. *John 5:18, 10:33*
- Jesus claimed to be the Messiah. *John 4:25,26*
- Jesus claimed to be the Christ. *Mark 14:61-62*
- Jesus claimed to be able to forgive sins; something only God can do. *Mark 2:1-13*

"He who has seen Me has seen the Father." *John 14:9*

"For in Him all the fulness of Deity dwells in bodily form." *Colossians 2:9*

2. Jesus pre-existed for eternity before He came to this earth. In fact, the world was made through Him.

"And He is the image of the invisible God, the firstborn of all creation. For in Him all things were created, both in the heavens and on earth, visible and invisible,...all things have been created through Him and for Him." *Colossians 1:15,16*

"All things came into being through Him: and apart from Him nothing came into being that has come into being." *John 1:3*

"But as for you, Bethlehem Ephrathah, too little to be among the clans of Judah, from you One will go forth for Me to be ruler in Israel. His goings forth are from long ago, from the days of eternity." *Micah 5:2*

3. Unlike others who have claimed to be God in the flesh, Jesus lived a perfect, sinless life.

"For we do not have a high priest who cannot sympathize with our weaknesses, but one who has been tempted in all things as we are, yet without sin." *Hebrews 4:15*

"And you know that He appeared in order to take away sins; and in Him there is no sin." *1 John 3:5*

4. Mankind is separated from God because of our sin. Jesus willingly gave His life as the only perfect, sinless sacrifice to pay the penalty for the sins of mankind and make us holy.

"But your iniquities have made a separation between you and your God, and your sins have hid His face from you, so that He does not hear." *Isaiah 59:2*

"For all have sinned and fall short of the glory of God." *Romans 3:23*

"God demonstrates His own love toward us in that while we were yet sinners, Christ died for us." *Romans 5:8*

"He made Him who knew no sin to be sin on our behalf, that we might become the righteousness of God in Him." *2 Corinthians 5:21*

5. **All the religions of the world offer various ways to improve ourselves, do good deeds, gain wisdom, reach enlightenment, etc. Christianity also encourages us to do good and gain wisdom. But Christianity is unique because it never teaches that these are ways to reach God. Only through Christ can we have access to God because His payment for our sin is the only way to obtain forgiveness and be allowed into God's presence. Salvation is not something we achieve – it's something we receive.**

"Jesus said to him, 'I am the way, and the truth, and the life; no one comes to the Father but through Me.'" *John 14:6*

"I am the door; if anyone enters through Me, he shall be saved, and shall go in and out, and find pasture. The thief comes only to steal and kill and destroy; I came that they might have life, and might have it abuntantly" *John 10:9,10*

"For there is salvation in no one else; for there is no other name under heaven that has been given among men, by which we must be saved." *Acts 4:12*

"For the wages of sin is death, but the free gift of God is eternal life in Christ Jesus our Lord." *Roman 6:23*

"For there is one God, and one mediator also between God and men, the man Christ Jesus, who gave Himself as a ransom for all." *1 Timothy 2:5,6a*

6. **One thing that separates Jesus from Paul Twitchell is that Twitchell is still dead. After Jesus died, He rose from the dead to verify that He was indeed God's Son.**

Jesus was, "declared with power to be the Son of God by the resurrection from the dead." *Romans 1:4*

"Christ died for our sins... He was buried... He was raised on the third day according to the Scriptures... He appeared to Peter, then to the twelve. After that He appeared to more than five hundred..." *1 Corinthians 15:3-6*

7. **Paul Twitchell actually said that if we want to know the truth we should avoid thinking!**

"To see the perfect truth of ECK as IT is demands and compels the subjugation of Soul. This is the Everlasting gospel which in Its majesty and uniqueness of pure truth necessitates a suspension of the personal activity of thought." *(Shariyat, p. 24)*

8. **But Christ encouraged us to use our minds in our service to God.**

"And you shall love the Lord your God with all your heart, and with all your soul, and with all your mind, and with all your strength." *Mark 12:30*

9. **Christ told us to be on the alert to the many false messiahs and teachers who would come after Him, and warned us not to be misled.**

"See to it that no one mislead you. For many will come in My name, saying, 'I am the Christ,' and will mislead many. And many false prophets will arise, and will mislead many. Then if any one says to you, 'Behold, here is the Christ,' or 'There He is, do not believe him. For false Christs and false prophets will arise and will show great signs and wonders, so as to mislead, if possible, even the elect. Behold, I have told you in advance." *Matthew 24:4,5,11,23-25*.

10. **Unlike the living Eck Master, the fully divine Jesus Christ willingly accepted the worship of His followers.**

"And those who were in the boat worshiped Him, saying, 'You are certainly God's Son!'" *Matthew 14:33*

11. **To know God personally and experience His love and forgiveness for you, simply receive Christ into your life as your only Savior and Lord.**

"For God so loved the world, that He gave His only begotten Son, that whoever believes in Him shall not perish, but have everlasting life." *John 3:16*

"But as many as received Him, to them He gave the right to become children of God, even to those who believe in His name." *John 1:12*

11 Evolutionism (Darwinism, Naturalism)

Charles Darwin (1809-1882) theorized that all complex life forms – every spider monkey, swordfish, pine tree, horseshoe crab, bald eagle, dandelion, or human – have descended from a common ancestor. In his book, "Origin of the Species," Darwin tells of being an avid pigeon breeder, and how man has been able to produce many different varieties of pigeons by breeding individual specimens with traits that man might find desirable; whether it be fancier tail feathers, shorter beaks, color variations, or whatever. He wrote that if man can manipulate animals in this way, in what he called "artificial selection," then nature could produce the amazing varieties of life we have today through "natural selection." He taught that it was through natural selection, and descent with modification, that certain specimens with slight advantages over others were able to pass on their genes to the next generation, and through countless eons of time, we have the enormous variety of living organisms today.

When debating intelligent design vs. evolution, it's not a matter of faith vs. evidence. It's a matter of evidence vs. evidence. Darwin was honest enough in his book to include a chapter called, "On the Imperfection of the Geological Record." Here he explained that the fossil record does not contain the countless transitional forms required to prove his theory. As he expressed it: "I do not pretend that I should have ever suspected how poor was the record in the best preserved geological sections, had not the absence of innumerable transitional links between species which lived at the commencement and close of each formation, pressed so hardly on my theory." He speculated that conditions on earth that were favorable to the formation of fossils were very sporadic, and only occasionally were ideal enough to record the various specimens alive at any given time. He hoped that with enough digging, the chain of transitional fossils could be found to prove his theory. But with over a century and a half of digging since his book was published, the huge gaps in the fossil record remain. We hear about the search for the "missing link," but for Darwin to be proven true we're not simply looking for a missing link – we're looking for a missing chain.

Darwin was also perplexed by the sudden appearance of massive numbers of fully formed fossil remains in the rock layer called the "Cambrian Explosion," with no prior fossil evidence of what these animals evolved from. He was honest enough to admit this as a major challenge to his theory: "The case at present must remain inexplicable; and may be truly urged as a valid argument against the views here entertained." His best explanation was that these animals must have evolved some place on the earth (which had yet to be discovered), then migrated throughout the world. Again, he expressed optimism that with enough digging, that location would someday be found. But it hasn't.

Christians have no problem with evolution within a species (micro-evolution). Dogs, pigeons, or horses can be bred to produce all kinds of varieties within their species. But what the evidence has been unable to prove is macro-evolution, where one species changes into another, then another, and so on. To try to prove macro-evolution using examples of micro-evolution is not good science.

Something Darwin did not know about was the complexity of information stored inside DNA. For his theory to be true, this complex information had to have come into existence by chance. But this information is so complex, it's like finding the entire works of Shakespeare written in the sand on a beach and concluding it got there by the wind and surf hitting the sand over time. The more we learn about the complexity of DNA, the less likely it appears to have come into existence by chance. Reasonable minds would at least have to be willing to consider the possibility that this extremely complex information was put there by an intelligent creator.

Based on Darwin's theory of natural selection, living things must be able to reproduce in order to change and bring diversity. But what Darwin's theories of natural selection can't even begin to explain is how all nonliving, nonreproducing, inorganic matter, with all its complexities, has come into existence. Did the universe evolve from a speck of dust? And where did the speck of dust come from?

Darwinism is more than just the study of animals and fossils. Darwinism brings a worldview called "naturalism," which allows for nothing but what exists in nature. Anything outside the natural world is considered supernatural, which would include Christianity and all religions. Naturalism carries with it the lack of meaningful purpose to life. If humans evolved by chance from a speck of dust, without help from a supreme being, then we are a fluke of the universe. But if God created us, He probably did it for a purpose.

Both Darwin's theory and the theory of intelligent design take faith to believe; neither can be totally proven by science. But which takes more faith to believe; Darwin's theory of evolution – which is not fully supported by fossil evidence – or the creation story described in the Bible where animals appeared fully formed? Does the evidence for God's existence outweigh the evidence for God's nonexistence?

---

1. The Bible may not tell us exactly how everything came into being, but it does tell us who created it all.

"All things came into being through Him, and apart from Him nothing came into being that has come into being." *John 1:3*

2. The fossil record doesn't show the gradual, transitional forms to prove Darwin right. The missing chain is still missing. Genesis says God created animals fully developed, "after their kind," which is how they appear in the fossil record.

"Then God said, 'Let the earth bring forth living creatures after their kind: cattle and creeping things and beasts of the earth after their kind'; and it was so. And God made the beasts of the earth after their kind, and the cattle after their kind, and everything that creeps on the ground after its kind; and God saw that it was good." *Genesis 1:24,25*

3. The only way inorganic matter can bring forth reproducing life forms is through an act of God; it clearly doesn't happen by chance. If it happens by chance, why doesn't it keep happening? Why can't scientists create animals in a lab?

"Then the Lord God formed man of dust from the ground, and breathed into his nostrils the breath of life; and man became a living being." *Genesis 2:7*

4. If humans evolved from simpler life forms, we have something in common with every other creature; we are all an accident. But the Bible tells us man is no accident, and we have great worth because we are created in God's image.

"When I consider Your heavens, the work of Your fingers, the moon and the stars, which You have ordained; what is man that You take thought of him, and the son of man that You care for him? Yet You have made him a little lower than God, and You crown him with glory and majesty!" *Psalm 8:3-5*

"Then God said, 'Let Us make man in Our image, according to Our likeness.' And God created man in His own image, in the image of God He created him; male and female He created them." *Genesis 1:26,27*

5. We revere animals, plants, stars, and galaxies with great awe. But we should hold the creator of all these in even higher regard. The complexity and beauty of creation are meant to lead us to believe in God, not to reject Him.

"From the time the world was created, people have seen the earth and sky and all that God made. They can clearly see his invisible qualities – his eternal power and divine nature. So they have no excuse whatsoever for not knowing God." *Romans 1:20 (NLT)*

6. Darwin was focused on the link between man and the animals. But the Bible is far more focused on the link between man and God. Fortunately, God provided a link or mediator between man and God: Jesus Christ.

"For there is one God, and one mediator also between God and men, the man Christ Jesus, who gave Himself as a ransom for all." *1 Timothy 2:5,6a*

7. It's not enough just to go from believing in evolution to believing in some supreme, divine force. We start by accepting God as our Creator, but it must lead to accepting God as our Savior. We are so valuable to God that He sent His Son Jesus to reconcile us back to Him by paying the penalty of all the sins of mankind.

"For God so loved the world, that He gave His only begotten Son, that whoever believes in Him shall not perish, but have everlasting life." *John 3:16*

12 Existentialism

Not all existentialist philosophers share identical views. Some have been very religious (though not necessarily Christian), and some have been secular, agnostic, or atheistic. But there are important traits shared by all existentialists.

To think existentially is to think with inward passion. Existentialists feel the loneliness and anguish of human existence far more deeply than most average people. And one thing all existentialists share is despair over the human predicament. They see man's purpose as elusive, and human existence as not completely describable or understandable. Anxiety characterizes the human state, and man is viewed as incomplete and frail. Most existentialists share a deep angst or dread which comes from realizing that our future is undetermined, and the only thing that can fill our emptiness is our freely chosen actions.

Is there a way we can find purpose in life, and fill our emptiness?

1. Existentialists believe we exist apart from God.

According to Sartre, an atheistic existentialist: "The existentialist... thinks it very distressing that God does not exist, because all possibility of finding values... disappears along with Him.... Nowhere is it written that the Good exists, that we must be honest, that we must not lie: because the fact is we are on a plane where there are only men. Dostoevsky said, 'If God didn't exist, everything would be possible.' That is the very starting point of existentialism. Indeed, everything is permissible if God does not exist, and as a result man is forlorn, because neither within him nor without does he find anything to cling to." (*Existentialism and Human emotions*, NY, The Citadel Press, *pp. 22,23*)

But Jesus said, "I am the vine, you are the branches; he who abides in me, and I in him, he bears much fruit; for apart from Me you can do nothing." *John 15:5*

2. Existentialism maintains that if there is a God, we are separated from Him. Actually, the Bible gives us the reason we feel separated from God. It's because we are! And the reason we are separated from God is because of our sin.

"But your iniquities have made a separation between you and your God, and your sins have hid His face from you, so that He does not hear." *Isaiah 59:2*

"For all have sinned and fall short of the glory of God." *Romans 3:23*

3. Pascal, the great mathematician, said that inside each of us is a "God-shaped vacuum" which can only be filled by God; not by our actions, possessions, careers, relationships, or anything else.

Jesus said, "The thief comes only to steal, and kill, and destroy; I came that they might have life, and might have it abundantly." *John 10:10*

"Whoever drinks of the water that I shall give him shall never thirst; but the water that I shall give him shall become in him a well of water springing up to eternal life." *John 4:14*

4. Existentialists tell us "existence precedes essence;" that is, our value comes from the fact that we exist, even if our existence is futile. But the Bible tells us man's value comes from the fact that we are created by God in His image.

"When I consider Your heavens, the work of Your fingers, the moon and the stars, which You have ordained; what is man that You take thought of him, and the son of man that You care for him? Yet You have made him a little lower than God, and You crown him with glory and majesty!" *Psalm 8:3-5*

"Then God said, 'Let Us make man in Our image, according to Our likeness...' And God created man in His own image, in the image of God He created him; male and female He created them." *Genesis 1:26,27*

"For You formed my inward parts; You wove me in my mother's womb. I will give thanks to You, for I am fearfully and wonderfully made; wonderful are Your works, and my soul knows it very well." *Psalm 139:13,14*

5. Even the atheist Sartre eventually came to realize that he could not have existed without God.

In 1980, in the last months before his death, Sartre wrote in the *Nouvel Observateur*, "I do not feel that I am the product of chance, a speck of dust in the universe, but someone who was expected, prepared, prefigured. In short, a being whom only a Creator could put here: And this idea of a creating hand refers to God."

6. **Existentialists often refer to "objective truth," meaning what is said, and "subjective truth," meaning how it is said. If the objective truth is that God exists and loves us, the subjective truth is how He said it; by sending His Son Jesus to demonstrate His love and reconcile us to God by paying the penalty for our sins.**

   "But God demonstrates His own love for us in that while we were yet sinners Christ died for us." *Romans 5:8*

7. **Christ is the only way to find fulfillment and have access to God.**

   "Jesus said, 'I am the way, and the truth, and the life; no one comes to the Father but through Me.'" *John 14:6*

   "I am the door; if anyone enters through Me, he will be saved, and will go in and out and find pasture." *John 10:9*

   "For there is salvation in no one else; for there is no other name under heaven that has been given among men, by which we must be saved." *Acts 4:12*

   "For there is one God, and one mediator also between God and men, the man Christ Jesus, who gave Himself as a ransom for all." *1 Timothy 2:5,6a*

8. **The Bible is not anti-philosophy, but it warns that philosophy can become something that distracts us from properly focusing on Christ.**

   "See to it that no one takes you captive through philosophy and empty deception, according to the tradition of men, according to the elementary principles of the world, rather than according to Christ. For in Him all the fulness of deity dwells in bodily form." *Colossians 2:8,9*

9. **God wants us to use our minds and gain wisdom, but He warns us not to rely on our own wisdom as the final source for guidance. God's understanding is infinite, but ours is limited.**

   "Trust in the Lord with all your heart and do not lean on your own understanding. In all your ways acknowledge Him, and He will make your paths straight. Do not be wise in your own eyes; fear the Lord and turn away from evil. It will be healing to your body and refreshment to your bones." *Proverbs 3:5-8*

10. **Mankind suffers not because God has forsaken us. Mankind suffers because we have forsaken God. Suffering was not present on earth prior to sin. When Adam and Eve sinned, not only did sin enter into the world, but suffering and death entered in as well. Suffering is a universal curse which has come upon us because as humans, we have universally rebelled against God. After Adam and Eve disobeyed and tried to become like God by eating the fruit, God told them:**

    "I will greatly multiply your pain in childbirth, in pain you shall bring forth children... Cursed is the ground because of you; in toil you shall eat of it all the days of your life. Both thorns and thistles it shall grow for you; and you shall eat the plants of the field; by the sweat of your face you shall eat bread till you return to the ground, because from it you were taken; for you are dust, and to dust you shall return." *Genesis 3:16-19*

11. **Existentialists feel the pain and emptiness that results from separation from God. We must each establish a personal relationship with God by trusting Christ to pay the penalty for our sins and give us access to God. Then one's new life with meaning will begin.**

    "For God so loved the world, that He gave His only begotten Son, that whoever believes in Him shall not perish, but have everlasting life." *John 3:16*

    "For the wages of sin is death, but the free gift of God is eternal life in Christ Jesus our Lord." *Romans 6:23*

    "Behold, I stand at the door and knock; if any one hears My voice and opens the door, I will come in to him, and will dine with him, and he with me." *Revelation 3:20*

13 The Forum (EST, Erhard Seminar Training, Landmark Forum)

The Forum was started in 1985 by Werner Erhard and Fernardo Flores. Prior to starting the Forum, Erhard had also become famous for a somewhat similar movement called Erhard Seminar Training (also known as EST) which he had started in 1971. In 1991, Erhard sold his intellectual property rights to the Forum and the new group revamped the movement under the name Landmark Education, which offers training under the name Landmark Forum.

According to Erhard, (originally known as John Paul Rosenberg), "Life is always perfect just the way it is." ("What's So Wrong," January 1975) Part of Erhard's training involves helping people discover and understand this perfection, and their personal potential. Erhard has also said, "But don't get me wrong, I don't think the world needs EST; I don't think the world needs anything; the world already is and that's perfect." (Adam Smith, "Powers of Mind, Part 2: The EST Experience," New York, Sept 29, 1975, p 284)

But is life really as perfect as Erhard maintains?

Just watching the nightly news, where we see the terrible suffering that people inflict upon each other, makes us wonder if something is fundamentally imperfect about this world.

The Bible gives us simple answers to this question.

---

1. In the beginning, the world indeed was perfect.

"And God saw all that He had made, and behold, it was very good." *Genesis 1:31*

2. The world became imperfect when sin entered in.

"Therefore, just as through one man sin entered into the world, and death through sin, and so death spread to all men, because all sinned." *Romans 5:12*

"Cursed in the ground because of you; in toil you shall eat of it all the days of your life. Both thorns and thistles it shall grow for you." *Genesis 3:17-18*

3. The only perfect world is the next world – heaven.

"And He shall wipe away every tear from their eyes; and there shall no longer be any death; there shall no longer be any mourning, or crying, or pain; the first things have passed away." *Revelation 21:4*

"And there shall no longer be any curse." *Revelation 22:3*

4. Our sin is what makes us imperfect, and sin is what makes this world imperfect. Sin is also what separates us from God.

"The Lord has looked down from heaven upon the sons of men, to see if there are any who understand, who seek after God. They have all turned aside; together they have become corrupt; there is no one who does good, not even one." *Psalm 14:1-3*

"But your iniquities have made a separation between you and your God, and your sins have hid His face from you, so that He does not hear." *Isaiah 59:2*

"For all have sinned and fall short of the glory of God." *Romans 3:23*

5. If we pretend we are perfect, and do not face up to the fact that we are fallen sinners, we are only fooling ourselves.

"If we say that we have no sin, we are deceiving ourselves, and the truth is not in us." *1 John 1:8*

6. The only way to experience life as it was meant to be is by knowing God and living by His commands and guidelines.

"The thief comes only to steal, and kill, and destroy; I came that they might have life, and might have it abundantly." *John 10:10*

"Everyone who drinks of this water shall thirst again; but whoever drinks of the water that I shall give him shall never thirst; but the water that I shall give him shall become in him a well of water springing up to eternal life." *John 4:14*

7. To know God, you must first accept the fact that you are a sinner, and far from perfect.

"If we confess our sins, He is faithful and righteous to forgive us our sins and to cleanse us from all unrighteousness. If we say that we have not sinned, we make Him a liar, and His word is not in us." *1 John 1:9,10*

8. Next, you must accept the payment for your sins which Christ has paid by dying for you.

"But God demonstrates His own love toward us, in that while we were yet sinners, Christ died for us." *Romans 5:8*

"For Christ also died for sins once for all, the just for the unjust, in order that He might bring us to God, having been put to death in the flesh, but made alive in the spirit." *1 Peter 3:18*

9. As we submit to letting Christ be Lord of our lives, He gradually perfects us.

"...fixing our eyes on Jesus, the author and perfector of faith." *Hebrews 12:2*

"The God of all grace who called you to His eternal glory in Christ, will Himself perfect, confirm, strengthen and establish you." *1 Peter 5:10*

10. By filllling our minds with God's truths, we slowly begin to recognize God's will for our lives.

"Therefore I urge you, brethren, by the mercies of God, to present your bodies a living and holy sacrifice, acceptable to God, which is your spiritual service of worship. And do not be conformed to this world, but be transformed by the renewing of your mind, so that you may prove what the will of God is, that which is good and acceptable and perfect." *Romans 12:1,2*

11. The Forum, as well as religions and philosophical movements throughout the world, teach that we can reach God or reach perfection under our own power. Each religion has their own way to reach God through doing good deeds, or gaining enlightenment, etc. But Christianity is unique among all the religions of the world because it teaches that our good deeds don't bring us to God. Access to God can only come through Christ.

"Jesus said to him, 'I am the way, and the truth, and the life; no one comes to the Father but through Me.'" *John 14:6*

"For there is salvation in no one else; for there is no other name under heaven that has been given among men, by which we must be saved." *Acts 4:12*

12. Even once you become a Christian and obtain forgiveness, we still do not become perfect until we get to heaven.

"Not that I have already obtained it or have already become perfect, but I press on in order that I may lay hold of that for which also I was laid hold of by Christ Jesus. Brethren, I do not regard myself as having laid hold if it yet; but one thing I do: forgetting what lies behind and reaching forward to what lies ahead." *Philippians 3:12,13*

13. To become a Christian right now, simply confess your sinfulness to God and ask Christ into your life.

"Behold, I stand at the door and knock; if any one hears my voice and opens the door, I will come in to him, and will dine with him, and he with Me." *Revelation 3:20*

"Therefore if any man is in Christ, he is a new creature; the old things passed away; behold, new things have come." *2 Corinthians 5:17*

"Come to Me, all who are weary and heavy-laden, and I will give you rest. Take My yoke upon you and learn from Me, for I am gentle and humble in heart, and you will find rest for your souls. For My yoke is easy and My burden is light." *Matthew 11:28-30*

14 Freemasonry (Masons, Knights Templar, Rosicrucians)

Most Masons see Freemasonry as a benevolent, fraternal organization that exists to serve and help others. If you are a Mason, you have been given explanations for the mysterious symbols and rituals of Freemasonry. But have you ever been told the full, or true significance of these symbols and rituals, or of the Masonic Order as a whole?

The most comprehensive book which best defines the beliefs of Freemasonry is the 861 page "Morals and Dogma of the Ancient and Accepted Scottish Rite of Freemasonry" (commonly referred to as "Morals and Dogma"), written in 1871 by the Sovereign Grand Commander of the Southern Supreme Council, Albert Pike (1809-1891). Even to this day, Masonic leaders refer to this work as the "Bible of Masonry." If you've never examined the teachings of this definitive book, you may be surprised to find out there is more to Freemasonry than you ever imagined.

1. **If you are a Mason, particularly in the early stages of the Blue Lodge, you have been given explanations for the teachings and rituals you have been through. But *Morals and Dogma* states plainly that these explanations are false!**

   "The Blue Degrees are but the outer court or portico of the Temple. Part of the symbols are displayed to the Initiate, but he is intentionally misled by false interpretations. It is not intended that he shall understand them, but it is intended that he shall imagine he understands them. Their true explication is reserved for the Adepts, the Princes of Masonry." (p. 819)

   "The truth must be kept secret, and the masses need a teaching proportioned to their imperfect reason." (p.103)

   "Masonry... conceals its secrets from all except the Adepts and Sages, or the Elect, and uses false explanations and misinterpretations of its symbols to mislead those who deserve only to be misled; to conceal the truth, which it calls Light, from them, and to draw them away from it." (p. 104)

2. **According to *Morals and Dogma,* who or what is the source of the "Light" that must be hidden from the general public, as well as lower Masonic members, but only revealed to the highest members of Masonry?**

   "Lucifer, the Light-bearer!... Lucifer, the Son of the Morning! Is it he who bears the Light?... Doubt it not!" (p. 321)

3. **Since Lucifer is the source of the "Light," it is no wonder that the real meanings of Masonic teachings are cloaked in deception. According to Scripture, Lucifer (Satan) is the father of lies.**

   "He was a murderer from the beginning, and does not stand in the truth, because there is no truth in him. Whenever he speaks a lie, he speaks from his own nature; for he is a liar, and the father of lies." *John 8:44,45*

4. **God's Word teaches that those who really have the truth should not hide it from others, and must never attempt to conceal the truth or draw others away from it as taught in *Morals and Dogma*. (p. 104)**

   "You are the light of the world. A city set on a hill cannot be hidden. Nor do men light a lamp, and put it under the peck-measure, but on the lampstand; and it gives light to all who are in the house. Let your light shine before men in such a way that they may see your good works, and glorify your Father who is in heaven." *Matthew 5:14-16*

   "But all things become visible when they are exposed by the light, for everything that becomes visible is light." *Ephesians 5:13*

   "And this is the message that we have heard from Him and announce to you, that God is light, and in Him there is no darkness at all. If we say that we have fellowship with Him and yet walk in darkness, we lie and do not practice the truth; but if we walk in the light as He Himself is in the light, we have fellowship with one another, and the blood of Jesus His Son cleanses us from all sin. If we say we have no sin, we are deceiving ourselves, and the truth is not in us." *1 John 1:5-8*

5. **Even though Freemasonry does help in many humanitarian causes, and their teachings make frequent references to God, the Bible warns us that such things can be used as a disguise for evil.**

"Satan disguises himself as an angel of light. Therefore it is not surprising if his servants also disguise themselves as servants of righteousness." *2 Corinthians 11:14,15*

"Beware of the false prophets, who come to you in sheep's clothing, but inwardly are ravenous wolves.... Not everyone who says to Me, 'Lord, Lord,' will enter the kingdom of heaven; but he who does the will of My Father, who is in heaven. Many will say to Me on that day, 'Lord, Lord did we not prophesy in Your name, and in Your name cast out demons, and in Your name perform many miracles?' And then I will declare to them, 'I never knew you; depart from Me, you who practice lawlessness.'" *Matthew 7:15,21*-23

6. According to *Morals and Dogma,* Freemasonry is not simply a fraternal organization, it is clearly a religion.

"Every Masonic Lodge is a temple of religion; and its teachings are instruction in religion." (p.213)

"It (Masonry) is the universal, eternal, immutable religion, such as God planted it in the heart of universal humanity." (p. 219)

7. Within the religious teachings of Freemasonry, the Bible is viewed with less regard than the Kabbalah, an ancient book of occult teachings. Its followers believe the Kabbalah reveals the true yet hidden meanings of stories from the Bible.

"The Bible, with all the allegories it contains, expresses, in an incomplete and veiled manner only, the religious science of the Hebrews. (p. 744)

"The Kabbalah alone consecrates the alliance of the Universal Reason and the Divine Word... it alone reconciles Reason with Faith, Power with Liberty, Science with Mystery; it has the keys of the Present, the Past, and the Future." (p. 744)

8. Masons tend to believe that we reach God through our good works, symbolized in Masonic rituals by the climbing of the ladder and the wearing of the white apron. In other words, they teach that salvation is something we achieve. But the Bible teaches that salvation is something we receive, as a free gift that comes only by faith in Christ. We're not saved as a result of good works; we're saved, and good works are the result.

"He saved us, not on the basis of deeds which we have done in righteousness, but according to His mercy, by the washing of regeneration and renewing by the Holy Spirit, whom He poured out upon us richly through Jesus Christ our Savior." *Titus 3:5,6*

"The wages of sin is death, but the free gift of God is eternal life in Christ Jesus our Lord." *Romans 6:23*

"For all of us have become like one who is unclean, and all our righteous deeds are like a filthy garment; and all of us wither like a leaf, and our iniquities, like the wind, take us away. There is no one who calls on Your name, who arouses himself to take hold of You; for You have hidden Your face from us and have delivered us into the power of our iniquities." *Isaiah 64:6,7*

9. Because good works can't save us, the only way to be certain you will be allowed in heaven is to receive Christ as your personal Savior who paid for your sins.

"But God demonstrates His own love for us in that while we were yet sinners Christ died for us." *Romans 5:8*

"For God so loved the world, that He gave His only begotten Son, that whoever believes in Him shall not perish, but have everlasting life." *John 3:16*

"Jesus said to him, 'I am the way, and the truth, and the life; no one comes to the Father but through Me.'" *John 14:6*

"Behold, I stand at the door and knock; if any one hears My voice and opens the door, I will come in to him, and dine with him, and he with Me." *Revelation 3:20*

"But as many as received Him, to them He gave the right to become children of God, even to those who believe in His name." *John 1:12*

15 Hare Krishna

The Hare Krishna faith, as taught by A.C. Bhaktivedanta Swami Prabhupada (who died in 1977) tells us that when this life is over, we can obtain salvation and be freed from the cycle of reincarnation only if our bad deeds are outweighed by our good deeds. These deeds include things such as, "chanting the name of God, hearing and singing his praises, meditation upon the divine play and deeds of KRSNA, and engaging in the rites and ceremonies of worship. One must also repeat the name of God to the count of beads." (Abhay Charan de Bhaktivedanta Swami Prabhupada, "Bhagavad-Gita As It Is," p. 326) The faith teaches that if our good deeds are not adequate to atone for our bad deeds, then we once again return to this life to keep trying.

Both Christianity and Hare Krishna stress the importance of doing good deeds. Both faiths also teach that there can be a better life in the hereafter. But even though Christianity stresses the importance of doing good works, we do them for a totally different reason or motivation.

What is it about Christianity that is different?

---

1. God expects us to do good works, in fact we have been created for the purpose of doing good works.

"For we are His workmanship, created in Christ Jesus for good works, which God prepared beforehand, that we should walk in them." *Ephesians 2:10*

"Even so faith, if it has no works, is dead, being by itself.... For just as the body without the spirit is dead, so also faith without works is dead." *James 2:17,26*

2. Even though we are commanded to do good works, they are not what save us.

"For all our righteous deeds are like a filthy garment." *Isaiah 64:6*

"He saved us, not on the basis of deeds which we have done in righteousness, but according to His mercy, by the washing of regeneration and renewing by the Holy Spirit, whom He poured out upon us richly through Jesus Christ our Savior." *Titus 3:5,6*

3. Salvation is not like wages which are earned. It is not something we achieve. The Bible tells us that salvation is a free gift which is received.

"For the wages of sin is death, but the free gift of God is eternal life in Christ Jesus our Lord." *Romans 6:23*

"For by grace you have been saved through faith; and that not of yourselves, it is the gift of God; not as a result of works, that no one should boast." *Ephesians 2:8,9*

4. Our salvation is not based on what we do, but on what only Christ could do. He is the only perfect, sinless man to ever live.

"But God demonstrates His own love for us in that while we were yet sinners Christ died for us. Much more then, having now been justified by His blood, we shall be saved from the wrath of God through Him." *Romans 5:8,9*

"For Christ also died for sins once for all, the just for the unjust, in order that He might bring us to God." *1 Peter 3:18*

"This is good and acceptable in the sight of God our Savior, who desires all men to be saved. For there is one God, and one mediator between God and men, the man Christ Jesus, who gave Himself as a ransom for all." *1 Timothy 2:4-6a*

"Jesus said to him, 'I am the way, and the truth, and the life; no one comes to the Father but through Me.'" *John 14:6*

5. Christ was not only fully man; He was also fully God.

"For in Him all the fulness of Deity dwells in bodily form." *Colossians 2:9*

6. **By trusting in Christ's death to pay the penalty for our bad deeds, His perfect righteousness is credited to us! We now look to God through Christ, and God looks at us through Christ.**

"But now God has shown us a different way of being right in his sight – not by obeying the law but by the way promised in the Scriptures long ago. We are made right in God's sight when we trust in Jesus Christ to take away our sins. And we all can be saved in this same way, no matter who we are or what we have done." *Romans 3:21,22 (NLT)*

7. **Many people will someday stand before the Lord when their lives are over, and expect to be received into heaven based on their good deeds. But Jesus tells us that trusting in our good deeds instead of in His sacrificial death will result in being rejected from heaven.**

"Not everyone who says to Me, 'Lord, Lord,' will enter the kingdom of heaven; but he who does the will of My Father, who is in heaven. Many will say to Me on that day, 'Lord, Lord, did we not prophesy in Your name, and in Your name cast out demons, and in Your name perform many miracles?' And then I will declare to them, 'I never knew you; depart from Me, you who practice lawlessness.'" *Matthew 7:21-23*

8. **Other religions teach that we reach God through good deeds, gaining wisdom, etc. But the Bible tells us Jesus is unique among all spiritual teachers. He was fully God, fully man, He lived a sinless life, and His sacrificial death provides our only access to God. We don't trust in our righteousness; we trust in Christ's righteousness to save us.**

"For there is salvation in no one else; for there is no other name under heaven that has been given among men, by which we must be saved." *Acts 4:12*

9. **After we trust Christ, then we do good works to bring glory to God, not to ourselves.**

"He died for all, that they who live should no longer live for themselves, but for Him who died and rose again on their behalf." *2 Corinthians 5:15*

"In humility receive the word implanted, which is able to save your souls. But prove yourselves doers of the word, and not merely hearers who delude themselves." *James 1:21,22*

10. **When this life is over, we will all be judged for the works we have done. But more importantly, we will be judged for what we have believed.**

"Then they asked Him, 'What must we do to do the works God requires?' Jesus answered, 'The work of God is this: to believe in the One He has sent.'" *John 6:28,29*

"For God so loved the world, that He gave His only begotten Son, that whoever believes in Him shall not perish, but have everlasting life." *John 3:16*

11. **This judgment has nothing to do with whether or not we will be reincarnated back to earth, but determines where we go in the next life. The Bible teaches that we are never reincarnated.**

"It is appointed for men to die once, and after this comes judgment." *Hebrews 9:27*

12. **The Bible warns us to be on the alert to religious leaders that promise salvation but who are actually false and misleading.**

"But even if we, or an angel from heaven, should preach to you a gospel contrary to what we have preached to you, he is to be accursed! As we have said before, so I say again now, if any man is preaching to you a gospel contrary to what you received, he is to be accursed! For am I now seeking the favor of men, or of God? Or am I striving to lease men? If I were still trying to please men, I would not be a bondservant of Christ." *Galatians 1:8-10*

13. **Because our good works cannot save us, the only way to be certain you will be allowed in heaven is to receive Christ as your personal savior who paid the penalty for your sins.**

"I stand at the door and knock; if any one hears My voice and opens the door, I will come in to him." *Revelation 3:20*

"But as many as received Him, to them He gave the right to become children of God, even to those who believe in His name." *John 1:12*

16 Hedonism

Pleasure and personal happiness are the main pursuits of the hedonist, or "lifestyle worshiper." And God is certainly not opposed to us enjoying life. After all, He gave us life and created pleasures for us to enjoy.

But God wants us to keep things in balance and not live for pleasure, or love pleasure more than we love Him. A lot of people reject the idea of becoming a Christian simply because they think the non-Christian lifestyle is more fun. Hmmm: Sex, drugs, and rock & roll; or abstinence, sobriety, and hymns?

Does God want us to have fun in life, or is He a Cosmic Killjoy who wants us to live dull, boring lives? Is the Christian life really as dull and boring as non-Christians think? And compared to the benefits of the Christian life, is the non-Christian lifestyle overrated?

What does the Bible tell us about God's view of pleasure, the pursuit of individuial happiness, and the meaning of life?

---

1. God has given us many pleasures to enjoy.

"There is nothing better for a man than to eat and drink and tell himself that his labor is good. This also I have seen, that it is from the hand of God. For who can eat and who can have enjoyment without Him?" *Ecclesiastes 2:24,25*

2. In fact, in heaven we will enjoy many pleasures.

"You will make known to me the path of life; in Your presence is fullness of joy; in Your right hand there are pleasures forever. " *Psalm 16:11*

3. The problem with pleasure is that we can love pleasure more than we love God.

"But realize this, that in the last days difficult times will come. For men will be lovers of self, lovers of money... without self-control... lovers of pleasure rather than lovers of God..." *2 Timothy 3:4*

"And the seed which fell among the thorns, these are the ones who have heard, and as they go on their way they are choked with worries and riches and pleasures of this life..." *Luke 8:14*

4. Even though God created all pleasures, they can be misused or become the main focus of our lives. This is when pleasure turns to sin. It results in the internal war between pleasing our flesh or pleasing God. Does the hedonistic, non-Christian life offer thrills? Of course! It would be exhilarating to jump off the Empire State Building, but the consequences would be terrible. The deeds of the flesh have one set of results, and the spiritual life submitted to God will have a completely different set of results.

"For the flesh sets its desire against the Spirit, and the Spirit against the flesh; for these are in opposition to one another.... Now the deeds of the flesh are evident, which are: immorality, impurity, sensuality... jealousy, outbursts of anger... drunkenness, carousings, and things like these, of which I forewarn you... that those who practice such things shall not inherit the kingdom of God. But the fruit of the Spirit is love, joy, peace, patience, kindness, goodness, faithfulness, gentleness, self-control." *Galatians 5:17,19-23*

5. The difference between the Christian or non-Christian lifestyle basically comes down pleasing God or pleasing yourself; living for the Spirit or living for the flesh; living by God's definition of right and wrong or making up your own definition of right and wrong. The fleshly lifestyle is about indulging one's physical desires and appetites on demand, while the spiritual lifestyle is about submitting to Christ as Lord over every area of your life, and only indulging in physical desires and appetites within His allowed parameters. These two forces of the flesh and the spirit are always in a never-ending battle to dominate our lives.

"For those who are according to the flesh set their minds on the things of the flesh, but those who are according to the Spirit, the things of the Spirit. For the mind set on the flesh is death, but the mind set on the Spirit is life and peace, because the mind set on the flesh is hostile toward God; for it does not subject itself to the law of God, for it is not even able to do so, and those who are in the flesh cannot please God. However, you are not in the flesh but in the Spirit, if indeed the Spirit of God dwells in you. But if anyone does not have the Spirit of Christ, he does not belong to Him." *Romans 8:5-9*

6. **Rather than making the pursuit of pleasure our chief goal in life, we should be seeking God as our chief goal in life. If we do this, He will provide the pleasures we need. If God is what makes us happy, everything else does, too. If God is not what makes us happy, nothing else will either.**

"But seek first His kingdom, and His righteousness, and all these things shall be added to you." *Matthew 6:33*

7. **If our purpose in life is to simply please our flesh by living for pleasure instead of living for God, we end up enjoying life less, not more.**

"She who gives herself to wanton pleasure is dead even while she lives." *1 Timothy 5:6*

"The thief comes only to steal, and kill, and destroy. I came that they might have life, and might have it abundantly." *John 10:10*

8. **One of the most deceptive things about sin is that it eventually has power over you. Living for the flesh makes you a slave of sin, and only through the power of God's help can you overcome it.**

"Jesus said to the people who believed in him, 'You are truly my disciples if you keep obeying my teachings. And you will know the truth, and the truth will set you free.' 'But we are descendants of Abraham,' they said. 'We have never been slaves to anyone on earth. What do you mean, "set free"?' Jesus replied, 'I assure you that everyone who sins is a slave of sin. A slave is not a permanent member of the family, but a son is part of the family forever. So if the Son sets you free, you will indeed be free.'" *John 8:31-36 (NLT)*

9. **The Bible says non-Christians will always struggle to understand why Christians prefer the Christian lifestyle.**

"But people who aren't Christians can't understand these truths from God's Spirit. It all sounds foolish to them because only those who have the Spirit can understand what the Spirit means. We who have the Spirit understand these things, but others can't understand us at all." *1 Corinthians 2:14,15 (NLT)*

10. **Physical or sensual pleasures are only temporary, and too much indulgence can result in self-destruction. But God also offers spiritual pleasures, which are eternal.**

"For the one who sows to his own flesh shall from the flesh reap corruption, but the one who sows to the Spirit shall from the Spirit reap eternal life." *Galatians 6:8*

"By faith Moses, when he had grown up, refused to be called the son of Pharaoh's daughter; choosing to endure ill-treatment with the people of God, than to enjoy the passing pleasures of sin; considering the reproach of Christ greater riches than the treasures of Egypt; for he was looking to the reward." *Hebrews 11:24-26*

"Have you found honey? Eat only what you need, that you not have it in excess and vomit it." *Proverbs 25:16*

11. **Christ sacrificed His life to pay for our sins so that we can come to heaven and enjoy the pleasure of being with Him forever.**

"But God demonstrates His own love for us in that while we were yet sinners Christ died for us." *Romans 5:8*

"For God so loved the world, that He gave His only begotten Son, that whoever believes in Him shall not perish, but have everlasting life." *John 3:16*

"For we also once were foolish ourselves, disobedient, deceived, enslaved to various lusts and pleasures. But when the kindness of God our Savior and His love for mankind appeared, He saved us, not on the basis of deeds which we have done in righteousness, but according to His mercy." *Titus 3:3-5*

"Behold, I stand at the door and knock; if any one hears My voice and opens the door, I will come in to him, and will dine with him, and he with Me." *Revelation 3:20*

"But as many as received Him, to them He gave the right to become children of God, even to those who believe in His name." *John 1:12*

17 Hinduism

To the Hindu, salvation is the liberation of the soul from the wheel of karma (the reincarnation cycle of birth, death, and rebirth) so that the soul can enter nirvana, the place of fulness or completeness. It is there that we become one with the "Impersonal All," in much the same way that a drop of water merges with the ocean. The Bhagavad-Gita, which is the sacred book of Hinduism, teaches that there are three different ways to obtain salvation:

- *The Way of Works (Karma Marga): The carrying out of prescribed religious duties, rites, and ceremonies.*
- *The Way of Knowledge (Jhana Marga): Through self-discipline and meditating, the individual reaches a state of consciousness and frees himself from the wheel of karma.*
- *The Way of Devotion (Bhakti Marga): The devotion to a deity reflected in acts of love and worship.*

Jesus once told a man named Nicodemus, "Unless one is born again, he cannot see the kingdom of God." (John 3:3) But was Jesus referring to the Hindu concept of birth, death, and rebirth, or was He offering a way of salvation that was entirely different?

---

1. When Jesus told Nicodemus that he needed to be born again, Nicodemus did not understand.

"Jesus answered and said to him, 'Truly, truly, I say to you, unless one is born again he cannot see the kingdom of God.' Nicodemus said to Him, 'How can a man be born when he is old? He cannot enter a second time into his mother's womb and be born, can he?'" (*John 3:3,4*)

2. Jesus was not talking about being reborn physically. He was telling Nicodemus he needed to be reborn spiritually.

"Jesus answered, 'Unless one is born of water (meaning physically, from the womb) and the Spirit, he cannot enter the kingdom of God. That which is born of the flesh is flesh, and that which is born of the Spirit is spirit.'" *John 3:6*

"Therefore if any man is in Christ, he is a new creature; the old things passed away; behold, new things have come." *2 Corinthians 5:17*

3. The way to be reborn spiritually is simply by believing in Jesus.

"For God so loved the world, that He gave His only begotten Son, that whoever believes in Him should not perish, but have eternal life." *John 3:16*

Believing in Jesus does not mean simply believing that someone named Jesus once lived and taught, as did Buddha, Confucius, or Plato. To "believe in Jesus" means to place one's total trust in Him as the only means to obtain forgiveness and salvation. It means fully trusting Him to pay the price for our sins; something none of us can do ourselves.

4. Jesus did not teach that salvation is obtained through "the Way of Works," "the Way of Knowledge," or "the Way of Devotion." Jesus taught that He is the one and only way!

"Jesus said to him, 'I am the way, and the truth, and the life. No one comes to the Father except through Me.'" *John14:6*

"I am the door; if anyone enters through Me, he will be saved, and will go in and out and find pasture. The thief comes only to steal and kill and destroy; I came that they may have life, and have it abundantly." *John 10:9,10*

5. Jesus is different from other religious leaders because He is both fully man and fully God!

"For in Him all the fullness of Deity dwells in bodily form." *Colossians 2:9*

"For there is one God, and one mediator also between God and men, the man Christ Jesus, who gave Himself as a ransom for all." *1 Timothy 2:5,6a*

6. When we place our trust in Jesus, our sins are placed onto Him and His perfect holiness is credited to us.

"For Christ also died for sins once for all, the just for the unjust, in order that He might bring us to God." *1 Peter 3:18*

"He made Him who knew no sin to be sin on our behalf, that we might become the righteousness of God in Him." *2 Corinthians 5:21*

"For the wages of sin is death, but the free gift of God is eternal life in Christ Jesus." *Romans 6:23*

"For we also once were foolish ourselves, disobedient, deceived, enslaved to various lusts and pleasures, spending our life in malice and envy, hateful, hating one another. But when the kindness of God our Savior and His love for mankind appeared, He saved us, not on the basis of deeds which we have done in righteousness, but according to His mercy, by the washing of regeneration and renewing by the Holy Spirit, whom He poured out upon us richly through Jesus Christ our Savior." *Titus 3:3-6*

7. The Bible teaches that there is no such thing as successive lives, or reincarnation. Therefore, it is imperative that we believe in Christ during this lifetime.

"It is appointed for men to die once, and after this comes judgment." *Hebrews 9:27*

"Remember Him before the silver cord is broken and the golden bowl is crushed, the pitcher by the well is shattered and the wheel at the cistern is crushed; then the dust will return to the earth as it was, and the spirit will return to God who gave it." *Ecclesiastes 12:6,7*

8. Because Jesus paid the price of salvation for us, salvation is a free gift which He offers to us. Because it is a gift, salvation is something that is *received*, not something that is *achieved*.

"For by grace you have been saved through faith; and that not of yourselves, it is the gift of God; not as a result of works, so that no one may boast. For we are His workmanship, created in Christ Jesus for good works, which God prepared beforehand so that we would walk in them." *Ephesians 2:8-10*

"Then they asked Him, 'What must we do to do the works God requires?' Jesus answered, 'The work of God is this: to believe in the One He has sent." *John 6:28,29*

9. Jesus taught that all people will someday stand before Him at their final judgment. Those who have trusted in their good deeds to get them into heaven will be shocked to find out that their good deeds won't get them in.

"Not everyone who says to Me, 'Lord, Lord,' will enter the kingdom of heaven, but he who does the will of My Father who is in heaven will enter. Many will say to Me on that day, 'Lord, Lord, did we not prophesy in Your name, and in Your name cast out demons, and in Your name perform many miracles?' And then I will declare to them, 'I never knew you; Depart from Me, you who practice lawlessness.'" *Matthew 7:21-23*

"Therefore they said to Him, 'What shall we do, so that we may work the works of God?' Jesus answered and said to them, 'This is the work of God, that you believe in Him whom He has sent.'" *John 6:28,29*

10. To receive your free gift of salvation, simply confess your sins to God and ask Christ into your life, trusting in His payment for your sins instead of your own good deeds.

"If we say that we have no sin, we are deceiving ourselves and the truth is not in us. If we confess our sins, He is faithful and righteous to forgive us our sins and to cleanse us from all unrighteousness. If we say that we have not sinned, we make Him a liar and His word is not in us. My little children, I am writing these things to you so that you may not sin. And if anyone sins, we have an Advocate with the Father, Jesus Christ the righteous; and He Himself is the propitiation for our sins; and not for ours only, but also for those of the whole world." *1 John 1:8 – 2:2*

"Behold, I stand at the door and knock; if any one hears my voice and opens the door, I will come in to Him, and dine with him, and he with Me." *Revelation 3:20*

"But as many as received Him, to them He gave the right to become children of God, even to those who believe in His name." *John 1:12*

18 Homosexuality

If the Bible teaches love, what does it say about loving someone of the same sex?

1. The Bible makes it clear that God loves everyone, and He wants everyone to love Him, and to love each other.

"Beloved, let us love one another, for love is from God, and everyone who loves is born of God and loves God. The one who does not love does not know God, for God is love." *1 John 4:7,8*

2. The way God shows that He loves us is by sending His Son to give His life for us.

"God demonstrates His own love toward us, in that while we were yet sinners, Christ died for us." *Romans 5:8*

3. The way we demonstrate to God that we love Him is by following His commandments.

"By this we know that we love the children of God, when we love God and observe His commandments. For this is the love of God, that we keep His commandments; and His commandments are not burdensome." *1 John 5:2,3*

4. Love is such a powerful force, God gives us instructions on what we should love and what we should not love.

We are to love:
- the Lord your God – *Deuteronomy 6:5*
- your neighbor as yourself – *Leviticus 19:18*
- what is good – *Amos 5:15, Titus 1:8*
- discipline and knowledge – *Proverbs 12:1*
- your enemies – *Matthew 5:44*
- husbands are to love wives – *Ephesians 5:25*
- wives are to love husbands – *Titus 2:4*

We are not to love:
- money – *Hebrews 13:5, 1 Timothy 6:10*
- the world – *1 John 2:15, James 4:4*
- pleasure – *2 Timothy 3:4*
- sleep – *Proverbs 20:13*
- falsehood – *Zechariah 8:17*
- praise – *Matthew 6:5*

5. When the Bible talks about the love people have for each other, it uses three different Greek words to convey three different types of love.

- Phileo – the brotherly love one feels for a friend
- Eros – the erotic, romantic, or sexual love one feels for a lover
- Agapé (or agapao) – the unconditional love that is not earned, nor based on merit

(Some homosexuals contend that Jesus and His disciple John were homosexual lovers because John is referred to as "the disciple Jesus loved," in John 13:23 and John 19:26. However, the original language makes no reference whatsoever to any sexual overtones in their relationship.)

6. We are permitted – in fact commanded – to love one another in the "agapé" sense, but what does the Bible teach about loving someone of the same sex in an "eros" or sexual type of love?

"God gave them over in the lusts of their hearts to impurity, that their bodies might be dishonored among them.... For this reason God gave them over to degrading passions; for their women exchanged the natural function for that which is unnatural, and in the same way also the men abandoned the natural function of the woman and burned in their desire towards one another, men with men committing indecent acts and receiving in their own persons the due penalty of their error." *Romans 1:24,26,27*

7. Homosexuality is not the only sin that can separate us from God. Any sin is enough to keep us out of heaven. Fortunately, God loves us so much that He sent His Son Jesus to pay the penalty for every possible sin.

"For all have sinned and fall short of the glory of God." *Romans 3:23*

"For whoever keeps the whole law and yet stumbles in one point, he has become guilty of all." *James 2:10*

But God demonstrates His own love toward us, in that while we were yet sinners, Christ died for us." *Romans 5:8*

8. Many homosexuals try to reconcile their gay lifestyle with the Bible. They agree that the Old Testament law declared homosexuality to be a sin, but feel when Christ abolished the law in the New Testament, then homosexu-

ality was no longer considered sin. It's true that dietary, ceremonial, and civil laws were done away when the law was abolished; however, there were no moral or sexual laws which were abolished. In the New Testament, adultery is still sin, stealing is still sin, murder is still sin, incest is still sin, and yes, homosexuality is still considered a sin.

From the Old Testament:

"You shall not lie with a male as one lies with a female; it is an abomination." *Leviticus 18:22*

From the New Testament:

"Or do you not know that the unrighteous shall not inherit the kingdom of God? Do not be deceived; neither fornicators, nor idolaters, nor adulterers, nor effeminate, nor homosexuals, nor thieves, nor covetous, nor drunkards, nor revilers, nor swindlers, shall inherit the kingdom of God. And such were some of you; but you were washed, but you were sanctified, but you were justified in the name of the Lord Jesus Christ, and in the Spirit of our God."
1 Corinthians 6:9-11

9. **If a person claims to love God, but defiantly disobeys God by embracing a gay lifestyle, it reveals he or she does not love God enough to obey Him, and that their real god is their lifestyle. Every gay person who claims to be a follower of Christ must ask themselves: "Are you a gay person first, or a disciple of Christ first?"**

"And by this we know that we have come to know Him, if we keep His commandments. The one who says, 'I have come to know Him,' and does not keep his commandments, is a liar, and the truth is not in Him; but whoever keeps His word, in him the love of God has truly been perfected." *1 John 2:3-5*

"For no man can serve two masters. Either he will hate the one and love the other, or he will hold to one and despise the other." *Matthew 6:24*

10. **God loves us just the way we are, and loves us too much to let us stay just the way we are. To obtain God's forgiveness and His power to conquer any sinful habit, we must confess our sin and invite Christ into our lives.**

"If we say that we have no sin, we are deceiving ourselves, and the truth is not in us. If we confess our sin, He is faithful and righteous to forgive us our sins and to cleanse us from all unrighteousness." *1 John 1:8,9*

God never made anyone materialistic, or dishonest, or a liar, or racist, or hateful, or gay, or greedy. If that were true, people could just blame God for their own particular sin. Adulterers would say God made them adulterers. Greedy people would say God made them greedy, etc. The way to obtain forgiveness for any sin is to admit that we are responsible for our disobedient choices. This is what confession is; agreeing with God that our sin is sin.

11. **Without Christ, we lack the power to conquer sin. But once He indwells us, He can give us the power we need to break old patterns and habits.**

"And now, all glory to God, who is able to keep you from stumbling, and who will bring you into his glorious presence innocent of sin and with great joy. All glory to him, who alone is God our Savior, through Jesus Christ our Lord. Yes, glory, majesty, power, and authority belong to him, in the beginning, now, and forevermore. Amen." *Jude 24,25 (NLT)*

"No temptation has overtaken you but such as is common to man; and God is faithful, who will not allow you to be tempted beyond what you are able, but with the temptation will provide the way of escape also, that you may be able to endure it." *1 Corinthians 10:13*

"The Lord knows how to rescue the godly from temptation." *2 Peter 2:9*a

"Delight yourself in the Lord and He will give you the desires of your heart." *Psalm 37:4*

12. **Every person, gay or straight, must individually receive Christ to obtain forgiveness from all sins, as well as the power to redirect our passions and desires to conquer sin in the future.**

"Jesus said to him, 'I am the way, and the truth, and the life; no one comes to the Father but through me.'" *John 14:6*

"For the wages of sin is death, but the free gift of God is eternal life in Christ Jesus." *Romans 6:23*

19 Humanism (Secular Humanism)

According to the ancient Greek philosopher Protagoras, "Man is the measure of all things." Paul Kurtz expanded on this concept when he wrote "The Humanist Manisfesto" in 1933 along with input from other leading secular humanists. Kurtz defines Humanism as "faith in the supreme value and self-perfectability of human personality."

Humanism places all its hopes on man to solve our problems. According to his manifesto: "Man is at last becoming aware that he alone is responsible for the realization of the world of his dreams, that he has within himself the power for its achievement."

Even though the human race did not exactly prove its ability to perfect itself over the next forty years after he wrote his first manifesto, Kurtz wrote "The Humanist Manifesto II" in 1973, which included the same basic premise that humans have within us the ability to perfect ourselves.

The Bible does agree with Kurtz that humans have supreme value, but the Scriptures give us a different view on how we can be perfected.

---

1. Humanism begins and ends with man.

"As non-theists, we begin with humans not God, nature not deity." (Kurtz, from *First Resolution, Manifesto II.*)

2. But the Scriptures tell us not to begin with ourselves, but with God.

"I am the Alpha and the Omega, the first and the last, the beginning and the end." *Revelation 22:13*

"Know that the Lord Himself is God; it is He who has made us, and not we ourselves." *Psalm 100:3*

3. Humanism believes that Christianity, or any belief in God, is obsolete.

"As in 1933, humanists still believe that traditional theism, especially faith in the prayer-hearing God, assumed to love and care for persons, to hear and understand their prayers, and to be able to do something about them, is an unproved and outmoded faith." (Kurtz, *Manifesto II*)

4. But the teachings, principles, and truths of Christianity found in God's enduring Bible have been around much longer than Humanism. The Bible's assessment of the human condition continues to prove itself totally accurate.

"For the word of God is living and active, and sharper than any two-edged sword" *Hebrews 4:12*

"Heaven and earth will pass away, but My words will not pass away." *Matthew 24:35*

5. The belief that humans alone can solve our own problems has been disproven again and again throughout history.

"Thus says the Lord, 'Cursed is the man who trusts in mankind and makes flesh his strength, and whose heart turns away from the Lord. For he will be like a bush in the desert and will not see when prosperity comes, but will live in stony wastes in the wilderness, a land of salt without inhabitant. Blessed is the man who trusts in the Lord and whose trust is the Lord. For he will be like a tree planted by the water, that extends its roots by a stream and will not fear when the heat comes; but its leaves will be green, and it will not be anxious in a year of drought nor cease to yield fruit.'" *Jeremiah 17:5-8*

6. The Bible teaches that God scoffs at man's prideful efforts to rid ourselves of His commands and instructions.

"Why are the nations in an uproar and the peoples devising a vain thing? The kings of the earth take their stand and the rulers take counsel together against the Lord and against His Anointed, saying, 'Let us tear their fetters apart and cast away their cords from us!' He who sits in the heavens laughs, the Lord scoffs at them." *Psalm 2:1-4*

7. God is the only One who can perfect us.

"And after you have suffered for a little, the God of all grace, who called you to His eternal glory in Christ, will Himself perfect, confirm, strengthen and establish you." 1 Peter 5:10

8. The first step God takes towards perfecting us is by forgiving our sins.

"If we say that we have no sin, we are deceiving ourselves, and the truth is not in us. If we confess our sin, He is faithful and righteous to forgive us our sins and to cleanse us from all unrighteousness." *1 John 1:8,9*

9. Only when God's children meet the Lord will we be completely perfected.

"Beloved, now we are children of God, and it has not appeared as yet what we shall be. We know that, when He appears, we shall be like Him, because we shall see Him just as He is. And everyone who has this hope fixed on Him purifies himself, just as He is pure." *1 John 3:2,3*

10. Humanism states that we must save ourselves.

"But we can discover no divine purpose or providence for the human species. While there is much that we do not know, humans are responsible for what we are or will become. No deity will save us; we must save ourselves." (Kurtz, *First Resolution, Manifesto II*)

11. Paul Kurtz does not elaborate on what he feels we need to be saved from. But history has shown that man is at his worst when we decide that there is no divine purpose for humanity, nor any responsibility to stand accountable before God. Kurtz says we must save ourselves, but the Bible makes it clear that we need to be saved *from* ourselves, and that we can only be saved by trusting in Christ.

"And she will bear a Son; and you shall call His name Jesus, for it is He who will save His people from their sins." *Matthew 21:1*

"And there is salvation in no one else; for there is no other name under heaven that has been given among men, by which we must be saved." *Acts 4:12*

"I am the door; if anyone enters through Me, he shall be saved, and shall go in and out, and find pasture." *John 10:9*

12. Paul Kurtz wrote that "reasonable minds" will reject the gospel.

"Salvationism, based on mere affirmation, still appears as harmful, diverting people with false hopes of heaven hereafter. Reasonable minds look to other means for survival." (from the Preface of *Humanist Manifesto II*)

13. But the Bible tells us that those who are not spiritually minded will never understand the things of God.

"But we know these things because God has revealed them to us by his Spirit, and his Spirit searches out everything and shows us even God's deep secrets. No one can know what anyone else is really thinking except that person alone, and no one can know God's thoughts except God's own Spirit. And God has actually given us his Spirit (not the world's spirit) so we can know the wonderful things God has freely given us. When we tell you this, we do not use words of human wisdom. We speak words given to us by the Spirit, using the Spirit's words to explain spiritual truths. But people who aren't Christians can't understand these truths from God's Spirit. It all sounds foolish to them because only those who have the Spirit can understand what the Spirit means. We who have the Spirit understand these things, but others can't understand us at all. How could they? For, 'Who can know what the Lord is thinking? Who can give him counsel?' But we can understand these things, for we have the mind of Christ." *1 Corinthians 2:10-16 (NLT)*

14. Salvation through Christ is simple. It does not require works – just faith.

"'Sirs, what must I do to be saved?' And they said, 'Believe in the Lord Jesus, and you shall be saved.'" *Acts 16:30,31*

"For by grace you have been saved through faith; and that not of yourselves, it is the gift of God; not as a result of works, that no one should boast." *Ephesians 2:8,9*

"Behold, I stand at the door and knock; if any one hears my voice, and opens the door, I will come into him, and dine with him, and he with Me." *Revelation 3:20*

"But as many as received Him, to them He gave the right to become children of God, even to those who believe in His name." *John 1:12*

20 Islam

Out of respect for Jesus, most Muslims prefer to believe that He did not actually die on a cross. But Christians place a great emphasis on Christ's death and resurrection. We invite our Muslim friends to not only join us in the discussion of "if" Jesus died on the cross, but also to discuss the question of "why" He died.

---

1. Surah 4:157, translated from the Koran, tells us that Jesus was the Messiah. However, it sheds doubt on whether or not He was actually crucified.

"And because of their saying: We slew the Messiah Jesus, Son of Mary, Allah's messenger – They slew him not nor crucified, but it appeared so unto them; and lo! those who disagree concerning it are in doubt thereof; they have no knowledge thereof save pursuit of a conjecture: they slew him not for certain."

2. Was the death of Jesus "for certain?" Throughout the gospels, Jesus spoke openly of His upcoming death and resurrection, and when He spoke about it, His own disciples did not yet fully understand why He had to die. Out of respect they tried to talk Him out of it.

"From that time on Jesus began to show His disciples that He must go to Jerusalem, and suffer many things, from the elders and chief priests and scribes, and be killed, and be raised up on the third day. And Peter took Him aside and began to rebuke Him, saying, 'God forbid it, Lord! This shall never happen to You.'" *Matthew 16:21-22.*

3. Christ also said that He gave up His life willingly; He would not be killed by force.

"For this reason the Father loves me, because I lay down my life that I may take it up again. No one has taken it from Me, for I lay it down on my own initiative, I have authority to lay it down and I have authority to take it up again. This commandment I received from My Father." *John 10:17,18*

4. When Jesus' followers found His tomb empty, an angel reminded them that Jesus had predicted His own death.

"'He is not here, but He has risen. Remember how He spoke to you while He was still in Galilee, saying that the Son of Man must be delivered into the hands of sinful men, and be crucified, and the third day rise again.' And they remembered His words." *Luke 24:6-8*

5. Why was Jesus so determined to give His life? Because He knew that only He was qualified to pay the penalty for all the sins of mankind, so that we could obtain forgiveness.

"He Himself bore our sins in His body on the cross, that we might die to sin and live to righteousness; for by His wounds you were healed." *1 Peter 2:24*

"Christ also died for sins once for all, the just for the unjust, in order that He might bring us to God." *1 Peter 3:18*

6. Jesus' resurrection is important because it is the ultimate, undeniable proof that He was indeed God's Son.

Jesus was "declared with power to be the Son of God by the resurrection from the dead." *Romans 1:4*

"If Christ has not been raised, your faith is worthless; you are still in your sins." *1 Corinthians 15:17*

7. If Jesus did not die on the cross, then it raises many important questions:

- If Jesus escaped the cross altogether, and someone else was mistakenly crucified in His place, then why did Jesus foretell His own death and resurrection if He had not intended to go through with it?
- Why wasn't the body of the person supposedly executed in His place still buried in the tomb?
- If Jesus wasn't crucified, how did He get the nail wounds in His hands and feet, or the spear wound in His side?
- Why did the angel lie to the disciples at the tomb by telling them Jesus had risen from the dead?

8. One of Jesus' disciples, "Doubting Thomas," is like many people who doubt Christ's resurrection today. But once he saw Jesus was alive, look at the conclusion he reached about who Jesus was:

"'Unless I shall see in His hands the imprint of the nails, and put my finger into the place of the nails, and put my hand into His side, I will not believe.' And after eight days again His disciples were inside, and Thomas with them. Jesus came, the doors having been shut, and stood in their midst, and said, 'Peace be with you.' Then He said to Thomas, 'Reach here your finger, and see My hands; and reach here your hand, and put it into My side; and be not unbelieving, but believing.' Thomas answered and said to Him, 'My Lord and my God!'" *John 20:25-28*

9. So who was Jesus? A teacher? A prophet? Jesus once asked His disciples who the people thought He was:

"And they said, 'Some say John the Baptist; some, Elijah; and others Jeremiah, or one of the prophets.'" *Matthew 16:14*

10. After His disciples had answered Jesus' question, He asked them this important follow-up question:

"He said to them, 'But who do you say that I am?' And Simon Peter answered and said, 'You are the Christ, the Son of the living God.'" *Matthew 16:15,16*

11. Many people respect Jesus as a prophet, but He claimed to be more than a prophet. He claimed to be God's Son.

"But Jesus remained silent. The high priest said to him, "I charge you under oath by the living God: Tell us if you are the Christ, the Son of God.' 'Yes, it is as you say,' Jesus replied." *Matthew 26:63,64a (NIV)*

12. The Bible teaches that there is one God, and God exists in three distinct "Persons:" God the Father, God the Son, and God the Holy Spirit. (Much like H20 exists in three forms; liquid/water, solid/ice, and gas/steam.)

"Then God said, 'Let Us make man in Our image, according to Our likeness.'" *Genesis 1:26*

"May the grace of our Lord Jesus Christ, the love of God, and the fellowship of the Holy Spirit be with you all. *2 Corinthians 13:13 (NLT)*

13. As God's Son, Jesus was both fully God and fully man. His death is important because that is how He paid for our sins. By taking our sins onto Himself, His sacrificial death makes it possible for us to have access to God the Father.

"For God so loved the world, that He gave His only begotten Son, that whoever believes in Him shall not perish, but have everlasting life." *John 3:16*

"But God demonstrates His own love toward us, in that while we were yet sinners, Christ died for us." *Romans 5:8*

14. Many people respect Jesus as a good teacher and prophet, but often reject His teachings that He was God in the flesh. To reject this important truth means to say that Jesus was a liar and a deceiver.

"The Jews answered Him, 'For a good work we do not stone You, but for blasphemy; and because You, being a man, make Yourself out to be God.'" *John 10:33*

"For this reason therefore the Jews were seeking all the more to kill Him, because He not only was breaking the Sabbath, but also was calling God His own Father, making Himself equal with God." *John 5:18*

"For in Him (Jesus) all the fulness of Deity dwells in bodily form." *Colossians 2:9*

15. When it comes to how we obtain salvation, the Koran and the Bible have very different views. The Koran teaches to trust in our good deeds to get us to heaven. It describes a set of scales where our good deeds are placed on one side, and our bad deeds in the other. If the good deeds outweighs the bad, we go to heaven.

"On that day all shall be weighed with justice. Those whose scales are heavy shall triumph, but those whose scales are light shall lose their souls, because they have denied Our revelations." *(From the Koran, Surah 7:8,9)*

16. But the Bible teaches that our only way to have access to God is by trusting in Christ's death to pay for our sins. No amount of good deeds will outweigh our sins. We must individually believe Jesus Christ was God's Son who paid the penalty for our sins by dying on a cross, then proved He was telling the truth by rising from the dead.

"Jesus said, 'I am the way, and the truth, and the life; no one comes to the Father, but through Me.'" *John 14:6*

"For the wages of sin is death, but the free gift of God is eternal life in Christ Jesus our Lord." *Romans 6:23*

21 Jehovah's Witnesses (Watchtower Bible and Tract Society)

Charles Taze Russell (1852-1916) attended a protestant church while growing up in Pennsylvania. As he reached adulthood, he found various areas of traditional Christian theology with which he disagreed. Being an independent thinker, he began to develop and teach his own theology. He gained a following, and in 1884 incorporated his growing organization and called it the Watchtower Bible and Tract Society. Mr. Russell would certainly agree that his teachings are different from the teachings of traditional Christianity. Most of the differences concern two key issues: Who exactly was Jesus Christ, and how can we obtain salvation? But which views are true?

Jesus gave us a very simple way to know the truth: "If you abide in My word, then you are truly disciples of Mine; and you shall know the truth, and the truth shall make you free." (John 8:31,32) By looking to God's Word, we can compare Jehovah's Witness teachings to those of traditional, orthodox Christianity. After all, if a person believes the teachings which are not the truth, it will have eternal consequences.

1. Jehovah's Witnesses teach that Jesus is our Savior, but that He was only a perfect man and not God.

"The justice of God would not permit that Jesus as a ransom be more than a perfect man. And certainly not the supreme God almighty in the flesh." (Charles Russell, *Let God Be True*)

2. But if Jesus Christ was only a man and not God, His sacrificial death on the cross does nothing to help us obtain forgiveness. According to Scripture, only God can be our Savior.

"I am the Lord your God, the Holy One of Israel, your Savior... Before Me there was no God formed, and there will be none after Me. I, even I, and the Lord; and there is no savior besides Me." *Isaiah. 43:3,10,11*

"And all flesh will know that I, the Lord, am your Savior, and your redeemer the Mighty One of Jacob." *Isaiah 49:26*

"Yet I have been the Lord your God and you were not to know any god except Me, since the land of Egypt; for there is no savior besides Me." *Hosea 13:4*

For it is for this we labor and strive, because we have fixed our hope on the living God, who is the Savior of all men." *1 Timothy 4:10*

"And we have beheld and bear witness that the Father has sent the Son to be the Savior of the world." *1 John 4:14*

"God has brought to Israel a Savior, Jesus." *Acts 13:23*b

"For in Him (Jesus) all the fulness of Deity dwells in bodily form." *Colossians 2:9*

"For this cause the Jews were seeking all the more to kill Him, because not only was He breaking the Sabbath, but also was calling God His own Father, making Himself equal with God." *John 5:18*

3. Jehovah's Witnesses teach that Jesus was created, and that He has not pre-existed for all eternity as God the Father has. But what does the Bible say about this?

"But as for you, Bethlehem Ephrathah, too little to be among the clans of Judah, from you One will go forth for Me to be ruler in Israel. His goings forth are from long ago from the days of eternity." *Micah 5:2*

"'Your father Abraham rejoiced to see My day, and he saw it and was glad.' So the Jews said to Him, 'You are not yet fifty years old, and have You seen Abraham?' Jesus said to them, 'Truly, truly, I say to you, before Abraham was born, I AM.' Therefore they picked up stones to throw at Him; but Jesus hid Himself, and went out of the temple." *John 8:56-59*

(In this verse, Jesus refers to Himself using the exact same name ("I AM") that God called Himself when speaking to Moses from the burning bush! When His listeners clearly understood that Jesus was claiming to be God, they viewed this as heresy and were ready to stone Him for it. However, the Jehovah's Witness version of the Bible, the New World

Translation, changes the wording to remove Jesus' clear claim to divinity. In the NWT, verse 58 reads: "Jesus said to them: 'Most truly I say to you, before Abraham came into existence, I have been.'" But this watered down claim would not have been considered heresy, or motivated His listeners to call for a stoning.)

4. Even though Charles Russell taught his followers not to worship Jesus, Jesus was indeed worshiped by His followers.

"And they came into the house and saw the Child with Mary His mother; and they fell down and worshiped Him." Matthew 2:11

"And he said, 'Lord, I believe.' And he worshiped Him." *John 9:38*

"And those who were in the boat worshiped Him, saying, 'You are certainly God's Son!'" *Matthew 14:33*

"And behold, Jesus met them and greeted them. And they came up and took hold of His feet and worshiped Him." *Matthew 28:9*

"The Father... has given all judgment to the Son, in order that all may honor the Son, even as they honor the Father. He who does not honor the Son does not honor the Father who sent Him." *John 5:22,23*

5. Christ was fully God, and He died for us.

"'I am the Alpha and the Omega,' says the Lord God, 'who is and who was and who is to come, the Almighty.... Do not be afraid; I am the first and the last, and the living One; and I was dead, and behold, I am alive forevermore, and I have the keys of death and of Hades." *Revelation 1:8,17,18*

This passage is clearly talking about God. But if Jesus was not God, then when did God die?

6. Mr. Russell taught that trusting in Jesus Christ's death on the cross does not fully pay for our individual sin.

According to Mr. Russell, "...each for himself, may have a full chance to prove, by obedience or disobedience, their worthiness of life eternal." (*Studies in the Scriptures,* Vol. 1, p.298)

7. But the Scriptures tell us that good works can't help earn our salvation. It is a gift based totally on faith.

"Many will say to Me on that day, 'Lord, Lord, did we not prophesy in Your name, and in Your name cast out demons, and in Your name perform many miracles?' And then I will declare to them, 'I never knew you; depart from Me, you who practice lawlessness.'" *Matthew 7:22,23*

"For by grace you have been saved through faith; and that not from yourselves, it is the gift of God, not as a result of works, that no one should boast." *Ephesians 2:8,9*

"The wages of sin is death, but the free gift of God is eternal life in Christ Jesus our Lord." *Romans 6:23*

"He saved us, not on the basis of deeds we have done in righteousness, but according to His mercy, by the washing of regeneration and renewing of the Holy Spirit, whom He poured out upon us richly through Jesus Christ our Savior." *Titus 3:5,6*

8. What happens to people who distort the gospel, or teach a different plan of salvation from the Bible?

"But even if we, or an angel from heaven, should preach to you a gospel contrary to what we have preached to you, he is to be accursed! As we have said before, so I say again now, if any man is preaching to you a gospel contrary to what you received, he is to be accursed!" *Galatians 1:8,9*

9. The final question is: Do you want to trust your entire eternal destiny to the teachings of a man who disagreed with what the Bible clearly teaches? Or will you trust what the Bible says?

"These things I have written to you who believe in the name of the Son of God, in order that you may know that you have eternal life." *1 John 5:13*

"Then they asked Him, 'What must we do to do the works God requires?' Jesus answered, 'The work of God is this: to believe in the One He has sent.'" *John 6:28,29*

22 Judaism

Many Jews tend to reject Jesus as the Messiah because He did not set up His kingdom on earth. But there is also another mission for the Messiah as described in the Hebrew Bible.

The shedding of blood by a perfect, innocent sacrifice was a recurring theme in regard to appeasing God's judgment to receive His mercy and the forgiveness of sins. The Passover lamb is a perfect example. But was the shed blood of the Passover lamb symbolic of how the Messiah Himself would shed His own blood so our sins could be forgiven? Jesus certainly shed His blood, but if He was the Messiah then why didn't He set up His earthly kingdom while He was here?

1. At the first Passover, those who were protected by the blood of the lamb received God's mercy. Those not protect ed by the blood of the lamb received God's judgment.

"Then Moses summoned all the elders of Israel and said to them, 'Go at once and select the animals for your families and slaughter the Passover lamb. Take a bunch of hyssop, dip it into the blood in the basin and put some of the blood on the top and both sides of the doorframe. Not one of you shall go out the door of his house until morning. When the Lord goes through the land to strike down the Egyptians, He will see the blood on the top and sides of the doorframe and He will not permit the destroyer to enter your houses and strike you down.'" *Exodus 12:21-23*

2. Isaiah wrote that the Lord would take our sins onto Himself and give His life much like a sacrificial lamb.

"But He was pierced through for our transgressions, He was crushed for our iniquities; the chastening for our well-being fell upon Him, and by His scourging we are healed. All of us like sheep have gone astray, each of us has turned to his own way; but the Lord has caused the iniquity of us all to fall on Him. He was oppressed and He was afflicted, yet He did not open His mouth; like a lamb that is led to slaughter, and like a sheep that is silent before its shearers, so He did not open His mouth." *Isaiah 53:5-7*

3. When Jesus began His ministry in Israel, John the Baptist introduced Him to the Jews as the "Lamb of God."

"The next day John saw Jesus coming toward him and said, 'Look, the Lamb of God who takes away the sin of the world!'" *John 1:29*

4. Isaiah did not say when it would happen, but he predicted the Messiah would set up a kingdom on earth.

"For to us a child is born, to us a child is given, and the government will be on his shoulders. And he will be called Wonderful Counselor, Mighty God, Everlasting Father, Prince of Peace. Of the increase of his government and peace there will be no end. He will reign on David's throne and over his kingdom, establishing and upholding it with justice and righteousness from that time on and forever." *Isaiah 9:6,7 (NIV)*

5. The religious leaders of His day felt Jesus' claim to be equal with God was blasphemy, a crime which the Mosaic law condemned. And since the proof they were looking for was the setting up of an earthly kingdom, they thought Jesus did not qualify to be the Messiah. They wanted Him executed for making these claims:

- Jesus claimed to be the Messiah. *John 4:25,26*
- Jesus claimed to be the Christ. *Mark 14:62-64*
- Jesus claimed to be King of the Jews. *Matthew 27:11*
- Jesus claimed to be God's Son, making Himself equal with God. *John 5:18, 10:33, Luke 22:70*
- Jesus claimed to be able to forgive sins, something only God can do. *Mark 2:1-12*
- Jesus claimed to be the only way to have access to God. *John 14:6*
- Jesus called Himself the same name God used from the burning bush. *John 8:56-59*

6. The Jews of Jesus' time understood that the Messiah was predicted to set up His kingdom on earth, and they were hoping Jesus would free them from the Romans. But they did not grasp that only the Messiah was qualified to be the perfect sacrifice God would accept as payment for sins. This is why He allowed Himself to die. The crowds thought that if He was the Messiah, He should save Himself. But He had come to save *them*.

"And the inscription of the charge against Him read, 'The King of the Jews'.... And those passing by were hurling abuse at Him, wagging their heads, and saying, 'Ha! You who were going to destroy the temple and rebuilt it in three days, save Yourself, and come down from the cross!' In the same way the chief priests along with the scribes were also mocking Him among themselves and saying, 'He saved others; He cannot save Himself. Let this Christ, the King of Israel, now come down from the cross so that we may see and believe!'" *Mark 15:26,29-32*

7. When God provided the sacrifice to take the place of Abraham's son Isaac, it was the perfect foreshadowing of how God would provide the ultimate sacrifice in Jesus.

"Isaac spoke to Abraham his father and said, 'My father!' And he said, 'Here I am, my son.' And he said, 'Behold, the fire and the wood, but where is the lamb for the burnt offering?' Abraham said, 'God will provide for Himself the lamb for the burnt offering, my son.' So the two of them walked on together.... Then Abraham raised his eyes and looked, and behold, behind him a ram caught in the thicket by his horns; and Abraham went and took the ram and offered him up for a burnt offering in the place of his son." *Genesis 22:7,8,13*

8. The ultimate proof that Jesus was God's Son was His resurrection from the dead.

Jesus was "declared with power to be the Son of God by the resurrection from the dead." *Romans 1:4*

"Christ died for our sins according to the Scriptures... He was buried... He was raised on the third day according to the Scriptures, and after that He appeared to Cephas (Peter), then to the twelve. After that He appeared to more than five hundred brethren at one time." *1 Corinthians 15:3-6*

9. Today, Christ's blood pays for our forgiveness and protects us from judgment – much like the Passover Lamb.

"You were not redeemed with perishable things like silver or gold from your futile way of life inherited from your forefathers, but with precious blood, as of a lamb unblemished and spotless, the blood of Christ." *1 Peter 1:18,19*

"But God demonstrates His own love toward us, in that while we were yet sinners, Christ died for us. Much more then, having now been justified by His blood, we shall be saved from the wrath of God through Him." *Romans 5:8,9*

10. So if Jesus is the Messiah, why has He waited so long to return to earth and set up His kingdom? His own disciples asked Him this same question after His resurrection.

"And so when they had come together, they were asking Him, saying, 'Lord is it at this time You are restoring the kingdom to Israel?' He said to them, 'It is not for you to know.'" *Acts 1:6*

11. God is obviously more patient than we are, because He is waiting for His salvation message to reach all the world so they can believe in Jesus as the Messiah and be saved. When Jesus does return, He will finally reign as King.

"And as He was sitting on the Mount of Olives, the disciples came to Him privately, saying, 'Tell us, when will these things be, and what will be the sign of Your coming, and of the end of the age?' And Jesus said to them, 'See to it that no one misleads you... And this gospel of the kingdom shall be preached in the whole world for a witness to all the nations, and then the end shall come.'" *Matthew 24:3,4,14*

12. Jews and Christians worship the same God, but through different access. Jews tend to believe we can access God by doing good works and being righteous. But Christians believe we can only access God through faith in Christ, because we are far from perfect and only He can qualify as the perfect sacrifice who could atone for our sins – just like the spotless Passover lamb that was a symbol of the future Messiah of Israel.

"What shall we say then? That Gentiles, who did not pursue righteousness, attained righteousness, even the righteousness which is by faith; but Israel, pursuing a law of righteousness, did not arrive at that law. Why? Because they did not pursue it by faith, but as though it were by works." *Romans 9:30-32*

"Jesus said to him, 'I am the way, and the truth, and the life; no one comes to the Father, but through Me.'" *John 14:6*

"I am the door; if anyone enters through Me, he will be saved, and will go in and out and find pasture. The thief comes only to steal and kill and destroy; I came that they may have life, and have it abundantly." *John 10:9,10*

23 Kabbalah

The practice of Kabbalah is said to date back thousands of years, and reached its peak in medieval Spain. Traditionally, it was only taught to Jewish men over forty, but in recent years there has been a resurgence of popularity even beyond the Jewish faith, with many celebrity followers. The central Kabbalah teachings are found in a multi-volume book called The Zohar, which contains commentaries, sermons, treatises, etc. It brings esoteric and mystical insights into the teachings of the Torah (the first five books of the Hebrew Bible, also known as the Old Testament.) It teaches that the Torah can only make sense by understanding the symbolic, encoded, hidden meanings in the text – the Bible is not to be understood merely at face value; its real meaning only emerges through the lens of the Zohar and the teachings of Kabbalah.

The goal of Kabbalah is to restore the oneness and unbroken relationship mankind enjoyed with God in the original Garden of Eden. They believe that the creator God, known as Ein Sof, can only be known or reached through the Tree of Life. God's light flows downward to humanity through the Tree of Life which has ten branches, or "emanations of God." As we increase our understanding and master these ten truths, we climb these branches like "rungs on a ladder to enlightenment." As we ascend, we draw nearer to God by increasing our capacity to contain more of God's light, and eventually reunite with the Divine.

Kabbalah and the Bible agree that mankind has fallen from the perfect relationship with God that we enjoyed in the Garden of Eden. And both agree that we desperately need to be reconciled with our Creator. But the Bible offers a different perspective on how we can restore our original intimacy with God.

---

1. The Garden of Eden was a place of total perfection, where Adam and Eve had a close relationship with God.

"Then God said, 'Let there be light'; and there was light. God saw that the light was good; and God separated the light from the darkness." *Genesis 1:3*

"The Lord God planted a garden toward the east, in Eden; and there He placed the man whom He had formed. Out of the ground the Lord God caused to grow every tree that is pleasing to the sight and good for food; the tree of life also in the midst of the garden, and the tree of the knowledge of good and evil." *Genesis 2:8,9*

2. The world is now far from perfect, and is marred by the effects of sin which separates us from God.

"So He drove the man out; and at the east of the Garden of Eden He stationed the cherubim and the flaming sword which turned every direction to guard the way to the tree of life." *Genesis 3:24*

"But your iniquities have made a separation between you and your God, and your sins have hidden His face from you so that He does not hear.... Therefore justice is far from us, and righteousness does not overtake us; we hope for light, but behold, darkness, for brightness, but we walk in gloom." *Isaiah 59:2,9*

3. How can we restore our relationship with God? Good deeds and spiritual learning can make us better people, but fall far short of bridging the gap that sin has created between sinful man and our holy God.

"For all of us have become like one who is unclean, and all our righteous deeds are like a filthy garment; and all of us wither like a leaf, and our iniquities, like the wind, take us away." *Isaiah 64:6*

"For all have sinned and fall short of the glory of God." *Romans 3:23*

4. The Bible teaches that we must be holy to be allowed into God's presence. That is why God sent His Son Jesus to earth. Jesus was fully God and fully man, and as the only perfect, sinless human, He provides the only acceptable payment for our sin. This is why He allowed Himself to be crucified on the cross.

"For God so loved the world, that He gave His only begotten Son, that whoever believes in Him shall not perish, but have eternal life. For God did not send the Son into the world to judge the world, but that the world might be saved through Him." *John 3:16,17*

"This is good and acceptable in the sight of God our Savior, who desires all men to be saved and to come to the knowledge of the truth. For there is one God, and one mediator also between God and men, the man Christ Jesus, who gave Himself as a ransom for all, the testimony given at the proper time." *1 Timothy 2:3-6*

"We are Christ's ambassadors, and God is using us to speak to you. We urge you, as though Christ himself were here pleading with you, 'Be reconciled to God!' For God made Christ, who never sinned, to be the offering for our sin, so that we could be made right with God through Christ." *2 Corinthians 5:20,21 (NLT)*

5. Does God bury important truths in the Bible by cloaking them in deep mystery that only the enlightened people could possibly understand? Jesus' own disciples asked Him a similar question when He kept teaching the multitudes by using parables. Jesus told them the only requirement to understanding God's teachings is the willingness to seek God's truths and submit to Him by becoming His disciple. Rebellion obstructs spiritual clarity.

"His disciples came and asked him, 'Why do you always tell stories when you talk to the people?' Then he explained to them, 'You have been permitted to understand the secrets of the Kingdom of Heaven, but others have not. To those who are open to my teaching, more understanding will be given, and they will have an abundance of knowledge. But to those who are not listening, even what they have will be taken away from them. That is why I tell these stories, because people see what I do, but they don't really see. They hear what I say, but they don't really hear, and they don't understand. This fulfills the prophecy of Isaiah, which says: "You will hear my words, but you will not understand; you will see what I do, but you will not perceive its meaning. For the hearts of these people are hardened, and their ears cannot hear, and they have closed their eyes – so their eyes cannot see, and their ears cannot hear, and their hearts cannot understand, and they cannot turn to me and let me heal them.""" *Matthew 13:10-15 (NLT)*

"So Jesus was saying to those Jews who had believed Him, 'If you continue in My word, then you are truly disciples of Mine; and you will know the truth, and the truth will make you free.'" *John 8:31,32*

6. If Kabbalah has been around as long as people say, then it was around when Jesus lived. But He never said to follow its teachings or to seek God through climbing the Tree of Life. He claimed that we can only reach God through Him. Christianity is not about reaching God in our own strength; Christianity is about God reaching down to man through Jesus Christ to do what we could never do in our own strength.

"Jesus said to him, 'I am the way, and the truth, and the life; no one comes to the Father but through Me.'" *John 14:6*

"And there is salvation in no one else; for there is no other name under heaven that has been given among men by which we must be saved." *Acts 4:12*

"He who does not enter by the door into the fold of the sheep, but climbs up some other way, he is a thief and a robber.... I am the door; if anyone enters through Me, he will be saved, and will go in and out and find pasture. The thief comes only to steal and kill and destroy; I came that they may have life, and have it abundantly." *John 10:1,9,10*

7. Only those whose sins are paid for by Christ will be allowed into heaven. There we will eat from the Tree of Life, and enjoy deep intimacy with God.

"He who has an ear, let him hear what the Spirit says to the churches. To him who overcomes, I will grant to eat of the tree of life which is in the Paradise of God." *Revelation 2:7*

"Then he showed me a river of the water of life, clear as crystal, coming from the throne of God and of the Lamb, in the middle of its street. On either side of the river was the tree of life, bearing twelve kinds of fruit, yielding its fruit every month; and the leaves of the tree were for the healing of the nations. There will no longer be any curse; and the throne of God and of the Lamb will be in it, and His bond-servants will serve Him; they will see His face, and His name will be on their foreheads. And there will no longer be any night; and they will not have need of the light of a lamp nor the light of the sun, because the Lord God will illumine them; and they will reign forever and ever." *Revelation 22:1-5*

8. To begin a relationship with God, confess your sins and place your trust in Jesus instead of your own good deeds.

"But as many as received Him, to them He gave the right to become children of God, even to those who believe in His name." *John 1:12*

24 Lifespring

Founded in 1974 by John P. Hanley, Randy Revell, and three others, Lifespring is based on seeking the betterment of their followers to reach their full potential. Lifespring teaches, "At the essence, or core, of each of us is a perfect, loving, and caring being." (Self Acceptance: Real Encounter, front page)

Christianity also seeks the betterment of its followers, but through a very different way. The Bible teaches that there has only been one perfect, loving, and caring being – Jesus Christ – and He came to make us perfect, loving, caring beings. So, how does the Bible say we can become the perfect, loving, and caring beings we were meant to be?

1. Lifespring teaches that our power to become perfect comes from within.

"Each of us already has everything necessary to achieve and be all we want in our lives." *(Questions and Answers about Lifespring, p. 3)*

2. The Bible has a very different view concerning what is within us.

"The heart is deceitful above all things and beyond cure. Who can understand it?" *Jeremiah 17:9*

3. The Apostle Paul wrote very openly about the reality of his own personal struggle with doing what is right.

"I don't understand myself at all, for I really want to do what is right, but I don't do it. Instead, I do the very thing I hate. I know perfectly well that what I am doing is wrong, and my bad conscience shows that I agree that the law is good. But I can't help myself, because it is sin inside me that makes me do these evil things. I know I am rotten through and through so far as my old sinful nature is concerned. No matter which way I turn, I can't make myself do right. I want to, but I can't. When I want to do good, I don't. And when I try not to do wrong, I do it anyway. But if I am doing what I don't want to do, I am not really the one doing it; the sin within me is doing it. It seems to be a fact of life that when I want to do what is right, I inevitably do what is wrong. I love God's law with all my heart. But there is another law at work within me that is at war with my mind. This law wins the fight and makes me a slave to the sin that is still within me. Oh, what a miserable person I am! Who will free me from this life that is dominated by sin?" *Romans 7:15-24 (NLT)*

4. The strength needed to improve ourselves cannot come from within ourselves, but only from God.

"Not that we are adequate in ourselves to consider anything as coming from ourselves. But our adequacy is from God." *2 Corinthians 3:5*

"Thus says the Lord, 'Cursed is the man who trusts in mankind and makes flesh his strength, and whose heart turns away from the Lord. For he will be like a bush in the desert and will not see when prosperity comes, but will live in stony wastes in the wilderness, a land of salt without inhabitant. Blessed is the man who trusts in the Lord and whose trust is the Lord. For he will be like a tree planted by the water, that extends its roots by a stream and will not fear when the heat comes; but its leaves will be green, and it will not be anxious in a year of drought nor cease to yield fruit.'" *Jeremiah 17:5-8*

5. The first step to becoming a "perfect, loving, caring being" is to admit you are not a "perfect, loving, caring being." Then you must admit that you need help beyond yourself to overcome our struggles, addictions, harmful thoughts, and destructive behavior patterns.

"The Lord has looked down from heaven upon the sons of men, to see if there are any who understand, who seek after God. They have all turned aside; together they have become corrupt; there is no one who does good, not even one." *Psalm 14:1-3*

"If we say that we have no sin, we are deceiving ourselves, and the truth is not in us. If we confess our sins, He is faithful and righteous to forgive us our sins and to cleanse us from all unrighteousness. If we say that we have not sinned, we make Him a liar, and His word is not in us." *1 John 1:8-10*

"But your iniquities have made a separation between you and your God, and your sins have hid His face from you, so that He does not hear." *Isaiah 59:2*

"For all have sinned and fall short of the glory of God." *Romans 3:23*

6. Jesus is the only perfect person to have ever lived, and He never sinned. That's because He was both fully God and fully man.

"For we do not have a high priest who cannot sympathize with our weaknesses, but one who has been tempted in all things as we are, yet without sin." *Hebrews 4:15*

"And you know that He appeared in order to take away sins; and in Him there is no sin." *1 John 3:5*

"For in Him all the fulness of Deity dwells in bodily form." *Colossians 2:9*

"For there is one God, and one mediator also between God and men, the man Christ Jesus, who gave Himself as a ransom for all." *1 Timothy 2:5,6a*

7. Because Jesus was perfect, He is the only acceptable sacrifice who could pay the penalty for the sins of all who are not perfect.

"But God demonstrates His own love for us in that while we were yet sinners Christ died for us." *Romans 5:8*

"But He was pierced through for our transgressions, He was crushed for our iniquities; the chastening for our well-being fell upon Him, and by His scourging we are healed. All of us like sheep have gone astray, each of us has turned to his own way; but the Lord has caused the iniquity of us all to fall on Him." *Isaiah 53:5,6*

"John saw Jesus coming toward him and said, 'Look, the Lamb of God who takes away the sin of the world!'" *John 1:29*

"He made Him who knew no sin to be sin on our behalf, that we might become the righteousness of God in Him." *2 Corinthians 5:21*

8. We can be forgiven in this life; however, we will not become perfect in this life. With God's help we can grow towards perfection in this life, but we won't achieve perfection until we see the Lord.

"Not that I have already obtained it or have already become perfect, but I press on in order that I may lay hold of that for which also I was laid hold of by Christ Jesus." *Philippians 3:12*

"And after you have suffered for a little while, the God of all grace, who called you to His eternal glory in Christ, will Himself perfect, confirm, strengthen, and establish you." *1 Peter 5:10*

"We know that when He appears, we shall be like Him, because we shall see Him just as He is." *1 John 3:2*

9. In order to receive God's power to overcome bad patterns and habits, we must first individually receive Christ as the payment for our sins. Once God lives within us, He empowers us to become better and better people. As we grow closer to God and benefit from the gifts of other believers, we grow in spiritual maturity.

"Behold, I stand at the door and knock; if any one hears My voice and opens the door, I will come in to him, and will dine with him, and he with me." *Revelation 3:20*

"But as many as received Him, to them He gave the right to become children of God, even to those who believe in His name." *John 1:12*

10. As Christians, we can have the deepest possible joy by being Christ-centered, not self-centered.

John the Baptist said regarding Jesus: "By this my joy has been made full. He must increase, but I must decrease." *John 3:29b,30a*

Jesus once told a woman who was drawing water from a well, "Whoever drinks of the water that I shall give him shall never thirst; but the water that I shall give him shall become in him a well of water springing up to eternal life." *John 4:14*

25 Marxism (Communism, Leninism)

Karl Marx (1818-1883) was a German philosopher and revolutionary socialist. He was an atheist who believed that the material world is all that exists. He saw religion as a tool of the ruling class to manipulate the suppressed working class with hopes of a better life in the hereafter. To Marx, the great "classless society" could only exist once all religion was abolished, paving the way for the perfection of society through the process of change he called "dialectical materialism." In his own words, "Religion is the opiate of the people and the enemy of all progress." He thought that God did not create man, but man created God. Marx felt that class reform is man's top priority. He fought strongly against class suppression, even if it meant fighting it by suppressing religion.

Many years have passed since Marx gave the world his formula for society's happiness. Unfortunately, history has proven that when any society ceases to believe in God, or to be accountable to Him, suppression does not cease – it increases dramatically! Was his mistake to base his philosophy on the premise that the material world is all that exists?

1. First of all, the Bible teaches that the material world is not all that exists.

"The fool has said in his heart, 'There is no God.'" *Psalm 14:1*

"The wicked, in the haughtiness of his countenance, does not seek Him. All his thoughts are, 'There is no God.'" *Psalm 10:4*

"Know that the Lord Himself is God; it is He who has made us, and not we ourselves. We are His people and the sheep of His pasture." *Psalm 100:3*

"The natural man does not accept the things of the Spirit of God; for they are foolishness to Him, and he cannot understand them, because they are spiritually appraised." *1 Corinthians 2:14*

2. While Marx taught that the material world is all that exists, the Bible teaches that the most convincing proof that God exists is the material world that He created.

"The heavens are telling of the glory of God; and their expanse is declaring the work of His hands. Day to day pours forth speech, and night to night reveals knowledge. There is no speech, nor are there words; their voice is not heard. Their line has gone out through all the earth, and their utterances to the end of the world." *Psalm 19:1-4*

"For since the creation of the world His invisible attributes, His eternal power and divine nature, have been clearly seen, being understood through what has been made, so that they are without excuse." *Romans 1:20*

"It is I who made the earth, and created man upon it. I stretched out the heavens with My hands, and I ordained all their host." *Isaiah 45:12*

3. Often the reason a person has never found God is because that person has never seriously sought God. The Bible promises those who seriously seek God will find Him. Then it's up to us to either accept or reject Him.

"The God who made the world and all things in it... made from one, every nation of mankind to live on all the face of the earth... that they should seek God, if perhaps they might grope for Him and find Him, though He is not far from each one of us." *Acts 17:24,26,27*

"And you will seek Me and find Me, when you search for Me with all your heart." *Jeremiah 29:13*

"If you seek Him, He will let you find Him; but if you forsake Him, He will reject you forever." *1 Chronicles 28:9*

4. The Bible tells us what to expect for those who reject God and trust in themselves. And history proves it true.

"Thus says the Lord, 'Cursed is the man who trusts in mankind and makes flesh his strength, and whose heart turns away from the Lord. For he will be like a bush in the desert and will not see when prosperity comes, but will live in stony wastes in the wilderness, a land of salt without inhabitant. Blessed is the man who trusts in the Lord and whose trust is the Lord. For he will be like a tree planted by the water, that extends its roots by a stream and will not fear when the heat comes; but its leaves will be green, and it will not be anxious in a year of drought nor cease to yield fruit.'" *Jeremiah 17:5-8*

5. God sent His Son Jesus to the earth. By learning from God's Son, we learn about God the Father.

"God... has spoken to us in His Son, whom He appointed heir of all things, through whom also He made the world. And He is the radiance of His glory and the exact representation of His nature, and upholds all things by the word of His power. When He had made purification of sins, He sat down at the right hand of the Majesty on high." *Hebrews 1:1-3*

"And He is the image of the invisible of God." *Colossians 1:15*

"For in Him all the fulness of Deity dwells in bodily form." *Colossians 2:9*

6. Jesus gave His life so that we can be forgiven and begin a new relationship with God, who is holy.

"For God so loved the world that He gave His only begotten Son, that whoever believes in Him shall not perish but have everlasting life." *John 3:16*

"But God demonstrates His own love for us in that while we were yet sinners, Christ died for us." *Romans 5:8*

"For there is salvation in no one else; for there is no other name under heaven that has been given among men, by which we must be saved." *Acts 4:12*

"For there is one God, and one mediator also between God and men, the man Christ Jesus, who gave Himself as a ransom for all." *1 Timothy 2:5,6a*

"Jesus said to him, 'I am the way, and the truth, and the life; no one comes to the Father, but through Me.'" *John 14:6*

7. To begin to get to know God, ask Jesus into your heart. Then your new relationship with God will begin.

"But as many as received Him, to them He gave the right to become children of God, even to those who believe in His name." *John 1:12*

"Behold, I stand at the door and knock; if any one hears My voice and opens the door, I will come into him, and dine with him, and he with Me." *Revelation 3:20*

8. Belief in God not only results in a better hereafter, but in a better now.

"The thief comes only to steal, and kill, and destroy; I came that they might have life, and might have it abundantly." *John 10:10*

9. Karl Marx taught that the ruling class promoted religion as a way to manipulate and suppress the lower class. But countries who have embraced Marxism are well known for suppressing the freedoms of their citizens. In spite of Marx's views toward religion, fully devoted followers of Christ constantly proclaim that their relationship of submission to God is a source of great freedom.

"So Jesus was saying to those Jews who had believed Him, 'If you abide in My word, then you are truly disciples of Mine; and you will know the truth, and the truth will make you free.... So if the Son makes you free, you will be free indeed.'" *John 8:31,32,36*

10. Jesus came to set us free from suppression, but in a very different way that Karl Marx taught. Jesus empowers us to overcome our inner slavery to sin. Only through Him can we obtain the power to overcome our human pride and fleshly addictions.

"For I joyfully concur with the law of God in the inner man, but I see a different law in the members of my body, waging war against the law of my mind, and making me a prisoner of the law of sin which is in my members. Wretched man that I am! Who will set me free from the body of this death? Thanks be to God through Jesus Christ our Lord!" *Romans 7:22-25*

26 Materialism

Material blessings are one of many types of blessings God holds in His hand. However, the Bible gives us certain guidelines regarding material blessings. For instance, Solomon (one of the richest men to ever live) wrote, "He who loves money will not be satisfied with money." (Ecclesiastes 5:16)

Sadly, a dangerous way of thinking has crept into the theology of many Churches and ministries who teach that material prosperity is proof of an obedient life. Unscrupulous preachers have manipulated Christians with the promise that if they give money to their church, God will reward them tenfold or more. The motive to give has been corrupted away from giving out of love to giving out of greed. On the other hand, misguided Christians aren't the only ones who have an imbalanced view of their material possessions. People of many faiths, as well as people with no belief in God, often place too much emphasis on the things they own.

What else does the Bible say regarding God's material blessings for us?

1. Material blessings are from the Lord.

"Every good thing bestowed and every perfect gift is from above, coming down from the Father of lights." *James 1:17*

2. Before God brought the Hebrews into the Promised Land, He reminded them that the power to make wealth came from Him.

"Otherwise, you may say in your heart, 'My power and the strength of my hand made me this wealth.' But you shall remember the Lord your God, for it is He who is giving you power to make wealth, that He may confirm His covenant which He swore to your fathers, as it is this day." *Deuteronomy 8:17,18*

3. The down side of material blessings is that if we love the riches God bestows, it can distract us from our primary task of seeking God Himself.

"Do not store up for yourselves treasures on earth, where moth and rust destroy, and where thieves break in and steal. But store up for yourselves treasures in heaven, where neither moth nor rust destroys, and where thieves do not break in or steal; for where your treasure is, there your heart will be also.... No one can serve two masters; for either he will hate the one and love the other, or he will hold to one and despise the other. You cannot serve God and wealth." *Matthew 6:19-21,24*

"Do not be anxious then, saying, 'What shall we eat?' or 'What shall we drink?' or 'With what shall we clothe ourselves?'.... But seek first His kingdom and His righteousness; and all these things shall be added to you." *Matthew 6:31,33*

4. We are allowed to have money, but we are not to love money. The Bible says contentment brings us peace.

"But those who want to get rich fall into temptation and a snare and many foolish and harmful desires which plunge men into ruin and destruction. For the love of money is a root of all sorts of evil, and some by longing for it have wandered away from the faith, and pierced themselves with many a pang." *1 Timothy 6:8-10*

"Let your character be free from the love of money, being content with what you have; for He Himself has said, 'I will never desert you, nor will I ever forsake you.'" *Hebrews 13:5*

"Not that I speak from want, for I have learned to be content in whatever circumstances I am." *Philippians 4:11*

5. Material blessings can actually choke out our spiritual growth, if we love them more than we love God.

"And the one on whom seed was sown among the thorns, this is the man who hears the word, and the worry of the world, and the deceitfulness of riches choke the word, and it becomes unfruitful." *Matthew 13:22*

6. According to Scripture, if we love money more than welove God, we are guilty of idolatry.

"Therefore consider the members of your earthly body as dead to immorality, impurity, passion, evil desire, and greed, which amounts to idolatry." *Colossians 3:5*

7. Material blessings are given to us so that we can enjoy them, and enjoy sharing them with others.

"Instruct those who are rich in this present world not to be conceited or to fix their hope on the uncertainty of riches, but on God, who richly supplies with all things to enjoy. Instruct them to do good, to be rich in good works, and to be generous and ready to share, storing up for themselves the treasure of a good foundation for the future, so that they may take hold of that which is life indeed." *1 Timothy 6:17-19*

8. Material blessings are good, but God has given us a far greater gift; His own Son.

"He who did not spare His own Son, but delivered Him up for us all, how will He not also with Him freely give us all things?" *Romans 8:32*

"For God so loved the world, that He gave His only begotten Son, that whoever believes in Him shall not perish, but have eternal life." *John 3:16*

"For in Him all the fulness of Deity dwells in bodily form." *Colossians 2:9*

9. Why is knowing Jesus Christ more valuable than material riches? Because through Jesus we can have access to God the Father and enjoy eternity with Him.

"For there is salvation in no one else; for there is no other name under heaven that has been given among men, by which we must be saved." *Acts 4:12*

"For there is one God, and one mediator also between God and men, the man Christ Jesus, who gave Himself as a ransom for all." *1 Timothy 2:5,6a*

"But God demonstrates His own love toward us, in that while we were yet sinners, Christ died for us." *Romans 5:8*

10. The Bible describes heaven as being a place of incredible wealth where the streets are paved with gold. So why spend your short life trying to acquire what is abundant in heaven?

"And the twelve gates were twelve pearls; each one of the gates was a single pearl. And the street of the city was pure gold, like transparent glass." *Revelation 21:21*

"He is no fool who gives what he cannot keep to gain that which he cannot lose." (Quote from Jim Elliot, a missionary who gave his life sharing the gospel with unreached people groups in Ecuador in 1956,)

11. God also wants to give us the gift of free salvation, which was paid for by Christ's sacrificial death, and comes only through believing in Christ.

"For the wages of sin is death, but the free gift of God is eternal life in Christ Jesus our Lord." *Romans 6:23*

"For by grace you have been saved through faith; and that not from yourselves, it is the gift of God, not as a result of works, that no one should boast." *Ephesians 2:8,9*

12. To receive God's greatest blessing which surpasses any material blessing, simply ask Christ into your heart.

"Jesus said to him, 'I am the way, and the truth, and the life; no one comes to the Father, but through Me.'" *John 14:6*

"I am the door; if anyone enters through Me, he shall be saved, and shall go in and out, and find pasture." *John 10:9*

"But as many as received Him, to them He gave the right to become children of God, even to those who believe in His name." *John 1:12*

"If you abide in My word, then you are truly disciples of Mine; and you shall know the truth, and the truth shall make you free." *John 8:31,32*

27 Mormonism (Church of Jesus Christ of Latter Day Saints, LDS)

Brigham Young (1801-1877) was a disciple of Joseph Smith (1805-1844) and an early leader of the Latter Day Saints. Young taught his followers, "Believe in God, believe in Jesus, and believe in Joseph (Smith) his prophet, and Brigham his successor, and I add, if you will believe in your hearts and confess with your mouth that Jesus is the Christ, that Joseph was a prophet, and that Brigham is his successor, you shall be saved in the kingdom of God." (Journal of Discourses, 6:229)

Perhaps the most telling phrase in his quote is, "...and I add." Does the original plan of salvation that Jesus Himself taught really need anything added to it?

Mormonism also teaches that God was once a human as we are now, and that we can also someday become the god of our own universe. As for the Bible, Mormons hold it in high regard but consider the more recent writings of Joseph Smith and church elders to be more definitive of God's truths. So how do Mormon teachings about God, the Bible, and "grace coupled with works" compare to traditional, biblical Christian teachings?

1. First of all, the Scriptures in the Bible have not been corrupted or changed to the point of being untrustworthy. God has promised to protect His words.

"For as the rain and snow come down from heaven, and do not return there without watering the earth, and making it bear and sprout, and furnishing seed to the sower and bread to the eater; so shall My word be which goes forth from My mouth; it shall not return to Me empty, without accomplishing what I desire, and without succeeding in the matter for which I sent it." *Isaiah 55:10,11*

"Heaven and earth will pass away, but My words will not pass away." *Matthew 24:35*

2. The Bible makes it clear that there is only one God, and He exists in three distinct "persons;" God the Father, God the Son, and God the Holy Spirit.

"Then God said, 'Let Us make man in Our image, according to Our likeness.'" *Genesis 1:26*

"Then I heard the voice of the Lord, saying, 'Whom shall I send, and who will go for Us?'" *Isaiah 6:8*

"Go therefore and make disciples of all the nations, baptizing them in the name of the Father and the Son and the Holy Spirit." *Matthew 28:19*

"And after being baptized, Jesus went up immediately from the water; and behold, the heavens were opened, and He saw the Spirit of God descending as a dove, and coming upon Him; and behold, a voice out of the heavens, saying, 'This is My beloved Son, in whom I am well pleased.'" *Matthew 3:16,17*

3. The Bible teaches that no other gods exist anywhere in the universe other than the one, true God.

"Before Me there was no God formed, and there will be none after Me. I, even I, and the Lord; and there is no savior besides Me." *Isaiah 43:10,11*

"Is there any God besides Me, or is there any other Rock? I know of none." *Isaiah 44:8*

4. Jesus, being fully God and fully man, is uniquely qualified to make it possible for us to have access to the Father.

"For in Him all the fulness of Deity dwells in bodily form." *Colossians 2:9*

"For there is one God, and one mediator also between God and men, the man Christ Jesus, who gave Himself as a ransom for all." *1 Timothy 2:5,6a*

"But now in Christ Jesus you who formerly were far off have been brought near by the blood of Christ... for through Him we both have our access in one Spirit to the Father." *Ephesians 2:13,18*

5. Salvation is free, but it's only free to us. A price has been paid, and it was paid by Jesus Christ Himself.

"For the wages of sin is death, but the free gift of God is eternal life in Christ Jesus our Lord." *Romans 6:23*

"God demonstrates His own love for us in that while we were yet sinners Christ died for us." *Romans 5:8*

"For Christ also died for sins once for all, the just for the unjust, in order that He might bring us to God, having been put to death in the flesh, but made alive in the spirit." *1 Peter 3:18*

"John saw Jesus coming toward him and said, 'Look, the Lamb of God who takes away the sin of the world!'" *John 1:29*

6. Even though good works are commanded, we cannot do enough good works to blot out our sin and get us to heaven, or prove ourselves worthy of salvation. According to the Scriptures, our good works have nothing to do with obtaining the free gift of salvation.

"All our righteous deeds are like a filthy garment." *Isaiah 64:6*

"He saved us, not on the basis of deeds which we have done in righteousness, but according to His mercy, by the washing of regeneration and renewing by the Holy Spirit, whom He poured out upon us richly through Jesus Christ our Savior." *Titus 3:5-6*

"For by grace you have been saved through faith; and that not of yourselves, it is the gift of God ; not as a result of works, so that no one may boast." *Ephesians 2:8,9*

"But as many as received Him, to them He gave the right to become children of God, even to those who believe in His name." *John 1:12*

"If you confess with your mouth Jesus as Lord, and believe in your heart that God raised Him from the dead, you shall be saved." *Romans 10:9*

7. Because salvation is a gift, based on faith not works, we can know we are saved.

"And this is the testimony: God has given us eternal life, and this life is in His Son. He who has the Son has life; he who does not have the Son of God does not have the life. I write these things to you who believe in the name of the Son of God so that you may know that you have eternal life." *1 John 5:11-13*

"For this reason it is by faith, that it might be in accordance with grace, in order that the promise may be certain to all the descendants." *Romans 4:16*

8. Faith in God is how people have been saved throughout all of Scripture.

"If, in fact, Abraham was justified by works, he had something to boast about – but not before God. What does the Scripture say? 'Abraham believed God and it was credited to him as righteousness.'" *Romans 4:2,3*

"...and after he (the Philippian jailer) brought them (Paul and Silas) out, he said, 'Sirs, what must I do to be saved?' And they said, 'Believe in the Lord Jesus, and you shall be saved, you and your household.'" *Acts 16:30,31*

9. Beware of any plan of salvation which differs from the traditional, historic gospel presented in the Bible.

"But even if we, or an angel from heaven, should preach to you a gospel contrary to what we have preached to you, he is to be accursed! As we have said before, so I say again now, if any man is preaching to you a gospel contrary to what you received, he is to be accursed!" *Galatians 1:8,9*

10. To know that you are saved, place 100% of your trust in Christ – not your works. God simply requires that we believe in Christ!

"Then they asked Him, 'What must we do to do the works God requires?' Jesus answered, 'The work of God is this: to believe in the One He has sent.'" *John 6:28,29*

28 Nation of Islam

One of the primary goals of the Nation of Islam is to act as a catalyst within the black community to promote the rights of blacks, and help undo the injustices caused by slavery. To do this they welcome the cooperation of black Christian churches as well. Muslims and Christians may have similar views on fighting injustice in the world, but even though the Nation of Islam wants to work with Christian churches to prevent injustice, are the core beliefs of Islam compatible with the core beliefs of Christianity?

1. **Men like W.D. Fard, Elijah Mohammed, Malcom X, and Louis Farrakhan have fought against the injustices of slavery, but Jesus has triumphed over a type of slavery no other human could conquer – our slavery to sin.**

   "Jesus answered them, 'Truly, truly, I say to you, every one who commits sin is the slave of sin.... If therefore the Son shall make you free, you shall be free indeed.'" *John 8:34,36*

   The Apostle Paul wrote: "For I joyfully concur with the law of God in the inner man, but I see a different law in the members of my body, waging war against the law of my mind, and making me a prisoner of the law of sin which is in my members. Wretched man that I am! Who will set me free from the body of this death? Thanks be to God through Jesus Christ our Lord!" *Romans 7:22-25*

2. **Why is Jesus qualified to set us free from sin? The Bible says that Jesus is God's only begotten Son. To beget means to create an offspring of the same nature as the parent, so a human can only beget another human. Yet the Koran teaches that God does not beget, which means Jesus was not God's Son.**

   "He (God) begetteth not, nor is He begotten; and there is none like unto Him." *(From the Koran, Surah 112:3)*

3. **When it comes to who Jesus is, the Koran and the Bible present different viewpoints. The Bible teaches that Jesus is indeed God's only begotten Son. Therefore, as God the Son, Jesus is every bit as divine as God the Father.**

   "For God so loved the world, that He gave His only begotten Son, that whoever believes in Him shall not perish, but have everlasting life." *John 3:16*

   "For in Him (Jesus) all the fulness of Deity dwells in bodily form." *Colossians 2:9*

4. **When it comes to how we obtain salvation, the Koran and the Bible also have very different views. The Koran describes a set of scales where our good deeds are placed on one side, and our bad deeds in the other. If the good deeds outweighs the bad, we go to heaven.**

   "On that day all shall be weighed with justice. Those whose scales are heavy shall triumph, but those whose scales are light shall lose their souls, because they have denied Our revelations." *(From the Koran, Surah 7:8,9)*

5. **But the Bible tells us that we can never pay for our own sins by doing good works. Our salvation is a free gift of God's mercy when we accept Christ as our Savior who died on the cross to pay the penalty for our sins.**

   "He Himself bore our sins in His body on the cross, that we might die to sin and live to righteousness; for by His wounds you were healed." *1 Peter 2:24*

   "The wages of sin is death, but the free gift of God is eternal life in Christ Jesus our Lord." *Romans 6:23*

6. **The Koran and the Bible have different views of Christ's death. The Koran teaches that it never happened.**

   "And because of their saying: We slew the Messiah Jesus, Son of Mary, Allah's messenger – They slew him not nor crucified, but it appeared so unto them; and lo! those who disagree concerning it are in doubt thereof; they have no knowledge thereof save pursuit of a conjecture: they slew him not for certain." *(From the Koran, Surah 4:157)*

7. **Was the death of Jesus "for certain?" Jesus Himself spoke openly of His upcoming death and resurrection, and His own disciples did not yet understand why He had to die. Out of respect they tried to talk Him out of it.**

   "From that time on Jesus began to show His disciples that He must go to Jerusalem, and suffer many things, from the elders and chief priests and scribes, and be killed, and be raised up on the third day. And Peter took Him aside and began to rebuke Him, saying, 'God forbid it, Lord! This shall never happen to You.'" *Matthew 16:21-22.*

8. Christ said that He gave up His life willingly; it would not taken from Him by force.

"For this reason the Father loves me, because I lay down my life that I may take it up again. No one has taken it from Me, for I lay it down on my own initiative. I have authority to lay it down and I have authority to take it up again. This commandment I received from My Father." *John 10:17,18*

9. Once Jesus had died, some of His followers went to His tomb and found it empty. An angel appeared and reminded them that Christ had predicted his own death and resurrection.

"'He is not here, but He has risen. Remember how He spoke to you while He was still in Galilee, saying that the Son of Man must be delivered into the hands of sinful men, and be crucified, and the third day rise again.' And they remembered His words." *Luke 24:6-8*

10. After Jesus had died and come back to life, He showed His followers physical proof of His crucifixion; the wounds in his hands and side. No other living person bore scars of crucifixion.

"Then He said to Thomas, 'Reach here your finger, and see My hands; and reach here your hand, and put it into My side; and be not unbelieving, but believing.' Thomas answered and said to Him, 'My Lord and my God!'" *John 20:27-29*

11. If Jesus did not die on the cross, then it raises many important questions:

- How did Jesus get the nail wounds in His hands and feet, or the spear wound in His side?
- Why did the angel lie to the disciples at the tomb by telling them Jesus had risen from the dead?
- Why did Jesus foretell His own death and resurrection if He had not intended to go through with it?
- Why wasn't the body of the person supposedly executed in His place still buried in the tomb?

12. Jesus' resurrection was the final proof that He was indeed God's Son.

Christ was: "declared with power to be the Son of God by the resurrection from the dead." *Romans 1:4*

"If Christ has not been raised, your faith is worthless; you are still in your sins." *1 Corinthians 15:17*

13. Louis Farrakhan tells his followers to view him as the Messiah, and that the historical Jesus of the Bible is simply a "type" of the Messiah who would come later. But Jesus warned us not to be misled by such claims.

"Then if anyone says to you, 'Behold, here is the Christ,' or 'There He is,' do not believe him. For false Christs and false prophets will arise and will show great signs and wonders, so as to mislead, if possible, even the elect. Behold I have told you in advance." *Matthew 24:23-25*

14. As God's Son, Jesus was fully God and fully man, and provides the only way for man to reach God. We can be saved only by trusting in His payment for our sin.

"For there is salvation in no one else; for there is no other name under heaven that has been given among men, by which we must be saved." *Acts 4:12*

"Jesus said to him, 'I am the way, and the truth, and the life; no one comes to the Father, but through Me.'" *John 14:6*

"For there is one God, and one mediator also between God and men, the man Christ Jesus, who gave Himself as a ransom for all." *1 Timothy 2:5,6a*

"If you confess with your mouth Jesus as Lord, and believe in your heart that God raised Him from the dead, you shall be saved." *Romans 10:9*

29 Nazism

Nazism, a shortened word for National Socialism, was the driving force behind Germany's Third Reich. And in Adolf Hitler's own words, "Whoever wants to understand National Socialist Germany must know Wagner." Even though Richard Wagner was a brilliant composer, he believed deeply in the superiority of the Aryan (German) race, and saw the Jews as vastly inferior. Wagner also claimed to have had a revelation that Jesus Christ had been born of Aryan stock. Houston Chamberlain, son-in-law of Richard Wagner, wrote in "The Foundations of the Nineteenth Century:" "Whoever claimed that Jesus was a Jew was either stupid or telling a lie... Jesus was not a Jew. He was an Aryan."

The Third Reich cannot be understood without understanding their belief that only through racial purity and a pure bloodline can humanity achieve its fullest potential. To Hitler and the Nazis, the very existence of other "subhuman" races hindered the development of the master race. In Hitler's own words, "I do not look upon Jews as animals, they are further removed from animals than we are.... Therefore it is not a crime to exterminate them, since they do not belong to humanity at all." (Trevor Ravenscroft, "The Spear of Destiny," York Beach, Maine: Weiser, 1982, p. 251) Detailed lectures were given in schools and to SS troops in which Aryan and Jewish skulls were compared in an attempt to prove that Aryans were vastly superior. And because Hitler saw Jews as inferior and weak, Darwinism gave him the "permission" to exterminate the Jews, seeing as how only the "fittest" had the right to survive. According to Hitler, "Man has every right to be as cruel as nature."

But what does the Bible have to say about the importance of the Jews?

---

1. Jews are biological descendants of Abraham. God promised to bless Abraham and his descendants forever.

"And I will make you a great nation, and I will bless you, and make your name great; and so you shall be a blessing; and I will bless those who bless you, and the one who curses you I will curse. And in you all the families of the earth shall be blessed." *Genesis 12:2,3*

2. God also made promises to Abraham's grandson Jacob (whose name was later changed to "Israel"), and he became the father of the twelve Jewish tribes.

"Your descendants shall also be like the dust of the earth, and you shall spread out to the west and to the east and to the north and to the south; and in you and in your descendants shall all the families of the earth be blessed. And behold, I am with you, and will keep you wherever you go, and will bring you back to this land; for I will not leave you until I have done what I have promised you." *Genesis 28:14,15*

3. God continued to express His commitment to Israel during the forty years they wandered in the wilderness under Moses, and even after they came to dwell in the Promised Land.

"For you are a holy people to the Lord your God; the Lord your God has chosen you to be a people for His own possession out of all the peoples who are on the face of the earth." *Deuteronomy 7:6*

"For the Lord will not abandon His people on account of His great name, because the Lord has been pleased to make you a people for Himself." *1 Samuel 12:22*

God has not finished fulfilling His promises to His chosen people. That's probably why Satan would like to see the Jews destroyed. If they all die out, God cannot fulfill His promises, which would make God appear to be untrustworthy.

4. Jesus was a direct descendant of Abraham, Jacob, and King David. The Bible leaves no doubt that Jesus was indeed Jewish, and was called in Scripture the "King of the Jews."

"He will be great, and will be called the Son of the Most High; and the Lord God will give Him the throne of His father David; and He will reign over the house of Jacob forever; and His kingdom will have no end." *Luke 1:32,33*

"They are the people of Israel, chosen to be God's special children. God revealed his glory to them. He made covenants with them and gave his law to them. They have the privilege of worshiping him and receiving his wonderful promises. Their ancestors were great people of God, and Christ himself was a Jew as far as his human nature is concerned. And he is God, who rules over everything and is worthy of eternal praise! Amen." *Romans 9:4,5 (NLT)*

5. For centuries, the Jews were God's primary people for letting the world know who He was. As Paul put it in Romans 3:2, "they were entrusted with the oracles of God." It's clear there would be no Christianity if there were no Judaism. Christianity has been called "the blossom on the stem of Judaism." In the following passage, Paul describes how non-Jews have been "grafted in" to the olive tree of Judaism:

"But if some of the branches were broken off, and you, being a wild olive, were grafted in among them and became partaker with them of the rich root of the olive tree, do not be arrogant toward the branches; but if you are arrogant, remember that it is not you who supports the root, but the root supports you." *Romans 11:17,18*

6. Even though a person may not have been born Jewish, we can all become partakers of the promises God made to the Jews if we simply believe in Jesus, the King of the Jews.

"There is neither Jew nor Greek, there is neither slave nor free man, there is neither male nor female; for you are all one in Christ Jesus. And if you belong to Christ, then you are Abraham's offspring, heirs according to promise." *Galatians 3:28,29*

7. Through Christ's death God has provided a way for Jews and non-Jews to have peace with one another.

"Therefore remember, that formerly you, the Gentiles in the flesh... remember that you were at that time separate from Christ, excluded from the commonwealth of Israel, and strangers to the covenants of promise, having no hope and without God in the world. But now in Christ Jesus you who formerly were far off have been brought near by the blood of Christ. For He himself is our peace, who made both groups into one, and broke down the barrier of the dividing wall, by abolishing in His flesh the enmity... that in Himself He might make the two into one new man, thus establishing peace, and might reconcile them both in one body to God through the cross, by it having put to death the enmity." *Ephesians 2:11-16*

8. Christ not only makes it possible for Jews and non-Jews to make peace and be reconciled with each other, but even more importantly, He makes it possible for everyone make peace and be reconciled with God!

"For there is one God, and one mediator also between God and man, the man Christ Jesus, who gave Himself as a ransom for all." *1 Timothy 2:5,6a*

"But God demonstrates His own love toward us, in that while we were yet sinners, Christ died for us. Much more then, having now been justified by His blood, we shall be saved from the wrath of God through Him. For if while we were enemies, we were reconciled to God through the death of His Son, much more having been reconciled, we shall be saved by His life. And not only this, but we also exult in God through our Lord Jesus Christ, through whom we have now received the reconciliation." *Romans 5:8-11*

9. Hitler was obsessed with purity of race, but God is far more concerned with purity of heart.

"Blessed are the pure in heart, for they shall see God." *Matthew 5:8*

"But the goal of our instruction is love from a pure heart and a good conscience and a sincere faith." *1 Timothy 1:5*

10. If you claim to love God yet hate your fellow man, it's like a window into your heart to reveal what's inside.

"If someone says, 'I love God,' and hates his brother, he is a liar; for the one who does not love his brother whom he has seen, cannot love God whom he has not seen." *1 John 4:20*

11. Even though you may have been a hater of Jews, and guilty of other sins, God is willing to forgive you and reconcile with you right now if you will confess your sins and receive Christ into your heart.

"If we confess our sins, He is faithful and righteous to forgive us our sins, and to cleanse us from all unrighteousness." *1 John 1:9*

30 New Age Movement

Although it's not easy to define the entire New Age movement, it is fairly well summed up by prominent New Age spokesperson Shirley Maclaine: "The New Age is man being divine, man can become God. Man does not need a savior, he can save himself through cyclic rebirth and reincarnation." (Time magazine, December 7, 1987)

New Age followers believe that through our efforts over several lifetimes, we can each achieve the level of "Ascended Master," and become fully perfected, divine beings.

New Age followers believe that once humans realize our divine potential, mankind can then evolve to a higher plane; and the more people who believe this, the sooner it will happen. Christians are often seen as slowing down mankind's next evolutionary step because of our dogmatic insistence that Jesus is mankind's savior and our only way to God.

Jesus is certainly highly respected by New Age followers. But they embrace Him more for His teachings on love than for His sacrificial death to pay for sins on our behalf.

Did Christ's death really have any significance in regard to helping us reach God? Or on the other hand, if we can save ourselves, does mankind really need a savior?

1. **Within New Age, God is viewed as a force which we are all part of; yet not necessarily as a knowable, intelligent being. But according to the Bible, God is knowable and is infinitely intelligent!**

   "'For My thoughts are not your thoughts, neither are your ways My ways,' declares the Lord. 'For as the heavens are higher than the earth, so are My ways higher than your ways, and My thoughts than your thoughts.'" *Isaiah 55:8,9*

   "He counts the number of the stars; He gives names to all of them. Great is our Lord, and abundant in strength; His understanding is infinite." *Psalm 147:4,5*

   "As for you my son Solomon, know the God of your father, and serve Him with a whole heart and a willing mind; for the Lord searches all hearts, and understands every intent of the thoughts. If you seek Him, He will let you find Him; but if you forsake Him, He will reject you forever." *1 Chronicles 28:9*

2. **God is also seeking those who truly want to know Him!**

   "For the eyes of the Lord move to and fro throughout the earth that He may strongly support those whose heart is completely His." *2 Chronicles 16:9*

   "Draw near to God and He will draw near to you." *James 4:8*

3. **The human race has problems not because we have forgotten that we are gods, but because we have forgotten that God is God.**

   "Know that the Lord Himself is God; it is He who has made us, and not we ourselves; we are His people and the sheep of His pasture." *Psalm 100:3*

4. **The desire to become a god is nothing new; the angel Lucifer tried it himself.**

   "But you said in your heart, 'I will ascend to heaven; I will raise my throne above the stars of God... I will ascend above the heights of the clouds; I will make myself like the Most High.'" *Isaiah 14:13,14*

5. **The desire to become gods is what tempted Adam and Eve to sin, and humanity has been separated from God ever since.**

   "And the serpent said to the woman, 'You shall surely not die! For God knows that in the day you eat from it your eyes will be opened, and you will be like God, knowing good and evil.'" *Genesis 3:4,5*

   "Therefore, just as through one man (Adam) sin entered into the world, and death through sin, and so death spread to all men, because all sinned." *Romans 5:12*

"For all have sinned and fall short of the glory of God." *Romans 3:23*

6. Even though we humans cannot become gods, God did become a man! God came to earth in human form as Jesus Christ, who was both fully man and fully God!

"For in Him all the fulness of Deity dwells in bodily form." *Colossians 2:9*

"For there is one God, and one mediator also between God and men, the man Christ Jesus, who gave Himself as a ransom for all." *1 Timothy 2:5,6a*

7. God loves us and wants us to know Him intimately, and He sent His Son Jesus to make that possible.

"For as through the one man's disobedience (Adam) the many were made sinners, even so through the obedience of the One the many will be made righteous." *Romans 5:19*

"God was in Christ reconciling the world to Himself, not counting their trespasses against them." *2 Corinthians 5:19*

"For God so loved the world, that He gave His only begotten Son, that whoever believes in Him shall not perish, but have everlasting life." *John 3:16*

"For the Son of Man has come to seek and save that which was lost." *Luke 19:10*

"Jesus said to him, 'I am the way, and the truth, and the life; no one comes to the Father, but through Me.'" *John 14:6*

"For there is salvation in no one else; for there is no other name under heaven that has been given among men, by which we must be saved." *Acts 4:12*

8. New Age followers emphasize Jesus' teachings on love more than His teachings on why He had to die for us. But Jesus' death was the ultimate expression of His love.

"God demonstrates His own love for us in that while we were yet sinners Christ died for us." *Romans 5:8*

"This is My commandment, that you love one another, just as I have loved you. Greater love has no one than this, that one lay down his life for his friends." *John 15:12,13*

"I am the good shepherd, and I know My own, and My own know Me... and I lay down My life for the sheep." *John 10:14,15*

"For the Son of Man did not come to be served, but to serve, and to give His life as a ransom for many." *Matthew 20:28*

9. Jesus never taught His followers the concept of reincarnation, but He did teach the concept of being "born again." When we give our lives to Him, we get a completely new start in life.

"Truly, truly I say to you, unless one is born again, he cannot see the kingdom of God." *John 3:3*

"Therefore if any man is in Christ, he is a new creature; the old things passed away; behold new things have come." *2 Corinthians 5:17*

10. To begin your relationship with God, simply confess to God that you are a sinner, and ask Christ to come into your heart as your Savior.

"If we confess our sins, He is faithful and righteous to forgive us our sins and to cleanse us from all unrighteousness. If we say that we have not sinned, we make Him a liar, and His word is not in us." *1 John 1:9,10*

"Behold, I stand at the door and knock; if any one hears My voice and opens the door, I will come in to him, and dine with him, and he with Me." *Revelation 3:20*

"But as many as received Him, to them He gave the right to become children of God, even to those who believe in His name." *John 1:12*

31 Occultism

Occultism is a broad field encompassing many practices that seek a deeper level of contact with the spirit world. People seek help from spirits to bring power, success, love, or to learn hidden secrets about this life and the next. Many who practice occultism use Tarot Cards, Ouija Boards, Fortune Telling, Palmistry, Astrology, Psychics, Channeling, etc. Many who delve into these practices admit they are not 100% accurate, but claim they can sometimes produce amazing results.

Many who practice occultism profess to believe in God, and some have mingled these practices with Christianity or Catholicism. But are there any dangers in communicating with the spirit world through occultism? And does God really speak to us through occult practices?

1. Even though some people who offer fortune telling or other services are totally fake, the Bible describes instances where people have been able to accomplish surprising results, signs, and wonders by the power of spirits.

"So Moses and Aaron came to Pharaoh, and thus they did just as the Lord had commanded; and Aaron threw his staff down before Pharaoh and his servants, and it became a serpent. Then Pharaoh also called for the wise men and the sorcerers, and they also, the magicians of Egypt, did the same with their secret arts. For each one threw down his staff and they turned into serpents. But Aaron's staff swallowed up their staffs." *Exodus 7:10-12*

"When He (Jesus) got out of the boat, immediately a man from the tombs with an unclean spirit met Him, and he had his dwelling among the tombs. And no one was able to bind him anymore, even with a chain; because he had often been bound with shackles and chains, and the chains had been torn apart by him and the shackles broken in pieces, and no one was strong enough to subdue him." *Mark 5:2-4*

"Then that lawless one will be revealed whom the Lord will slay with the breath of His mouth and bring to an end by the appearance of His coming; that is, the one whose coming is in accord with the activity of Satan, with all power and signs and false wonders, and with all the deception of wickedness for those who perish, because they did not receive the love of the truth so as to be saved." *2 Thessalonians 2:8-10*

2. According to the Bible, all spirits are ultimately subject to Christ.

"At the name of Jesus every knee should bow, of those who are in heaven, and on earth, and under the earth, and that every tongue should confess that Jesus Christ is Lord to the glory of God the Father." *Philippians 2:10,11*

"And it happened that as we were going to the place of prayer, a certain slave-girl having a spirit of divination met us, who was bringing her masters much profit by fortunetelling... But Paul... turned and said to the spirit, 'I command you in the name of Jesus Christ to come out of her!' And it came out that very moment. But when her masters saw that their hope of profit was gone, they seized Paul and Silas and dragged them into the market place before the authorities." *Acts 16:16-19*

3. Even though all spirits are ultimately subject to Christ, they are not all obedient to Him. If a spirit communicates with us, we can't be certain it is telling the truth. If a message comes to you from occult practices, and God is not the one speaking to you, then who is?

"Dear friends, do not believe everyone who claims to speak by the Spirit. You must test them to see if the spirit they have comes from God. For there are many false prophets in the world." *1 John 4:1 (NLT)*

"But the Spirit explicitly says that in later times some will fall away from the faith, paying attention to deceitful spirits and doctrines of demons." *1 Timothy 4:1*

"Satan disguises himself as an angel of light. Therefore it is not surprising if his servants also disguise themselves as servants of righteousness." *2 Corinthians 11:14,15*

4. Because of the dangerously deceptive nature of demonic spirits, the Bible makes it clear that communication with the spirit world by any occult practice is non-compatible with faith in God; and warns us never to do it.

"There shall not be found among you... one who uses divination, one who practices witchcraft, or one who interprets omens, or a sorcerer, or one who casts a spell, or a medium, or a spiritist or one who calls up the dead. For whoever does these things is detestable to the Lord." Deuteronomy 18:10-12

"But for the cowardly and unbelieving and abominable and murderers and immoral persons and sorcerers and idolaters and all liars, their part will be in the lake that burns with fire and brimstone, which is the second death." *Revelation 21:8*

5. **When you call for the help of spirits, it gives them permission to become part of your life. Once spirits or demons are in your life, they exert more and more control over you. Even though they might be able to bring you success, powers, or hidden information, demons are deceptive and you will someday regret the decision to seek their involvement. Rather than turning to spirits we can't trust, turn directly to God, whom we can trust!**

"And when they say to you, 'Consult the mediums and the spiritists who whisper and mutter,' should not a people consult their God? Should they consult the dead on behalf of the living?" *Isaiah 8:19*

6. **We don't need any spirits to intercede between God and us. God has already sent His Son as the only acceptable mediator to provide direct access to God! By offering His Son Jesus as the payment for our sins, God will forgive our sins and make us holy, which makes it possible for us to have direct access to Him!**

"For there is one God, and one mediator also between God and men, the man Christ Jesus, who gave Himself as a ransom for all." *1 Timothy 2:5,6a*

"Jesus said to him, 'I am the way, and the truth, and the life; no one comes to the Father but through Me.'" *John 14:6*

"I am the door; if anyone enters through Me, he will be saved, and will go in and out and find pasture. The thief comes only to steal and kill and destroy; I came that they may have life, and have it abundantly." *John 10:9,10*

"But God demonstrates His own love toward us, in that while we were yet sinners, Christ died for us." *Romans 5:8*

7. **To obtain the forgiveness from occult practices or any other sin, you must first simply admit you are a sinner and need to be forgiven.**

"For all have sinned and fall short of the glory of God." *Romans 3:23*

"But your iniquities have made a separation between you and your God, and your sins have hid His face from you, so that He does not hear." *Isaiah 59:2*

"If we say that we have no sin, we are deceiving ourselves, and the truth is not in us. But if we confess our sins, He is faithful and righteous to forgive us our sins and to cleanse us from all unrighteousness." *1 John 1:8,9*

8. **Without Christ in your life, you won't have the power to break demonic involvement. Ask Christ into your life and your direct access to God will begin.**

"I am the door; if anyone enters through Me, he shall be saved, and shall go in and out, and find pasture." *John 10:9*

"Behold, I stand at the door and knock; if any one hears my voice and opens the door, I will come in to him, and will dine with him, and he with Me." *Revelation 3:20*

"But as many as received Him, to them He gave the right to become children of God, even to those who believe in His name." *John 1:12*

9. **Once a person trusts Christ, there must be no mingling of occultism with Christianity; there must be a complete break with all occult practices.**

"Many also of those who had believed kept coming, confessing and disclosing their practices. And many of those who practiced magic brought their books together and began burning them in the sight of all; and they counted up the price of them and found it fifty thousand pieces of silver. So the word of the Lord was growing mightily and prevailing." *Acts 19:18-20*

32 Pantheism

In pantheism, there is no distinction between the creation and the creator. God is all that exists, and everything that exists is God. God is all and in all. Therefore, pantheism stresses the oneness and interconnectedness of all that exists, with nothing being separated from anything else, because everything is all part of the same infinite, yet impersonal and unknowable God, known as Brahman.

To achieve oneness with God, or Brahman, pantheists believe it doesn't really matter which path you take, as long as one heads in the right direction. Matters of doctrine and specific beliefs are not as important to the pantheist as is the technique one takes to arrive at oneness with Brahman. Some chant, some meditate, and some practice physical disciplines. Almost all the techniques require quiet and solitude so that the mind can be emptied. To the pantheist, what you believe is not as important as what you become.

Both the pantheist and the Christian believe in God. But the God revealed in the Bible is a very different God than the Brahman of pantheism.

What exactly does the Bible have to say about God's character and how we can know Him?

---

1. God is infinite, but He is also personal and unknowable. If we will seek God, He will let us find Him.

"He counts the number of the stars; He gives names to all of them. Great is our Lord, and abundant in strength; His understanding is infinite." *Psalm 147:4,5*

"The God who made the world and all things in it... made from one, every nation of mankind to live on all the face of the earth... that they should seek God, if perhaps they might grope for Him and find Him, though He is not far from each one of us." *Acts 17:24,26,27*

"And you will seek Me and find Me, when you search for Me with all your heart." *Jeremiah 29:13*

"Draw near to God and He will draw near to you." *James 4:8*

"If you seek Him, He will let you find Him; but if you forsake Him, He will reject you forever." *1 Chronicles 28:9*

2. God wants us to know Him and has revealed Himself to mankind in several ways. One of the ways is through His creation.

"The heavens are telling of the glory of God; and their expanse is declaring the work of His hands. Day to day pours forth speech, and night to night reveals knowledge. There is no speech, nor are there words; their voice is not heard. Their line has gone out through all the earth, and their utterances to the end of the world." *Psalm 19:1-4a*

"For since the creation of the world His invisible attributes, His eternal power and divine nature, have been clearly seen, being understood through what has been made, so that they are without excuse." *Romans 1:20*

3. God created the universe, but there is a clear separation between the Creator and the creation. We are clearly told to only worship God, but not the creation. By removing the distinction between Creator and creation, it either deifies the earth and all of creation, or it lowers God to the level of plants, animals, and rocks.

"For they exchanged the truth of God for a lie, and worshiped and served the creature rather than the Creator, who is blessed forever. Amen." *Romans 1:25*

4. In pantheism, there is no distinction between man and God. But the Bible tells us that God is infinitely greater than man, and trying to be God is what caused mankind to become separated from God. This is referred to as "the original sin."

"'For My thoughts are not your thoughts, neither are your ways My ways,' declares the Lord. 'For as the heavens are higher than the earth, so are My ways higher than your ways, and My thoughts than your thoughts.'" *Isaiah 55:8,9*

"And the serpent said to the woman, 'You shall surely not die! For God knows that in the day you eat from it your eyes will be opened, and you will be like God, knowing good and evil.'" *Genesis 3:4,5*

"Therefore, just as through one man (Adam) sin entered into the world, and death through sin, and so death spread to all men, because all sinned." *Romans 5:12*

"But your iniquities have made a separation between you and your God, and your sins have hid His face from you, so that He does not hear." *Isaiah 59:2*

"For all have sinned and fall short of the glory of God." *Romans 3:23*

5. **Fortunately, God loves mankind so much that He has provided a way for us to be reunited with Him. He sent His own sinless Son Jesus to the earth, who gave His life as the payment for our sins. Jesus was both fully God and fully man.**

"For God so loved the world, that He gave His only begotten Son, that whoever believes in Him shall not perish, but have everlasting life." *John 3:16,17*

"God demonstrates His own love for us in that while we were yet sinners Christ died for us." *Romans 5:8*

"The wages of sin is death, but the free gift of God is eternal life in Christ Jesus our Lord." *Romans 6:23*

6. **Because Jesus is the only perfect man to ever live, and because He was both fully God and fully man, He is therefore the only acceptable payment for our sins. This is why He is the only way to heaven.**

"Jesus said to him, 'I am the way, and the truth, and the life; no one comes to the Father, but through Me.'" *John 14:6*

"For there is salvation in no one else; for there is no other name under heaven that has been given among men, by which we must be saved." *Acts 4:12*

"God our Savior... desires all men to be saved and to come to the knowledge of the truth. For there is one God, and one mediator also between God and men, the man Christ Jesus, who gave Himself as a ransom for all." *1 Timothy 2:3-6a*

"For in Him (Jesus) all the fulness of Deity dwells in bodily form." *Colossians 2:9*

7. **Now that Jesus Christ has paid for the sins of the world, all we have to do in order to have that payment apply to our sins is to confess to God that we are sinners, and accept Christ's offer of forgiveness by receiving Him into our lives.**

"I acknowledged my sin to You, and my iniquity I did not hide; I said, 'I will confess my transgressions to the Lord;' and You forgave the guilt of my sin." *Psalm 32:5*

"If we say that we have no sin, we are deceiving ourselves, and the truth is not in us. If we confess our sins, He is faithful and righteous to forgive us our sins and to cleanse us from all unrighteousness. If we say that we have not sinned, we make Him a liar, and His word is not in us." *1 John 1:8-10*

8. **To the pantheist, what we become is more important than what we believe. But the Bible tells us that if we first believe in Christ, we will become children of God. If you will ask Christ into your life, you will be allowed to start a personal relationship with God, and you can spend eternity in Heaven with the God who created you.**

"Behold, I stand at the door and knock; if any one hears My voice and opens the door, I will come in to him, and will dine with him, and he with Me." *Revelation 3:20*

"But as many as received Him, to them He gave the right to become children of God, even to those who believe in His name." *John 1:12*

33 Rastafarianism

Rastafarianism began in Jamaica in 1930, but the roots of their beliefs go back to ancient times when the Queen of Sheba went from Ethiopia to visit King Solomon. Rastafarians believe that during their visit they conceived a child, and when the Queen returned, the child started a dynasty of Ethiopian rulers who were the true and rightful descendants to the throne of Israel, and are therefore God's chosen people.

In 1892, a new prince of this royal family was born whose name was Tafari Makonnen. In 1916 he became a Duke and was called Ras (Duke) Tafari. Also in 1916, a Jamaican political and religious leader named Marcus Garvey told his black followers in a speech, "Look to Africa for the crowning of a Black king; he shall be the Redeemer." In 1930, when Ras Tafari became Emperor of Ethiopia, he took the name Haile Selassie 1, which means Power of the Trinity. He is viewed by Rastafarians as the fulfillment of Garvey's prophecy. The year 1930 was also when Rastafarianism as a religion began. As a leader, Haile Salassie worked for economic and social reforms.

Some of the main beliefs of Rastafarians are:
- *Ethiopia is heaven.*
- *Selassie would arrange for the return of all African descendants to Africa.*
- *White people are wicked and inferior to blacks. (In some groups in Jamaica, whites and others are welcome into the religion if they believe Selassie is a god.)*

Selassie died in 1975, but Rastafarians believe he was the living God, Redeemer, and the true Messiah. They refer to him as "King of Kings," and the "Conquering Lion of the Tribe of Judah." As a form of homage to their leader, his followers wear their hair in dreadlocks to resemble the mane of a lion.

But is Haile Selassie really the one true Messiah, or is Jesus Christ?

---

1. First of all, Jesus claimed to be not just a messenger from God, Jesus claimed to be God.

- Jesus claimed to be the Messiah. *John 4:25,26*
- Jesus claimed to be the Christ. *Mark 14:62-64*
- Jesus claimed to be King of the Jews. *Matthew 27:11*
- Jesus claimed to be God's Son, making Himself equal with God. *John 5:18, 10:33*
- Jesus claimed to be able to forgive sins, something only God can do. *Mark 2:1-12*
- Jesus claimed to be the God of the Old Testament, by giving Himself the same name as God. *John 8:56-59*

"He who has seen Me has seen the Father." *John 14:9*

"For in Him all the fulness of Deity dwells in bodily form." *Colossians 2:9*

"For this reason therefore the Jews were seeking all the more to kill Him, because He not only was breaking the Sabbath, but also was calling God His own Father, making Himself equal with God." *John 5:18*

2. Jesus pre-existed for eternity before He came to this earth. In fact, the world was made through Him.

"And He is the image of the invisible God, the firstborn of all creation. For in Him all things were created, both in the heavens and on earth, visible and invisible... all things have been created through Him and for Him." *Colossians 1:15,16*

"All things came into being through Him: and apart from Him nothing came into being that has come into being." *John 1:3*

3. Jesus is from the tribe of Judah, and the documented heir to the throne of Israel.

- The genealogy of Jesus' adopted father Joseph is traced in Matthew 1 to King David's son Solomon.
- The genealogy of Jesus' mother Mary is traced in Luke 3 to King David through his son Nathan.

4. The Old Testament predicted the Messiah would be born in Bethlehem, not Ethiopia.

"But as for you, Bethlehem Ephrathah, too little to be among the clans of Judah, from you One will go forth for Me to be ruler in Israel. His goings forth are from long ago, from the days of eternity." *Micah 5:2*

5. Unlike others who have claimed to be God in the flesh, Jesus lived a perfect, sinless life.

"For we do not have a high priest who cannot sympathize with our weaknesses, but one who has been tempted in all things as we are, yet without sin." *Hebrews 4:15*

6. Jesus gave His life as the only perfect, sinless sacrifice to pay the penalty for the sins of mankind and make us holy.

"For Christ also died for sins once for all, the just for the unjust, in order that He might being us to God." *1 Peter 3:18*

"God demonstrates His own love toward us in that while we were yet sinners, Christ died for us." *Romans 5:8*

"He made Him who knew no sin be sin on our behalf, that we might become the righteousness of God in Him." *2 Corinthians 5:21*

7. Because Christ led the only sinless life, His payment for our sin is the only way to obtain forgiveness so that we can be allowed into God's presence.

"Jesus said to him, 'I am the way, and the truth, and the life; no one comes to the Father but through Me.'" *John 14:6*

"I am the door; if anyone enters through Me, he shall be saved, and shall go in and out, and find pasture." *John 10:9*

"For there is salvation in no one else; for there is no other name under heaven that has been given among men, by which we must be saved." *Acts 4:12*

"For there is one God, and one mediator also between God and men, the man Christ Jesus, who gave Himself as a ransom for all." *1 Timothy 2:5,6a*

8. One clear difference between Jesus and Haile Selassie is that Selassie is still dead. After Jesus died, He rose from the dead to give us the ultimate proof that He was indeed God's Son.

Jesus was, "declared with power to be the Son of God by the resurrection from the dead." *Romans 1:4*

"Christ died for our sins... He was buried... He was raised on the third day according to the Scriptures... He appeared to Cephas, then to the twelve. After that He appeared to more than five hundred." *1 Corinthians 15:3-6*

"If Christ has not been raised, your faith is worthless; you are still in your sins." *1 Corinthians 15:17*

9. Christ predicted that false messiahs would come after Him, and warned us not to be misled.

"See to it that no one mislead you. For many will come in My name, saying, 'I am the Christ,' and will mislead many.... And many false prophets will arise, and will mislead many.... Then if any one says to you, 'Behold, here is the Christ,' or 'There He is,' do not believe him. For false Christs and false prophets will arise and will show great signs and wonders, so as to mislead, if possible, even the elect. Behold, I have told you in advance." *Matthew 24:4,5,11,23-25.*

10. According to the Bible, God only had one Son who was of the same divine nature as God the Father; and that was Jesus.

"For God so loved the world, that He gave His only begotten Son, that whoever believes in Him shall not perish, but have eternal life. *John 3:16*

11. To know God personally and experience His love and forgiveness for you, simply receive Christ into your life as your only Savior and Lord.

"Behold I stand at the door and knock; if any one hears My voice and opens the door, I will come in to him, and will dine with him, and he with Me." *Revelation 3:20*

"But as many as received Him, to them He gave the right to become children of God, even to those who believe in His name." *John 1:12*

34 Santeria

Santeria (Spanish for "the worship of saints") is a blend of Catholicism with an ancient African religion originating from slaves brought from the West African Yoruba tribe, by way of the Caribbean. Santerians worship gods from African religions along with certain Catholic saints that they consider to be divine. Santerians believe that although the universe was created by one supreme God, the care of the world had been entrusted to many smaller gods, called "orishas." One orisha becomes the Santerian's guardian angel.

Experts say slaves blended their African religions with Catholicism to protect their African religion while appearing to be Catholic converts. One of the central rituals of Santerians is bloodletting through animal sacrifice, mostly of goats and chickens, for the purpose of "cleansing."

The Bible speaks a great deal about our need to be cleansed from sin. And even though God's Word states the importance of shed blood to receive cleansing, the Bible offers a very different way to receive cleansing than with the blood of animal sacrifices.

1. The Bible clearly states that cleansing from sin can come only by way of shedding blood.

"All things are cleansed with blood, and without shedding of blood there is no forgiveness." *Hebrews 9:22*

2. In the Old Testament, God told His people to sacrifice a lamb once a year at Passover. Those who were protected by the blood of the lamb received God's mercy. Those not protected by the blood received God's judgment.

"Then Moses summoned all the elders of Israel and said to them, 'Go at once and select the animals for your families and slaughter the Passover lamb. Take a bunch of hyssop, dip it into the blood in the basin and put some of the blood on the top and both sides of the doorframe. Not one of you shall go out the door of his house until morning. When the Lord goes through the land to strike down the Egyptians, He will see the blood on the top and sides of the doorframe and He will not permit the destroyer to enter your houses and strike you down.'" *Exodus 12:21-23*

3. God told His people in the Old Testament to sacrifice animals, but not because animal sacrifices could cleanse us from sin. Animal sacrifices were simply a symbol to remind God's people that forgiveness comes only through the shedding of blood.

"But in those sacrifices there is a reminder of sins year by year. For it is impossible for the blood of bulls and goats to take away sins." *Hebrews 10:4*

4. The only worthy sacrifice acceptable to God to cleanse us from sin is the sacrifice which God Himself has provided; Jesus, His only Son, who was fully God and fully man.

"And Abraham said, 'God will provide for Himself the lamb for the burnt offering.'" *Genesis 22:8*

"The next day John saw Jesus coming toward him and said, 'Look, the Lamb of God who takes away the sin of the world!'" *John 1:29*

"But He was pierced through for our transgressions, He was crushed for our iniquities; the chastening for our well-being fell upon Him, and by His scourging we are healed. All of us like sheep have gone astray, each of us has turned to his own way; but the Lord has caused the iniquity of us all to fall on Him. He was oppressed and He was afflicted, yet He did not open His mouth; like a lamb that is led to slaughter, and like a sheep that is silent before its shearers, so He did not open His mouth." *Isaiah 53:5-7*

5. Just as those who were protected by the blood of the Passover lamb received God's mercy, Christ's blood protects us from the punishment we deserve for our sins.

"In Him we have redemption through His blood, the forgiveness of our trespasses, according to the riches of His grace, which He lavished upon us." *Ephesians 1:7,8*

"But God demonstrates His own love toward us, in that while we were yet sinners, Christ died for us. Much more then, having now been justified by His blood, we shall be saved from the wrath of God through Him." *Romans 5:8,9*

"You were not redeemed with perishable things like silver or gold from your futile way of life inherited from your fore-fathers, but with precious blood, as of a lamb unblemished and spotless, the blood of Christ." *1 Peter 1:18,19*

6. Christ's sacrifice is the only sacrifice needed to obtain cleansing for all of mankind. No others will ever be necessary!

"And what God wants is for us to be made holy by the sacrifice of the body of Jesus Christ once for all time. Under the old covenant, the priest stands before the altar day after day, offering sacrifices that can never take away sins. But our High Priest offered himself to God as one sacrifice for sins, good for all time. Then he sat down at the place of highest honor at God's right hand.... For by that one offering he perfected forever all those whom he is making holy." *Hebrews 10:10,12,14 (NLT)*

7. The Bible says there are many spirits, but none of them should be considered gods. Even though all spirits are ultimately subject to Christ, they are not all obedient to Him. The Bible prohibits mingling the worship of other spirits or saints with the worship of the true God.

"Beloved, do not believe every spirit, but test the spirits to see whether they are from God." *1 John 4:1*

"But the Spirit explicitly says that in later times some will fall away from the faith, paying attention to deceitful spirits and doctrines of demons." *1 Timothy 4:1*

"Satan disguises himself as an angel of light. Therefore it is not surprising if his servants also disguise themselves as servants of righteousness." *2 Corinthians 11:14,15*

8. Because of the deceptive nature of demonic spirits, the Bible makes it clear that communication with the spirit world by any occult practice is totally non-compatible with faith in God; and warns us never to do it.

"There shall not be found among you... one who uses divination, one who practices witchcraft, or one who interprets omens, or a sorcerer, or one who casts a spell, or a medium, or a spiritist or one who calls up the dead. For whoever does these things is detestable to the Lord." *Deuteronomy 18:10-12*

"But for the cowardly and unbelieving and abominable and murderers and immoral persons and sorcerers and idolaters and all liars, their part will be in the lake that burns with fire and brimstone, which is the second death." *Revelation 21:8*

9. One of the sins we need to be cleansed from is that of worshiping other gods or spirits. We must forsake all other gods because they are false.

"You shall have no other gods before Me. You shall not make for yourself an idol, or any likeness of what is in heaven above or on the earth beneath or in the water under the earth. You shall not worship them or serve them; for I, the Lord your God, am a jealous God." *Exodus 20:3-5*

"Know therefore today, and take it to your heart, that the Lord, He is God in heaven above and on the earth below; there is no other." *Deuteronomy 4:39*

"Now to the King eternal, immortal, invisible, the only God, be honor and glory forever and ever. Amen." *1 Timothy 1:15*

10. To have Christ's blood pay the penalty for your sins, confess your sins to Him and ask Christ into your heart.

"If we say that we have no sin, we are deceiving ourselves, and the truth is not in us. If we confess our sins, He is faithful and righteous to forgive us our sins and to cleanse us from all unrighteousness. If we say that we have not sinned, we make Him a liar, and His word is not in us." *1 John 1:8-10*

"Jesus said to him, 'I am the way, and the truth, and the life; no one comes to the Father, but through Me.'" *John 14:6*

"For there is salvation in no one else; for there is no other name under heaven that has been given among men, by which we must be saved." *Acts 4:12*

35 Satanism

It comes as no surprise that Jesus Christ is not held in high regard by Satanists. Anton LaVey founded the Church of Satan in 1966. In his famous Satanic Bible, published in 1969, he wrote: "I dip my forefinger in the watery blood of your impotent mad redeemer, and write over his thorn-torn brow: The TRUE prince of evil – the king of the slaves!" (p. 30) LaVey goes on to mock Christ's death on the cross: "Behold the crucifix; what does it symbolize? Pallid incompetence hanging on a tree." (p. 31)

Satanists view the cross is a symbol of Christ's weakness, and are taught that Christ's death on the cross was a humiliating defeat for followers of the "right hand path." But did Christ die because He was overpowered by stronger forces, or did He willingly allow Himself to be crucified? And if Jesus allowed Himself to be crucified, then why?

The Satanic Bible also provides a different view of the afterlife than what is described in the Holy Bible: "Life is the great indulgence – death, the great abstinence. Therefore, make the most of life – HERE AND NOW! There is no heaven of glory bright, and no hell where sinners roast. Here and now is our day of torment! Here and now is our day of joy! Here and now is our opportunity! Choose ye this day, this hour, for no redeemer liveth! Say unto thine own heart, 'I am mine own redeemer.'" (p. 33) But surprisingly, LaVey does add something that agrees with the teachings of the Holy Bible: "Too long right and wrong, good and evil have been inverted by false prophets!" (p.31)

So the question is: Who is lying and who is telling the truth? Should we trust Satan and his carnal followers, or should we trust Christ?

---

1. The Bible tells us Lucifer was a beautiful angel created by God, and was the highest ranking angel in heaven.

"You had the seal of perfection, full of wisdom and perfect in beauty. You were in Eden, the garden of God; every precious stone was your covering: the ruby, the topaz and the diamond; the beryl, the onyx and the jasper; the lapis lazuli, the turquoise and the emerald; and the gold, the workmanship of your settings and sockets, was in you. On the day that you were created they were prepared. You were the anointed cherub who covers, and I placed you there. You were on the holy mountain of God; you walked in the midst of the stones of fire. You were blameless in your ways from the day you were created until unrighteousness was found in you." *Ezekiel 28:12-15*

2. Lucifer was cast out of heaven because he tried to make himself like God.

"But you said in your heart, 'I will ascend to heaven; I will raise my throne above the stars of God, and I will sit on the mount of assembly in the recesses of the north. I will ascend above the heights of the clouds; I will make myself like the Most High.' Nevertheless you will be thrust down to Sheol, to the recesses of the pit." *Isaiah 14:13-15*

3. After he was removed from heaven, Lucifer, speaking through the serpent, tempted Adam and Eve by making them think they could also become like God. When they sinned, all of mankind became separated from God.

"And the serpent said to the woman, 'You shall surely not die! For God knows that in the day you eat from it your eyes will be opened, and you will be like God, knowing good and evil.'" *Genesis 3:4,5*

"Therefore, just as through one man (Adam) sin entered into the world, and death through sin, and so death spread to all men, because all sinned." *Romans 5:12*

4. Once sin entered into the world, God took the punishment we deserve onto Himself by sending His Son Jesus to die on the cross and reconcile man back to God.

"He Himself bore our sins in His body on the cross, that we might die to sin and live to righteousness; for by His wounds you were healed." *1 Peter 2:24*

"For Christ also died for sins once for all, the just for the unjust, in order that He might bring us to God, having been put to death in the flesh, but made alive in the Spirit." *1 Peter 3:18*

5. When Jesus died on the cross, it was not a demonstration of weakness, it was a demonstration of His love. Jesus

willingly allowed Himself to be crucified. It was actually Satan who did not want Jesus to be crucified.

"From that time on Jesus began to show His disciples that He must go to Jerusalem, and suffer many things, from the elders and chief priests and scribes, and be killed, and be raised up on the third day. And Peter took Him aside and began to rebuke Him, saying, 'God forbid it, Lord! This shall never happen to You.' But He turned and said to Peter, 'Get behind Me, Satan! You are a stumbling block to Me, for you are not setting your mind on God's interests, but man's.'" *Matthew 16:21-23*

"For this reason the Father loves me, because I lay down my life that I may take it up again. No one has taken it from Me, for I lay it down on my own initiative." *John 10:17,18*

"God demonstrates His own love for us in that while we were yet sinners Christ died for us." *Romans 5:8*

6. Jesus proved He was God's Son by triumphantly rising from the dead!

"'He is not here, but He has risen. Remember how He spoke to you while He was still in Galilee, saying that the Son of Man must be delivered into the hands of sinful men, and be crucified, and the third day rise again.' And they remembered His words." *Luke 24:6-8*

Jesus Christ was: "declared with power to be the Son of God by the resurrection from the dead." *Romans 1:4*

7. Jesus is infinitely more powerful than Satan and will destroy him and his followers.

"Little Children, let no one deceive you; the one who practices righteousness is righteous, just as He is righteous; the one who practices sin is of the devil; for the devil has sinned from the beginning. The Son of God appeared for this purpose, that He might destroy the works of the devil." *1 John 3:7,8*

"And then that lawless one will be revealed whom the Lord will slay with the breath of His mouth and bring to an end by the appearance of His coming." *2 Thessalonians 2:8*

8. Even though Satan can offer some fun in this life, his followers can only look forward to spending a joyless eternity away from God, punished in the flames of hell.

"And all the nations will be gathered before Him; and He will separate them from one another, as the shepherd separates the sheep from the goats; and He will put the sheep on His right, and the goats on the left. Then the King will say to those on His right, 'Come you who are blessed of My Father, inherit the kingdom prepared for you from the foundation of the world.' ...Then He will say to those on His left, 'Depart from Me, accursed ones, into the eternal fire which has been prepared for the devil and his angels.'" *Matthew 25:32,33,41*

9. Satan is a liar and does not want you to understand what happens after death, or accept God's forgiveness.

"You are of your father the devil, and you want to do the desires of your father. He was a murderer from the beginning, and does not stand in the truth, because there is no truth in him. Whenever he speaks a lie, he speaks from his own nature; for he is a liar, and the father of lies. But because I speak the truth, you do not believe Me." *John 8:44,45*

10. To become a Christian and break Satan's grip on you, confess your sins and ask Christ into your heart.

"If you confess with your mouth Jesus as Lord, and believe in your heart that God raised Him from the dead, you shall be saved." *Romans 10:9*

"In addition to all, taking up the shield of faith, with which you will be able to extinguish all the flaming missiles of the evil one." *Ephesians 6:16*

11. When a person comes to Christ, there must be a complete break with satanic practices and occultism.

"Many also of those who had believed kept coming, confessing and disclosing their practices. And many of those who practiced magic brought their books together and began burning them in the sight of all; and they counted up the price of them and found it fifty thousand pieces of silver. So the word of the Lord was growing mightily and prevailing." *Acts 19:18-20*

36 Scientology

When we observe the world around us, it's easy to see that mankind has fallen short of our potential. L. Ron Hubbard started the Church of Scientology in 1954 to help mankind regain our full potential. Scientology has high regard for human creativity, and many celebrities have said great things about Scientology, but its teachings continue to generate controversy.

Mr. Hubbard taught that humans are actually members of a long-lost civilization from the planet Helatrobus. Its divine citizens were known as "thetans," but were driven away by evil forces forty-trillion years ago. These defeated thetans found their way to earth, but over the ages have forgotten their divine nature and immense potential. Scientology offers a way to help its followers regain their original powers and potential. Hubbard invented the discipline of "dianetics," designed to heal psychosomatic illnesses by cleansing the mind of harmful mental images. One way to help achieve this is by having trained auditors guide their fellow Scientologists through a clearing process to erase "engrams," which are negative mental images resulting from experiences accumulated during former lives throughout the ages. The auditors use a device called an "E meter" to detect and discard the engrams which hold us back from fully grasping the divine force which is our fundamental nature.

Christianity agrees with Hubbard that mankind has fallen far short of our potential, and that we are spiritual beings who need to be purified. But Christianity offers a very different method to make us pure and achieve our full potential.

1. All humans have fallen far short of our potential.

"There is none righteous, not even one; there is none who understands, there is none who seeks for God; all have turned aside, together they have become useless; there is none who does good, Not even one.... Destruction and misery are in their paths, and the path of peace they have not known. There is no fear of God before their eyes.... For all have sinned and fall short of the glory of God." *Romans 3:10-12,16-18,23*

2. According to the Bible, man's problems are not a result of having forgotten we are gods; but because we have forgotten that only God is God.

"Know that the Lord Himself is God; it is He who has made us, and not we ourselves; we are His people and the sheep of His pasture." *Psalm 100:3*

"Before Me there was no God formed, and there will be none after Me. I, even I, and the Lord; and there is no savior besides Me." *Isaiah 43:10,11*

"Is there any God besides Me, or is there any other Rock? I know of none." *Isaiah 44:8*

3. Man was created perfect, full of potential, and enjoyed an intimate relationship with God. But the desire to be like God and become divine caused Adam and Eve to fall from their full potential and be removed from the Garden of Eden. Mankind has continued sinning and been separated from God ever since.

"And the serpent said to the woman, 'You shall surely not die! For God knows that in the day you eat from it your eyes will be opened, and you will be like God, knowing good and evil.'" *Genesis 3:4,5*

"Therefore, just as through one man (Adam) sin entered into the world, and death through sin, and so death spread to all men, because all sinned." *Romans 5:12*

"But your iniquities have made a separation between you and your God, and your sins have hid His face from you, so that He does not hear." *Isaiah 59:2*

4. In order to purify us from our sin and reconcile us back to our holy God, He sent His Son Jesus Christ to make us holy by paying the penalty for our sin.

"But God demonstrates His own love for us in that while we were yet sinners Christ died for us." Romans 5:8

"He made Him who knew no sin to be sin on our behalf, that we might become the righteousness of God in Him." 2 Corinthians 5:21

"For God so loved the world, that He gave His only begotten Son, that whoever believes in Him shall not perish, but have everlasting life." *John 3:16*

"But He was pierced through for our transgressions, He was crushed for our iniquities; the chastening for our well-being fell upon Him, and by His scourging we are healed. All of us like sheep have gone astray, each of us has turned to his own way; but the Lord has caused the iniquity of us all to fall on Him." *Isaiah 53:5,6*

5. Christ is our only way to obtain forgiveness and thus have access to God.

"Jesus said to him, 'I am the way, and the truth, and the life; no one comes to the Father but through Me.'" *John 14:6*

"For there is salvation in no one else; for there is no other name under heaven that has been given among men, by which we must be saved." *Acts 4:12*

6. We have only one lifetime, so it is important to get things right with God before this life is over.

"It is appointed for men to die once, and after this comes judgment." *Hebrews 9:27*

"Remember Him before the silver cord is broken and the golden bowl is crushed... then the dust will return to the earth as it was, and the spirit will return to God who gave it." *Ecclesiastes 12:6,7*

7. The Bible teaches us to rise above negative input from the world's value system by filling our minds with good teachings.

"Therefore I urge you, brethren, by the mercies of God, to present your bodies a living and holy sacrifice, acceptable to God, which is your spiritual service of worship. And do not be conformed to this world, but be transformed by the renewing of your mind, so that you may prove what the will of God is, that which is good and acceptable and perfect." *Romans 12:12*

"Finally, brethren, whatever is true, whatever is honorable, whatever is right, whatever is pure, whatever is lovely, whatever is of good repute, if there is any excellence and if anything worthy of praise, dwell on these things." *Philippians 4:8*

8. Scientology doesn't necessarily stress the importance of living a holy lifestyle, but the Bible teaches that obedience to God is what opens the door to a deeper, more intimate relationship with Him.

"He who has My commandments and keeps them is the one who loves Me; and he who loves Me will be loved by My Father, and I will love him and will disclose Myself to him." *John 14:21*

9. Each of us need to do more than cleanse our minds from negative thoughts. We must each cleanse our hearts by individually confessing our sins and receive Christ.

"If we say that we have no sin, we are deceiving ourselves, and the truth is not in us. If we confess our sins, He is faithful and righteous to forgive us our sins and to cleanse us from all unrighteousness. If we say that we have not sinned, we make Him a liar, and His word is not in us." *1 John 1:8-10*

"Behold, I stand at the door and knock; if any one hears My voice and opens the door, I will come in to him, and will dine with him, and he with Me." *Revelation 3:20*

"But as many as received Him, to them He gave the right to become children of God, even to those who believe in His name." *John 1:12*

10. Receiving Christ is the first step toward reaching our full potential. The final step comes in the next life when all believers meet the Lord face to face and are completely transformed.

"Beloved, now we are children of God, and it has not appeared as yet what we shall be. We know that, when He appears, we shall be like Him, because we shall see Him just as He is. And everyone who has this hope fixed on Him purifies Himself just as He is pure." *1 John 3:2,3*

37 Shinto

Shinto is the ancient, indigenous faith tradition of Japan. Its practice can take many forms; to some followers, Shinto is a form of religion, to others it is a philosophy, and to others a mythology that helps explain Japan's proud history. Many Shinto shrines are scattered throughout Japan, where people perform various rituals.

The Japanese call their country "Nippon," which literally means "sun origin." This is why the Japanese flag proudly displays the emblem of the bright, red sun. Even though Shinto literally means "the way of the gods," and Shintoists believe in many deities, or "kami," they believe the world was created by the most powerful of the all gods, the sun-goddess Amaterasu. She created the Japanese islands and people first, and made them most blessed in all of creation. Shinto is based on this pride in Japan as a nation, and as the pre-eminent race of people.

For centuries the Japanese were taught as children that their emperors were divine descendants of the sun-goddess Amaterasu, who gave the imperial house their divine right to rule. But in a radio broadcast to the Japanese people in 1946, after centuries of Japanese emperors who claimed to be divine, Emperor Hirohito renounced his own divinity and his family's divine right to rule.

Even though Hirohito and the other emperors turned out to be just as human as the rest of us, the Bible teaches there was once a man on earth who was both fully man and fully God. His name was Jesus Christ. But who exactly was Jesus, why did He come to earth, why did He die, and what does His death mean to us?

1. According to the Bible, there is only one God.

"Know therefore today, and take it to your heart, that the Lord, He is God in heaven above and on the earth below; there is no other." *Deuteronomy 4:39*

"Before Me there was no God formed, and there will be none after Me. I, even I, and the Lord; and there is no savior besides Me." *Isaiah 43:10,11*

"Is there any God besides Me, or is there any other Rock? I know of none." *Isaiah 44:8*

2. Even though God is one, He exists in three distinct persons, much like H20 can exist as a liquid (water), as a solid (ice), and as a gas (steam).

"Go therefore and make disciples of all the nations, baptizing them in the name of the Father and the Son and the Holy Spirit." *Matthew 28:19*

3. Jesus was born around 2,000 years ago in a small town in Israel. He was fully God and fully human.

"For in Him all the fulness of Deity dwells in bodily form." *Colossians 2:9*

4. There are other gods in Shinto besides Amaterasu, and some of the gods misbehave just as humans do. But Jesus was perfect, and never sinned.

"For we do not have a high priest who cannot sympathize with our weaknesses, but one who has been tempted in all things as we are, yet without sin." *Hebrews 4:15*

"And you know that He appeared in order to take away sins; and in Him there is no sin." *1 John 3:5*

5. All of mankind has been separated from God because of our sins.

"For all have sinned and fall short of the glory of God." *Romans 3:23*

"But your iniquities have made a separation between you and your God, and your sins have hid His face from you, so that He does not hear." *Isaiah 59:2*

6. **When Jesus allowed Himself to be crucified on a cross, He took ours sins onto Himself. He fully paid the penalty for our sins, and gave His righteousness to us so that we could be reunited with God.**

"But God demonstrates His own love for us in that while we were yet sinners Christ died for us." *Romans 5:8*

"For the wages of sin is death, but the free gift of God is eternal life in Christ Jesus our Lord." *Romans 6:23*

"God was in Christ reconciling the world to Himself, not counting their trespasses against them. He made Him who knew no sin to be sin on our behalf, that we might become the righteousness of God in Him." *2 Corinthians 5:19,21*

"For God so loved the world, that He gave His only begotten Son, that whoever believes in Him shall not perish, but have everlasting life. For God did not send the Son into the world to judge the world; but that the world should be saved through Him." *John 3:16,17*

7. **After Jesus was crucified, He rose from the dead; proving He was indeed God's Son.**

Jesus was "declared with power to be the Son of God by the resurrection from the dead." *Romans 1:4*

"Christ died for our sins according to the Scriptures... He was buried... He was raised on the third day according to the Scriptures, and after that He appeared to Cephas, then to the twelve. After that He appeared to more than five hundred brethren at one time." *1 Corinthians 15:3-6*

"If Christ has not been raised, your faith is worthless; you are still in your sins." *1 Corinthians 15:17*

8. **Jesus provides the only way for sinful humans to be forgiven and get to heaven.**

"Jesus said to him, 'I am the way, and the truth, and the life; no one comes to the Father, but through Me.'" *John 14:6*

"For there is salvation in no one else; for there is no other name under heaven that has been given among men, by which we must be saved." *Acts 4:12*

"For there is one God, and one mediator also between God and men, the man Christ Jesus, who gave Himself as a ransom for all." *1 Timothy 2:5,6a*

9. **In Shinto, the Japanese people have been taught that they are pre-eminent among the world's races. But Christianity teaches we are all equal before God.**

"There is neither Jew nor Greek, there is neither slave nor free man, there is neither male nor female; for you are all one in Christ Jesus." *Galatians 3:28*

"In this new life, it doesn't matter if you are a Jew or a Gentile, circumcised or uncircumcised, barbaric, uncivilized, slave, or free. Christ is all that matters, and he lives in all of us." *Colossians 3:11 (NLT)*

10. **Shintoists can plead with their gods for forgiveness of sins, yet even its gods are guilty of immoralities. But Christ can offer us total forgiveness because He actually lived a sinless life and paid the penalty for our sins. When we trust in His payment for our sins, His righteousness is given to us. All we must do is simply confess our sins and place our faith in Him as we invite Christ into our lives.**

"If we say that we have no sin, we are deceiving ourselves, and the truth is not in us. If we confess our sins, He is faithful and righteous to forgive us our sins and to cleanse us from all unrighteousness. If we say that we have not sinned, we make Him a liar, and His word is not in us." *1 John 1:8-10*

"Behold, I stand at the door and knock; if any one hears My voice and opens the door, I will come in to him., and will dine with him, and he with me." *Revelation 3:20*

"But as many as received Him, to them He gave the right to become children of God, even to those who believe in His name." *John 1:12*

38 Skepticism

Socrates summed up the view of a skeptic: "All I know, is that I know nothing." The skeptic is certain about one thing: that nothing can be known for certain. But can we be certain about that? As soon as a skeptic says with certainty that we can know nothing for certain, he has sawn off the branch on which he is sitting.

Skeptics sometimes ponder questions as basic as "do we really exist?" So you'd think that the question of whether or not God exists would be even more mind-boggling. But if God exists, He would most likely have infinite power to be able to create the universe. Therefore if God is infinite, how will our three-pound brains ever fully comprehend the infinite nature of God? It's as if the thimble, because it cannot contain the volume of an ocean, declares with certainty that it can't be certain the ocean exists.

Does God exist? And has God communicated with mankind? When a genius wants to communicate with a child, he must speak at the child's own level. Christians believe that is what God has done with us by revealing Himself in the Scriptures. Even though the Bible does not give us every answer we could ever ask about God, it does tell us in that God exists, He is knowable, and He loves us dearly.

1. Many writers of the Bible who knew God best admitted they did not know God fully.

Moses: "The secret things belong to the Lord our God, but the things revealed belong to us and to our sons forever." *Deuteronomy 29:29*

David: "Such knowledge is too wonderful for me; it is too high, I cannot attain to it." *Psalm 139:6* "He counts the numbers of the stars; He gives names to all of them. Great is our Lord, and abundant in strength; His understanding is infinite." *Psalm 147:4,5*

Paul: "Oh, the depth of the riches both of the wisdom and knowledge of God! How unsearchable are His judgments and unfathomable His ways!" *Romans 11:33*

Isaiah: "Who is able to advise the Spirit of the Lord? Who knows enough to be his teacher or counselor?" *Isaiah 40:13 (NLV)*

"'For My thoughts are not your thoughts, neither are your ways My ways,' declares the Lord. 'For as the heavens are higher than the earth, so are My ways higher than your ways, and My thoughts than your thoughts.'" *Isaiah 55:8,9*

2. The most indisputable evidence that God exists is that His creation exists. He has created the infinite universe which functions with the precision of a gigantic clock.

'The heavens are telling of the glory of God; and the firmament is declaring the work of His hands. Day to day pours forth speech, and night to night reveals knowledge.... Their line has gone out through all the earth, and their utterances to the end of the world." *Psalm 19:1,2,4*

"For since the creation of the world His invisible attributes, His eternal power and divine nature, have been clearly seen, being understood through what has been made, so that they are without excuse." *Romans 1:20*

3. Another type of evidence that shows the reality of God's power is the huge number of Christians who will gladly testify how knowing God has changed their lives.

"Therefore if anyone is in Christ, he is a new creature; the old things passed away; behold, new things have come.... Therefore, we are ambassadors for Christ, as though God were making an appeal through us; we beg you on behalf of Christ, be reconciled to God." *2 Corinthians 5:17,20*

4. God is also knowable! God has promised that if we seek Him, He will let us find Him. He is also seeking us.

"The God who made the world and all things in it… made from one, every nation of mankind to live on all the face of the earth… that they should seek God, if perhaps they might grope for Him and find Him, though He is not far from each one of us." *Acts 17:24,26,27*

"And you will seek Me and find Me, when you search for Me with all your heart." *Jeremiah 29:13*

"For the eyes of the Lord move to and fro throughout the earth that He may strongly support those whose heart is completely His." *2 Chronicles 16:9*

"Draw near to God and He will draw near to you." *James 4:8*

"True worshipers shall worship the Father in spirit and truth; for such people the Father seeks to be His worshipers." *John 4:23*

5. God sent His fully divine Son Jesus to the earth to reconcile mankind to God.

"For in Him (Jesus) all the fulness of Deity dwells in bodily form." *Colossians 2:9*

"For there is one God, and one mediator also between God and men, the man Christ Jesus, who gave Himself as a ransom for all." *1 Timothy 2:5,6a*

"God...has spoken to us in His Son, whom He appointed heir of all things, through whom also He made the world. And He is the radiance of His glory and the exact representation of His nature, and upholds all things by the word of His power. When He had made purification of sins, He sat down at the right hand of the Majesty on high." *Hebrews 1:1-3*

6. Jesus taught us about God, and gave His life to pay the penalty for our sins so that we can be reconciled with God who is completely holy.

"God demonstrates His own love for us in that while we were yet sinners Christ died for us." *Romans 5:8*

"For God so loved the world that He gave His only begotten Son, that whoever believes in Him shall not perish but have everlasting life." *John 3:16*

7. The complexity of creation, and of the atom itself, provides evidence that everything must have had a designer. But no amount of scientific evidence will completely prove everything we are told in the Bible. That's why the Christian faith is called the Christian faith. We believe the Bible not simply because we have all the convincing evidence we could hope for, but because we have enough evidence to believe God is trustworthy.

"And without faith it is impossible to please Him, for he who comes to God must believe that He is, and that He is a rewarder of those who seek Him." *Hebrews 11:6*

"Faith is the assurance of things hoped for, the conviction of things not seen." *Hebrews 11:1*

8. Does it take a huge amount of faith to become a Christian? As long as a tiny amount of faith is properly placed in the true God, it can accomplish great things.

"Truly I say to you, if you have faith the size of a mustard seed, you will say to this mountain, 'Move from here to there,' and it will move; and nothing will be impossible to you." *Matthew 17:20*

9. To begin your relationship with God, confess to Him that you are a sinner, and ask Jesus into your heart.

"If we say that we have no sin, we are deceiving ourselves, and the truth is not in us. If we confess our sins, He is faithful and righteous to forgive us our sins and to cleanse us from all unrighteousness." *1 John 1:8,9*

"I stand at the door and knock; if any one hears My voice and opens the door, I will come into him." *Revelation 3:20*

"But as many as received Him, to them He gave the right to become children of God, even to those who believe in His name." *John 1:12*

10. Our access to God is based on what Christ did, not on our good works, so we can know we have eternal life.

"These things I have written to you who believe in the name of the Son of God in order that you may know that you have eternal life." *1 John 1:13*

39 Spiritism (Necromancy)

Both the Spiritist and the Christian believe that when a person dies, the spirit lives on. The Bible also contains numerous mentions of the spirit world and the practice of spiritism.

Today, many psychics, mediums, and channellers offer to help people get in touch with the spirit world to learn hidden secrets about our future, our love lives, our careers, or to communicate with departed loved ones. Sometimes a channeller will yield his or her body to be controlled by a departed spirit who then communicates messages to the living.

Many of those who practice spiritism think it is perfectly compatible with Christianity. They see themselves as using their unique gifts in the service of others. But what does the Bible have to say about the practice of spiritism?

1. According to the Bible, all spirits are subject to Christ.

"At the name of Jesus every knee should bow, of those who are in heaven, and on earth, and under the earth, and that every tongue should confess that Jesus Christ is Lord to the glory of God the Father." *Philippians 2:10,11*

"And it happened that as we were going to the place of prayer, a certain slave-girl having a spirit of divination met us, who was bringing her masters much profit by fortunetelling... But Paul... turned and said to the spirit, 'I command you in the name of Jesus Christ to come out of her!' And it came out that very moment." *Acts 16:16-18*

2. Even though all spirits are ultimately subject to Christ, they are not all obedient to Him. So if a spirit communicates with us, we can't necessarily be certain it is telling the truth.

"But the Spirit explicitly says that in later times some will fall away from the faith, paying attention to deceitful spirits and doctrines of demons." *1 Timothy 4:1*

"Beloved, do not believe every spirit, but test the spirits to see whether they are from God." *1 John 4:1*

"Satan disguises himself as an angel of light. Therefore it is not surprising if his servants also disguise themselves as servants of righteousness." *2 Corinthians 11:14,15*

3. Some people claiming to communicate with spirits are totally fake, and take advantage of gullible people. But the Bible describes instances where people have accomplished surprising results by the power of spirits.

"So Moses and Aaron came to Pharaoh, and thus they did just as the Lord had commanded; and Aaron threw his staff down before Pharaoh and his servants, and it became a serpent. Then Pharaoh also called for the wise men and the sorcerers, and they also, the magicians of Egypt, did the same with their secret arts. For each one threw down his staff and they turned into serpents. But Aaron's staff swallowed up their staffs." *Exodus 7:10-12*

"When He (Jesus) got out of the boat, immediately a man from the tombs with an unclean spirit met Him, and he had his dwelling among the tombs. And no one was able to bind him anymore, even with a chain; because he had often been bound with shackles and chains, and the chains had been torn apart by him and the shackles broken in pieces, and no one was strong enough to subdue him." *Mark 5:2-4*

"Then that lawless one will be revealed whom the Lord will slay with the breath of His mouth and bring to an end by the appearance of His coming; that is, the one whose coming is in accord with the activity of Satan, with all power and signs and false wonders, and with all the deception of wickedness for those who perish, because they did not receive the love of the truth so as to be saved." *2 Thessalonians 2:8-10*

4. The spirits of dead people are limited in their activities by boundaries that God has set. Since departed humans are restricted in their ability to communicate with the living, if a spirit claims to be a departed friend or loved one, then it must be some other kind of spirit, most likely a demon, pretending to be someone it is not.

"Between us and you there is a great chasm fixed, in order that those who wish to come over from here to you may not be able, and that none may cross over from there to us." *Luke 16:26*

5. **People who communicate with spirits might be convinced they are doing something helpful. But because of the deceptive nature of some spirits the Bible makes it clear that the practice of spirit communication is totally non-compatible with obedience to God, and warns us never to do it.**

   "There shall not be found among you... one who uses divination, one who practices witchcraft, or one who interprets omens, or a sorcerer, or one who casts a spell, or a medium, or a spirititst, or one who calls up the dead. For whoever does these things is detestable to the Lord." *Deuteronomy 18:10-12*

6. **There may be some areas of our lives that God wants us to simply trust Him with, rather than trying to gain information from some deceptive spirit. Rather than talking to spirits we can't trust, we can talk directly to God.**

   "The secret things belong to the Lord, but the things revealed belong to us and to our sons forever, that we may observe all the words of this law." *Deuteronomy 29:29*

   "And when they say to you, 'Consult the mediums and the spiritists who whisper and mutter,' should not a people consult their God? Should they consult the dead on behalf of the living?" *Isaiah 8:19*

7. **We don't need any spirits to intercede between God and us. God has already sent His Son as the only acceptable mediator to provide direct access to God! By offering His Son Jesus as the payment for our sins, God will forgive our sins and make us holy, which makes it possible for us to have direct access to Him!**

   "For there is one God, and one mediator also between God and men, the man Christ Jesus, who gave Himself as a ransom for all." *1 Timothy 2:5,6a*

   "Jesus said to him, 'I am the way, and the truth, and the life; no one comes to the Father but through Me.'" *John 14:6*

   "I am the door; if anyone enters through Me, he will be saved, and will go in and out and find pasture. The thief comes only to steal and kill and destroy; I came that they may have life, and have it abundantly." *John 10:9,10*

   "For through Him (Jesus) we both have our access in one Spirit to the Father." *Ephesians 2:18*

8. **To obtain the forgiveness Christ offers, you must first admit you are a sinner and need to be forgiven. Then ask Christ into your life as your personal Savior and your direct relationship with God will begin.**

   "For all have sinned and fall short of the glory of God." *Romans 3:23*

   "If we say that we have no sin, we are deceiving ourselves, and the truth is not in us. But if we confess our sins, He is faithful and righteous to forgive us our sins and to cleanse us from all unrighteousness." *1 John 1:8,9*

   "Behold, I stand at the door and knock; if any one hears my voice and opens the door, I will come in to him, and will dine with him, and he with me." *Revelation 3:20*

   "But as many as received Him, to them He gave the right to become children of God, even to those who believe in His name." *John 1:12*

9. **God has given us guidance in His Word, and if there is something else we want to know about the future or whatever, we should simply trust God rather than seeking guidance from the spirit world.**

   "All Scripture is inspired by God and profitable for teaching, for reproof, for correction, for training in righteousness; so that the man of God may be adequate, equipped for every good work." *2 Timothy 3:16,17*

   "For the word of God is living and active and sharper than any two-edged sword, and piercing as far as the division of soul and spirit, of both joints and marrow, and able to judge the thoughts and intentions of the heart." *Hebrews 4:12*

10. **Once a person trusts Christ, there must be a complete break with all occult practices.**

    "Many also of those who had believed kept coming, confessing and disclosing their practices. And many of those who practiced magic brought their books together and began burning them in the sight of all; and they counted up the price of them and found it fifty thousand pieces of silver. So the word of the Lord was growing mightily and prevailing." *Acts 19:18-20*

40 Sufism (Islamic Mysticism, Path Of Love)

Sufism is a generally anti-dogmatic system of beliefs. Sufism means "fusion," and seeks to attract, digest, and integrate prevailing religious, scientific, and creative ideas of the times. There is also a great emphasis on exploring the mysteries within the self. Sufis believe in the oneness of all the world's religions, so they collect and treasure the teachings of religious masters from many faiths. They see no finer example of a perfect human being than Jesus Christ.

Naturally, Christians also hold Jesus in high regard. But Christians are less interested in fusing the varied teachings of the world's religions than are Sufis. But why are Christians so stubbornly dogmatic about Jesus Christ being the only way to heaven? Did Jesus teach this about Himself? Is Jesus basically equal with other religious masters of the world, or does He somehow stand apart from them all?

1. Jesus did not claim to be just a messenger from God, He claimed to be God.

- Jesus claimed to be the Messiah. *John 4:25,26*
- Jesus claimed to be the Christ. *Mark 14:62-64*
- Jesus claimed to be King of the Jews. *Matthew 27:11*
- Jesus claimed to be God's Son, making Himself equal with God. *John 5:18, 10:33*
- Jesus claimed to be able to forgive sins, something only God can do. *Mark 2:1-12*

"For in Him all the fulness of Deity dwells in bodily form." *Colossians 2:9*

2. Jesus is set apart from the founders of other religions because through Jesus the world was made.

"All things came into being through Him; and apart from Him nothing came into being that has come into being." *John 1:3*

"For by Him all things were created, both in the heavens and on earth, visible and invisible, whether thrones or dominions or rulers or authorities – all things have been created through Him and for Him." *Colossians 1:16*

3. The religious founders of other faiths give conflicting accounts about God Himself. Krishna taught there are many gods. Moses, Jesus, and Muhammed taught there is one God. Zoroaster taught there are two primary gods; one good, one evil. Jesus taught He would rise from the dead. Muhammed taught Jesus did not rise from the dead. By fusing all these teachings, one can only assume that God is contradictory and deceptive regarding how He reveals Himself to mankind. But the Bible teaches that God is truthful and does not change.

"For I, the Lord, do not change." *Malachi 3:6*

"God...cannot lie." *Titus 1:2*

"Jesus Christ is the same yesterday, today, yes and forever." *Hebrews 13:8*

4. Unlike other religious teachers, Jesus lived a perfect, sinless life.

"For we do not have a high priest who cannot sympathize with our weaknesses, but one who has been tempted in all things as we are, yet without sin." *Hebrews 4:15*

"And you know that He appeared in order to take away sins; and in Him there is no sin." *1 John 3:5*

5. Sufis believe the best way to find God is by looking within oneself. According to the Hadith (the book considered by Muslims to be second in authority to the Koran): "He who knows himself knows God." But if we examine ourselves honestly, we have to admit that we are sinful, and sin is what separates mankind from God. The Christian version of this statement would be: "He who knows himself knows he needs a savior."

"The heart is more deceitful than all else and is desperately sick; who can understand it?" *Jeremiah 17:9*

"For all have sinned and fall short of the glory of God." *Romans 3:23*

"If we say that we have no sin, we are deceiving ourselves, and the truth is not in us." *1 John 1:8*

"For I know that nothing good dwells in me, that is, in my flesh; for the wishing is present in me, but the doing of the good is not." *Romans 7:18*

6. God loves us so much that He sent His son Jesus, who gave His life on the cross to pay for our sins.

"For this reason the Father loves Me, because I lay down my life that I may take it up again. No one has taken it from Me, for I lay it down on my own initiative." *John 10:17,18*

"But God demonstrates His own love toward us, in that while we were yet sinners, Christ died for us. Much more then, having now been justified by His blood, we shall be saved from the wrath of God through Him." *Romans 5:8,9*

"He made Him who knew no sin be sin on our behalf, that we might become the righteousness of God in Him." *2 Corinthians 5:21*

7. Because Christ led the only sinless life, He is the only acceptable sacrifice to pay the penalty for our sins.

"Jesus said to him, 'I am the way, and the truth, and the life; no one comes to the Father, but through Me.'" *John 14:6*

"For there is salvation in no one else; for there is no other name under heaven that has been given among men, by which we must be saved." *Acts 4:12*

"For there is one God, and one mediator also between God and men, the man Christ Jesus, who gave Himself as a ransom for all." *1 Timothy 2:5,6a*

8. There is some truth in every religion, and all truth is God's truth. But other religions contain certain teachings about God that oppose what the Bible teaches. Jesus valued unity, but He valued adherence to the truth even higher. This is why Christians cannot embrace every teaching of every religion, and divisions result.

"Do you suppose that I (Jesus) came to grant peace on earth? I tell you, no, but rather division; for from now on five members in one household will be divided, three against two, and two against three." *Luke 12:51,52*

9. After Jesus died, He rose from the dead to prove He was indeed God's Son, and as God's Son everything He said was true.

"Christ died for our sins... He was buried... He was raised on the third day according to the Scriptures... He appeared to Cephas, then to the twelve. After that He appeared to more than five hundred." *1 Corinthians 15:3-6*

Jesus Christ was: "declared with power to be the Son of God by the resurrection from the dead." *Romans 1:4*

"If Christ has not been raised, your faith is worthless; you are still in your sins." *1 Corinthians 15:17*

10. Sufis teach holistic purification of the body through diet, the use of herbs, aromatherapy, etc. But Christ focused on our need for inner, spiritual purification by obtaining forgiveness from our sins, which only He can perform.

"First clean the inside of the cup, and of the dish, so the outside of it may become clean also." *Matthew 23:26*

11. To experience God's love and forgiveness for you, simply confess your sinfulness and receive Christ into your life as your only Savior and Lord.

"If we confess our sins, He is faithful and righteous to forgive us our sins and to cleanse us from all unrighteousness." *1 John 1:9*

"Jesus said to the people who believed in him, 'You are truly my disciples if you keep obeying my teachings. And you will know the truth, and the truth will set you free.... So if the Son sets you free, you will indeed be free.'" *John 8:31,32,36 (NLT)*

"But as many as received Him, to them He gave the right to become children of God, even to those who believe in His name." *John 1:12*

41 Taoism (Daoism)

Lao Tzu founded Taoism around 550 B.C. in China. He sought to achieve harmony with the "natural flow" of the universe. Taoists approach life with the goal of "taking no action that is contrary to Nature."

To a Taoist, the universe is made up of, and held together by the eternal balance of two opposite and equal forces, yin (the negative) and yang (the positive). These two forces both complement and contradict each other. A mysterious, hidden force known as "chi" connects the universe, and can be mastered through meditation, physical exercises, breathing exercises, etc. As for a sense of right and wrong, Taoist philosophy tends to stay away from strict distinctions of good and bad, in preference to the idea of all things maintaining harmony and balance.

As every follower of Taoism knows, the word "Tao" basically means "the way." In his book the "Tao Te King or The Way and Its Power," Lao-tzu wrote, "The way is nameless and hidden, yet all things gain their fulfillment in it." Jesus also spoke of something He called "the way." In His famous sermon on the mount, Jesus said, "Enter by the narrow gate; for the gate is wide, and the way is broad that leads to destruction, and many are those who enter by it. For the gate is small, and the way is narrow that leads to life, and few are those who find it." (Matthew 7:13,14)

One might assume that "the way" Jesus described might be similar to "the way" Lao-tzu described. However, "the way" Jesus was referring to is actually quite unique. According to Jesus, He is the way.

1. **Jesus is unique among founders of other religions. According to the Bible, He was not merely a teacher; He was fully God and fully man, and the world was made through Him.**

   "For in Him all the fulness of Deity dwells in bodily form." *Colossians 2:9*

   "For there is one God, and one mediator also between God and men, the man Christ Jesus, who gave Himself as a ransom for all." *1 Timothy 2:5,6a*

   "All things came into being through Him; and apart from Him nothing came into being that has come into being." *John 1:3*

   "And He is the image of the invisible God, the firstborn of all creation. For in Him all things were created, both in the heavens and on earth, visible and invisible... all things have been created through Him and for Him." *Colossians 1:15,16*

2. **Jesus taught that God loves all people of the world, and provided the way for us to spend eternity with God.**

   "For God so loved the world, that He gave His only begotten Son, that whoever believes in Him should not perish, but have eternal life." *John 3:16*

3. **The Bible doesn't blur the distinction between good and evil. The reason mankind is separated from God is because we are sinful and God is holy.**

   "But your iniquities have made a separation between you and your God, and your sins have hid His face from you, so that He does not hear." *Isaiah 59:2*

   "The Lord has looked down from heaven upon the sons of men, to see if there are any who understand, who seek after God. They have all turned aside; together they have become corrupt; there is no one who does good, not even one." *Psalm 14:1-3*

   "For all have sinned and fall short of the glory of God." *Romans 3:23*

4. **The Bible tells us that neither philosophy, wisdom, physical disciplne, breathing exercises, nor spiritual enlightenment can reconcile us back to God.**

   "See to it that no one takes you captive through philosophy and empty deception, according to the tradition of men, according to the elementary principles of the world, rather than according to Christ." *Colossians 2:8*

5. Even though we are sinful, God loves us and sent His only Son Jesus to reconcile mankind back to God.

"He made Him who knew no sin to be sin on our behalf, that we might become the righteousness of God in Him." *2 Corinthians 5:21*

"But God demonstrates His own love for us in that while we were yet sinners Christ died for us." *Romans 5:8*

"God was in Christ reconciling the world to Himself, not counting their trespasses against them." *2 Corinthians 5:19*

6. Jesus lived a perfect, sinless life, and allowed Himself to be put to death on a cross. By giving His life for us, He took the punishment we deserve for our sins onto Himself. This is the only way we can obtain forgiveness.

"And you know that He appeared in order to take away sins; and in Him there is no sin." *1 John 3:5*

"For Christ also died for our sins once for all, the just for the unjust, in order that He might bring us to God." *1 Peter 3:18*

7. After Jesus was crucified, three days later He rose from the dead, proving once and for all that He was God's Son.

"Christ died for our sins... He was buried... He was raised on the third day according to the Scriptures... He appeared to Cephas, then to the twelve. After that He appeared to more than five hundred." *1 Corinthians 15:3-6*

Jesus Christ was "declared with power to be the Son of God by the resurrection from the dead." *Romans 1:4*

"If Christ has not been raised, your faith is worthless; you are still in your sins." *1 Corinthians 15:17*

8. God wants to forgive you and allow you to have eternal life. And His forgiveness is a free gift that we do not have to work for. It has been paid for by Jesus' death.

"For the wages of sin is death, but the free gift of God is eternal life in Christ Jesus our Lord." *Romans 6:23*

"For by grace you have been saved through faith; and that not from yourselves, it is the gift of God, not as a result of works, that no one should boast." *Ephesians 2:8,9*

"He saved us, not on the basis of deeds we have done in righteousness, but according to His mercy, by the washing of regeneration and renewing of the Holy Spirit, whom He poured out upon us richly through Jesus Christ our Savior." *Titus 3:5,6*

9. To obtain God's forgiveness, Jesus asks that we admit we are sinners, and believe in Him.

"If we say that we have no sin, we are deceiving ourselves, and the truth is not in us. If we confess our sins, He is faithful and righteous to forgive us our sins and to cleanse us from all unrighteousness." *1 John 1:8,9*

10. Jesus taught that He Himself is "the way" that we can have salvation and go to heaven.

"Jesus said to him, 'I am the way, the truth, and the life; no one comes to the Father but through Me.'" *John 14:6*

"I am the door; if anyone enters through Me, he shall be saved, and shall go in and out, and find pasture." *John 10:9*

"And there is salvation in no one else, for there is no other name under heaven that has been given among men, by which we must be saved." *Acts 4:12*

11. Receive (or invite) Jesus Christ into your life, and you will receive forgiveness and be able to go to heaven.

"If you confess with your mouth Jesus as Lord, and believe in your heart that God raised Him from the dead, you shall be saved." *Romans 10:9*

"I stand at the door and knock; if any one hears My voice and opens the door, I will come in to him." *Revelation 3:20*

"But as many as received Him, to them He gave the right to become children of God, even to those who believe in His name." *John 1:12*

42 Theosophy

Helena Petrovna Blavatsky (1831-1891) founded the Theosophical Society in 1875. "Theosophy" means "divine wisdom," and she wrote extensively to explain the wisdom underlying all religions.

One of the main teachings was that all religions are basically the same at their core: "What we desire to prove is, that underlying every once popular religion was the same ancient wisdom-doctrine, one and identical." ("The Purpose of Theosophy," 1888, p. 25)

When Ms. Blavatsky founded Theosophy, she gave it the motto, "There is no Religion higher than Truth." The quest for truth was a major theme in her teachings: "Hence the first and chief necessity of chelaship (discipleship) is a spirit of absolute unselfishness and devotion to Truth; then follow self-knowledge and self-mastery." ("Col. Wr." Volume XI p. 301) She saw truth as something that should be pursued, yet not with the expectation of finding absolute truth: "There is no room for absolute truth upon any subject whatsoever, in a world as finite and conditioned as man is himself. But there are relative truths, and we have to make the best we can of them." ("Lucifer," February 1888)

But if there was one specific religion that angered Ms. Blavatsky, it would have to be Christianity. "The name has been used in a manner so intolerant and dogmatic, especially in our day, that Christianity is now the religion of arrogance, par excellence, a stepping-stone for ambition, a sinecure for wealth, sham, and power; a convenient screen for hypocrisy." (H.P. Blavatsky, "Studies in Occultism," Theosophical University Press, p. 138) She was right to condemn hypocrisy and pride; even Jesus did the same. But what seems to have annoyed Ms. Blavatsky even more is the way Christians are so dogmatic about considering their faith to be the only way to heaven; something she saw as arrogant.

Is it true that Christianity is basically the same as other world religions, or is there a reason why Christians are so stubbornly dogmatic about their faith being unique?

1. **Christians believe Christianity is unique because Jesus was different from the founders of other religions.**

   - Jesus claimed to be the Messiah. *John 4:25,26*
   - Jesus claimed to be the Christ. *Mark 14:62-64*
   - Jesus claimed to be King of the Jews. *Matthew 27:11*
   - Jesus claimed to be God's Son, making Himself equal with God. *John 5:18, 10:33*
   - Jesus claimed to be able to forgive sins, something only God can do. *Mark 2:1-12*

   "All things came into being through Him: and apart from Him nothing came into being that has come into being." *John 1:3*

   "For in Him all the fulness of Deity dwells in bodily form." *Colossians 2:9*

2. **If major world religions are based on the same basic wisdom, then they shouldn't be so contradictory. The founders of other faiths give conflicting accounts about God Himself. Krishna taught there are many gods. Moses, Jesus, and Muhammed taught there is one God. Zoroaster taught there are two primary gods. Jesus taught He would rise from the dead. Muhammed taught Jesus did not rise from the dead. By accepting all these teachings, one can only assume that truth is like rubber, or that God is contradictory and deceptive regarding how He reveals Himself to mankind. But the Bible teaches that God is truthful and does not change.**

   "For I, the Lord, do not change." *Malachi 3:6*

   "God...cannot lie." *Titus 1:2*

   "Jesus Christ is the same yesterday, today, yes and forever." *Hebrews 13:8*

3. **Members of the Theosophical Society are not given strict instructions on moral discipline, and are free to decide what moral guidelines work best for them. But the Bible teaches that there is great danger in rejecting God's standards of holy living. When we ignore or reject God's commands, our sin separates from an intimate relationship with God.**

"But your iniquities have made a separation between you and your God, and your sins have hid His face from you, so that He does not hear." *Isaiah 59:2*

"For all have sinned and fall short of the glory of God." *Romans 3:23*

4. When we willingly submit to God's teachings, it brings inner freedom – not enslavement.

"If you abide in My word, then you are truly disciples of Mine; and you shall know the truth, and the truth shall make you free.... If therefore the Son shall make you free, you shall be free indeed." *John 8:31,32,36*

5. God loves sinful humans so much that He sent His Son Jesus to willingly give His life to pay for our sins.

"For this reason the Father loves Me, because I lay down my life that I may take it up again. No one has taken it from Me, for I lay it down on my own initiative." *John 10:17,18*

"God demonstrates His own love toward us in that while we were yet sinners, Christ died for us." *Romans 5:8*

6. Jesus claimed He was the only way to reach God. Was He being arrogant, or simply telling us the truth?

"Jesus said to him, 'I am the way, and the truth, and the life; no one comes to the Father but through Me.'" *John 14:6*

"For there is salvation in no one else; for there is no other name under heaven that has been given among men, by which we must be saved." *Acts 4:12*

"For there is one God, and one mediator also between God and men, the man Christ Jesus, who gave Himself as a ransom for all." *1 Timothy 2:5,6a*

7. Other religions teach that we reach God by doing good deeds or attaining great wisdom, rather than through faith in Christ. Even though Jesus valued unity, He valued adherence to the truth even higher. This is why Christians are "dogmatic," and must exclude other religions of the world. Sometimes this can be divisive.

Jesus said: "Do you suppose that I came to grant peace on earth? I tell you, no, but rather division; for from now on five members in one household will be divided, three against two, and two against three." *Luke 12:51,52*

8. Ms. Blavatsky practiced spirit communication by channeling "adepts." But God would prefer that we talk directly to Him in prayer, and study His Word for guidance.

"And when they say to you, 'Consult the mediums and the spiritists who whisper and mutter,' should not a people consult their God? Should they consult the dead on behalf of the living?" *Isaiah 8:19*

9. After Jesus died, He rose from the dead to verify that He was indeed God's Son and His teachings were truth.

"Christ died for our sins... He was buried... He was raised on the third day according to the Scriptures... He appeared to Cephas, then to the twelve. After that He appeared to more than five hundred." *1 Corinthians 15:3-6*

Jesus Christ was: "declared with power to be the Son of God by the resurrection from the dead." *Romans 1:4*

"If Christ has not been raised, your faith is worthless; you are still in your sins." *1 Corinthians 15:17*

10. Christ predicted that false messiahs and teachers would come after Him, and warned us not to be misled.

"See to it that no one mislead you. For many will come in My name, saying, 'I am the Christ,' and will mislead many.... And many false prophets will arise, and will mislead many.... Then if any one says to you, 'Behold, here is the Christ,' or 'There He is, do not believe him. For false Christs and false prophets will arise and will show great signs and wonders, so as to mislead, if possible, even the elect. Behold, I have told you in advance." *Matthew 24:4,5,11,23-25.*

11. To know God and experience His love and forgiveness, receive Christ into your life as your Savior and Lord.

"But as many as received Him, to them He gave the right to become children of God, even to those who believe in His name." *John 1:12*

43 Trancendental Meditation

Maharishi Mahesh Yogi (1917 - 2008), also known as MMY, founded this movement in 1958 in India, and brought it to America in 1959. He has taught TM to many famous people, including the Beatles. His teachings appeared new to the western world, but were deeply rooted in ancient Hinduism. It is not surprising that some see TM as a gateway to deeper involvement in Hinduism. TM is basically a technique to help people relax. People who join must participate in initiation ceremonies that involve the reading in Sanskrit of the "puja," a collection of prayers to Hindu deities. Initiates are then assigned a sacred, Hindu, one-word mantra, which is usually the name of a Hindu deity. The mantra is repeated over and over. This blocks out thoughts or thinking of any kind, and as a result is said to be relaxing and bring peace.

In TM there is a deep emphasis on not thinking. "It is only childish and ridiculous to base one's life on the level of thinking. Thinking can never be a profound basis of living. Being is the natural basis... thinking, on the other hand, is only imaginary." (Maharishi, Trancendental Meditation, p. 99)

But MMY does think enough to have formed definite opinions on Jesus Christ: "Due to not understanding the life of Christ and not understanding the message of Christ, I don't think Christ ever suffered or Christ could suffer... It's a pity that Christ is talked of in terms of suffering... it is a wrong interpretation of the life of Christ and the message of Christ... How could suffering be associated with the One who has been all joy, all bliss, who claims all that? It's only the misunderstanding of the life of Christ." (MMY Meditations of MMY pp. 123,124)

If you are the thinking type, make up your own mind concerning what the Bible says about Christ's life, death, and sufferings.

---

1. Hundreds of years before Jesus was born, Old Testament prophecies foretold Christ's sufferings.

"But He was pierced through for our transgressions, He was crushed for our iniquities; the chastening for our well-being fell upon Him, and by His scourging we are healed. All of us like sheep have gone astray, each of us has turned to his own way; but the Lord has caused the iniquity of us all to fall on Him." *Isaiah 53:5,6*

2. According to all four gospels, Jesus suffered and endured an agonizing death in front of many witnesses.

"Then Pilate therefore took Jesus, and scourged Him. And the soldiers wove a crown of thorns and put it on His head, and arrayed Him in a purple robe; and they began to come up to Him, and say, 'Hail, King of the Jews!' and to give him blows in the face." *John 19:1-3*

"And when they came to the place called The Skull, there they crucified Him and the criminals, one on the right and the other on the left.... And the people stood by, looking on. And even the rulers were sneering at Him.... And the soldiers also mocked Him." *Luke 23:33,35,36*

3. Jesus' sufferings were so apparent that Thomas, one of Jesus' close disciples, said he would not recognize the resurrected Jesus unless he saw the scars on Jesus' body that were suffered during His crucifixion.

"Unless I shall see in His hands the imprint of the nails, and put my finger into the place of the nails, and put my hand into His side, I will not believe." *John 20:25*

4. Why did Jesus suffer? Because He willingly gave Himself as the only sinless and acceptable sacrifice who could pay the penalty for our sins.

"For Christ also died for sins once for all, the just for the unjust, in order that He might bring us to God, having been put to death in the flesh, but made alive in the spirit." *1 Peter 3:18*

"And you know that He appeared in order to take away sins; and in Him there is no sin." *1 John 3:5*

"God demonstrates His own love for us in that while we were yet sinners Christ died for us." *Romans 5:8*

"For the wages of sin is death, but the free gift of God is eternal life in Christ Jesus our Lord." *Romans 6:23*

5. Christ took the punishment we deserve for our sin so that we can take on His righteousness.

"God was in Christ reconciling the world to Himself, not counting their trespasses against them." *2 Corinthians 5:19*

"He made Him who knew no sin to be sin on our behalf, that we might become the righteousness of God in Him." *2 Corinthians 5:21*

"For God so loved the world, that He gave His only begotten Son, that whoever believes in Him shall not perish, but have everlasting life." *John 3:16*

6. Christ was raised from the dead proving that He was indeed God's Son.

Jesus Christ was: "declared with power to be the Son of God by the resurrection from the dead." *Romans 1:4*

"Then He said to Thomas, 'Reach here your finger, and see My hands; and reach here your hand, and put it into My side; and be not unbelieving, but believing.' Thomas answered and said to Him, 'My Lord and my God!'" *John 20:27,28*

7. Christ suffered and died so that we can be at peace with God. And the key to being able to relax and be at peace is to first make peace with God and trust Him fully.

"Be anxious for nothing, but in everything by prayer and supplication with thanksgiving let your requests be made known to God. And the peace of God, which surpasses all comprehension, will guard your hearts and your minds in Christ Jesus." *Phillipians 4:6,7*

"You will keep in perfect peace him whose mind is steadfast, because he trusts in You." *Isaiah 26:3*

"Let go, relax and know that I am God." *Psalm 46:10*

"Come to Me, all who are weary and heavy laden, and I will give you rest. Take My yoke upon you, and learn from Me, for I am gentle and humble in heart; and you shall find rest for your souls." *Matthew 11:28,29*

8. The Bible tells us to meditate, but not the type of meditation that empties our minds. We are told to fill our minds by meditating on God's Word, and He promises it will benefit us greatly.

"How blessed is the man who does not walk in the counsel of the wicked, nor stand in the path of sinners, nor sit in the seat of scoffers! But his delight is in the law of the Lord, and in His law he meditates day and night. And he will be like a tree firmly planted by streams of water, which yields its fruit in its season, and its leaf does not wither; and in whatever he does, he prospers." *Psalm 1:1-3*

"This book of the law shall not depart from your mouth, but you shall meditate on it day and night, so that you may be careful to do according to all that is written in it; for then you will make your way prosperous, and then you will have success." *Joshua 1:8*

"Therefore I urge you, brethren, by the mercies of God, to present your bodies a living and holy sacrifice, acceptable to God, which is your spiritual service of worship. And do not be conformed to this world, but be transformed by the renewing of your mind, so that you may prove what the will of God is, that which is good and acceptable and perfect." *Romans 12:1,2*

"Finally, brethren, whatever is true, whatever is honorable, whatever is right, whatever is pure, whatever is lovely, whatever is of good repute, if there is any excellence and if anything worthy of praise, dwell on these things." *Philippians 4:8*

9. By confessing your sins and trusting Christ for forgiveness, you can be saved and be at peace with God.

"If we say that we have no sin, we are deceiving ourselves, and the truth is not in us. If we confess our sins, He is faithful and righteous to forgive us our sins and to cleanse us from all unrighteousness." *1 John 1:8,9*

"I stand at the door and knock; if any one hears My voice and opens the door, I will come in to him." *Revelation 3:20*

"But as many as received Him, to them He gave the right to become children of God, even to those who believe in His name." *John 1:12*

44 The Unification Church ("Moonies")

Reverend Sun Myung Moon (1920-2012) founded the Unification Church in South Korea in 1954, which has now spread throughout the world. In his book "Divine Principle," Reverend Moon made a number of comments on the life and mission of Jesus Christ:

- *"Jesus failed in his Christly mission. His death on the cross was not an essential part of God's plan for redeeming sinful man." (pp. 142,143)*
- *"We therefore must realize that Jesus did not come to die on the cross." (p.178)*
- *"However great his value may be, he cannot assume any value greater than that of a man." (p. 255)*
- *"It is plain that Jesus is not God Himself" (p. 258)*

As for himself, Reverend Moon has also made amazing claims. In 1976, Time Magazine quoted him saying: "He (God) is living in me and I am the incarnation of Himself. The whole world is in my hands, and I will conquer and subjugate the world." As for Christianity, he said: "God is now throwing Christianity away and is now establishing a new religion, and this new religion is Unification Church."

Are Reverend Moon's views about himself and Jesus true? Jesus gave us a simple test to separate truth from falsehood. He said, "If you abide in My word, then you are truly disciples of Mine; and you shall know the truth, and the truth shall make you free." (John 8:31,32) By looking directly to God's Word, and staying within its teachings, we can examine Reverend Moon's comments in light of what the Scriptures tell us. After all, if a person believes teachings that are not the truth, it will have eternal consequences.

---

1. Jesus spoke openly of His upcoming death and resurrection, because He knew He had come to be crucified.

"From that time on Jesus began to show His disciples that He must go to Jerusalem, and suffer many things, from the elders and chief priests and scribes, and be killed, and be raised up on the third day." *Matthew 16:21*

"The Son of Man did not come to be served, but to serve, and to give His life a ransom for many." *Matthew 20:28*

2. Christ said He would give up His life willingly; it would not be taken by force, nor was His death an accident.

"For this reason the Father loves me, because I lay down my life that I may take it up again. No one has taken it from Me, for I lay it down on my own initiative. I have authority to lay it down and I have authority to take it up again. This commandment I received from My Father." *John 10:17,18*

3. Once Jesus had died, some of His followers went to His tomb and found it empty. An angel appeared and reminded them that Christ had predicted His own crucifixion and resurrection.

"'He is not here, but He has risen. Remember how He spoke to you while He was still in Galilee, saying that the Son of Man must be delivered into the hands of sinful men, and be crucified, and the third day rise again.' And they remembered His words." *Luke 24:6-8*

4. Why did Jesus die? He was the only sinless, acceptable sacrifice who could pay the penalty for the sins of mankind.

"He Himself bore our sins in His body on the cross, that we might die to sin and live to righteousness; for by His wounds you were healed." *1 Peter 2:24*

"For Christ also died for sins once for all, the just for the unjust, in order that He might bring us to God, having been put to death in the flesh, but made alive in the Spirit." *1 Peter 3:18*

"And you know that He appeared in order to take away sins; and in Him there is no sin." *1 John 3:5*

5. His death is even more significant in view of the Bible's teaching that Jesus was fully God and fully man.

"In the beginning was the Word, and Word was with God, and the Word was God.... And the Word became flesh, and dwelt among us, and we saw His glory, glory as of the only begotten from the Father, full of grace and truth." *John 1:1,14*

"For in Him all the fulness of Deity dwells in bodily form." *Colossians 2:9*

"For there is one God, and one mediator also between God and men, the man Christ Jesus, who gave Himself as a ransom for all." *1 Timothy 2:5,6a*

"The Jews answered Him, 'For a good work we do not stone You, but for blasphemy; and because You, being a man, make Yourself out to be God.'" *John 10:33*

6. Did Jesus complete His mission to redeem mankind? His final words on the cross give us the answer.

"After this, Jesus, knowing that all things had already been accomplished, in order that the Scriptures might be fulfilled said, 'I am thirsty.' ...When Jesus therefore had received the sour wine, He said, 'It is finished!' And He bowed His head, and gave up His spirit." *John 19:28,30*

7. Reverend Moon teaches that he has taken up the messianic mission which Christ failed to complete. But Christ predicted that false messiahs would come after Him, and warned us not to be misled.

"See to it that no one mislead you. For many will come in My name, saying, 'I am the Christ,' and will mislead many.... And many false prophets will arise, and will mislead many.... Then if any one says to you, 'Behold, here is the Christ,' or 'There He is,' do not believe him. For false Christs and false prophets will arise and will show great signs and wonders, so as to mislead, if possible, even the elect. Behold, I have told you in advance." *Matthew 24:4,5,11,23-25*.

"Jesus said to him, 'I am the way, and the truth, and the life; no one comes to the Father, but through Me.'" *John 14:6*

"For there is salvation in no one else; for there is no other name under heaven that has been given among men, by which we must be saved." *Acts 4:12*

8. There is no mystery concerning how we will know the Messiah when He returns. We are told in Scripture that when Jesus returns, He will descend from heaven to the exact same spot from which He ascended into heaven.

"And after He had said these things, He was lifted up while they were looking on, and a cloud received Him out of their sight. And as they were gazing intently into the sky while He was departing, behold, two men in white clothing stood beside them; and they also said, 'Men of Galilee, why do you stand looking into the sky? This Jesus, who has been taken up from you into heaven, will come in just the same way as you have watched Him go into heaven.'" *Acts 1:9-11*

According to this passage, any potential messiah who does not come to earth the same way that Jesus left the earth would be automatically disqualified.

9. What happens to those who teach distorted forms of the gospel from the traditional, biblical Christian gospel?

"But even if we, or an angel from heaven, should preach to you a gospel contrary to what we have preached to you, he is to be accursed! As we have said before, so I say again now, if any man is preaching to you a gospel contrary to what you received, he is to be accursed!" *Galatians 1:8,9*

10. Do you want to trust your entire eternal destiny to the teachings of a man who disagrees with what the Bible clearly says, and makes false claims to be the Messiah? Or will you trust the words of Christ and the Bible teaches?

"I stand at the door and knock; if any one hears My voice and opens the door, I will come in to him." *Revelation 3:20*

"But as many as received Him, to them He gave the right to become children of God, even to those who believe in His name." *John 1:12*

"These things I have written to you who believe in the name of the Son of God, in order that you may know that you have eternal life." *1 John 5:13*

"If you confess with your mouth Jesus as Lord, and believe in your heart that God raised Him from the dead, you shall be saved." *Romans 10:9*

45 Unitarian

Unitarians tend to be anti-dogmatic when it comes to their beliefs. One might even say Unitarians are dogmatically anti-dogmatic. The individual member is generally left to arrive at his or her own beliefs, and those individual beliefs are respected by the rest of the congregation. But there is one doctrine held by Unitarians which comes close to being held in a dogmatic fashion. Unitarians believe that the conventional understanding of the Trinity, or triune nature of God, is not an accurate understanding of who God is; hence the term Unitarian (compared to Trinitarian).

What exactly does the Bible say in regard to this important issue?

---

1. God's Word tells us that we cannot know everything about God, at least not right now, because He is infinite and we are finite. Even people in the Bible were willing to admit they did not fully understand everything.

Moses: "The secret things belong to the Lord our God, but the things revealed belong to us and to our sons forever." *Deuteronomy 29:29*

Isaiah: "Who is able to advise the Spirit of the Lord? Who knows enough to be his teacher or counselor?" *Isaiah 40:13 (NLV)*

David: "Such knowledge is too wonderful for me; it is too high, I cannot attain to it." *Psalm 139:6*

Paul: "Oh, the depth of the riches both of the wisdom and knowledge of God! How unsearchable are His judgments and unfathomable His ways!" *Romans 11:33*

"For now we see in a mirror dimly, but then face to face; now I know in part, but then I shall know fully just as I also have been fully known." *1 Corinthians 13:12*

2. Judaism and Christianity are "monotheistic;" that is, we believe in and worship only one God.

"Hear O Israel! The Lord is our God, the Lord is one!" *Deuteronomy 6:4*

"Now to the King eternal, immortal, invisible, the only God, be honor and glory forever and ever. Amen." *1 Timothy 1:15*

"Know therefore today, and take it to your heart, that the Lord, He is God in heaven above and on the earth below; there is no other." *Deuteronomy 4:39*

3. Even though God hasn't revealed everything about Himself in the Bible, He sometimes refers to Himself as being plural in nature.

"Then God said, 'Let Us make man in Our image, according to Our likeness.'" *Genesis 1:26*

"Then I heard the voice of the Lord, saying, 'Whom shall I send, and who will go for Us?'" *Isaiah 6:8*

4. The Bible clearly tell us that there is only one God, and God consists of three distinct "Persons."

"Go therefore and make disciples of all the nations, baptizing them in the name of the Father and the Son and the Holy Spirit." *Matthew 28:19*

"And after being baptized, Jesus went up immediately from the water; and behold, the heavens were opened, and He saw the Spirit of God descending as a dove, and coming upon Him; and behold, a voice out of the heavens, saying, 'This is My beloved Son, in whom I am well pleased.'" *Matthew 3:16,17*

Perhaps the illustration that comes closest to explaining how God exists in three distinct Persons within the Trinity, each having different role or function, is the comparison to H2O. It can exist in three different states, all of which are fully H2O: Liquid (water), Solid (ice), Gas (steam). Each form of H20 has a different function; you can't skate on water, you can't drink steam, and clouds can't be blocks of ice.

5. Jesus made many claims about Himself. If any of His claims are not true, then He must be written off as a liar. But if

His claims are true, then He deserves to be worshiped.

- Jesus claimed to be the Messiah. *John 4:25,26*
- Jesus claimed to be the Christ. *Mark 14:62-64*
- Jesus claimed to be King of the Jews. *Matthew 27:11*
- Jesus claimed to be God's Son, making Himself equal with God. *John 5:18,10:33*
- Jesus claimed to be able to forgive sins, something only God can do. *Mark 2:1-12*

6. **When you reject the concept of the Trinity, it leads you to believe that Jesus Christ was just a man rather than God in the flesh. But the Bible tells us Jesus was fully God and fully man.**

   "In the beginning was the Word, and the Word was with God, and the Word was God.... And the Word became flesh, and dwelt among us, and we beheld His glory, glory as of the only begotten from the Father, full of grace and truth." *John 1:1,14*

   "For in Him all the fulness of Deity dwells in bodily form." *Colossians 2:9*

   "The Jews answered Him, 'For a good work we do not stone You, but for blasphemy; and because You, being a man, make Yourself out to be God.'" *John 10:33*

7. **If Jesus Christ was only a man, then His sacrificial death on the cross does nothing to help us obtain forgiveness. And we desperately need a Savior because our sin has separated us from God.**

   "But your iniquities have made a separation between you and your God, and your sins have hid His face from you, so that He does not hear." *Isaiah 59:2*

   "For all have sinned and fall short of the glory of God." *Romans 3:23*

   "By this we know that we abide in Him and He in us, because He has given us of His Spirit. And we have behold and bear witness that the Father has sent the Son to be the Savior of the world." *1 John 4:13,14*

8. **Christ's role within the Trinity is to make access to the Father possible. By being both fully God and a fully, sinless man, He took the penalty for our sins onto Himself and makes us holy so we can be allowed into God's presence.**

   "For there is one God, and one mediator also between God and men, the man Christ Jesus, who gave Himself as a ransom for all." *1 Timothy 2:5,6a*

   "Jesus said to him, 'I am the way, and the truth, and the life; no one comes to the Father, but through Me.'" *John 14:6*

   "God was in Christ reconciling the world to Himself, not counting their trespasses against them. He made Him who knew no sin to be sin on our behalf, that we might become the righteousness of God in Him." *2 Corinthians 5:19,21*

   "But now in Christ Jesus you who formerly were far off have been brought near by the blood of Christ... for through Him we both have our access in one Spirit to the Father." *Ephesians 2:13,18*

9. **A human can *create* a work of art, but a human can only *beget* another human – that is, another human of the same nature as the parent. As God's only begotten Son, Jesus is the same divine nature as God the Father.**

   "For God so loved the world, that He gave His only begotten Son, that whoever believes in Him shall not perish, but have everlasting life." *John 3:16*

10. **To obtain God's free gift of forgiveness, simply confess your sin and believe in Christ as God's Son.**

    "If we confess our sins, He is faithful and righteous to forgive us our sins and to cleanse us from all unrighteousness." *1 John 1:9*

    "I am the door; if anyone enters through Me, he will be saved, and will go in and out and find pasture." *John 10:9*

    "But as many as received Him, to them He gave the right to become children of God, even to those who believe in His name." *John 1:12*

46 Unity

When Charles and Myrtle Fillmore founded the Unity Church in 1889, one of their unique beliefs was: "There is no sin, sickness or death." ("Unity," Volume 47, No. 5, p. 403) In the Unity Statement of Faith, Article 22, their concept of death is explained more fully: "We believe that the dissolution of spirit, soul, and body caused by death, is annulled by rebirth of the same spirit and soul in another body here on earth. We believe the repeated incarnations of man to be a merciful provision of our loving Father to the end that all may have opportunity to attain immortality through regeneration, as did Jesus."

The Bible describes how our loving Father has given a merciful provision to mankind, but is it the one described above? The Fillmores looked to the Bible to read about Jesus, but are their conclusions in harmony with Jesus' own teachings regarding Himself and the reason He came to earth? What exactly does the Bible tell us about who Jesus was, why He came, and how His mission related to sin, sickness, and death?

---

1. If sin is not real, then mankind does not need a savior to save us from sin. If sin is not real, then why does the Bible spend so much time talking about it? To be perfectly honest, sin is very real and separates us from God.

"But your iniquities have made a separation between you and your God, and your sins have hid His face from you, so that He does not hear." *Isaiah 59:2*

"For all have sinned and fall short of the glory of God." *Romans 3:23*

2. Rebirth is a biblical concept. But Jesus spoke only of our spiritual rebirth through believing in Christ, and never even mentioned the possibility of a physical rebirth into another body.

"Jesus answered and said to him, 'Truly, truly, I say to you, unless one is born again, he cannot see the kingdom of God.' Nicodemus said to Him, 'How can a man be born when he is old? He cannot enter a second time into his mother's womb and be born, can he?' Jesus answered, 'Truly, truly, I say to you, unless one is born of water (meaning physically, from the womb) and the Spirit, he cannot enter the kingdom of God. That which is born of the flesh is flesh, and that which is born of the Spirit is spirit.'" *John 3:3-6*

"It is appointed for men to die once, and after this comes judgment." *Hebrews 9:27*

"Remember Him before the silver cord is broken and the golden bowl is crushed... then the dust will return to the earth as it was, and the spirit will return to God who gave it." *Ecclesiastes 12:6,7*

3. Spiritual rebirth only occurs when we trust in Christ as our Savior.

"For God so loved the world, that He gave His only begotten Son, that whoever believes in Him shall not perish, but have everlasting life." *John 3:16*

"God demonstrates His own love for us in that while we were yet sinners Christ died for us." *Romans 5:8*

"Therefore if any man is in Christ; he is a new creature; the old things passed away; behold, new things have come." *2 Corinthians 5:17*

4. God loves us in spite of our sin, and His "merciful provision" for us is Christ. Only Jesus can save us from our sin because He lived a sinless life.

"And you know that He appeared in order to take away sins; and in Him there is no sin." *1 John 3:5*

"God was in Christ reconciling the world to Himself, not counting their trespasses against them.... He made Him who knew no sin to be sin on our behalf, that we might become the righteousness of God in Him." *2 Corinthians 5:19,21*

"John saw Jesus coming toward him and said, 'Look, the Lamb of God who takes away the sin of the world!'" *John 1:29*

5. Jesus was not merely a wise teacher, He was fully God and fully man, and only through Him can mankind obtain forgiveness from sin.

"For in Him all the fulness of Deity dwells in bodily form." *Colossians 2:9*

"The Jews answered Him, 'For a good work we do not stone You, but for blasphemy; and because You, being a man, make Yourself out to be God.'" *John 10:33*

"For there is one God, and one mediator also between God and men, the man Christ Jesus, who gave Himself as a ransom for all." *1 Timothy 2:5,6a*

"For the grace of God has appeared, bringing salvation to all men, instructing us to deny ungodliness and worldly desires and to live sensibly, righteously and godly in the present age, looking for the blessed hope and the appearing of the glory of our great God and Savior, Christ Jesus; who gave Himself for us, that He might redeem us from every lawless deed and purify for Himself a people for His own posession, zealous for good deeds." *Titus 2:11-14*

6. Only those who have their sins forgiven will have access to the Father, and Christ is the only way to receive forgiveness.

"Jesus said to him, 'I am the way, and the truth, and the life; no one comes to the Father, but through Me.'" *John 14:6*

"For there is salvation in no one else; for there is no other name under heaven that has been given among men, by which we must be saved." *Acts 4:12*

7. Christ died for our sins, then rose from the dead to prove He was God's Son!

"Christ died for our sins according to the Scriptures... He was buried... He was raised on the third day according to the Scriptures, and after that He appeared to Cephas, then to the twelve. After that He appeared to more than five hundred brethren at one time." *1 Corinthians 15:3-6*

Jesus was: "declared with power to be the Son of God by the resurrection from the dead." *Romans 1:4*

"If Christ has not been raised, your faith is worthless; you are still in your sins." *1 Corinthians 15:17*

8. Not only does the Bible teach that sin is real, but that the universal curse of sickness and death was a direct result of sin.

"For the wages of sin is death, but the free gift of God is eternal life in Christ Jesus our Lord." *Romans 6:23*

9. In this life here on earth we have sin, sickness, and death. But only in heaven will these things be gone.

"He shall wipe away every tear from their eyes; and there shall no longer be any death; there shall no longer by any mourning, or crying, or pain; the first things have passed away." *Revelation 21:4*

10. The Fillmores believed that sin, sickness, and death were not real. Did they ever see a cemetery or a hospital? Or perhaps they simply lived in denial of the truth. They placed their faith on the concept that they would be reincarnated. But the Bible clearly teaches something very different – that the only way to know God is to admit that your sin is real, and ask Christ to be your Savior and Lord.

"If we say that we have no sin, we are deceiving ourselves, and the truth is not in us. If we confess our sins, He is faithful and righteous to forgive us our sins and to cleanse us from all unrighteousness. If we say that we have not sinned, we make Him a liar, and His word is not in us." *1 John 1:8-10*

"If you confess with your mouth Jesus as Lord, and believe in your heart that God raised Him from the dead, you shall be saved." *Romans 10:9*

"Behold, I stand at the door and knock; if any one hears My voice and opens the door, I will come in to him, and will dine with him, and he with Me." *Revelation 3:20*

47 Voodoo

Voodoo originated in Haiti in the late 1700s and has spread widely ever since. It is a mixture of certain elements of Catholicism combined with various African religious practices such as spirit communication and ancestor worship. Originally, it was a way for African slaves to continue practicing their religious beliefs, while appearing to use Christian symbols.

Voodoo teaches that the supreme being does not bother to intercede in the affairs of humans, so people must curry favor with the lesser spirits. The most common name for the leading god in Voodoo is Damballah, represented by the serpent. Many of the rituals are designed to curry favor with various spirits, or to obtain protection from harmful spirits. Another voodoo practice is the placing of hexes and spells on one's enemies, or the protection from hexes placed by others. During worship, some worshipers allow spirits to take over their bodies, to speak and act through them.

Even though voodoo originated in the 1700s, other similar spirit-related practices have been around for centuries, and the Bible gives us very specific instructions regarding such practices. But what exactly does the Bible say, and does the Bible give us permission to mingle Christian elements with spiritual practices of other faiths?

---

1. There are many spirits, but only one true God. He does not want His worship mingled with the worship of other spirits or false gods.

"You shall have no other gods before Me. You shall not worship them or serve them; for I, the Lord your God, am a jealous God." *Exodus 20:3,5*

"Before Me there was no God formed, and there will be none after Me. I, even I, and the Lord; and there is no savior besides Me." *Isaiah 43:10,11*

"Is there any God besides Me, or is there any other Rock? I know of none." *Isaiah 44:8*

"Know therefore today, and take it to your heart, that the Lord, He is God in heaven above and on the earth below; there is no other." *Deuteronomy 4:39*

2. According to the Bible, all spirits are subject to Christ because He is fully God.

"At the name of Jesus every knee should bow, of those who are in heaven, and on earth, and under the earth, and that every tongue should confess that Jesus Christ is Lord to the glory of God the Father." Philippians 2:10,11

"For in Him all the fulness of Deity dwells in bodily form." *Colossians 2:9*

"And it happened that as we were going to the place of prayer, a certain slave-girl having a spirit of divination met us, who was bringing her masters much profit by fortunetelling... But Paul... turned and said to the spirit, 'I command you in the name of Jesus Christ to come out of her!' And it came out that very moment." *Acts 16:16,18*

3. All spirits are ultimately subject to Christ, though not all are obedient to Him. If a spirit communicates with us, we can't be certain it is telling the truth.

"Dear friends, do not believe everyone who claims to speak by the Spirit. You must test them to see if the spirit they have comes from God. For there are many false prophets in the world." *1 John 4:1 (NLT)*

"But the Spirit explicitly says that in later times some will fall away from the faith, paying attention to deceitful spirits and doctrines of demons." *1 Timothy 4:1*

"Satan disguises himself as an angel of light. Therefore it is not surprising if his servants also disguise themselves as servants of righteousness." *2 Corinthians 11:14,15*

"Whenever he (the Devil) speaks a lie, he speaks from his own nature, for he is a liar and the father of lies." *John 8:44b*

4. Because of the dangerously deceptive nature of some spirits, the Bible makes it clear that communication with the spirit world by any occult practices is non-compatible with faith in God; and warns us never to do it.

"There shall not be found among you... one who uses divination, one who practices witchcraft, or one who interprets omens, or a sorcerer, or one who casts a spell, or a medium, or a spirititst, or one who calls up the dead. For whoever does these things is detestable to the Lord." *Deuteronomy 18:10-12*

"Do not turn to mediums or spiritists; do not seek them out to be defiled by them. I am the Lord your God." *Leviticus 19:31*

"But for the cowardly and unbelieving and abominable and murderers and immoral persons and sorcerers and idolaters and all liars, their part will be in the lake that burns with fire and brimstone, which is the second death." *Revelation 21:8*

5. Rather than communicate with spirits we can't trust, we can communicate directly with the God we can trust!

"And when they say to you, 'Consult the mediums and the spiritists who whisper and mutter,' should not a people consult their God? Should they consult the dead on behalf of the living?" *Isaiah 8:19*

6. Christ is infinitely more powerful than Damballah, or any spirit. Christ will ultimately defeat all evil spirits.

"And he laid hold of the dragon, the serpent of old, who is the devil and Satan... and threw him into the abyss, and shut it and sealed it over him, so that he should not deceive the nations any longer... And the devil who deceived them was thrown in the lake of fire and brimstone, where the beast and the false prophet are also, and they will be tormented day and night forever and ever." *Revelation 20:2,3,10*

7. We don't need any spirits to intercede between God and us. God has already sent His Son as the only acceptable mediator to provide direct access to God! By offering His Son Jesus as the payment for our sins, God will forgive our sins and make us holy, which makes it possible for us to have direct access to Him!

"Jesus said to him, 'I am the way, and the truth, and the life; no one comes to the Father but through Me.'" *John 14:6*

"I am the door; if anyone enters through Me, he will be saved, and will go in and out and find pasture. The thief comes only to steal and kill and destroy; I came that they may have life, and have it abundantly." *John 10:9,10*

"And there is salvation in no one else; for there is no other name under heaven that has been given among men by which we must be saved." *Acts 4:12*

"But God demonstrates His own love toward us, in that while we were yet sinners, Christ died for us." *Romans 5:8*

8. To obtain the forgiveness Christ offers, you must first simply admit you are a sinner and need to be forgiven.

"For all have sinned and fall short of the glory of God." *Romans 3:23*

"If we say that we have no sin, we are deceiving ourselves and the truth is not in us. If we confess our sins, He is faithful and righteous to forgive us our sins and to cleanse us from all unrighteousness." *1 John 1:8,9*

9. Ask Christ into your life and your direct access to the God of the universe will begin.

"I stand at the door and knock; if any one hears my voice and opens the door, I will come in to him" *Revelation 3:20*

"But as many as received Him, to them He gave the right to become children of God, even to those who believe in His name." *John 1:12*

10. Once a person becomes a Christian, there must be a complete break with all occult practices.

"Many also of those who had believed kept coming, confessing and disclosing their practices. And many of those who practiced magic brought their books together and began burning them in the sight of all; and they counted up the price of them and found it fifty thousand pieces of silver. So the word of the Lord was growing mightily and prevailing." *Acts 19:18-20*

48 The Way International

Victor Paul Weirwille, born in 1917, is the founder of The Way International and their famous introductory course "Power for Abundant Living." Regarding the source of his own unique teachings, Mr. Weirwille has said, "God spoke to me audibly, just like I'm talking to you now. He said he would teach me the word as it had not been known since the first century, if I would teach it to others." (Elena S Whiteside, "The Way: Living in Love," New Knoxville, Ohio: American Christian Press, p 178.)

Perhaps the simplest way to find out if this is true would be to compare Mr. Wierwille's teachings with what was being taught in the first century by those church leaders who had been taught by Jesus Himself, and used by God to write the Scriptures and launch the Christian church.

1. One of Wierwille's primary teachings is that Jesus Christ was only a perfect man, but not God.

Wierwille wrote: "If Jesus Christ is God and not the Son of God, we have not yet been redeemed." (*Jesus Christ Is Not God, p. 6*) He also writes, "Those who teach that Jesus Christ is God and God is Jesus Christ will never stand approved in rightly dividing God's word, for there is only one God, and 'Thou shalt have no other gods.'" (*p. 79*)

2. The Bible clearly tells us that there is only one God.

"Now to the King eternal, immortal, invisible, the only God, be honor and glory forever and ever. Amen."
1 Timothy 1:15

"Hear O Israel! The Lord is our God, the Lord is one!" *Deuteronomy 6:4*

"Know therefore today, and take it to your heart, that the Lord, He is God in heaven above and on the earth below; there is no other." *Deuteronomy 4:39*

3. Even though there is only one God, He describes Himself in the Bible as being plural in nature.

"Then God said, 'Let Us make man in Our image, according to Our likeness.'" *Genesis 1:26*

"Then I heard the voice of the Lord, saying, 'Whom shall I send, and who will go for Us?'" *Isaiah 6:8*

4. The Bible clearly tell us that there is only one God, and God consists of three distinct "Persons."

"Go therefore and make disciples of all the nations, baptizing them in the name of the Father and the Son and the Holy Spirit." *Matthew 28:19*

"And after being baptized, Jesus went up immediately from the water; and behold, the heavens were opened, and He saw the Spirit of God descending as a dove, and coming upon Him; and behold, a voice out of the heavens, saying, 'This is My beloved Son, in whom I am well pleased.'" *Matthew 3:16,17*

The grace of the Lord Jesus Christ, and the love of God, and the fellowship of the Holy Spirit, be with you all." *2 Corinthians 13:14*

This concept of three distinct Persons within the Trinity may seem confusing, but one thing can exist in three states: H20 can be a solid (ice), a liquid (water), or a gas (steam).

5. When you reject the concept of the Trinity, it leads you to believe that Jesus Christ was just a man rather than God in the flesh. But the Bible tells us Jesus was fully God and fully man.

"In the beginning was the Word, and the Word was with God, and the Word was God." *John 1:1*

"For in Him (Jesus) all the fulness of Deity dwells in bodily form." *Colossians 2:9*

"Then He (Jesus) said to Thomas, 'Reach here with your finger, and see My hands; and reach here your hand and put it into My side; and do not be unbelieving, but believing.' Thomas answered and said to Him, 'My Lord and my God'!" *John 20:27,28*

"But of the Son He says, 'Thy throne, O God, is forever and ever.'" *Hebrews 1:9*

6. Jesus has pre-existed throughout all of eternity past. just like God the Father.

"But as for you, Bethlehem Ephrathah, too little to be among the clans of Judah, from you One will go forth for Me to be ruler in Israel. His goings forth are from long ago, from the days of eternity." *Micah 5:2*

"'I am the Alpha and the Omega,' says the Lord God, 'who is and who was and who is to come, the Almighty.... Do not be afraid; I am the first and the last, and the living One; and I was dead, and behold, I am alive forevermore." *Revelation 1:8,17,18*

7. If Jesus was only a man, His death does nothing to help us obtain forgiveness. Only God can be our Savior.

"Before Me there was no God formed, and there will be none after Me. I, even I, and the Lord; and there is no savior besides Me." *Isaiah 43:10,11*

"For the grace of God has appeared, bringing salvation to all men, instructing us to deny ungodliness and worldly desires... looking for the blessed hope and the appearing of the glory of our great God and Savior, Christ Jesus; who gave Himself for us, that He might redeem us from every lawless deed and purify for Himself a people for His own possession, zealous for good deeds." *Titus 2:11-14*

8. Jesus clearly claimed to be God, and to His Jewish listeners this was blasphemy – a crime deserving death.

"For this cause the Jews were seeking all the more to kill Him, because not only was He breaking the Sabbath, but also was calling God His own Father, making Himself equal with God." *John 5:18*

"The Jews answered Him, 'For a good work we do not stone You, but for blasphemy; and because You, being a man, make Yourself out to be God.'" *John 10:33*

"So the Jews said to Him, 'You are not yet fifty years old, and have You seen Abraham?' Jesus said to them, 'Truly, truly, I say to you, before Abraham was born, I AM.' Therefore they picked up stones to throw at Him, but Jesus hid Himself and went out of the temple." *John 8:57-59*

"And they all said, 'Are You the Son of God, then?' And He said to them, 'Yes I am.' Then they said, "What further need do we have of testimony? For we have heard it for ourselves from His own mouth.'" *Luke 22:70,71*

9. A person can create a painting or a sculpture, but a human can only beget another human – an offspring of the same nature as the parent. As God's only begotten Son, Jesus is the same nature as God the Father.

"For God so loved the world, that He gave His only begotten Son, that whoever believes in Him shall not perish, but have everlasting life." *John 3:16*

10. By being both God and man, Christ's role within the Trinity is to provide access to the Father. He took the penalty for our sins onto Himself. Once we are holy, we can be allowed into God's presence.

"For there is one God, and one mediator also between God and men, the man Christ Jesus, who gave Himself as a ransom for all." *1 Timothy 2:5,6a*

"Jesus said to him, 'I am the way, and the truth, and the life; no one comes to the Father, but through Me. If you had known Me, you would have known My Father also; from now on you know Him, and have seen Him.' Philip said to Him, 'Lord, show us the Father, and it is enough for us.' Jesus said to him, 'Have I been so long with you, and yet you have not come to know Me, Philip? He who has seen Me has seen the Father." *John 14:6-9a*

11. To obtain Christ's payment for your sin and receive His gift of free forgiveness – as taught in the first century – simply confess your sin and believe in Christ as God's fully divine Son.

"I stand at the door and knock; if anyone hears My voice and opens the door, I will come into him." *Revelation 3:20*

"If we confess our sins, He is faithful and righteous to forgive us our sins and to cleanse us from all unrighteousness." *1 John 1:9*

49 Witchcraft (Wicca)

Beliefs within Witchcraft (also known as Wicca) can be quite varied. Most Wiccans are duotheistic, in that they venerate both a god and a goddess; which some Wiccans believe are actual beings while others see them as simply symbolic of positive and negative forces in nature. Still other Wiccans are monotheistic, while others are atheist or agnostic. Regardless of these differences, Witches believe that powers are available by tapping into the mystical forces of nature. Many Wiccans practice what they consider to be good witchcraft (white magic) to make good things happen, while other Wiccans admittedly cast harmful spells on their enemies (black magic). During certain rituals, Wiccans often stand within a circle for the purpose of protecting themselves from the same spiritual forces they are calling up.

In the Wizard of Oz, Glenda asked Dorothy, "Are you a good witch, or a bad witch?" But perhaps the question we should be asking today is: "Is Witchcraft good or bad?" What are the powers behind all Witchcraft? Are Witches simply calling upon forces of nature, or are there other forces involved that even Witches may not understand? And who is the ultimate recipient of the devotion from those who practice Witchcraft?

1. Nature has been created by God, and He has declared that His creation is good.

"The earth brought forth vegetation, plants yielding seed after their kind, and trees bearing fruit with seed in them, after their kind; and God saw that it was good." *Genesis 1:12*

2. Even though nature is good and should be respected as God's creation, it is not what we should venerate or worship. Doesn't it make more sense to worship the God who created nature?

"Professing to be wise, they became fools... For they exchanged the truth of God for a lie, and worshiped and served the creature rather than the Creator, who is blessed forever. Amen." *Romans 1:22,25*

3. The Bible says that activities which seek to curry favor with spirits or forces other than God are not something God approves or endorses in any way.

"There shall not be found among you... one who uses divination, one who practices witchcraft, or one who interprets omens, or a sorcerer, or one who casts a spell, or a medium, or a spiritist, or one who calls up the dead. For whoever does these things is detestable to the Lord." *Deuteronomy 18:10-12*

"But cowards who turn away from me, and unbelievers, and the corrupt, and murderers, and the immoral, and those who practice witchcraft, and idol worshipers, and all liars – their doom is in the lake that burns with fire and sulfur. This is the second death." *Revelation 21:8 (NLT)*

4. Since God is good, and He makes it clear that He does not approve of Witchcraft, then the powers behind Witchcraft certainly cannot be from God, and probably aren't even from nature. If you think Witchcraft is wholesome and good, it's possible you have been deceived.

"Every good thing given and every perfect gift is from above, coming down from the Father of lights, with whom there is no variation or shifting shadow." *James 1:17*

5. Witchcraft and white magic may appear to do good for those who practice it. But Satan is very deceptive and can fool many people into thinking something is good when it is not.

"...Satan disguises himself as an angel of light. Therefore it is not surprising if his servants also disguise themselves as servants of righteousness." *2 Corinthians 11:14,15*

"But the Spirit explicitly says that in later times some will fall away from the faith, paying attention to deceitful spirits and doctrines of demons." *1 Timothy 4:1*

6. Since the powers behind Witchcraft are not from God, and Witchcraft is clearly prohibited by God, then it simply stands to reason that these powers are from Satan or his demons.

"Little children, let no one deceive you; the one who practices righteousness is righteous, the one who practices sin is of the devil, for the devil has sinned from the beginning. The Son of God appeared for this purpose that He might destroy the works of the devil." *1 John 3:7,8*

"Therefore also God highly exalted Him (Jesus), and bestowed on Him the name which is above every name, that at the name of Jesus every knee should bow, of those who are in heaven, and on earth, and under the earth, and that every tongue should confess that Jesus Christ is Lord to the glory of God the Father." *Philippians 2:9-11*

"You are of your father the devil, and you want to do the desires of your father. He was a murderer from the beginning, and does not stand in the truth because there is no truth in him. Whenever he speaks a lie, he speaks from his own nature, for he is a liar and the father of lies. But because I (Jesus) speak the truth, you do not believe Me." *John 8:44,45*

7. The practice of Witchcraft, just like any other sin, must be confessed to be forgiven.

"If we say that we have no sin, we are deceiving ourselves, and the truth is not in us. If we confess our sins, He is faithful and righteous to forgive us our sins and to cleanse us from all unrighteousness. If we say that we have not sinned, we make Him a liar, and His word is not in us." *1 John 1:8-10*

8. Jesus is God's Son, and provides Himself as the payment for all sin. He loves us and is ready to forgive if we will simply accept His free gift.

"For God so loved the world, that He gave His only begotten Son, that whoever believes in Him shall not perish, but have everlasting life." *John 3:16*

"But God demonstrates His own love for us in that while we were yet sinners Christ died for us." *Romans 5:8*

"For the wages of sin is death, but the free gift of God is eternal life in Christ Jesus our Lord." *Romans 6:23*

"I am the door; if anyone enters through Me, he will be saved, and will go in and out and find pasture. The thief comes only to steal and kill and destroy; I came that they may have life, and have it abundantly." *John 10:9,10*

9. The reason Jesus is the only way to have sins forgiven is because He is both God and man, and He lived a sinless life. He willingly sacrificed His life as the only acceptable sacrifice to pay the penalty for our sin.

"For in Him all the fulness of Deity dwells in bodily form." *Colossians 2:9*

"For there is one God, and one mediator also between God and men, the man Christ Jesus, who gave Himself as a ransom for all." *1 Timothy 2:5,6a*

"Jesus said to him, 'I am the way, and the truth, and the life; no one comes to the Father, but through Me.'" *John 14:6*

"For there is salvation in no one else; for there is no other name under heaven that has been given among men, by which we must be saved." *Acts 4:12*

10. To become a Christian, simply confess your sins and invite Christ into your life.

"Behold, I stand at the door and knock; if any one hears My voice and opens the door, I will come in to him, and will dine with him, and he with Me." *Revelation 3:20*

"But as many as received Him, to them He gave the right to become children of God, even to those who believe in His name." *John 1:12*

11. When a person comes to trust in Christ, there must be a complete break with witchcraft and all occult practices.

"Many also of those who had believed kept coming, confessing and disclosing their practices. And many of those who practiced magic brought their books together and began burning them in the sight of all; and they counted up the price of them and found it fifty thousand pieces of silver. So the word of the Lord was growing mightily and prevailing." *Acts 19:18-20*

50 Zoroastrianism

Zoroaster (also known as Zarathustra) lived in the area of modern day Iraq or Iran somewhere around 650 BC. and possibly even earlier. It is one of the oldest of the world's religions. At the age of 30, he wrote that he received a vision in which a large figure appeared to him, calling himself Vohu Masna, or "good thought." He took Zoraster into the presence of Ahura Mazda, or "wise lord," and taught him this religion.

There are some similarities between Zoroastrianism and Christianity, such as a belief in heaven and hell, as well as punishment for the wicked and reward for the righteous. Within Zoroastrianism, there are also many other divine entities called "yazatas" (which means "worthy of worship"), and some people compare them to the angels of Christianity (although angels are not considered divine or worthy of worship). For centuries, Zoroastrians have studied the stars, and there is speculation that the Magi mentioned in Matthew who followed the star to Bethlehem might have been Zoroastrian priests.

In the Avesta (the sacred writings of Zorastrianism) the enemy of Ahura Mazda is called Angra Mainyu, or "the bad spirit." They are said to be co-equal, and co-eternal. According to the Avesta, these two equal powers have been at odds throughout eternity and continue their struggle throughout the ages. But even though there are some similarities between Zoroastrianism and Christianity, how are they different, and what makes those differences so significant?

1. **Zoroastrians worship only one god, but they believe in the existence of many deities; the two most powerful are Ahura Mazda and Angra Mainyu. Christians clearly believe in the existence of only one divine being – God.**

   "Before Me there was no God formed, and there will be none after Me. I, even I, and the Lord; and there is no savior besides Me." *Isaiah 43:10,11*

   "Is there any God besides Me, or is there any other Rock? I know of none." *Isaiah 44:8*

2. **Even though the Bible tells us there is only one God, He exists in three "persons" – God the Father, God the Son, and God the Holy Spirit.**

   "Go therefore and make disciples of all the nations, baptizing them in the name of the Father and the Son and the Holy Spirit." *Matthew 28:19*

3. **The Bible tells of how God expelled a rebellious angel and his followers out of heaven. This angel was originally called Lucifer but was later known as Satan. Satan's power is described as vastly inferior to God's, and Satan has not pre-existed throughout eternity.**

   "You were blameless in your ways from the day you were created until unrighteousness was found in you. By the abundance of your trade you were internally filled with violence, and you sinned; therefore I have cast you as profane from the mountain of God." *Ezekiel 28:15,16a*

4. **Satan is not like God, nor equal in power to God. Satan was cast out of heaven because he tried to make himself like God.**

   "But you said in your heart, 'I will ascend to heaven; I will raise my throne above the stars of God, and I will sit on the mount of assembly in the recesses of the north. I will ascend above the heights of the clouds; I will make myself like the Most High." *Isaiah 14:13,14*

5. **After he was removed from heaven, Lucifer became known as Satan, and speaking through a serpent he tempted the first humans, Adam and Eve, by making them think they could also become like God. When they fell into sin, the entire human race became separated from God because of our unholiness.**

   "And the serpent said to the woman, 'You shall surely not die for God knows that in the day you eat from it your eyes will be opened, and you will be like God, knowing good and evil.'" *Genesis 3:4,5*

   "Therefore, just as through one man (Adam) sin entered into the world, and death through sin, and so death spread to all men, because all sinned." *Romans 5:12*

"For all have sinned and fall short of the glory of God." *Romans 3:23*

6. In order to reconcile mankind back to Himself, God sent His Son Jesus to earth to pay the penalty for our sins. Jesus was fully God and fully man, and He took our sins onto Himself when He died on the cross.

"For in Him all the fulness of Deity dwells in bodily form." *Colossians 2:9*

"For God so loved the world, that He gave His only begotten Son, that whoever believes in Him shall not perish, but have everlasting life." *John 3:16*

"But God demonstrates His own love for us in that while we were yet sinners Christ died for us." *Romans 5:8*

"For there is one God, and one mediator also between God and men, the man Christ Jesus, who gave Himself as a ransom for all." *1 Timothy 2:5,6a*

7. After He died, Christ rose from the dead to prove He was God's Son.

Jesus was "declared with power to be the Son of God by the resurrection from the dead." *Romans 1:4*

"Christ died for our sins according to the Scriptures… He was buried… He was raised on the third day according to the Scriptures, and after that He appeared to Cephas, then to the twelve. After that He appeared to more than five hundred brethren at one time." *1 Corinthians 15:3-6*

8. Jesus is infinitely more powerful than Satan and will destroy him and his followers.

"The Son of God appeared for this purpose, that He might destroy the works of the devil." *1 John 3:8*

"Greater is He who is in you than he who is in the world." *1 John 4:4*

"The ruler of this world will be cast out." *John 12:31*

9. The way a person obtains salvation according to Zoroastrianism is more similar to Islam than Christianity. Islam and Zoroastrianism teach that good deeds get us to heaven. But the Bible tells us that even though good works are important, we cannot do enough good works to get to heaven. That is why Christ died, to do what we could never achieve. He paid the penalty for our sins and make it possible for us to go to heaven.

"For by grace you have been saved through faith; and that not from yourselves, it is the gift of God, not as a result of works, that no one should boast." *Ephesians 2:8,9*

"For Christ also died for sins once for all, the just for the unjust, in order that He might bring us to God, having been put to death in the flesh, but made alive in the Spirit." *1 Peter 3:18*

"He Himself bore our sins in His body on the cross, that we might die to sin and live to righteousness; for by His wounds you were healed." *1 Peter 2:24*

"For the wages of sin is death, but the free gift of God is eternal life in Christ Jesus our Lord." *Romans 6:23*

10. To receive God's gift of free salvation, simply confess your sins and receive Christ into your life.

"If we say that we have no sin, we are deceiving ourselves, and the truth is not in us. If we confess our sins, He is faithful and righteous to forgive us our sins and to cleanse us from all unrighteousness. If we say that we have not sinned, we make Him a liar, and His word is not in us." *1 John 1:8-10*

"'Behold, I stand at the door and knock; if anyone hears My voice and opens the door, I will come in to him and will dine with him, and he with Me.'" *Revelation 3:20*

"But as many as received Him, to them He gave the right to become children of God, even to those who believe in His name." *John 1:12*

Section Two

C8

Biblical Answers to Tough Questions

51 Was Jesus God?

No name is more famous in all of human history than Jesus of Nazareth. Even the calendar is divided into two periods; before His birth or after. Mankind is somehow drawn to Him; either to love Him or to hate Him. Two thousand years after He walked the earth, millions of people still follow His teachings. On the other hand, millions of others are hostile to His teachings and His followers.

Jesus remains the most controversial person in history. So who was He? Many outside Christianity acknowledge His great skill as a teacher. But was He more than just a great teacher or philosopher? Could it be that Jesus Christ was actually fully God and fully man? Could He have been the human incarnation of the infinite God who created the universe? What does the Bible say about who Jesus was, why is He so important to mankind, and was He truly divine?

1. **Unlike other religious founders, predictions of Jesus' birth and other events in His life had already been recorded in the Old Testament centuries before His birth.**

   - He would be born into the Hebrew tribe of Judah. *Genesis 49:10, Matthew 1:2, Revelation 5:5*
   - He would be born in Bethlehem. *Micah 5:2, Matthew 2:1*
   - He would be born of a virgin. *Isaiah 7:14, Matthew 1:18-25*
   - He would work miracles. *Isaiah 61:1, Matthew 11:1-5, Luke 4:16-21*
   - He would be betrayed for exactly thirty pieces of silver. *Zechariah 11:12, Matthew 26:14-16*
   - The money to betray Him would be used to buy the Potter's Field. *Zechariah 11:12,13, Matthew 27:3-10*
   - His hands and feet would be pierced. *Psalm 22:16, John 19:35,37, John 20:24-28*
   - He would be the payment for our sins by taking our sins onto Himself. *Isaiah 53:5,6, 2 Corinthians 5:21*
   - People would gamble for his clothing by casting lots. *Psalm 22:18, John 19:23,24*
   - He would be executed along with criminals. *Isaiah 53:9,12, Luke 23:32,33*
   - He would be buried in a rich man's tomb. *Isaiah 53:9, Matthew 27:57-60*
   - His body would not decay, but would be resurrected. *Psalm 16:8-11, Luke 24:1-43, Romans 1:4*

2. **Jesus Himself claimed to be fully God.**

   - Jesus claimed to be the Messiah and the Christ. *John 4:25,26, Mark 14:62-64*
   - Jesus claimed to be King of the Jews. *Matthew 27:11*
   - Jesus claimed to be God's Son, making Himself equal with God. *John 5:18, 10:33, Luke 22:70*
   - Jesus claimed to be able to forgive sins, something which only God can do. *Mark 2:1-12*
   - Jesus claimed to be the only way to reach God. *John 14:6*
   - Jesus claimed to be the God of the Old Testament, having eternally pre-existed before coming to earth. *John 8:56-59*

3. **It was Jesus' claim to be God that resulted in His death sentence at His trial. The priests knew that if He claimed to be God they could execute Him for blasphemy.**

   "The Jews answered Him, 'For a good work we do not stone You, but for blasphemy; and because You, being a man, make Yourself out to be God.'" *John 10:33*

   "And they all said, 'Are You the Son of God, then?' And He said to them, 'Yes I am.' And they said, 'What further need do we have of testimony? For we have heard it for ourselves from His own mouth.'" *Luke 22:70,71*

4. **If Jesus was God, then He could have done some truly amazing things. And He did! The Bible describes many of HIs miracles, but the ultimate proof that Jesus was God's fully divine Son came when He rose from the dead.**

   Jesus was "declared with power to be the Son of God by the resurrection from the dead." *Romans 1:4*

   "Christ died for our sins according to the Scriptures... He was buried... He was raised on the third day according to the Scriptures, and after that He appeared to Cephas, then to the twelve. After that He appeared to more than five hundred brethren at one time." *1 Corinthians 15:3-6*

5. To understand Christ's deity, we must understand the concept of the Trinity and Jesus' role within the Trinity.

Perhaps the illustration that comes closest to explaining how God exists in three distinct Persons within the Trinity, each having different a function, is the comparison to H2O. It can exist in three different states, all of which are fully H2O and have different functions. For example, you can't skate on water, you can't drink steam, and clouds can't be blocks of ice; yet they are all equally H2O. Christ's chief function within the Trinity is to be the link or mediator between God and man so that we can have access to God.

"For there is one God, and one mediator also between God and men, the man Christ Jesus, who gave Himself as a ransom for all." *1 Timothy 2:5,6a*

"Jesus said to him, 'I am the way, and the truth, and the life; no one comes to the Father, but through Me.'" *John 14:6*

"For there is salvation in no one else; for there is no other name under heaven that has been given among men, by which we must be saved." *Acts 4:12*

"For in Christ the fullness of God lives in a human body." *Colossians 2:9 (NLT)*

6. Why is Jesus the only way to God? Because as the only sinless person to ever live, He is the only qualified sacrifice God the Father would accept to pay the price for our sins so that we could be made holy.

"For Christ also died for sins once for all, the just for the unjust, in order that He might bring us to God." *1 Peter 3:18*

"God was in Christ reconciling the world to Himself, not counting their trespasses against them. He made Him who knew no sin to be sin on our behalf, that we might become the righteousness of God in Him." *2 Corinthians 5:19,21*

"And you know that He appeared in order to take away sins; and in Him there is no sin." *1 John 3:5*

7. Jesus willingly allowed Himself to be crucified as a substitute on our behalf because of His great love for us.

"God demonstrates His own love for us in that while we were yet sinners Christ died for us." *Romans 5:8*

"For this reason the Father loves Me, because I lay down My life so that I may take it again. No one has taken it away from Me, but I lay it down on My own initiative. I have authority to lay it down, and I have authority to take it up again. This commandment I received from My Father." *John 10:17,18*

8. Even when Christ walked the earth there were a variety of opinions regarding who He was. He once asked His disciples who the people said He was:

"And they said, 'Some say John the Baptist; some, Elijah; and others Jeremiah, or one of the prophets.'" *Matthew 16:14*

9. After His disciples had answered Jesus' question, He asked an even more important follow-up question:

"He said to them, 'But who do you say that I am?' And Simon Peter answered and said, 'You are the Christ, the Son of the living God.'" *Matthew 16:15,16*

10. Author C.S. Lewis wrote the book *Mere Christianity* in 1952. It includes this statement about Jesus:

"A man who was merely a man and said the sort of things Jesus said would not be a great moral teacher. He would either be a lunatic – on the level with a man who says he is a poached egg – or he would be the devil of hell. You must take your choice. Either this was, and is, the Son of God, or else a madman or something worse. You can shut Him up for a fool or you can fall at His feet and call Him Lord and God. But let us not come with any patronizing nonsense about His being a great human teacher. He has not left that open to us."

11. If Jesus is the Son of God as He claimed – and proved by rising from the dead – then we can be certain His claim of being the only way to God is also true. If we accept Him as our Savior, our sins will be forgiven. If we reject Him as our Savior we will spend eternity away from God's presence.

"For God so loved the world, that He gave His only begotten Son, that whoever believes in Him shall not perish, but have everlasting life." *John 3:16*

52 Is Jesus Really The Only Way To Heaven?

Some people consider the claim that Jesus is the only way to heaven to be somewhat arrogant; as if Christians think we have a monopoly on the truth. But the reason Christians believe Jesus is the only way to heaven is because this was one of Jesus' primary teachings.

Is Jesus truly the only way to heaven? There are certainly plenty of other religions to choose from, and they offer alternative beliefs about how to get to heaven.

Many of those who do not believe in Jesus feel it doesn't matter what you believe, as long as you believe it. And yet many people have walked out onto frozen lakes believing the ice was thick enough to support their weight, only to find out it wasn't. The point is, faith is only as good as the object in which it is placed. If the claims of Christ are true, then He is the only way to heaven. But if His credibility is destroyed, then it's anybody's guess how to get to heaven.

What exactly did Jesus claim, and what does the Bible say about this important issue?

---

1. **First of all, if you compare the teachings of the other world religions, they can't all be right because they contradict each other on basic teachings about God.**

   • Krishna taught there are many gods.
   • Moses, Jesus, and Muhammed taught there is one God.
   • Zoroaster taught there are two primary gods; one good, one evil.
   • Jesus taught He was God's Son and would rise from the dead.
   • Muhammed taught that Jesus was not God's Son and did not rise from the dead.

2. **What, or Who, did Jesus claim to be?**

   • Jesus claimed to be God's Son, making Himself equal with God. *John 5:18, 10:33, Luke 22:70*
   • Jesus claimed to be the Messiah and the Christ. *John 4:25,26, Mark 14:62-64*
   • Jesus claimed to be able to forgive sins, something only God can do. *Mark 2:1-12*
   • Jesus claimed to have eternally pre-existed before coming to earth. *John 8:56-59*
   • Jesus claimed to be the only way to reach God. *John 14:6, John 10:9*

3. **Something that sets Christ apart from other religious founders and greatly increases His credibility is the fact that so many details of His life were written centuries before He was even born, and verified by the Dead Sea Scrolls.**

   • He would be born in Bethlehem. *Micah 5:2, Matthew 2:1*
   • He would be born of a virgin. *Isaiah 7:14, Matthew 1:18-25*
   • He would work miracles. *Isaiah 61:1, Matthew 11:1-5, Luke 4:16-21*
   • He would be betrayed for exactly thirty pieces of silver. *Zechariah 11:12, Matthew 26:14-16*
   • His hands and feet would be pierced. *Psalm 22:16, John 19:35,37, John 20:24-28*
   • People would gamble for his clothing by casting lots. *Psalm 22:18, John 19:23,24*
   • He would be executed along with criminals. *Isaiah 53:9,12, Luke 23:32,33*
   • He would be buried in a rich man's tomb. *Isaiah 53:9, Matthew 27:57-60*
   • His body would not decay, but would be resurrected. *Psalm 16:8-11, Luke 24:1-43, Romans 1:4*

4. **After Jesus was crucified as a criminal, He rose from the dead! This is the ultimate proof that He was the true Son of God, and therefore we can trust what He said.**

   "Christ died for our sins... He was buried... He was raised on the third day according to the Scriptures... He appeared to Cephas, then to the twelve. After that He appeared to more than five hundred." *1 Corinthians 15:3-6*

   Jesus was "declared with power to be the Son of God by the resurrection from the dead." *Romans 1:4*

   "If Christ has not been raised, your faith is worthless; you are still in your sins." *1 Corinthians 15:17*

5. **According to the Scriptures, God created the entire universe through Christ.**

"All things came into being through Him: and apart from Him nothing came into being that has come into being." *John 1:3*

6. Now that we know who Jesus claimed to be and what His credentials are, how does His plan of salvation work? It's very simple. It is based on trusting in Jesus to pay for our sins.

"For God so loved the world, that He gave His only begotten Son, that whoever believes in Him shall not perish, but have everlasting life." *John 3:16*

7. Mankind is sinful, and sin separates us from God. But God loves us so much that He sent His Son Jesus to pay the penalty for the sins of mankind by giving His life so that we could be forgiven and reunited with God.

"But your iniquities have made a separation between you and your God, and your sins have hid His face from you, so that He does not hear." *Isaiah 59:2*

"For all have sinned and fall short of the glory of God." *Romans 3:23*

"God demonstrates His own love for us in that while we were yet sinners Christ died for us." *Romans 5:8*

"He (God the Father) made Him (Jesus) who knew no sin be sin on our behalf, that we might become the righteousness of God in Him." *2 Corinthians 5:21*

8. Jesus was the only man who was God in the flesh and completely sinless, so He is the only acceptable sacrifice to pay for our sins. That's why He's the only way to heaven!

"For in Him (Jesus) all the fulness of Deity dwells in bodily form." *Colossians 2:9*

"And you know that He appeared in order to take away sins; and in Him there is no sin." *1 John 3:5*

"Jesus said to him, 'I am the way, and the truth, and the life; no one comes to the Father but through Me.'" *John 14:6*

"For there is one God, and one mediator also between God and men, the man Christ Jesus, who gave Himself as a ransom for all." *1 Timothy 2:5,6a*

9. Author C.S. Lewis wrote the famous book *Mere Christianity* in 1952. It includes this statement about Jesus:

"A man who was merely a man and said the sort of things Jesus said would not be a great moral teacher. He would either be a lunatic – on the level with a man who says he is a poached egg – or he would be the devil of hell. You must take your choice. Either this was, and is, the Son of God, or else a madman or something worse. You can shut Him up for a fool or you can fall at His feet and call Him Lord and God. But let us not come with any patronizing nonsense about His being a great human teacher. He has not left that open to us."

10. Other religions teach that we reach God by being good. That is where Christianity is unique. The Bible teaches that we can only reach God because He reached down to us by coming in the form of a man; Jesus.

"For by grace you have been saved through faith; and that not from yourselves, it is the gift of God, not as a result of works, that no one should boast." *Ephesians 2:8,9*

Imagine if all the founders of all the world's religions were on the bank of a lake, and you were drowning. Muhammed, Buddha, Confucius, L. Ron Hubbard, Joseph Smith, and all the others would be shouting instructions on how you could to swim to shore and save yourself. But Jesus would be different. He would dive in, swim out to you, and offer to bring you back to shore. If you accept His offer, you would be rescued. That is what makes Jesus unique among other religious founders. He has done the work for us! Our salvation is based on what He has done, not what we do.

11. To have Christ's payment apply to your sins so that you can be forgiven and go to heaven, simply confess your sins and place your faith in Christ as your personal Savior.

"I stand at the door and knock; if any one hears My voice and opens the door, I will come in to him." *Revelation 3:20*

"The wages of sin is death, but the free gift of God is eternal life in Christ Jesus our Lord." *Romans 6:23*

53 Did Jesus Really Rise From The Dead?

Of all the miracles in the Bible, the most significant – and the most scrutinized – is Jesus rising from the dead. Critics of the faith have known for centuries that if you can disprove the resurrection, you disprove Christianity. The resurrection is either the greatest event in human history, or the greatest lie ever told. Christianity is not just based on faith in a crucified Messiah, but faith in a resurrected Messiah! Ever since accounts of the resurrection began to circulate, especially among the people closest to the evidence, the debate never focused on whether or not Jesus' tomb was empty; but how it became empty. Was His body removed by human or divine intervention? When the apostles first began preaching about the resurrection to the people closest to the evidence, their opponents never produced a body to disprove the story.

To dismiss the resurrection is to ignore many ancient historical writings. The resurrection is mentioned in the Bible, and in writings by first and second century historians such as Clement of Rome, Polycarp, Justin Martyr, Tertullian, Josephus, and Ignatius. None of these writers were eyewitnesses to the risen Christ; they simply recorded historical events. Obviously, the testimony of eyewitnesses would have far more credibility. Fortunately, those accounts are available in the Bible. But there really aren't any eyewitness accounts by non-Christians who saw the risen Lord. Why? Probably because anybody who saw the risen Lord immediately became a believer!

So what happened to Jesus' body? If you visit the tomb of Buddha, Confucius, or Muhammed, their tombs are occupied. But the tomb of Jesus is empty! Does the empty tomb prove Christianity is true?

---

1. **The Christian faith is based on Jesus being God's only Son who paid for our sins with His death. The resurrection verifies that Jesus was indeed the Son of God. If He was not resurrected, our faith is worthless.**

   Jesus Christ was: "declared with power to be the Son of God by the resurrection from the dead." *Romans 1:4*

   "If Christ has not been raised, your faith is worthless; you are still in your sins." *1 Corinthians 15:17*

2. **Jesus' death and resurrection are the most thoroughly documented parts of His life. Half of John's gospel describes in detail the final week of Christ's life. We have far more eyewitness accounts about the death and burial of Christ than any other figure in ancient history. The four gospel accounts of the resurrection, as well as Paul's letters, were written while most of the hundreds of resurrection witnesses were still alive. If the accounts had been false, or if anyone knew where the body was hidden, there were plenty of people who could have raised a challenge. Paul wrote the following passage to the Corinthians in 56 A.D., 23 years after Christ died:**

   "For I delivered to you as of first importance what I also received, that Christ died for our sins according to the Scriptures, and that He was buried, and that He was raised on the third day according to the Scriptures, and that He appeared to Cephas, then to the twelve. After that He appeared to more than five hundred brethren at one time, most of whom remain until now, but some have fallen asleep; then He appeared to James, then to all the apostles; and last of all, as to one untimely born, He appeared to me also." *1 Corinthians 15:3-8*

3. **The gospels and New Testament letters were written by eyewitnesses of the resurrection, or by people who interviewed eyewitnesses.**

   "The one who existed from the beginning is the one we have heard and seen. We saw him with our own eyes and touched him with our own hands. He is Jesus Christ, the Word of life. This one who is life from God was shown to us, and we have seen him." *1 John 1:1,2a (NLT)*

   "For we did not follow cleverly devised tales when we made known to you the power and coming of our Lord Jesus Christ, but we were eyewitnesses of His majesty." *2 Peter 1:16*

4. **Other explanations for the resurrection raise more questions than they answer:**

   • If Jesus didn't die on the cross, but only fainted and then revived inside the tomb, how could He have survived the severe beatings, floggings, blood loss, the spear in his chest, and still have strength to escape by pushing open the huge stone at the tomb's entrance, then overpower and outrun the squad of Roman guards on severely wounded feet?

• If the hundreds of eyewitnesses were hallucinating when they saw the risen Lord, then why did their accounts match? And how could a figment of their imagination do things like eat, drink, cook, and allow His wounds to be examined?

• If the high priests or the Romans had taken the body of Jesus for safekeeping, why didn't they simply produce the body and put and end to the issue?

• If His body was merely tossed out to be eaten by dogs, then why did the priests have guards protect an empty tomb?

• If Jesus escaped the cross altogether, and someone else was mistakenly crucified in His place, then why had Jesus lied by foretelling His own death and resurrection before it happened? And how did Jesus get the nail wounds in His hands and feet, or the spear wound in His side which He showed Thomas in John 24? And if someone else was mistakenly executed, why wasn't that body still buried in the tomb?

• If the disciples stole the body from the tomb, how did they escape notice by the squad of trained Roman soldiers? And if they did succeed in stealing the body and creating a hoax, then why did they devote their lives to something they knew to be a lie, even when it meant beatings, stonings, torture, imprisonment, and execution?

5. Compare the results of two sermons preached by the apostles which described Jesus' resurrection. Paul preached in Athens, Greece (hundreds of miles from Jerusalem where Jesus was crucified and several years after the resurrection) to people who could not examine the evidence. The result was mixed:

"Now when they heard of the resurrection of the dead, some began to sneer, but others said, 'We shall hear you again concerning this.' But some men joined and believed." *Acts 17:32,34*

6. The other sermon was preached by Peter only six weeks after the resurrection in Jerusalem (where Jesus was crucified and resurrected) to the people most familiar with the events and who could easily examine the empty tomb and talk to witnesses. If they knew the story was false, Christianity would have been dead on arrival. But the result was overwhelming acceptance of Peter's message!

"Now when they heard this, they were pierced to the heart, and said to Peter and the rest of the apostles, 'Brethren, what shall we do?' ...So then, those who had received his word were baptized; and there were added that day about three thousand souls." *Acts 2:37,41*

7. One of Jesus' disciples, "Doubting Thomas," was like many people today. But once he saw Jesus was alive, look at the conclusion he reached about who Jesus was:

"The other disciples therefore were saying to him (Thomas), 'We have seen the Lord!' But he said to them, 'Unless I shall see in His hands the imprint of the nails, and put my finger into the place of the nails, and put my hand into His side, I will not believe.' And after eight days again His disciples were inside, and Thomas with them. Jesus came, the doors having been shut, and stood in their midst, and said, 'Peace be with you.' Then He said to Thomas, 'Reach here your finger, and see My hands; and reach here your hand, and put it into My side; and be not unbelieving, but believing.' Thomas answered and said to Him, 'My Lord and my God!'" *John 20:25-28*

8. As for proof outside of the Bible, there are ten mentions of Jesus from secular writings of the time, yet only nine mentions of the Roman Emperor Tiberius – the most powerful man on earth at the time of Christ. The following account of Jesus and His resurrection is from the writings of Jewish historian Josephus Flavius from the year 93 A.D.:

"At this time (the time of Pilate) there was a wise man who was called Jesus. And his conduct was good, and he was known to be virtuous. And many people from among the Jews and the other nations became his disciples. Pilate condemned him to be crucified and to die. And those who had become his disciples did not abandon his discipleship. They reported that he had appeared to them after his crucifixion and that he was alive; accordingly, he was perhaps the Messiah concerning whom the prophets have recounted wonders." *Josephus, Antiquities*

9. The Bible promises that all who believe in Christ will someday be resurrected! Today is your chance to believe!

"Jesus said to her, 'I am the resurrection and the life, he who believes in Me shall live even if he dies, and everyone who lives and believes in Me shall never die. Do you believe this?'" *John 11:25*

54 Is Jesus Coming Again?

Christians have been looking forward to the return of Christ since He left the earth 2,000 years ago. The Scriptures promise He will someday return to earth and reign as king in Jerusalem. Jesus' return will not be the end of the world, but will be the end of suffering for His followers, a time to reunite with departed loved ones, and the beginning of the best times ever on earth. But when will He come back? God in His wisdom has chosen not to tell us the exact time. He simply commands us to stay ready, expectant, and faithful until Christ returns. But He gives us signs that tell us when Christ's return is drawing near.

Jesus' disciples anxiously anticipated the coming of Christ's earthly reign as king, and they asked Him, "What will be the signs of Your coming?" At the time they asked this question, they didn't yet understand that His earthly kingdom would not come about until after He had fulfilled His mission of sacrificing His life to pay for the sins of the world. They assumed He would soon overthrow Israel's Roman occupiers.

Many of the Bible's predictions cannot be fully understood until after they occur. But it does give us a pretty good picture of future events, and has predicted many events with pinpoint accuracy. There are various views within Christianity as to the exact order of future events, but Bible-believing Christians all agree that Jesus will return. As years pass, more and more pieces of the puzzle fall into place.

1. **The second coming of Christ is often confused with another future event called "the rapture," which many theologians believe will occur prior to Christ's second coming, while others believe it will occur at the same time. Either way, it will be a joyous time for Christians because the dead will rise with new bodies to join the living in heaven.**

   "For the Lord Himself will descend from heaven with a shout, with the voice of the archangel, and with the trumpet of God; and the dead in Christ shall rise first. Then we who are alive and remain shall be caught up together with them in the clouds to meet the Lord in the air, and thus we shall always be with the Lord. Therefore comfort one another with these words." *1 Thessalonians 4:16-18*

2. **If the rapture occurs before the second coming, it will cause great chaos for those left on earth, and start the period known as the "tribulation." During this unprecedented anarchy, a global government will be led by the antichrist (a.k.a. the "beast"), who declares himself to be God and will deceive many into worshiping him and placing a mark of dedication on their bodies. This period lasts seven years and culminates with the battle of Armageddon.**

   "Let no one in any way deceive you, for it (Christ's return) will not come unless the apostasy comes first, and the man of lawlessness is revealed, the son of destruction, who opposes and exalts himself above every so-called god or object of worship, so that he takes his seat in the temple of God, displaying himself as being God. And then that lawless one will be revealed whom the Lord will slay with the breath of His mouth and bring to an end by the appearance of His coming." *2 Thessalonians 3:4,8*

3. **Christ will return for the battle of Armageddon and will defeat the armies led by the antichrist who is empowered by Satan. Christ will then set up His own global government which will last for a thousand years.**

   "And I saw the beast and the kings of the earth and their armies, assembled to make war against Him (Christ) who sat upon His horse, and against His army. And the beast was seized, and with him the false prophet who performed the signs in his presence, by which he deceived those who had received the mark of the beast and those who worshiped his image; these two were thrown alive into the lake of fire which burns with brimstone." *Revelation 19:19,20*

4. **After the thousand-year reign of Christ, Satan will be allowed to wreak havoc on earth for a limited amount of time, then he will be eternally bound. This earth will later be destroyed and replaced with an imperishable one.**

   "And he (an angel) laid hold of the dragon, the serpent of old, who is the devil and Satan, and bound him for a thousand years... so that he should not deceive the nations any longer, until the thousand years were completed; after these things he must be released for a short time. And when the thousand years are completed, Satan will be released from his prison, and will come out to deceive the nations... to gather them together for the war... and fire came down from heaven and devoured them. And the devil who deceived them was thrown into the lake of fire and brimstone, where the beast and the false prophet are also; and they will be tormented day and night for ever and ever.... And I saw a new heaven and a new earth; for the first heaven and the first earth passed away." *Revelation 20:2,3,7-10, 21:1*

5. So if Jesus is the Messiah, why has He waited so long to return to earth and set up His kingdom? His own disciples asked Him this question after His resurrection.

"And so when they had come together, they were asking Him, saying, 'Lord, is it at this time You are restoring the kingdom to Israel?' He said to them, 'It is not for you to know.'" *Acts 1:6,7a*

6. Jesus has waited to return so that the gospel can spread throughout the entire world in order for people of every nation to be offered salvation.

"The Lord is not slow about His promise, as some count slowness, but is patient toward you, not wishing for any to perish but for all to come to repentance." *2 Peter 3:9*

"And as He was sitting on the Mount of Olives, the disciples came to Him privately, saying, 'Tell us, when will these things be, and what will be the sign of Your coming, and of the end of the age?' And Jesus said to them, 'See to it that no one misleads you... And this gospel of the kingdom shall be preached in the whole world for a witness to all the nations, and then the end shall come.'" *Matthew 24:3,4,14*

7. Once people began seeing the miracles Jesus could perform, they wanted to make Him set up His kingdom. But He refused because the time was not yet right, and He had not yet fulfilled His mission of paying for our sins.

"Jesus therefore, perceiving that they were intending to take Him by force, to make Him king, withdrew again to the mountain by Himself alone." *John 6:15*

8. Jesus will return to the same spot from which He ascended; the Mount of Olives just outside Jerusalem. This is also about fifty miles south of where the battle of Armageddon will be fought.

"He was lifted up while they were looking on, and a cloud received Him out of their sight. And as they were gazing intently into the sky while He was departing, behold, two men, in white clothing stood beside them; and they also said, 'Men of Galilee, why do you stand looking into the sky? This Jesus, who has been taken up from you into heaven, will come in just the same way as you have watched Him go into heaven.' Then they returned to Jerusalem from the mount called Olivet, which is near Jerusalem." *Acts 1:9-12*

"And in that day His feet will stand on the Mount of Olives, which is in front of Jerusalem on the east; and the Mount of Olives will be split in its middle from east to west.... And the Lord will be king over all the earth; in that day the Lord will be the only one, and His name the only one." *Zechariah 14:4,9*

9. Here are some of the signs to watch for which tell us Christ's return is extremely close.

- Israel once again becoming a nation. *Ezekiel 36:1-12* (fulfilled in 1948)
- Increase of earthquakes in later times. *Matthew 24:7* (According to the U.S. Geological Survey, there were 2 quakes of 6.0 or greater between 1920 and 1930. Between 1980 and 1990, there were 86!)
- Many false imposters will claim to be the Christ. *Matthew 24:5* (Such as: David Koresh of the Branch Davidians, Shoko Asahara of the Japanese cult Aum Shinri Kyo, and Sun Myung Moon of the Unification Church)
- The rapture of all Christians. *1 Thessalonians 4:13-18, 1 Corinthians 15:51-54*
- The rise of the Antichrist. *2 Thessalonians 2:1-12, Revelation 13:1-8, Daniel 11:36,37*
- The great tribulation lasting 7 years. *Daniel 12:11-13, Revelation 11:2,13:5*

10. You can be ready for Christ's return by placing your trust in Him as your Savior and Lord.

"Therefore be on the alert, for you do not know which day your Lord is coming.... For this reason you be ready too; for the Son of Man is coming at an hour when you do not think He will." *Matthew 24:42,44*

"For God so loved the world, that He gave His only begotten Son, that whoever believes in Him shall not perish, but have everlasting life." *John 3:16*

55 What Is The Difference Between Making Jesus Your Savior And Making Him Lord?

We often hear Christians talk about how they made Jesus their personal Savior and Lord. This actually requires making two decisions; one decision to trust in Jesus as the Savior who forgives your sins so you can go to heaven, and another decision to submit every area of life in obedience to His Lordship. Sometimes people make both of these decisions at once, and sometimes they are made years apart. Sometimes people make Jesus their Savior (for what is often called "fire insurance") but they never allow Him to become their Lord over all areas of their life.

There's a saying that is probably a bit overstated, and yet there is some truth to it: "When you make Jesus your Savior, it brings your soul to heaven; when you make Him Lord, it brings heaven to your soul."

What exactly are the differences and results of each decision?

1. **Jesus is uniquely qualified from any other person to be our Savior who pays for our sins. The Bible tells us He is both fully God and fully human, and He lived a perfectly sinless life. He loved us enough to give His life on the cross, and by sacrificing His life He took the punishment for the world's sins to satisfy God's judgment.**

   "For there is one God, and one mediator also between God and men, the man Christ Jesus, who gave Himself as a ransom for all." *1 Timothy 2:5,6a*

   "For in Christ the fullness of God lives in a human body." *Colossians 2:9 (NLT)*

   "For there is salvation in no one else; for there is no other name under heaven that has been given among men, by which we must be saved." *Acts 4:12*

2. **How does a person make Jesus their personal Savior? We confess our sins and agree with God that we cannot save ourselves by doing good deeds or anything else. We trust fully in what Jesus has done on the cross rather than our own good deeds to obtain our salvation. And we willingly invite Christ into our lives.**

   "If we say that we have no sin, we are deceiving ourselves, and the truth is not in us. If we confess our sins, He is faithful and righteous to forgive us our sins and to cleanse us from all unrighteousness." *1 John 1:8,9*

   "Behold, I stand at the door and knock; if anyone hears My voice and opens the door, I will come in to him and will dine with him, and he with Me.." *Revelation 3:20*

3. **As our Savior, Jesus gives us access to God the Father – now, and for eternity. We look to God through Jesus, and God looks at us through Jesus. In God's eyes, we are as righteous as Jesus Himself.**

   "Jesus said to him, 'I am the way, and the truth, and the life; no one comes to the Father, but through Me.'" *John 14:6*

   "I am the door; if anyone enters through Me, he shall be saved, and shall go in and out, and find pasture. The thief comes only to steal, and kill, and destroy; I came that they might have life, and might have it abundantly." *John 10:9,10*

   "For no one can ever be made right in God's sight by doing what his law commands. For the more we know God's law, the clearer it becomes that we aren't obeying it. But now God has shown us a different way of being right in his sight – not by obeying the law but by the way promised in the Scriptures long ago. We are made right in God's sight when we trust in Jesus Christ to take away our sins. And we all can be saved in this same way, no matter who we are or what we have done. For all have sinned; all fall short of God's glorious standard. Yet now God in his gracious kindness declares us not guilty. He has done this through Christ Jesus, who has freed us by taking away our sins. For God sent Jesus to take the punishment for our sins and to satisfy God's anger against us. We are made right with God when we believe that Jesus shed his blood, sacrificing his life for us." *Romans 3:20-25 (NLT)*

   "God made him who had no sin to be sin for us, so that in him we might become the righteousness of God." *2 Corinthians 5:21 (NIV)*

4. **Making Jesus your Lord means submitting to His commandments and teachings over every area of your life, holding nothing back from His control. It doesn't mean you're perfect, but you start living for His glory rather than your own.**

"Trust in the Lord with all your heart and do not lean on your own understanding. In all your ways acknowledge Him, and He will make your paths straight." *Proverbs 3:5,6*

John the Baptist said: "So this joy of mine has been made full. He must increase, but I must decrease." *John 3:29b,30*

"And Mary said, 'Behold, the bondslave of the Lord; may it be done to me according to your word.'" *Luke 1:38a*

5. **God's love for us is unconditional, but our closeness and intimacy with God are conditional on our obedience to Him. When we make Him Lord, obey His commands, and trust in His wisdom, it gives us great peace and freedom from worry. As we obey, God discloses more of Himself to us and we grow closer to Him.**

"If you abide in My word, then you are truly disciples of Mine; and you shall know the truth, and the truth shall make you free." *John 8:31,32*

"He who has My commandments and keeps them is the one who loves Me; and he who loves Me will be loved by My Father, and I will love him and will disclose Myself to him." *John 14:21*

"You will keep in perfect peace all who trust in you, whose thoughts are fixed on you!" *Isaiah 26:3 (NLT)*

"Be anxious for nothing, but in everything by prayer and supplication with thanksgiving let your requests be made known to God. And the peace of God, which surpasses all comprehension, will guard your hearts and your minds in Christ Jesus." *Philippians 4:6,7*

6. **When people make Jesus their Savior, yet continue living a sinful lifestyle and refusing to allow Christ to be Lord over every area of their lives, they usually become more miserable than before they received Christ. Why? Because now they have the Holy Spirit indwelling them, constantly convicting them of their sins.**

"And when people escape from the wicked ways of the world by learning about our Lord and Savior Jesus Christ and then get tangled up with sin and become its slave again, they are worse off than before." *2 Peter 2:20 (NLT)*

7. **Jesus taught that many who made Him their Savior would later fall away because they didn't make Him their Lord.**

"The sower sows the word. These are the ones who are beside the road where the word is sown; and when they hear, immediately Satan comes and takes away the word which has been sown in them. In a similar way these are the ones on whom seed was sown on the rocky places, who, when they hear the word, immediately receive it with joy; and they have no firm root in themselves, but are only temporary; then, when affliction or persecution arises because of the word, immediately they fall away. And others are the ones on whom seed was sown among the thorns; these are the ones who have heard the word, but the worries of the world, and the deceitfulness of riches, and the desires for other things enter in and choke the word, and it becomes unfruitful. And those are the ones on whom seed was sown on the good soil; and they hear the word and accept it and bear fruit, thirty, sixty, and a hundredfold." *Mark 4:14-20*

8. **On the other hand, some people try to make Jesus their Lord by doing good deeds, but they make the mistake of trusting in their good deeds to get them to heaven instead of trusting in Christ as their Savior. None of us can do enough good deeds to outweigh our sin. As a result, those who trust in good deeds won't be allowed into heaven.**

"Not everyone who says to Me, 'Lord, Lord,' will enter the kingdom of heaven, but he who does the will of My Father who is in heaven will enter. Many will say to Me on that day, 'Lord, Lord, did we not prophesy in Your name, and in Your name cast out demons, and in Your name perform many miracles?' And then I will declare to them, 'I never knew you; depart from Me, you who practice lawlessness.'" *Matthew 7:21-23*

9. **Have you decided to make Jesus your personal Savior and Lord? Now is a great time to make both decisions.**

"As God's partners, we beg you not to reject this marvelous message of God's great kindness. For God says, 'At just the right time, I heard you. On the day of salvation, I helped you.' Indeed, God is ready to help you right now. Today is the day of salvation." *2 Corinthians 6:2,3 (NLT)*

56 Why Is Jesus Still Such A Controversial "Hot Potato?"

The Bible calls Jesus the "Prince of Peace," and yet arguably there has never been another human being more polarizing, more controversial, or who causes more disagreement and division. Some people devote their lives to His teachings, while others devote their lives to stamping out His teachings. Some people say Jesus has changed their lives, while others say that His teachings pull mankind down. Some people revere His name, while others use it as a curse word. Some people think He is mankind's only hope, while others think man's only hope is to stop the spread of His worship. During His lifetime, some considered Him God in the flesh, while others considered Him in league with the devil. Bring up Jesus in a conversation and see what happens. You'll see how He stirs people's passions. You rarely meet someone who has no opinion about Him. What is it about Jesus that stirs such a deep contrast in emotions?

1. Jesus knew of the polarizing nature His teachings and claims would bring. In fact, He often talked about it.

"Do you think I have come to bring peace to the earth? No, I have come to bring strife and division! From now on families will be split apart, three in favor of me, and two against – or the other way around. " *Luke 12:51,52 (NLT)*

2. Even while Jesus was teaching and performing miracles, the crowds had very polarized opinions of Him.

"There was a lot of discussion about him among the crowds. Some said, 'He's a wonderful man,' while others said, 'He's nothing but a fraud, deceiving the people.'" *John 7:12 (NLT)*

3. The people in His town of Nazareth were once so angry at Jesus that they tried to throw Him off a cliff!

"And they got up and drove Him out of the city, and led Him to the brow of the hill on which their city had been built, in order to throw Him down the cliff. But passing through their midst, He went His way." *Luke 4:29,30*

4. Another crowd was so thrilled after Jesus miraculously fed the 5,000 that they tried to force Him to be their king!

"Therefore when the people saw the sign which He had performed, they said, 'This is truly the Prophet who is to come into the world.' So Jesus, perceiving that they were intending to come and take Him by force to make Him king, withdrew again to the mountain by Himself alone." *John 6:14,15*

5. Jesus' teachings on "Love thy neighbor" or the "Golden Rule" aren't what stir up controversy. What riles people up are His bold claims about who He was.

- Jesus claimed to be the God of the Old Testament. *John 10:33, John 8:58*
- Jesus claimed to be God's Son, making Himself equal with God. *John 5:18, 10:33, Luke 22:70*
- Jesus claimed to be the only way to reach God. *John 14:6, John 10:9,10*
- Jesus claimed to be the Messiah and the Christ. *John 4:25,26, Mark 14:62-64*
- Jesus claimed to be King of the Jews. *Matthew 27:11*
- Jesus claimed to be able to forgive sins, something only God can do. *Mark 2:1-12*

6. The religious leaders hated Jesus for claiming to be God, and condemned Him to be executed for blasphemy.

"And they all said, 'Are You the Son of God, then?' And He said to them, 'Yes I am.' And they said, "What further need do we have of testimony? For we have heard it for ourselves from His own mouth.'" *Luke 22:70,71*

7. No other founder of a major world religion made the same claims Jesus did. Mohammed and Moses claimed to be prophets. Buddha and Confucius claimed to be teacher/philosophers. But Jesus claimed to be God!

"'I and the Father are one.' The Jews picked up stones again to stone Him. Jesus answered them, 'I showed you many good works from the Father; for which of them are you stoning Me?' The Jews answered Him, 'For a good work we do not stone You, but for blasphemy; and because You, being a man, make Yourself out to be God.'" *John 10:30-33*

8. Today, many non-Christians respect Jesus' teachings on love and forgiveness, but find His claim of being God and

the only way to reach heaven as being arrogant, egotistical, narrow-minded, or the ramblings of a crazy man. Christian author C.S. Lewis wrote the book *Mere Christianity* in 1952. It includes this important statement:

"A man who was merely a man and said the sort of things Jesus said would not be a great moral teacher. He would either be a lunatic – on the level with a man who says he is a poached egg – or he would be the devil of hell. You must take your choice. Either this was, and is, the Son of God, or else a madman or something worse. You can shut Him up for a fool or you can fall at His feet and call Him Lord and God. But let us not come with any patronizing nonsense about His being a great human teacher. He has not left that open to us."

9. **As eyewitnesses, Jesus' disciples were convinced He really was God in the flesh, that He rose from the dead, and that He was mankind's only hope for salvation. They were imprisoned, tortured, and killed for this belief. Jesus warned them to expect this kind of treatment from a world hostile to His teachings.**

"Then they will deliver you to tribulation, and will kill you, and you will be hated by all nations because of My name." *Matthew 24:9*

"If the world hates you, you know that it has hated Me before it hated you. If you were of the world, the world would love its own; but because you are not of the world, but I chose you out of the world, because of this the world hates you." *John 15:18,19*

"They will make you outcasts from the synagogue, but an hour is coming for everyone who kills you to think that he is offering service to God. These things they will do because they have not known the Father or Me." *John 16:2,3*

10. **Jesus' credibility hinges on one thing – the resurrection. If He really did rise from the dead, then it proves everything He claimed about Himself. If His body is still in the tomb, it proves He was a liar and deceiver.**

"And Jesus Christ our Lord was shown to be the Son of God when God powerfully raised him from the dead by means of the Holy Spirit." *Romans 1:4 (NLT)*

"And if Christ has not been raised, then our preaching is vain, your faith also is vain…. and if Christ has not been raised, your faith is worthless; you are still in your sins." *1 Corinthians 15:14,17*

"For I delivered to you as of first importance what I also received, that Christ died for our sins according to the Scriptures, and that He was buried, and that He was raised on the third day according to the Scriptures, and that He appeared to Cephas, then to the twelve. After that He appeared to more than five hundred brethren at one time, most of whom remain until now, but some have fallen asleep; then He appeared to James, then to all the apostles; and last of all, as to one untimely born, He appeared to me (Paul) also." *1 Corinthians 15:3-8*

11. **Why do millions of people live for Christ today, even though it brings rejection, ridicule, and harsh treatment from a world hostile to His teachings? Christians believe that what He said was true, and only through Christ can we live forever in heaven, which makes the hardships in this life pale by comparison.**

"For momentary, light affliction is producing for us an eternal weight of glory far beyond all comparison, while we look not at the things which are seen, but at the things which are not seen; for the things which are seen are temporal, but the things which are not seen are eternal." *2 Corinthians 4:17,18*

"For I consider that the sufferings of this present time are not worthy to be compared with the glory that is to be revealed to us." *Romans 8:18*

12. **Today, each of us must decide for ourselves who Jesus was. If He really was who He said He was, then what we believe about Him can make a difference for eternity. What is your decision? Was Jesus an egotistical mad man or God in the flesh? There's no middle ground! If you decide He was telling the truth about Himself, you can invite Him into your heart as your Savior and Lord.**

"For God so loved the world, that He gave His only begotten Son, that whoever believes in Him shall not perish, but have everlasting life." *John 3:16*

"Jesus said to him, "I am the way, and the truth, and the life ; no one comes to the Father but through Me." *John 14:6*

57 Was Jesus Merely A Great Man, But Not God?

Even people who aren't Christians will often acknowledge that Jesus was a great man. If you look at anyone's list of the greatest and most influential people who have ever lived, Jesus will usually appear somewhere on every list. He was not a military conqueror like Alexander the Great or Napoleon, nor was he a political leader like George Washington or Winston Churchill. He was a carpenter who never traveled more than 200 miles from where He was born, but His teachings have had a widespread influence throughout the world for centuries.

Since Jesus was a moral/religious leader who taught things like "Love thy neighbor" and the "Golden Rule," many people might put Him into a category with Buddha, Confucius, or Ghandi. One would certainly expect a moral teacher to be truthful and honest, but when you closely examine the things Jesus said about Himself, some people have concluded that He was a deceiver, or even insane. If you were to look at a list of the world's greatest people, how many of them have claimed to be the creator of the universe, or the only way people get to heaven, or the person who will judge the world, or to be God in the flesh? People who make such outrageous claims are more likely to show up on lists of the world's most egotistical, most deceitful, or most insane.

It's hard to see Jesus as a great man if you don't embrace His claims about who He was. When you honestly consider who He claimed to be, He was either God, or a liar, or an insane lunatic. Is viewing Jesus merely as a great man a true option for a person who made such sensational claims?

1. **After Jesus began making outrageous claims about who He was, and attracting attention for it, His own family members thought He had lost His mind!**

   "Then Jesus entered a house, and again a crowd gathered, so that he and his disciples were not even able to eat. When his family heard about this, they went to take charge of him, for they said, 'He is out of his mind.'" *Mark 3:20,21 (NIV)*

2. **Even while Jesus was teaching and performing miracles, the crowds had very polarized opinions of Him.**

   "There was a lot of discussion about him among the crowds. Some said, 'He's a wonderful man,' while others said, 'He's nothing but a fraud, deceiving the people.'" *John 7:12 (NLT)*

3. **Today, many non-Christians respect Jesus' teachings on love and forgiveness, but find His claim of being God and the only way to reach heaven as being arrogant, egotistical, or the ramblings of a crazy man. C.S. Lewis wrote the book *Mere Christianity* in 1952. He clearly summed up the options available when we try to conclude exactly who or what Jesus was:**

   "A man who was merely a man and said the sort of things Jesus said would not be a great moral teacher. He would either be a lunatic – on the level with a man who says he is a poached egg – or he would be the devil of hell. You must take your choice. Either this was, and is, the Son of God, or else a madman or something worse. You can shut Him up for a fool or you can fall at His feet and call Him Lord and God. But let us not come with any patronizing nonsense about His being a great human teacher. He has not left that open to us."

4. **So what exactly are the claims that Jesus made about who He was?**

   - Jesus claimed to be God's Son, making Himself equal with God. *John 5:18, 10:30-33, Luke 22:70*
   - Jesus claimed to be the Messiah, and the Christ. *John 4:25,26, Mark 14:62-64*
   - Jesus claimed to be King of the Jews. *Matthew 27:11*
   - Jesus claimed to be able to forgive sins, something only God can do. *Mark 2:1-12*
   - Jesus claimed to be the only way to reach God. *John 14:6, John 10:9*
   - Jesus claimed to be the God of the Old Testament, having eternally pre-existed before His birth. *John 8:56-59*
   - Jesus claimed He would someday judge all humans in the next life. *Matthew 25:31-46*
   - Jesus claimed to have all authority in heaven and on earth. *Matthew 28:18*

5. To add credibility, many details of Jesus' life were predicted in the Old Testament centuries before His birth.

- He would be born into the Hebrew tribe of Judah. *Genesis 49:10, Matthew 1:2, Revelation 5:5*
- He would be born in Bethlehem. *Micah 5:2, Matthew 2:1*
- He would perform miracles. *Isaiah 61:1, Matthew 11:1-5, Luke 4:16-21*
- He would be betrayed for exactly thirty pieces of silver. *Zechariah 11:12, Matthew 26:14-16*
- The money to betray Him would buy the Potter's Field. *Zechariah 11:12,13, Matthew 27:3-10*
- His hands and feet would be pierced. *Psalm 22:16, John 19:35,37, John 20:24-28*
- He would be the payment for our sins, taking them onto Himself. *Isaiah 53:5,6, 2 Corinthians 5:21, 1 Peter 2:24*
- People would gamble for his clothing by casting lots. *Psalm 22:18, John 19:23,24*
- He would be executed along with criminals. *Isaiah 53:9,12, Luke 23:32,33*
- He would be buried in a rich man's tomb. *Isaiah 53:9, Matthew 27:57-60*
- His body would not decay, but would be resurrected! *Psalm 16:8-11, Luke 24:1-43, 1 Corinthians 15:3-8*

6. It was Jesus' claim to be God that resulted in His death sentence. The religious leaders knew that if He claimed to be God, according to Jewish law they could execute Him for blasphemy.

"'I and the Father are one.' The Jews picked up stones again to stone Him. Jesus answered them, 'I showed you many good works from the Father; for which of them are you stoning Me?' The Jews answered Him, 'For a good work we do not stone You, but for blasphemy; and because You, being a man, make Yourself out to be God.'" *John 10:30-33*

"Then the high priest said to him, 'I demand in the name of the living God that you tell us whether you are the Messiah, the Son of God.' Jesus replied, 'Yes, it is as you say. And in the future you will see me, the Son of Man, sitting at God's right hand in the place of power and coming back on the clouds of heaven.' Then the high priest tore his clothing to show his horror, shouting, 'Blasphemy! Why do we need other witnesses? You have all heard his blasphemy. What is your verdict?' 'Guilty! they shouted. 'He must *die!*'" *Matthew 26:63b-66 (NLT)*

7. Even when Christ walked the earth, there were a variety of opinions regarding who He was. He once asked His disciples who the people said He was:

"And they said, 'Some say John the Baptist; some, Elijah; and others Jeremiah, or one of the prophets.'" *Matthew 16:14*

8. After His disciples had answered Jesus' question, He asked them an important follow-up question:

"He said to them, 'But who do you say that I am?' And Simon Peter answered and said, 'You are the Christ, the Son of the living God.'" *Matthew 16:15,16*

9. A man who makes grandiose claims about himself but can't back them up is quickly exposed as a fake. But Jesus proved that He really was God's Son by rising from the dead.

Jesus was "declared the Son of God with power by the resurrection from the dead." *Romans 1:4*

"Christ died for our sins according to the Scriptures... He was buried... He was raised on the third day according to the Scriptures, and after that He appeared to Cephas, then to the twelve. After that He appeared to more than five hundred brethren at one time." *1 Corinthians 15:3-6*

"And if Christ has not been raised, then our preaching is vain, your faith also is vain.... And if Christ has not been raised, your faith is worthless; you are still in your sins." *1 Corinthians 15:14,17*

10. Why is Jesus the only way to God? Because as the only sinless person to ever live, He is the only qualified sacrifice who could pay the price for our sins. Only by trusting in Christ can we be forgiven and made holy. If we accept Him as our Savior, our sins will be forgiven. If we choose to reject His offer of forgiveness, or merely view Him as a great man and nothing more, we will spend eternity away from God's presence.

"For God so loved the world, that He gave His only begotten Son, that whoever believes in Him shall not perish, but have everlasting life." *John 3:16*

"The wages of sin is death, but the free gift of God is eternal life in Christ Jesus our Lord." *Romans 6:23*

58 Was Jesus A Real, Historical Person – Or Just A Myth?

There are many famous figures from ancient history that historians agree to be real people; such as Plato, Alexander the Great, Cleopatra, Socrates, Aristotle, Herod, Tiberius, etc. There are also figures that historians agree to be simply mythical inventions; such as Zeus, Apollo, Mercury, Triton, Athena, Artemis, Hercules, etc. But which category does Jesus Christ belong in? To help us answer this question, we need to apply the same guidelines that help historians decide whether any ancient figure was real or invented:

- *There should be trustworthy, historical writings and documentation from reliable sources during the time period that tell us the person was real. Eyewitness accounts would be ideal.*
- *An actual person would have lived in actual places that can be verified by archeology, not in mythical locations like Mt. Olympus or Camelot.*
- *We should be able to pinpoint the accurate, historical timeframe of when the person lived and died.*
- *The person should have impacted the world through teachings, disciples, or followers.*

When we apply these standards to Jesus, does the evidence conclude He was real, or a myth?

1. Aside from biblical references that testify to the historicity of Jesus, there are also secular writings from that time period that clearly describe events from the life of Christ, and the impact of His teachings. These accounts are in clear harmony with the events the Bible describes.

"At this time (the time of Pilate) there was a wise man who was called Jesus. And his conduct was good, and he was known to be virtuous. And many people from among the Jews and the other nations became his disciples. Pilate condemned him to be crucified and to die. And those who had become his disciples did not abandon his discipleship. They reported that he had appeared to them after his crucifixion and that he was alive; accordingly, he was perhaps the Messiah concerning whom the prophets have recounted wonders." *Josephus, Antiquities*

There are ten known non-Christian sources that mention Jesus within 150 years of His death during the reign of Tiberius Caesar, the Emperor of Rome at the time. These writings are not as detailed as the gospel accounts, but harmonize perfectly with what the Bible tell us. The names of these sources from outside the Bible are: Josephus, Tacitus, Pliny the Younger, Phlegon, Thallus, Seutonius, Lucian, Celsus, Mar Bar-Serapion, and the Jewish Talmud. Surprisingly, over the same 150 years we have only nine mentions from secular writings of Tiberius Caesar himself – the most powerful man on earth at the time – and no serious historian doubts whether Tiberius was a real person or not.

2. None of the historical sources above were actual eyewitnesses of Jesus. Fortunately, the Bible provides many accounts of those who knew Jesus personally, and testified that He was quite real. Most of these eyewitnesses were persecuted, tortured, imprisoned, and even executed for their beliefs. They could have easily recanted their belief in Christ to save their lives, or switched to some Roman-approved, pagan religion. But they maintained their faith until the end. If these early believers had simply invented Christ as a mythical figure like Zeus or Apollo, why didn't they invent someone less controversial who wouldn't get them killed for believing in him?

"The one who existed from the beginning is the one we have heard and seen. We saw him with our own eyes and touched him with our own hands. He is Jesus Christ, the Word of life. This one who is life from God was shown to us, and we have seen him. And now we testify and announce to you that he is the one who is eternal life. He was with the Father, and then he was shown to us. We are telling you about what we ourselves have actually seen and heard, so that you may have fellowship with us. And our fellowship is with the Father and with his Son, Jesus Christ." *1 John 1:1-3 (NLT)*

"For we did not follow cleverly devised tales when we made known to you the power and coming of our Lord Jesus Christ, but we were eyewitnesses of His majesty." *2 Peter 1:16*

"So the other disciples were saying to him (Thomas), 'We have seen the Lord!' But he said to them, 'Unless I see in His hands the imprint of the nails, and put my finger into the place of the nails, and put my hand into His side, I will not believe.' After eight days His disciples were again inside, and Thomas with them. Jesus came, the doors having been shut, and stood in their midst and said, 'Peace be with you.' Then He said to Thomas, 'Reach here with your finger, and see My hands; and reach here your hand and put it into My side; and do not be unbelieving, but believing.' Thomas answered and said to Him, 'My Lord and my God!' Jesus said to him, 'Because you have seen Me, have you believed? Blessed are they who did not see, and yet believed.'" *John 20:25-29*

"Inasmuch as many have undertaken to compile an account of the things accomplished among us, just as they were handed down to us by those who from the beginning were eyewitnesses and servants of the word, it seemed fitting for me as well, having investigated everything carefully from the beginning, to write it out for you in consecutive order, most excellent Theophilus; so that you may know the exact truth about the things you have been taught." *Luke 1:1-4*

3. Luke's account allows us to pinpoint the timeframe of when Jesus was born, and tells us the specific location.

"Now in those days a decree went out from Caesar Augustus, that a census be taken of all the inhabited earth. This was the first census taken while Quirinius was governor of Syria. And everyone was on his way to register for the census, each to his own city. Joseph also went up from Galilee, from the city of Nazareth, to Judea, to the city of David which is called Bethlehem, because he was of the house and family of David, in order to register along with Mary, who was engaged to him, and was with child. While they were there, the days were completed for her to give birth." *Luke 2:1-6*

4. It's one thing to agree that Jesus was an actual person. But Jesus claimed to be more than just a person – He claimed to be God in the flesh. The same eyewitnesses who spent three years with Jesus, witnessed His miracles, and gave their lives for their belief, also testified that Jesus was crucified to pay for the sins of mankind, then rose from the grave to prove He was truly God's Son.

"And Jesus Christ our Lord was shown to be the Son of God when God powerfully raised him from the dead by means of the Holy Spirit." *Romans 1:4 (NLT)*

"Christ died for our sins... He was buried... He was raised on the third day according to the Scriptures... He appeared to Peter, then to the twelve. After that He appeared to more than five hundred brethren at one time." *1 Corinthians 15:3-6*

5. Since the gospel accounts were written by followers of Jesus, is the credibility of these accounts undermined by the fact that their writers believed in Jesus? Did they write these accounts so that they could benefit financially or gain worldly fame? Hardly! The men who wrote these accounts did so at great personal risk – which greatly enhances their reliability. Jesus even warned His followers to expect persecution for their faith.

"If the world hates you, you know that it has hated Me (Jesus) before it hated you. If you were of the world, the world would love its own; but because you are not of the world, but I chose you out of the world, because of this the world hates you. Remember the word that I said to you, 'A slave is not greater than his master.' If they persecuted Me, they will also persecute you; if they kept My word, they will keep yours also." *John 15:18-20*

"They will make you outcasts from the synagogue, but an hour is coming for everyone who kills you to think that he is offering service to God." *John 16:2*

"Indeed, all who desire to live godly in Christ Jesus will be persecuted." *2 Timothy 3:12*

"We are afflicted in every way, but not crushed; perplexed, but not despairing; persecuted, but not forsaken; struck down, but not destroyed; always carrying about in the body the dying of Jesus, so that the life of Jesus also may be manifested in our body. For we who live are constantly being delivered over to death for Jesus' sake, so that the life of Jesus also may be manifested in our mortal flesh." *2 Corinthians 4:8-11*

6. Jesus' teachings not only impacted His world, but continued impacting countless people throughout the centuries, and He has millions of followers today. One of His main teachings was that His death on the cross paid the penalty for all the sins of mankind. By confessing your sins and trusting in Christ's death, your sins can be forgiven today.

"But God demonstrates His own love toward us, in that while we were yet sinners, Christ died for us." *Romans 5:8*

"For God so loved the world, that He gave His only begotten Son, that whoever believes in Him shall not perish, but have eternal life." *John 3:16*

"But to all who believed him and accepted him, he gave the right to become children of God. They are reborn!" *John 1:12,13a (NLT)*

59 Why Did God Have To Sacrifice His Own Son To Save Us?

Some people have wondered why God would offer up His own Son to die such a painful death on the cross. This has led some people to wonder if maybe God is cruel in nature, rather than compassionate and loving. Did God not love His Son? Does God take delight in suffering?

The Bible tells us that Jesus' death paid the penalty for the sins of mankind. But was there any other way for the world to obtain forgiveness? The Bible teaches that God is extremely loving and compassionate. Even though everyone may not understand it, the Bible explains why the sacrifice of God's Son is actually the ultimate expression of God's love and compassion.

1. **The Bible tells us God hates sin. Sin is what makes us unholy and unworthy to be allowed into God's presence. To put it simply, sin separates us from God.**

   "But your iniquities have made a separation between you and your God, and your sins have hid His face from you, so that He does not hear." *Isaiah 59:2*

   "For all have sinned and fall short of the glory of God." *Romans 3:23*

2. **Before a criminal can be reunited with society, he must pay for his crime behind bars. In order for sinners to be reunited with a holy God, our sin must first be paid for. Unfortunately, we cannot pay for our sins in any way. Forgiveness from sin can only be paid for by the shedding of blood from a perfect and holy sacrifice.**

   "All things are cleansed with blood, and without shedding of blood there is no forgiveness." *Hebrews 9:22*

3. **In the Old Testament, God told His people to sacrifice a lamb at Passover. Those who were protected by the blood of the Passover lamb received God's mercy. Those not protected by the blood received God's judgment.**

   "Then Moses summoned all the elders of Israel and said to them, 'Go at once and select the animals for your families and slaughter the Passover lamb. Take a bunch of hyssop, dip it into the blood in the basin and put some of the blood on the top and both sides of the doorframe. Not one of you shall go out the door of his house until morning. When the Lord goes through the land to strike down the Egyptians, He will see the blood on the top and sides of the doorframe and He will not permit the destroyer to enter your houses and strike you down.'" *Exodus 12:21-23*

4. **God told His people in the Old Testament to sacrifice animals, but not because animal sacrifices could cleanse their sin. Animal sacrifices were simply a symbol to remind God's people that forgiveness comes only through the shed blood of an acceptable sacrifice.**

   "But in those sacrifices there is a reminder of sins year by year. For it is impossible for the blood of bulls and goats to take away sins." *Hebrews 10:4*

5. **The only sacrifice acceptable to God to cleanse us from sin is the one God Himself provided; Jesus, His only Son.**

   "And Abraham said, 'God will provide for Himself the lamb for the burnt offering.'" *Genesis 22:8*

   "The next day John saw Jesus coming toward him and said, 'Look, the Lamb of God who takes away the sin of the world!'" *John 1:29*

6. **Just as those who were protected by the blood of the Passover lamb received God's mercy, we can be protected by the blood of Christ, the Lamb of God, and receive God's mercy from the punishment sin deserves.**

   "You were not redeemed with perishable things like silver or gold... but with precious blood, as of a lamb unblemished and spotless, the blood of Christ." *1 Peter 1:18,19*

   "In Him we have redemption through His blood, the forgiveness of our trespasses, according to the riches of His grace, which He lavished upon us." *Ephesians 1:7,8*

   "And they sang a new song, saying, 'Worthy are You (Jesus) to take the book and to break its seals; for You were slain, and purchased for God with Your blood men from every tribe and tongue and people and nation.'" *Revelation 5:9*

7. **Why is Jesus the only worthy sacrifice? Because only He is fully God, fully man, and He lived a completely sinless life.**

"And you know that He appeared in order to take away sins; and in Him there is no sin." 1 John 3:5

"For in Him all the fulness of Deity dwells in bodily form." *Colossians 2:9*

8. **Christ's sacrifice is the one and only sacrifice needed to obtain cleansing for all of mankind. No others will ever be necessary! God set the highest possible price to pay for our sins, and then He paid it Himself!**

"We have been made holy through the sacrifice of the body of Jesus Christ once for all... But He having offered one sacrifice for sins for all time, sat down at the right hand of God. For by one offering He has perfected for all time those who are sanctified." *Hebrews 10:10,12,14 (NIV)*

9. **Imagine a judge declaring a criminal guilty, then loving the criminal so much that he went to prison in place of the criminal. That's basically what God has done! When Jesus – who was fully God – died on the cross to pay for our sins, it was the ultimate expression of God's love and compassion for mankind. God is holy and just, so He demands sin to be punished. Then He took the punishment Himself and paid a debt we could never pay.**

"But God demonstrates His own love toward us, in that while we were yet sinners, Christ died for us. Much more then, having now been justified by His blood, we shall be saved from the wrath of God through Him." *Romans 5:8,9*

"For God so loved the world, that He gave His only begotten Son, that whoever believes in Him shall not perish, but have everlasting life." *John 3:16*

10. **The sacrifice of Jesus was the only sacrifice that would please God's perfect standard, but the Father was still deeply grieved by the death of His Son. And Jesus was grieved from being separated from the Father.**

"But He was pierced through for our transgressions, He was crushed for our iniquities; the chastening for our well-being fell upon Him, and by His scourging we are healed. All of us like sheep have gone astray, each of us has turned to his own way; but the Lord has caused the iniquity of us all to fall on Him." *Isaiah 53:5,6*

11. **Jesus was not forced to endure the suffering of the cross, nor was He overpowered by the Romans who executed Him. He willingly submitted to the will of the Father by allowing Himself to be crucified.**

"I am the good shepherd, and I know My own and My own know Me, even as the Father knows Me and I know the Father; and I lay down My life for the sheep. I have other sheep, which are not of this fold; I must bring them also, and they will hear My voice; and they will become one flock with one shepherd. For this reason the Father loves Me, because I lay down My life so that I may take it again. No one has taken it away from Me, but I lay it down on My own initiative. I have authority to lay it down, and I have authority to take it up again. This commandment I received from My Father." *John 10:14-18*

12. **When Jesus died on the cross, our sins were paid for by His death. And when we accept Christ as our Savior, our sins are placed onto Him and His righteousness is placed onto us!**

"He (God the Father) made Him (Jesus) who knew no sin to be sin on our behalf, that we might become the righteousness of God in Him." *2 Corinthians 5:21*

13. **It's one thing to understand why God allowed His Son to give His life to pay for the sins of mankind. But to have Christ's payment apply to your own sins you must confess your sinful nature and ask Christ into your heart!**

"If we confess our sins, He is faithful and righteous to forgive us our sins and to cleanse us from all unrighteousness." *1 John 1:9*

"The wages of sin is death, but the free gift of God is eternal life in Christ Jesus our Lord." *Romans 6:23*

"I stand at the door and knock; if any one hears My voice and opens the door, I will come in to him." *Revelation 3:20*

"But as many as received Him, to them He gave the right to become children of God, even to those who believe in His name." *John 1:12*

60 If God Loves Us, Why Is There So Much Suffering In The World?

There is no escaping the fact that there's a great deal of suffering in the world. But just because there is suffering in the world, does that mean God does not care about us? Does it mean God has forsaken us? Does it mean the promises in the Bible aren't true?

Actually, the presence of suffering in the world is exactly what the Bible says we should expect. It teaches that God did not create the world intending for mankind to suffer, but He didn't create the world intending for mankind to sin, either. The Bible explains that suffering is not the result of God forsaking mankind, but the result of mankind forsaking God. And the Bible tells us exactly when and why suffering entered into the world.

Fortunately, God was willing to come to earth, in the form of Jesus Christ, and suffer right along with us, and for us, in order to make it possible for us to live forever with no suffering. Even though God gets no pleasure from seeing us suffer, the Bible tells us the reasons why we suffer, and how God uses suffering in our lives for various reasons.

1. **The suffering of mankind is a universal curse that has come upon us because we have rebelled against God. When Adam and Eve sinned, not only did sin enter into the world, but suffering entered in as well. After they disobeyed and tried to become like God by eating the forbidden fruit, God told them:**

   "To the woman He said, 'I will greatly multiply your pain in childbirth, in pain you will bring forth children; yet your desire will be for your husband, and he will rule over you.' Then to Adam He said, 'Because you have listened to the voice of your wife, and have eaten from the tree about which I commanded you, saying, "You shall not eat from it"; cursed is the ground because of you; in toil you will eat of it all the days of your life. Both thorns and thistles it shall grow for you; and you will eat the plants of the field; by the sweat of your face you will eat bread, till you return to the ground, because from it you were taken; for you are dust, and to dust you shall return.'" *Genesis 3:16-19*

2. **There will be no suffering in heaven, and all the effects of the universal curse that was given back in Genesis will be completely removed.**

   "'He shall wipe away every tear from their eyes; and there shall no longer by any death; there shall no longer be any mourning, or crying, or pain; the first things have passed away.' And He who sits on the throne said, 'Behold, I am making all things new.'" *Revelation 21:4,5*

   "For I consider that the sufferings of this present time are not worthy to be compared with the glory that is to be revealed to us." *Romans 8:18*

3. **When it comes to obedience, God has given us freedom of choice, but we do not have freedom of consequences that result from our choices. Even though God has granted mankind permission to exercise dominion over the earth, God still retains final sovereignty. When we suffer, He is fully aware of it and allows it to happen as a clear consequence of the sin mankind has chosen. However, God gets no pleasure from seeing us suffer.**

   "For the Lord will not reject forever, for if He causes grief, then He will have compassion according to His abundant lovingkindness. For He does not afflict willingly, or grieve the sons of men. Is it not from the mouth of the Most High that both good and ill go forth?" *Lamentations 3:31-33,38*

   "Shall we indeed accept good from the Lord and not accept adversity?" *Job 2:10*

4. **Today, God allows us to suffer for various reasons.**

   - Suffering is universal, and we all go through both sufferings and blessings sooner or later. *Ecclesiastes 8:14, Romans 8:18-25, Matthew 5:45*
   - Suffering can be used to discipline us, and teach us the consequences of sin. *Job 5:17,18, Galatians 6:7,8, Hebrews 12:6-11*
   - Suffering serves as a constant reminder of the original curse of sin, and therefore it also reminds us of our need

for forgiveness. *Genesis 3:16-19, Romans 6:23*

- Suffering can bring us into closer dependence on God, and help perfect us. *1 Peter 5:10, 2 Corinthians 21:7-10*
- We sometimes learn deep truths through suffering that we could not learn any other way. *Psalm 119:67,71,*
- Our sufferings uniquely equip us to comfort others who go through similar sufferings. *2 Corinthians 1:3-7*
- Our suffering can teach other people important lessons about trusting God as they observe us. *John 9:1-3, 11:*
- God rewards His followers for earthly sufferings when we reach the next life. *2 Corinthians 4:16-18*
- Suffering in this life serves as a foreshadowing of what awaits those in the hereafter who reject God's gracious offer of forgiveness through Christ. *Matthew 25:41, Luke 16:19-31*

5. Suffering was not the only consequence of mankind forsaking God. Our sin has also brought about a separation between our holy God and unholy man.

"But your iniquities have made a separation between you and your God, and your sins have hid His face from you, so that He does not hear." *Isaiah 59:2*

"For all have sinned and fall short of the glory of God." *Romans 3:23*

"The wages of sin is death, but the free gift of God is eternal life in Christ Jesus our Lord." *Romans 6:23*

6. Even though mankind is responsible for bringing suffering into the world, God still retains power over how much suffering takes place. Many people think God allows far too much suffering in the world, but we cannot know exactly how much suffering God prevents, or how much suffering there would be if God did not intervene. Suffering in this life is bad, but the suffering in hell, where there is total separation from God, is far worse.

"Then He will say to those on His left, 'Depart from Me, accursed ones, into the eternal fire which has been prepared for the devil and his angels.'" *Matthew 25:41*

7. God loves us, and has made it possible to have the curse of suffering removed. God gave us His Son Jesus, who was fully God and a fully, sinless man. Jesus took our sins onto Himself and paid the price for our sin. He came to earth and experienced the same sufferings as all of us. Jesus was willing to be tortured and crucified by being nailed to a cross because of His great love for us.

"God demonstrates His own love for us in that while we were yet sinners Christ died for us." *Romans 5:8*

"He Himself bore our sins in His body on the cross, that we might die to sin and live to righteousness, for by His wounds you were healed." *1 Peter 2:24*

"For there is one God, and one mediator also between God and men, the man Christ Jesus, who gave Himself as a ransom for all." *1 Timothy 2:5,6a*

8. Jesus left heaven, a place of no suffering, and came to earth where He suffered greatly as our substitute. Christ's payment made it possible for us to be forgiven and made holy so we can enter God's presence. Our sins are forgiven immediately when we accept Christ, but the curse of suffering remains with us until we reach the next life.

"For we know that all creation has been groaning as in the pains of childbirth right up to the present time. And even we Christians, although we have the Holy Spirit within us as a foretaste of future glory, also groan to be released from pain and suffering. We, too, wait anxiously for that day when God will give us our full rights as his children, including the new bodies he has promised us." *Romans 8:22,23 (NLT)*

9. How can we come to know Christ and experience His love and forgiveness, as well as obtain the gift of living forever without suffering? By simply confessing our sinful state and receiving Christ as our Savior!

"But as many as received Him, to them He gave the right to become children of God, even to those who believe in His name." *John 1:12*

"If we confess our sins, He is faithful and righteous to forgive us our sins and to cleanse us from all unrighteousness." *1 John 1:9*

"The thief comes only to steal and kill and destroy; I came that they may have life, and have it abundantly." *John 10:10*

61 If God Is Merciful, Why Should We Fear Him?

Some people have wondered if a God who is merciful is a God who needs to be feared. After all, why fear God or obey Him if He is just a big, tame, cuddly, teddy bear who forgives everyone no matter how bad they are? On the other hand, if God is someone we should fear, does that mean He is not merciful and loving? Is He a powerful, self-centered, cosmic dictator who delights in seeing us cower at His feet?

The Bible helps us discover the beautiful balance between fearing God and understanding His great mercy and love for mankind.

1. **What does it mean to fear the Lord? To fear God simply means to be in reverential awe of Him. Fear of God is the starting point of all wisdom. Our fear of God is expressed not in running from Him, but to Him; not by hiding from Him, but in drawing near in submission and obedience to His will, and by glorifying Him rather than ourselves.**

   "The fear of the Lord is the beginning of wisdom; a good understanding have all those who do His commandments; His praise endures forever." *Psalm 111:10*

2. **God is all-powerful, and we are totally dependent on Him to sustain us. It would be foolish not to be in awe of an all-powerful Creator who holds our lives in His hand.**

   "The God who made the world and all things in it, since He is Lord of heaven and earth... He Himself gives to all life and breath and all things." *Acts 17:24,25*

   "He counts the number of the stars; He gives names to all of them. Great is our Lord, and abundant in strength; His understanding is infinite." *Psalm 147:4,5*

   "For great is the Lord and greatly to be praised; He is to be feared above all gods. For all the gods of the peoples are idols, but the Lord made the heavens.... Ascribe to the Lord, O families of the peoples, ascribe to the Lord glory and strength. Ascribe to the Lord the glory of His name; bring an offering and come into His courts." *Psalm 96:4,5,7,8*

3. **The opposite of having fear of God is having pride in ourselves. Pride leads us to defy God and do whatever we want regardless of His clear warnings, This of course is sin; and sin separates us from our holy God.**

   "God is opposed to the proud but gives grace to the humble." *James 4:6*

   "But your iniquities have made a separation between you and your God, and your sins have hid His face from you, so that He does not hear." *Isaiah 59:2*

   "For all have sinned and fall short of the glory of God." *Romans 3:23*

4. **God has the power to punish us for sin, and the power to forgive sin. In His great love and mercy towards us, He provides the way for us to be forgiven. Because God holds the power to forgive sins, this leads us to fear Him.**

   "If You, Lord, should mark iniquities, O Lord, who could stand? But there is forgiveness with You, that You may be feared." *Psalm 130:3,4*

5. **It is not contradictory that God is both vengeful and merciful. He is vengeful because He holds us accountable for our sins which deserve punishment, and merciful because He took our punishment Himself.**

   "But He was pierced through for our transgressions, He was crushed for our iniquities; the chastening for our well-being fell upon Him, and by His scourging we are healed. All of us like sheep have gone astray, each of us has turned to his own way; but the Lord has caused the iniquity of us all to fall on Him." *Isaiah 53:5,6*

6. **How does God provide a way for us to receive forgiveness? Jesus, God's fully divine Son, paid the penalty for our sins by dying on the cross. This is the ultimate expression of God's love and mercy. It's like a judge who declares you guilty and deserving the death penalty, then steps down from the bench and goes to the chair in your place.**

   "For God so loved the world, that He gave His only begotten Son, that whoever believes in Him shall not perish, but have everlasting life." *John 3:16*

"But God demonstrates His own love toward us, in that while we were yet sinners, Christ died for us. Much more then, having now been justified by His blood, we shall be saved from the wrath of God through Him." *Romans 5:8,9*

7. Only Jesus is qualified to pay for our sins because He was fully God and a fully, sinless man. God requires the highest possible payment for sin, and Christ paid it.

"And you know that He appeared in order to take away sins; and in Him there is no sin." *1 John 3:5*

"For in Him (Christ) all the fulness of Deity dwells in bodily form." *Colossians 2:9*

"For there is one God, and one mediator also between God and men, the man Christ Jesus, who gave Himself as a ransom for all." *1 Timothy 2:5,6a*

"Jesus said to him, 'I am the way, and the truth, and the life; no one comes to the Father, but through Me.'" *John 14:6*

"For there is salvation in no one else; for there is no other name under heaven that has been given among men, by which we must be saved." *Acts 4:12*

8. Christ took our sins onto Himself when He died a sacrificial death on the cross. When we accept Him as our personal Savior, His righteousness is placed onto us. The wages of sin is death, and He paid that penalty for us.

"For the wages of sin is death, but the free gift of God is eternal life in Christ Jesus our Lord." *Romans 6:23*

"He (God the Father) made Him (God the Son) who knew no sin to be sin on our behalf, that we might become the righteousness of God in Him." *2 Corinthians 5:21*

9. It is a terrible mistake to reject God's offer of forgiveness through Christ, because then we only experience God as our vengeful judge and not as our loving Savior.

"It is a terrifying thing to fall into the hands of the living God." *Hebrews 10:31*

10. There are great benefits in this life when we live with a healthy, biblical fear of God.

- The fear of the Lord is the beginning of wisdom. *Psalm 111:10, Proverbs 1:7*
- The fear of the Lord prolongs life. *Proverbs 10:27*
- In the fear of the Lord there is strong confidence. *Proverbs 14:26*
- The fear of the Lord is a fountain of life. *Proverbs 14:27*
- Fear of the Lord brings great contentment. *Proverbs 15:16*
- The fear of the Lord leads to life. *Proverbs19:23*
- The fear of the Lord brings stability. *Isaiah 33:6*

11. When we fear God and submit to His authority, there is no reason to fear anything else! We are on the side of the most powerful force in the universe!

"If God is for us, who is against us?" *Romans 8:31*

"The Lord is for me; I will not fear; what can man do to me?" *Psalm 118:6*

"And do not fear those who kill the body, but are unable to kill the soul; but rather fear Him who is able to destroy both soul and body in hell." *Matthew 10:28*

12. The first step in fearing God is receiving His merciful gift of forgiveness. You can do this right now by confessing your sins and asking Christ into your heart.

"My dear children, I am writing this to you so that you will not sin. But if you do sin, there is someone to plead for you before the Father. He is Jesus Christ, the one who pleases God completely. He is the sacrifice for our sins. He takes away not only our sins but the sins of all the world." *1 John 2:1,2 (NLT)*

"If you confess with your mouth Jesus as Lord, and believe in your heart that God raised Him from the dead, you shall be saved." *Romans 10:9*

62 Why Would A Loving God Order The Killing Of Certain Groups In The Old Testament?

The Bible is famous for not pulling punches. Its followers could have easily edited out the Bible's unpleasant parts, but those parts have not been lost to tampering with the text. The Bible describes God's dealings with wicked people and gives graphic descriptions of their actions that brought God's judgment, so it's not rated G. Some parts are very unsettling to read. Due to God's decision to punish these groups with death, these accounts have made some people question God's love and goodness. In spite of these accounts describing God's punishment of the wicked, the Bible goes to great lengths to communicate the love God has for humanity. But if God is loving and merciful, why were there times when He had certain groups completely annihilated, including children? Some examples include: Flooding the earth in the time of Noah, raining fire and brimstone on Sodom and Gomorrah, the ten plagues of Egypt, plus the eradication of the Amalekites and other pagan groups within Israel. Can we reconcile the Bible's teaching that God loves humanity, even though the Bible also includes accounts where God ordered the deaths of the wicked?

1. **At least those who are unsettled by these accounts are viewing the events as factual, historical occurrences. Acceptance of the Bible as an accurate record of ancient history, and of God's nature, is the first step to understanding it.**

   "For this reason we also constantly thank God that when you received the word of God which you heard from us, you accepted it not as the word of men, but for what it really is, the word of God, which also performs its work in you who believe." *1 Thessalonians 2:13*

   "All Scripture is inspired by God and profitable for teaching, for reproof, for correction, for training in righteousness; so that the man of God may be adequate, equipped for every good work." *2 Timothy 3:16,17*

2. **God did not cause these deaths because He gets pleasure from seeing guilty people suffer.**

   "For the Lord will not reject forever, for if He causes grief, then He will have compassion according to His abundant lovingkindness. For He does not afflict willingly or grieve the sons of men." *Lamentations 3:31-33*

   "'For I have no pleasure in the death of anyone who dies,' declares the Lord God. 'Therefore, repent and live.'" *Ezekiel 18:32*

3. **The Bible doesn't go into explicit detail for every group that was exterminated, but it does give us specific details about the Baal-worshiping Amalekites that God wanted annihilated. It's important to understand the real problem God wanted to abolish; it wasn't just the people He was eradicating, it was their cruel worship practices. The pagan nations burned their children alive as sacrifices to curry favor for rain, better harvests, and prosperity.**

   "You shall not behave thus toward the Lord your God, for every abominable act which the Lord hates they have done for their gods; for they even burn their sons and daughters in the fire to their gods." *Deuteronomy 12:31*

   "Now go and strike Amalek and utterly destroy all that he has, and do not spare him; but put to death both man and woman, child and infant, ox and sheep, camel and donkey." *1 Samuel 15:3*

   "You shall consume all the peoples whom the Lord your God will deliver to you; your eye shall not pity them, nor shall you serve their gods, for that would be a snare to you." *Deuteronomy 7:16*

4. **God did not drive out pagan nations because the Israelites were so righteous, but because the pagan nations were exceedingly wicked.**

   "It is not for your righteousness or for the uprightness of your heart that you are going to possess their land, but it is because of the wickedness of these nations that the Lord your God is driving them out before you, in order to confirm the oath which the Lord swore to your fathers, to Abraham, Isaac and Jacob. Know, then, it is not because of your righteousness that the Lord your God is giving you this good land to possess, for you are a stubborn people." *Deuteronomy 9:5,6*

5. **Tragically, even though God ordered the Israelites to eradicate these people and their practices once and for all, they did not fully obey. Perhaps they doubted God's wisdom as many do today. Soon the Israelites adopted and perpetuated the same cruel practices they were ordered to eradicate.**

"They (the Israelites) did not destroy the peoples, as the Lord commanded them, but they mingled with the nations and learned their practices, and served their idols, which became a snare to them. They even sacrificed their sons and their daughters to the demons, and shed innocent blood, the blood of their sons and their daughters, whom they sacrificed to the idols of Canaan; and the land was polluted with the blood." *Psalm 106:34-38*

"Moreover, you took your sons and daughters whom you had borne to Me and sacrificed them to idols to be devoured. Were your harlotries so small a matter? You slaughtered My children and offered them up to idols by causing them to pass through the fire." *Ezekiel 16:20,21*

6. **These accounts are unsettling, but it's unreasonable to think that a loving God would passively look the other way and do nothing while these horrible burnings of live children continued unchecked from generation to generation. As a comparison, it's unfortunate that German civilians perished in the war against the Nazis, but to have allowed the Nazis to continue slaughtering millions of people would have resulted in vastly more deaths in the big picture.**

"There is an appointed time for everything. And there is a time for every event under heaven – a time to give birth and a time to die; a time to plant and a time to uproot what is planted. A time to kill and a time to heal; a time to tear down and a time to build up." *Ecclesiastes 3:1-3*

7. **As for the children who perished, as well as all young children who die before reaching the age of accountability, there is strong biblical evidence that they will be welcomed into heaven.**

"And they were bringing even their babies to Him (Jesus) so that He would touch them, but when the disciples saw it, they began rebuking them. But Jesus called for them, saying, 'Permit the children to come to Me, and do not hinder them, for the kingdom of God belongs to such as these. Truly I say to you, whoever does not receive the kingdom of God like a child will not enter it at all.'" *Luke 18:15-17*

8. **When an arm with gangrene or cancer is removed to prevent the disease from spreading, many healthy cells are also sacrificed but the person's life is spared. It's natural to wonder why God might have had the adults killed, but spared the children. Again, we have to look at the big picture. By eradicating the entire groups, their religion, their ritualistic burning of live children, and every trace of their culture, more lives would be saved for these reasons:**

- The practice of child burnings was ingrained in the culture, and would have been stopped once and for all.
- These deaths were a grim reminder to make people think twice before bringing back these horrible practices.
- A child who grows up in a different culture can tell by his looks that he's a different race than those around him. When he grows up, he would naturally want to rediscover and return to his own roots, heritage, culture, and religion, thus perpetuating the atrocities.
- These deaths were a clear reminder that it's not merely the sinner who reaps the consequences of his actions, but also the rest of society where they are practiced.

9. **God is just and requires punishment for sin; and all of us are sinners. Fortunately, God loves us so much that He took our punishment on the cross for all the sins of mankind – including yours. He gives us the free will to reject His free gift of salvation, or to accept it by receiving Christ as Savoir.**

"For the wages of sin is death, but the free gift of God is eternal life in Christ Jesus our Lord." *Romans 6:23*

"But God demonstrates His own love toward us, in that while we were yet sinners, Christ died for us." *Romans 5:8*

"For God so loved the world, that He gave His only begotten Son, that whoever believes in Him shall not perish, but have eternal life." *John 3:16*

"For there is one God, and one mediator also between God and men, the man Christ Jesus, who gave Himself as a ransom for all." *1 Timothy 2:5,6a*

63 Is The God Of The Old Testament Different From The God Of The New Testament?

People sometimes comment that the God of the Old Testament comes across as one who demands justice, whereas the God described in the New Testament seems more interested in forgiveness. In his "Letters from the Earth," humorist Mark Twain described the differences he observed: "The two Testaments are interesting, each in its own way. The Old one gives us a picture of these people's Deity as he was before he got religion, the other one gives us a picture of him as he appeared afterward." Some people have even gone as far as to conclude that the Bible describes two different Gods; the first who demands justice and punishment, and the second who is loving and merciful. Did God change from the Old Testament to the New? Are the stories from the Old Testament consistent with God's character traits described in the New Testament? And is Jesus Christ really the God of both the Old and the New Testaments?

1. **As a diamond turns and sparkles in the light, every new angle reveals more of its beauty; but the diamond itself is not changing. As the Scriptures slowly unveil new facets of God's character, God is not changing either. The only thing changing is our expanding knowledge of who He is. As the books of the Bible proceed from Genesis to Revelation, they reveal more and more of the various facets of God's character, but all the books are describing the same God. The Bible uses an analogy to describe getting to know God's multi-faceted nature. Getting to know God is like taking a tour through all the buildings and rooms of the city of Zion.**

    "Walk about Zion and go around her; count her towers; consider her ramparts; go through her palaces, that you may tell it to the next generation. For such is God, our God forever and ever." *Psalm 48:12-14*a

2. **Every book of the Bible reveals a little more about God and His character. But since He is infinite, eternal, and all-knowing, not even the Bible itself tells us everything there is to know about God. That's why we will continue getting to know God more and more throughout eternity in heaven.**

    "Oh, what a wonderful God we have! How great are his riches and wisdom and knowledge! How impossible it is for us to understand his decisions and his methods! For who can know what the Lord is thinking? Who knows enough to be his counselor?" *Romans 11:33,34 (NLT)*

3. **A child who chooses willful disobedience to his parents by engaging in dangerous or destructive activity would soon experience a different facet of his parents' character. The Bible describes how Adam and Eve lived in perfect harmony with God in the Garden of Eden until they chose sin over obedience. Prior to their rebellion, they only experienced God's love and fellowship. When they rebelled, they experienced the consequences of their sin and a facet of God's character they wouldn't have known otherwise.**

    "Then to Adam He said, 'Because you have listened to the voice of your wife, and have eaten from the tree about which I commanded you, saying, "You shall not eat from it"; cursed is the ground because of you; in toil you will eat of it all the days of your life. Both thorns and thistles it shall grow for you; and you will eat the plants of the field; by the sweat of your face you will eat bread, till you return to the ground, because from it you were taken; for you are dust, and to dust you shall return.'" *Genesis 3:17-19*

4. **In the Old Testament, there's a strong emphasis on following the many laws given to Moses. But it never teaches that the law was a way to work our way to Heaven. The Law was given to show us how far from perfect we really are, and how desperately we need a Savior. Once Christ came and fully revealed God's plan of salvation, He abolished our need to follow the ceremonial, dietary, and civil laws of Moses.**

    "The Law has become our tutor to lead us to Christ, so that we may be justified by faith. But now that faith has come, we are no longer under a tutor. For you are all sons of God through faith in Christ Jesus." *Galatians 3:24,25*

5. **In Peter's first epistle in the New Testament, he explained that redemption through Christ was part of God's ever unfolding plan, but many specifics had remained a mystery until Christ appeared on earth.**

    "This salvation was something the prophets wanted to know more about. They prophesied about this gracious salvation prepared for you, even though they had many questions as to what it all could mean. They wondered what the

Spirit of Christ within them was talking about when he told them in advance about Christ's suffering and his great glory afterward. They wondered when and to whom all this would happen. They were told that these things would not happen during their lifetime, but many years later, during yours. And now this Good News has been announced by those who preached to you in the power of the Holy Spirit sent from heaven." *1 Peter 1:10-12a (NLT)*

6. In the Old Testament, people trusted in a Savior (also called Redeemer, Messiah, or Christ) who had not yet come. Today, we trust in a Savior who has already come. But we're all trusting in the same Savior.

From the Old Testament:
- "And all flesh will know that I, the Lord, am your Savior and your Redeemer, the Mighty One of Jacob." *Isaiah 49:26b*
- "'The Redeemer will come to Zion, to those in Jacob who repent of their sins,' declares the Lord." *Isaiah 59:20*
- "As for me, I know that my Redeemer lives, and at the last He will take His stand on the earth." *Job 19:25*

From the New Testament:
- "The record of the genealogy of Jesus the Messiah, the son of David, the son of Abraham." *Matthew 1:1*
- "For today in the city of David there has been born for you a Savior, who is Christ the Lord." *Luke 2:11*
- "Jesus Christ is the same yesterday and today and forever." *Hebrews 13:8*
- "The woman said to Him, 'I know that Messiah is coming (He who is called Christ); when that One comes, He will declare all things to us.' Jesus said to her, 'I who speak to you am He.'" *John 4:25,26*

7. When God spoke to Moses from the burning bush in Exodus 3 of the Old Testament, God called Himself "I AM," a name revealing that God transcends time with His eternal, unchanging nature. Centuries later, Jesus claimed to be the same "I AM." His critics wanted to stone Him because they understood He was claiming to be the God of the Old Testament who spoke from the burning bush, which to them sounded like blasphemy and deserved execution.

"'Your father Abraham rejoiced to see My day, and he saw it and was glad.' So the Jews said to Him, 'You are not yet fifty years old, and have You seen Abraham?' Jesus said to them, 'Truly, truly, I say to you, before Abraham was born, I AM.' Therefore they picked up stones to throw at Him, but Jesus hid Himself and went out of the temple." *John 8:56-59*

8. The Old Testament tends to focus mainly on God's interactions with the Jews. In the New Testament, He continues His dealings with the Jews and broadens His outreach to gentiles. Through Christ, both groups are made into one. It's been said that Christianity is the blossom on the stem of Judaism. The Old Testament is the New Testament contained; the New Testament is the Old Testament explained.

"So, having obtained help from God, I stand to this day testifying both to small and great, stating nothing but what the Prophets and Moses said was going to take place; that the Christ was to suffer, and that by reason of His resurrection from the dead He would be the first to proclaim light both to the Jewish people and to the Gentiles." *Acts 26:22,23*

9. The sacrifice of the Passover Lamb, first performed in the Old Testament while the Israelites were slaves in Egypt, is a symbolic foreshadowing pointing to the future sacrificial death of Jesus, called the "Lamb of God" in the New Testament. In Exodus 12, those protected by the lamb's blood received God's mercy; those not protected by the lamb's blood received God's punishment. The same is true of those who allow Christ's blood to pay for their sins.

"The next day he (John the Baptist) saw Jesus coming to him and said, "Behold, the Lamb of God who takes away the sin of the world!" *John 1:29*

10. Some people say the concept of the Trinity only appears in the New Testament. But the Old Testament, as early as the first chapter of Genesis, gives us glimpses of the plural nature of God.

"Then God said, 'Let Us make man in Our image, according to Our likeness.'" *Genesis 1:26*

"The Lord says to my Lord: 'Sit at My right hand until I make Your enemies a footstool for Your feet.'" *Psalm 110:1*

11. When Adam and Eve sinned, mankind's perfect fellowship with God was broken. But that relationship can be restored now that Jesus Christ, has satisfied the penalty of sin. Salvation is a free gift we can all accept by faith.

"For the wages of sin is death, but the free gift of God is eternal life in Christ Jesus our Lord." *Romans 6:23*

64 What Is The Trinity?

Many people who believe in God reject the idea of the Trinity. People of other religions sometimes understand it to mean that Christians are polytheistic, worshiping three distinct Gods. The truth is, Christians worship three distinct Persons or members within the Trinity, but we still worship only one God. There is no question that the concept of the Trinity is difficult to understand, and has been confusing to many. The Bible tells us that even though we can know God, we cannot know everything about Him, at least right now, because He is infinite and we are finite. It's kind of like the difference between being able to wrap your arms around a tree trunk, but not around a football stadium.

The word "Trinity" does not appear anywhere in Scripture, but the concept of the Trinity appears throughout the Bible from the first chapter of Genesis (1:26) to the last chapter of Revelation (22:1,17). It is important to grasp this concept because each Person of the Trinity performs specific roles and tasks.

1. Christianity, which stemmed from Judaism, is "monotheistic." We believe in and worship only one God.

"Hear O Israel! The Lord is our God, the Lord is one!" *Deuteronomy 6:4*

"Now to the King eternal, immortal, invisible, the only God, be honor and glory forever and ever. Amen." *1 Timothy 1:17*

2. God sometimes refers to Himself in plural form, and He consists of three distinct "Persons" within the Trinity.

"Then God said, 'Let Us make man in Our image, according to Our likeness.'" *Genesis 1:26*

"And after being baptized, Jesus went up immediately from the water; and behold, the heavens were opened, and He saw the Spirit of God descending as a dove, and coming upon Him; and behold, a voice out of the heavens, saying, 'This is My beloved Son, in whom I am well pleased.'" *Matthew 3:16,17*

"Go therefore and make disciples of all the nations, baptizing them in the name of the Father and the Son and the Holy Spirit." *Matthew 28:19*

"The grace of the Lord Jesus Christ, and the love of God, and the fellowship of the Holy Spirit, be with you all." *2 Corinthians 13:14*

3. Perhaps the illustration that comes closest to explaining how God exists in three distinct Persons within the Trinity, each having different a function, is the comparison to H2O. It can exist in three different states, all of which are fully H2O: Liquid (water), Solid (ice), Gas (steam).

Each form of H20 has a different function. For instance, you can't skate on water, you can't drink steam, and clouds can't float in the sky as blocks of solid ice.

4. Who are the three Persons within the Trinity, and what are some of the roles or tasks each One performs?

God the Father
- He is an equal member of the Trinity. *John 5:18*
- He is eternal, pre-existing for all eternity. *1 Timothy 1:17*
- He is the ultimate recipient of our prayers. *Matthew 6:9*
- He has authority over the Son. *Matthew 26:39, Luke 10:16, 22:42, John 3:35, 4:34, 5:30, 6:38, 7:16, 8:28, 8:42, 10:18, 14:24,28,31, 15:1,10, 16:5, 1 Corinthians 11:3, 15:28, 1 John 4:13,14*
- He has authority over the Holy Spirit. *John 14:26, 15:26, 16:13*
- He disciplines us as a loving father for our good. *Hebrews 12:6-11*

God the Son (Jesus Christ)
- He is fully divine. *Mark 2:7, John 1:1-14, 5:18, 10:33, 14:9, 20:28, Colossians 1:19, 2:9, Hebrews 1:1-4*
- He is fully man, born of Mary while she was still a virgin. *Matthew 1:23,25, Luke 1:27,34*
- He was not a mere spirit, but was born a natural baby. *Luke 24:29-43,52, Galatians 4:4*
- He could be tempted but never sinned. *Hebrews 4:15, 2 Corinthians 5:21*

- He is eternal, pre-existing for all eternity. *Micah 5:2, John 8:58, 1 Timothy 1:17*
- He is an equal member of the Trinity. *John 5:18, 8:58*
- Through Him the world was made. *John 1:1-3, Colossians 1:15,16, Hebrews 1:2*
- He maintained all His divine attributes while on earth, but chose voluntary nonuse of certain attributes during His earthly life. *Philippians 2:6-8*
- He is head of the church. *Colossians 1:18, Ephesians 5:23*
- He will come again. *Acts 1:9-11, 1 Thessalonians 4:16-18*
- He is the Savior who provides the only way to have access to God by obtaining forgiveness. *John 3:16, 10:9, 14:6, Acts 4:12, 1 Timothy 2:5*
- He prays to the Father for us. *Romans 8:33,34, 1 John 2:1,2*

God the Holy Spirit (or Holy Ghost)
- He is eternal, and has pre-existed for all eternity. *1 Timothy 1:17*
- He is an equal member of the Trinity. *Matthew 28:19, Acts 5:3,4, 2 Corinthians 13:14*
- He is everywhere (omnipresent). *Psalm 139:7*
- He is our Helper. *John 14:16,26, 15:26, 16:7*
- He empowers us to do the things God wants us to do. *Acts 1:8*
- He prays to the Father for us. *Romans 8:26,27*
- He is our Teacher, and brings things to our remembrance. *John 14:26, 16:13*
- He participates in cleansing us for our salvation. *Titus 3:5*
- He seals us after we are saved so we can never lose our salvation. *Ephesians 1:13, 4:30*
- He makes us aware of our sin and our need for forgiveness. *John 16:8-11*
- He distributes spiritual gifts to every believer. *1 Corinthians 12:11*

5. **The problem in rejecting the Trinity is that it makes Jesus appear to be only a man and not God. His role within the Trinity is to provide us with our only access to God, through forgiveness of our sins. He achieved this by becoming a man, living a sinless life, then giving His life to pay the penalty for our sins. If Jesus was not God, then He cannot be our savior because only God can be our savior.**

   "For in Him (Jesus) all the fulness of Deity dwells in bodily form." *Colossians 2:9*

   "Jesus said to him, 'I am the way, and the truth, and the life; no one comes to the Father, but through Me.'" *John 14:6*

   "For there is one God, and one mediator also between God and men, the man Christ Jesus, who gave Himself as a ransom for all." *1 Timothy 2:5,6a*

   "For there is salvation in no one else; for there is no other name under heaven that has been given among men, by which we must be saved." *Acts 4:12*

   "But now in Christ Jesus you who formerly were far off have been brought near by the blood of Christ... for through Him we... have our access in one Spirit to the Father." *Ephesians 2:13,18*

   "I, even I, and the Lord; and there is no savior besides Me." *Isaiah 43:11*

   "And we have behold and bear witness that the Father has sent the Son to be the Savior of the world." *1 John 4:13,14*

6. **Since Christ is the only way to have access to God, if we reject Christ we reject God.**

   "The one who listens to you listens to Me, and the one who rejects you rejects Me; and he who rejects Me rejects the One who sent Me." *Luke 10:16*

7. **Christians often talk about "asking Christ into your heart," but when a person does this, all three members of the Trinity come to abide within him. Christ is the member of the Trinity who makes it all possible because He paid the price for our sins. Through Christ we can obtain the free gifts of forgiveness and eternal life. Our sinfulness is placed onto Christ, and His holiness is placed onto us so we can be allowed in God's holy presence.**

   "For God so loved the world, that He gave His only begotten Son, that whoever believes in Him shall not perish, but have everlasting life." *John 3:16*

65 Is The Bible Trustworthy?

Those who criticize the Bible tend to do so from two different viewpoints. The first critical viewpoint says that the Bible is human in origin rather than divinely inspired. The second critical viewpoint says that the Bible might have originally been divinely inspired, but over the centuries has lost much of its original meaning through sloppy copying, tampering, and other alterations to the original text.

Many people who shed doubt on the Bible's trustworthiness have never examined its credentials. It definitely stands out compared to ancient historical writings, or to the sacred writings of other religions.

1. The Bible is a record of God reaching out to man, and God has promised to protect His Word.

"Heaven and earth will pass away, but My words will not pass away." *Matthew 24:35*

"The Word of God is living and active and sharper than any two-edged sword." *Hebrews 4:12*

"All Scripture is inspired by God and profitable for teaching, for reproof, for correction, for training in righteousness; that the man of God may be adequate, equipped for every good work." *2 Timothy 3:16,17*

"But know this first of all, that no prophecy of Scripture is a matter of one's own interpretation, for no prophecy was ever made by an act of human will, but men moved by the Holy Spirit spoke from God." *2 Peter 1:20,21*

2. Unlike stories from Greek mythology and other religious writings, most of the Bible was written by eyewitnesses of the events described, or by people who had interviewed the eyewitnesses.

"For we did not follow cleverly devised tales when we made known to you the power and coming of our Lord Jesus Christ, but we were eyewitnesses of His majesty." *2 Peter 1:16*

"What was from the beginning, what we have heard, what we have seen with our eyes, what we beheld and our hands handled, concerning the Word of Life... what we have seen and heard we proclaim to you also." *1 John 1:1,3*

"Inasmuch as many have undertaken to compile an account of the things accomplished among us, just as those who from the beginning were eyewitnesses and servants of the Word have handed them down to us, it seemed fitting for me as well, having investigated everything carefully from the beginning, to write it you for you in consecutive order, most excellent Theophilus; so that you might know the exact truth about the things you have been taught." *Luke 1:1-4*

3. One convincing proof that the Bible is divinely inspired rather than human in origin is its amazing number of fulfilled predictions of the future – which is not something you find in the sacred writings of other faiths.

- The destruction of Tyre: Predicted in 570 B.C. in *Ezekiel 26:3-21,* ultimately fulfilled in 1291 A.D.
- The destruction of Edom: Predicted in 700 B.C. in *Isaiah 34:6-15,* fulfilled around 600 B.C.
- The destruction of Nineveh: Predicted in 661 B.C. in *Nahum 3:10-19,* fulfilled in 612 B.C.
- The destruction of Babylon: Predicted appx. 730 B.C. in *Isaiah 13:19-22,* fulfilled in 539 B.C.
- The destruction of Jerusalem's temple: Predicted 30 A.D. in *Matthew 24:1,2,* fulfilled in 70 A.D.
- The scattering of Israel as a nation: Predicted in 1420 B.C. in *Leviticus 26:31-33,* fulfilled 135 A.D.
- The reforming of Israel as a nation: Predicted appx. 580 B.C. in *Ezekiel 33:33-35,* fulfilled in 1948 A.D.

4. The Bible made accurate predictions of Jesus centuries before He was born, as verified by the Dead Sea Scrolls:

- He would be born in Bethlehem. *Micah 5:2, Matthew 2:1*
- He would be betrayed for exactly thirty pieces of silver. *Zechariah 11:12, Matthew 26:14-16*
- The betrayal money would also be used to buy the Potter's Field. *Zechariah 11:12,13, Matthew 27:3-10*
- His hands and feet would be pierced. *Psalm 22:16, John 19:35,37, John 20:24-28*
- He would pay for our sins by taking them onto Himself. *Isaiah 53:5,6, 2 Corinthians 5:21*
- People would gamble for his clothing by casting lots. *Psalm 22:18, John 19:23,24*
- He would be executed along with criminals. *Isaiah 53:9,12, Luke 23:32,33*
- He would be buried in a rich man's tomb. *Isaiah 53:9, Matthew 27:57-60*
- His body would not decay, but would be resurrected. *Psalm 16:8-11, Luke 24:1-43, Romans 1:4*

5. The most convincing proof that the original wording of the Bible has been preserved in tact is the large number of ancient, handwritten copies that still exist. These copies make it possible to cross-reference each other for any changes in wording. Most differences are the result of minor copyist errors like mispellings, etc. Only about 1% of the Bible's content contains variables, and none of these overturn major Bible teachings. These vast numbers of quality manuscripts make the Bible by far the most trustworthy of any piece of ancient literature. To reject the Bible's credentials would mean rejecting all known ancient literature and history. Here's how the number of Bible manuscripts compare with other ancient writings:

Author	Appx. Time Of Writing	Earliest Copy	# Of Ancient Copies
Plato	330 BC	900 AD	7
Ceasar	50 BC	900 AD	10
Aristotle	330 BC	1,100 AD	5
Euripedies	420 BC	1,100 AD	9
Pliny	100 AD	850 AD	7
Herodotus	430 BC	900 AD	8
New Testament	50-80 AD	130 AD	5,300+
Old Testament	1,500-400 BC	400 BC	14,000

6. For the Bible to be considered reliable in describing the next world, it certainly must be reliable in describing this world. Every new archaeological discovery continues to prove the Bible to be trustworthy.

The story of the birth of Christ starts out with these familiar words: "Now it came about in those days, that a decree went out from Caesar Augustus, that a census be taken of all the inhabited earth. This was the first census taken while Quirinius was governor of Syria." (*Luke 2:1,2*) This is a typical example of what makes the Bible unique among other religious writings. The events in the Bible are told in context with historically verifiable events. The writings of other religions tend to be collections of wise sayings, or stories with no relation to history or specific events, and therefore can't be proven. But through archaeology, the Bible has been proven reliable in its descriptions of ancient people, events, cultures, and civilizations. One excellent example of archaeology that supports the Bible is the Arch of Titus, finished in 81 A.D., which is still standing in Rome. On it you can see the Roman troops bringing back the spoils of their conquest of Jerusalem in 70 A.D., which Christ predicted decades before it actually occurred.

Many archaeologists searching ancient sites use the Bible as a guide. Through archaeology, much of the Bible has been proven, much is yet to be proven, but no part of it has ever been disproven. Other examples of real people mentioned in the Bible have also been verified by archaeology:

• Quirinius, Governor of Syria (*Luke 2:2*), verified by an inscription found in Antioch.
• Lysanias, Tetrarch of Abilene (*Luke 3:1*), verified by an inscription found near Damascus.
• Erastus, City Treasurer of Corinth (*Romans 16:23*), verified by an inscription found in Corinth.
• Gallio, Procousul of Achaia (*Acts 18:12*), verified by an inscription found in Delphi.
• Publius, "First Man" of Malta (*Acts 28:7*), verified by an inscription that calls him "First Man."
• Other figures from ancient empires such as Nebuchadnezzar, Sennacharib, Cyrus, Darius, Xerxes, Caesar Augustus, Belshazzar, Herod, Pilate, and many more.

7. The Bible is a small library of 66 books, written over 1,500 years, by about 40 different authors with unique writing styles, in three languages. The Bible's central theme is that man is separated from God because of our sin, but God loves us so much that He came to earth in human form as Jesus Christ who paid the price for our sins so that we could be reunited with God and live forever in heaven with Him.

"God demonstrates His own love for us in that while we were yet sinners Christ died for us." *Romans 5:8*

66 Can We Just Interpret The Bible However We Want?

When we read the newspaper or a history book, we naturally assume that what it says is what it means. But when some people read the Bible, they assume that everything is written in deep symbolism, with the true meaning obscured and open to subjective interpretation just like an abstract painting.

Parts of the Bible are written using literary techniques such as symbolism, figures of speech, metaphors, poetry, and allegory. And it takes some study to understand the meaning of these passages that one might not grasp from a superficial reading. But by far, the vast majority of the Bible is written quite matter-of-factly, without any symbolism or literary techniques that might confuse a first time reader.

The Bible is an amazing collection of ancient literature. It's a small library of 66 books, written over 1,500 years, by about 40 different authors. Like any library, there's a history section, poetry section, romance section, and a mystery section (that is, future events in Daniel, Revelation, etc.). There are even fictional parts where Jesus used stories, or "parables," to teach certain truths to His listeners. But most of the Bible is clearly to be understood as "nonfiction," and therefore taken as factual whenever possible.

So then, is the Bible a book we can subjectively interpret however we want?

---

1. **The Bible itself says that some parts are difficult to understand, and that when anything other than the true meaning of the Scripture is taught, it can be quite harmful.**

   "Some things are difficult to understand, which the untaught and unstable distort, as they do also the rest of the Scriptures, to their own destruction." *2 Peter 3:16*

2. **Why would God be so concerned that the meaning of the Scriptures be understood properly? It's because the Bible is inspired by God, and it is His love letter to mankind. If we misunderstand His words because of a wrong interpretation, then we miss out on what He wants us to know.**

   "But know this first of all, that no prophecy of Scripture is a matter of one's own interpretation, for no prophecy was ever made by an act of human will, but men moved by the Holy Spirit spoke from God." *2 Peter 1:20,21*

   "All Scripture is inspired by God and profitable for teaching, for reproof, for correction, for training in righteousness; that the man of God may be adequate, equipped for every good work." *2 Timothy 3:16,17*

   "Heaven and earth will pass away, but My words will not pass away." *Matthew 24:35*

3. **Even though some teachings in the Bible are difficult to understand, the most important teachings are difficult to misunderstand. God wants us to understand the Scriptures and will give us wisdom to help us understand it.**

   "But if any of you lacks wisdom, let him ask of God, who gives to all men generously and without reproach, and it will be given to him." *James 1:5*

   "And you will seek Me and find Me, when you search for Me with all your heart." *Jeremiah 29:13*

4. **For passages that are difficult to interpret, just remember that Scripture is best interpreted by other Scripture.**

   Even though the Bible is made up of 66 books, it still needs to be understood as a unit. The Bible could be compared to a magnificent tapestry; when you pull one thread, you find it is connected somewhere on the other side. A passage in one book, written in one century, is often best explained by seeking out other passages on the same topic that might have been written by different authors living in different centuries. That's the beauty of the Scripture. Even though God used humans to write it down, every passage has been inspired by God. In other words, the content and truths are from the Lord, but the style of writing varies from author to author.

5. **Why are there offshoot groups, cults, or sects who don't agree with the mainstream Christian interpretation of certain passages? Usually because they have either taken a verse out of context and twisted its meaning, or they have ignored certain sections of Scripture which provide the full biblical view of a topic.**

   In *Matthew 19:16-26*, when the rich, young ruler asked Jesus how he could have eternal life, Jesus initially responded, "Keep the commandments." But Jesus was not teaching that we work our way to heaven, as some people have interpreted this passage when they stop reading at that point. A few verses later, Jesus concluded His answer to the man's question by saying, "With men this is impossible, but with God all things are possible." He was actually saying we must be holy to get to heaven, but it is impossible to become holy based on our own good works, and that holiness must be imparted to us from God. Taking a verse out of context to twist the meaning is nothing new. Even Satan quoted Scripture in a twisted way when he tempted Jesus in the wilderness. (See *Luke 4:1-13*)

6. The Bible doesn't give us the option to "pick and choose" which passages to believe and which to reject.

Also in Matthew 19 when Christ told the rich, young ruler to keep the commandments, the man immediately responded, "Which ones?" Some Bibles print the words of Christ in red, but if one believes the Bible to be God's Word, then all the words are from the Lord, and none should be discarded.

7. The Bible does use symbolism and figures of speech at times.

Christ said in *John 10:9*, "I am the door; if anyone enters through Me, he shall be saved." Christ was not saying He was a literal wooden door, but simply that He is the way we have access to God. Again, Scripture is best interpreted by other Scripture, and a verse which helps interpret this one is *John 14:6* which reads, "Jesus said to him, 'I am the way, and the truth, and the life; no one comes to the Father, but through Me.'"

8. The Bible was written in Hebrew, Greek, and Aramaic. Sometimes when a figure of speech is translated from the original language it can be difficult to understand, and requires some study to avoid misinterpretation.

If a person said, "Bring me a donut, and step on it," and then that saying was translated literally into another language, some confusion would result. Good Bible study reference books can be a valuable tool in understanding difficult verses, and are available at Christian bookstores or on the internet.

9. Understanding the culture, or times, in which the passage was written helps understand the difference between a timeless precept or a wisdom principle.

In *1 Timothy 2:9*, Paul urged women not to wear their hair in braids. Archaeology has uncovered statues of pagan cult prostitutes who wore their hair in braids which identified them with their pagan religion. Paul was simply saying that Christian women should not let a fashion trend identify them with the wrong value system. Cultures vary; truths don't.

10. There is one central truth the Bible teaches over and over again. It is that man is separated from God because of our sin, but God loved mankind so much that He came to earth in human form as Jesus Christ. He paid the price for our sins so that we could be reunited with God and live forever in heaven with Him.

"God demonstrates His own love for us in that while we were yet sinners Christ died for us." *Romans 5:8*

"For God so loved the world, that He gave His only begotten Son, that whoever believes in Him shall not perish, but have everlasting life." *John 3:16*

"For the wages of sin is death, but the free gift of God is eternal life in Christ Jesus our Lord." *Romans 6:23*

11. Obedience to God results in much more spiritual clarity, whereas disobedience tends to cloud spiritual clarity.

"So Jesus was saying to those Jews who had believed Him, 'If you continue in My word, then you are truly disciples of Mine; and you will know the truth, and the truth will make you free.'" *John 8:31,32*

12. There are many Bible study reference books that help us understand the Bible better. But by far the greatest help to understanding the Bible is to have the same God who inspired the Bible dwell within you! If God does not dwell within you, then you will never fully understand what the Bible is talking about. Invite Christ in today!

"But people who aren't Christians can't understand these truths from God's Spirit. It all sounds foolish to them because only those who have the Spirit can understand what the Spirit means. We who have the Spirit understand these things, but others can't understand us at all. How could they?" *1 Corinthians 2:14-16a (NLT)*

67 Did The Miracles In The Bible Really Happen?

The miracles in the Bible are meant to help us believe. Yet to many people, the miracles are what keep them from believing. Throughout the Bible, periods of sensational miracles which defied the laws of nature were sporadic, and were more the exception rather than the rule. Many of the most familiar names in the Bible never performed such a miracle.

No one alive today saw the Red Sea parting or Jesus walk on water. But the Bible gives us detailed accounts written by eyewitnesses, and describes six categories of miracles – some of which we can witness today. And when you think about it, who wants to worship a God who is too wimpy to perform miracles?

1. The miracles described in the Bible fall into six basic categories:

(1) Natural Miracles, where God utilized the forces of nature to accomplish the miracle.
- The Red Sea parted by a strong wind blowing all night. *Exodus 14:2*
- Manna and quail provided daily. *Exodus 16:31, Numbers 11:31,32*
- The first nine plagues of Egypt; a series of natural ecological catastrophes. *Exodus 7:14-10:29*
- Ravens brought food to Elijah twice a day. *1 Kings 17:6*
- Jonah swallowed and transported by the whale. *Jonah 1:15-2:10*
- The huge catches of fish. *Luke 5:1-11, John 21:1-11*

(2) Unnatural Miracles, where God broke all the rules of nature to accomplish the miracle.
- Moses' staff turning into a snake, then back again. *Exodus 4:1-9*
- The sun standing still. *Joshua 10:12-15*
- The virgin birth. *Luke 1:26-38*
- Turning water into wine. *John 2:1-11*
- Walking on water. *Matthew 14:24-33, Mark 6:45-52*
- Feeding of the 5,000. *Mark 6:34-44*
- Instant healings, or instant onset of disease. *John 9:1-38, Luke 8:43,44, Matthew 8:13, Numbers 12:1-10*
- Jesus bringing Lazarus and others back to life. *John 11:1-46, Luke 7:11-17, Matthew 9:18-26*
- Jesus' resurrection. *Matthew 28:1-10, Mark 16:1-8, Luke 24:1-53, John 20:1-29*

(3) Prophetic Miracles, where specific events are described years, and even centuries before they occur.
- The destruction of various cities and nations such as Tyre (*Ezekiel 26:3-21*), Edom (*Isaiah 34:6-15*), Nineveh (*Nahum 3:10-19*), Babylon (*Isaiah 13:19-22*), Jerusalem (*Matthew 24:1,2*).
- The scattering and regathering of Israel as a nation. *Leviticus 26:31-33, Ezekiel 33:33-35.*
- Specific, detailed predictions of events in the life of Jesus, such as being born in Bethlehem (*Micah 5:2*), betrayed for exactly thirty pieces of silver (*Zechariah 11:12*), His hands and feet would be pierced (*Psalm 22:16*), people would gamble for His clothing by casting lots (*Psalm 22:18*), He would be executed along with criminals (*Isaiah 53:9,12*), He would be buried in a rich man's tomb (*Isaiah 53:9*), His body would be resurrected (*Psalm 16:8-11*).
- Accurate predictions give evidence that the Bible is divine in origin. *Isaiah 42:9, John 13:19, John 14:29*

(4) Everyday Miracles, which are events in everyday life that are truly acts of God, but people forget these miracles because they're so common. We call it a miracle for a blind person to then see, but what about the eye that can already see? Even if we don't witness the other types of miracles, we can all witness these.
- The birth of a child. *Psalm 139:13-16*
- The seeing eye and hearing ear. *Proverbs 20:12, Exodus 4:11, Psalm 94:9*
- The unexplainable aspects of nature. *Psalm 19:1-6, Psalm 8, Proverbs 30:18-28*
- The ongoing cycles of nature. *Acts 14:17*

(5) The Miracle of the Existence of Matter, defying the First Law of Thermodymanics (also called the Law of the Conservation of Matter) which states that matter cannot be created nor destoyed. All the matter in the universe was miraculously created out of nothing. If science says matter can't be created, where did it come from?
- God created the heavens and the earth. *Genesis 1:1, Isaiah 40:25,26, Isaiah 48:13, Isaiah 66:1,2, Colossians 1:16*
- Only God can call into being that which does not exist. *John 1:3, Romans 4:17*

(6) Changed-Life Miracles, when people's lives are changed in ways that can't be explained by simple willpower. There are also examples where God chooses not to change a difficult situation, but He changes our hearts to not only accept the situation as is, but to actually be grateful for the adversity.

- When a sinner is "born again" and becomes "a new creature." *Ezekiel 36:26, 2 Corinthians 5:17, John 3:1-6*
- Paul's change of heart that allowed him to thank God for the "thorn in the flesh." *2 Corinthians 12:7-9*
- David gave thanks for his afflictions because they brought him closer to God. *Psalm 119:71*

2. Skeptics may not accept the belief that God created the universe, but science can only speculate, and not explain, how all the matter that exists has burst forth out of nothing. How can nothing create something? Matter is not continuing to come into existence; it only happened once. The creation of all matter is the first act of God, or "miracle," found in the first verse of the Bible. The Bible makes it clear that the miracle of God's creation provides ample evidence for us to believe that God exists. And if God could perform this first miracle, is anything else too difficult?

"Ah Lord God! Behold, You have made the heavens and the earth by Your great power and by your outstretched arm! Nothing is too difficult for you" *Jeremiah 32:17*

"From the time the world was created, people have seen the earth and sky and all that God made. They can clearly see his invisible qualities – his eternal power and divine nature. So they have no excuse whatsoever for not knowing God." *Romans 1:20 (NLT)*

3. Why does God perform miracles? Supernatural miracles in Bible times authenticated a messenger and the message, as when Moses proved himself to Pharaoh. The messenger who did the most miracles was Jesus. What was His message? That He was God's divine Son who provides the only way for us to be forgiven and have access to God.

"Now when John (the Baptist) in prison heard of the works of Christ, he sent word by his disciples, and said to Him, 'Are You the Coming One, or shall we look for someone else?' And Jesus answered and said to them, 'Go and report to John the things which you hear and see: the blind receive sight and the lame walk, the lepers are cleansed and the deaf hear, and the dead are raised up, and the poor have the gospel preached to them. And blessed is he who keeps from stumbling over Me.'" *Matthew 11:2-6*

"Many other signs therefore Jesus also performed in the presence of the disciples, which are not written in this book; but these have been written that you may believe that Jesus is the Christ, the Son of God; and that believing you may have life in His name." *John 20:30,31*

4. Jesus' critics didn't try to discredit His supernatural powers, because His miracles were too well known.

"Therefore the chief priests and the Pharisees convened a council, and were saying, 'What are we doing? For this man is performing many signs. If we let Him go on like this, all men will believe in Him.'" *John 11:47,48*

5. The most important of all the miracles in the Bible would be Christ's resurrection, because this is the miracle which authenticates Him as the true Son of God. The entire Christian faith hinges on this miracle being legitimate.

"And Jesus Christ our Lord was shown to be the Son of God when God powerfully raised him from the dead by means of the Holy Spirit." *Romans 1:4 (NLT)*

"Christ died for our sins according to the Scriptures... He was buried... He was raised on the third day according to the Scriptures, and after that He appeared to Cephas, then to the twelve. After that He appeared to more than five hundred brethren at one time." *1 Corinthians 15:3-6*

6. Miracles that can be observed today include the millions of lives that have been transformed by following Christ. If you choose to confess your sins and accept Christ as your Savior and Lord, this same miracle can happen to you.

"And I will give you a new heart with new and right desires, and I will put a new spirit in you. I will take out your stony heart of sin and give you a new, obedient heart." *Ezekiel 36:26 (NLT)*

"Therefore if any man is in Christ; he is a new creature; the old things passed away; behold, new things have come." *2 Corinthians 5:17*

68 Is The Bible Full Of Contradictions?

Many people say the Bible is full of contradictions. If this is true, it would certainly undermine the idea that the Bible is divine in origin. To help bring clarity to this issue – which has kept many people from embracing the Bible as God's Word – it helps to understand the background of this important book.

The Bible is a small library of sixty-six individual books written by forty different authors, over a span of about 1,500 years, on three continents, in three original languages, and touches on hundreds of subjects. One would expect any normal book that contained writings by forty authors to include some contradictions here and there. But Christians believe the Bible is not a normal book. If it really is God's Word, it should be held to the highest possible standard. It should show evidence that it is divinely inspired and not a mere collection of various writings. Bible-believing Christians would agree that some verses do appear to contradict each other at a superficial reading. But when we do some digging and research, these conflicting verses can be understood and the contradictions disappear. When it comes to accurately understanding these problem verses, here are some guidelines that can help.

1. Differences in details between passages are not necessarily contradictions.

A football game was played, and was written about the next day by three newspapers. One mentioned a fumble and an interception. Another paper mentioned the interception but not the fumble, and also mentioned a blocked field goal. A third paper didn't describe any of these plays, but did mention a punt return and what song the band played at halftime. Fortunately, all three articles gave the same final score. But because of the differences in the details, should we conclude the game was never played? Of course not; these differences are to be expected.

2. Particularly in the four gospels, accounts of events in the life of Jesus can highlight slightly different details.

Matthew 20:30 mentions two unnamed blind men as Jesus was leaving Jericho. *Mark 10:46* mentions one blind man named Bartimaeus as Jesus was leaving Jericho. *Luke 18:35* mentions one blind man named Bartimaeus as Jesus was entering Jericho. John doesn't mention the event at all. These different details actually provide credibility that the four gospel authors did not collaborate to get all the details exactly the same. Matthew chose to describe two blind men but never gave either man's name. Mark and Luke focused on only one of the men, and added that his name was Bartimaeus. John chose to focus on other events during Jesus' ministry and didn't mention this event at all. But was Jesus entering or leaving Jericho? That leads to the next point.

3. Understanding geography, history, culture, and customs helps reconcile verses that appear to contradict.

In the verses above, Matthew and Mark mention that Jesus was leaving Jericho, while Luke says Jesus was entering Jericho. Archeology explains why this is not a contradiction. During the time of Jesus, there were two towns close to each other that were both called Jericho. The Old Testament town of Jericho (which was conquered by Joshua and the Israelites in Joshua 6) was a small village lying mostly among the ruins of the original town. (Joshua commanded that the town not be rebuilt in *Joshua 6:26*.) About two miles south was the new town of Jericho built by Herod the Great. Amazingly, this is the only town mentioned in the New Testament that existed in two separate locations, so it was completely possible to be leaving one Jericho while entering the next Jericho. As we compare all the verses, it helps us pinpoint that Jesus was between the two Jerichos, bringing even more clarity to the story.

4. None of the gospel accounts are exhaustive, or try to describe every single detail of Jesus' life and ministry. Each author will have his own emphasis and observations.

"Therefore many other signs Jesus also performed in the presence of the disciples, which are not written in this book; but these have been written so that you may believe that Jesus is the Christ, the Son of God; and that believing you may have life in His name." *John 20:30,31*

5. If a verse is taken out of context, it can appear to contradict other passages.

In *Matthew 19:16-26*, a rich man asked Jesus, "Teacher, what good thing shall I do that I may obtain eternal life?" The first part of Jesus' answer was: "If you wish to enter into life, keep the commandments." Many people stop reading there and conclude that this verse teaches we get to heaven by being good which contradicts other verses that say we are saved by faith in Christ. But sadly, the rich man left before Jesus concluded His answer with these remarks: "When the disciples heard this, they were very astonished and said, 'Then who can be saved?' And looking at them Jesus said to them, 'With people this is impossible, but with God all things are possible.'" (*Matthew 19:25,26*)

Jesus' full answer was that none of us are good enough to go to heaven because none of us have kept every commandment – we're all sinners. The salvation impossible for us to achieve was achieved by God Himself through the death of Christ. If we take the early verse out of context, it appears to contradict other Bible teachings on grace, and we miss the main point.

Paul clearly taught that salvation comes by faith not works: "For by grace you have been saved through faith; and that not of yourselves, it is the gift of God; not as a result of works, so that no one may boast." (*Ephesians 2:8,9*) But some critics have taken passages out of context from James and charged that James taught salvation comes by doing good works; contradicting Paul:

"You see that a man is justified by works and not by faith alone." (*James 2:24*) But reading James in context, we realize he was talking about justifying the genuineness of our faith to other people, not to God. Earlier in his book he clearly set forth the premise that we are saved by receiving Christ in faith, but we justify, or prove our conversion to other people as they observe our works: "Therefore, putting aside all filthiness and all that remains of wickedness, in humility receive the word implanted, which is able to save your souls. But prove yourselves doers of the word, and not merely hearers who delude themselves." (*James 1:21,22*) James goes on to write, "But someone may well say, 'You have faith and I have works; show me your faith without the works, and I will show you my faith by my works.'" (*James 2:18*) James' teaching is in perfect harmony with Paul, and with what Christ taught in *Matthew 7:15-20* about how deeds are a good way to indicate the genuineness of a person's faith: "Beware of the false prophets, who come to you in sheep's clothing, but inwardly are ravenous wolves. You will know them by their fruits. Grapes are not gathered from thorn bushes nor figs from thistles, are they? So every good tree bears good fruit, but the bad tree bears bad fruit. A good tree cannot produce bad fruit, nor can a bad tree produce good fruit. Every tree that does not bear good fruit is cut down and thrown into the fire. So then, you will know them by their fruits."

6. If you come across passages that appear to contradict, research them in the original language.

If man goes into a donut shop in a foreign country and says, "Bring me a donut and step on it," and then his comment is translated into the language of the person behind the counter, a very flat donut would result. Similar difficulties can result if we don't understand the original wording and nuances of certain Bible passages. *Acts 9:7* says that when Christ appeared to Paul on his way to Damascus, the other men heard a voice. But *Acts 22:7* says the other men did not hear a voice. By studying the original Greek, the contradiction disappears. The wording of the first verse conveys, "hearing a sound as a noise," but the wording of the second verse conveys, "hearing a voice that communicates a message." Putting the verses together we conclude the other men heard a sound, but only Paul could decipher what was being said. This is much like what happened in *John 12:28,* when God the Father spoke to Jesus; some people thought it was only thunder, while others perceived a voice speaking.

7. Christian author E. Paul Hovey wrote, "Men do not reject the Bible because it contradicts itself, but because it contradicts them." The only way to understand the Bible is by fully obeying what it says, then clarity will come.

"If you abide in My word, then you are truly disciples of Mine; and you shall know the truth, and the truth shall make you free." *John 8:31,32*

8. The Bible's authors maintain the same central storyline – God's redemption of man. Old Testament authors looked to a Messiah who had not yet come, and New Testament authors looked to a Messiah who had already come, but they were all looking to the same Messiah. Jesus Christ is the Bible's culmination of God's love for mankind. Only through Him can we receive the forgiveness and redemption we could never achieve on our own.

"For God so loved the world, that He gave His only begotten Son, that whoever believes in Him shall not perish, but have eternal life." *John 3:16*

"For the wages of sin is death, but the free gift of God is eternal life in Christ Jesus our Lord." *Romans 6:23*

69 Has The Bible Borrowed Ideas From Other Ancient Religions?

The ancient Mesopotamian story of Gilgamesh told how he built a huge boat and loaded it with animals to survive a massive flood. Sound familiar? Even many Native American traditions include an extremely similar story of a man who built a large boat loaded with animals to survive a flood. Coincidence?

But the comparisons to stories from the Bible aren't limited to just Noah. There's an ancient Mesopotamian clay seal in the British Museum that depicts a man, a woman, a tree, and a snake. It's hard to miss the similarity to the story of Adam and Eve. The story of the Tower of Babel also shows up in Chaldean writings. Even specific people mentioned in the Bible have shown up in the histories of other cultures, such as Nimrod being mentioned in Chaldean writings. The Hebrew culture and religion originated with Abraham, who lived in the fertile crescent of Mesopotamia (often called the "Cradle of Civilization"), which is the same region where the Chaldean/Babylonian culture began, so it's entirely possible that these cultures shared a common understanding of history. But does the fact that other ancient cultures share commonalities with the Bible undermine or strengthen the biblical accounts?

1. **It could be argued that since these stories have commonalities among other ancient cultures of the region, then maybe it should lend credibility that they were based on actual events, and were not simply made up in a vacuum. Here are four options of how these similar stories might have orignated:**

   • The Bible borrowed these stories from other cultures.
   • Other cultures borrowed these ideas from the Bible.
   • The Bible and these other stories are all based on the same fables that were passed around the ancient world.
   • The Bible and these other stories are all based on the same historical events, retold through different cultures.

   We do know that the ancient Hebrews were extremely dedicated to preserving written history as accurately as possible, which is why we have the Bible today. Is there a Chaldean Bible? Or an Assyrian Bible? Or a Sumerian Bible? No other culture in the region was as meticulous when it came to preserving the details of history. Based on the Hebrew culture's obsession with record keeping, it makes sense to assume the Hebrew account has the highest level of credibility from the region.

2. **But what about similarities to Jesus found in other ancient religions? For example, the ancient religion of Zoroastrianism taught that its founder, a man named Zoroaster, would impregnate a virgin who would give birth to a savior who would judge the world and raise the dead. His name was Mithras, who became the Persian sun god, and was often depicted with beams of light from his head like a halo. Devotion to him was said to enable his followers to earn salvation. But there is no historical evidence that Mithras ever actually lived, and was likely a mythical pagan figure like Hercules. Other pagan accounts or predictions of resurrection have been found, usually centered around agricultural harvest cycles, but none have been documented historically like the resurrection of Jesus. This is what sets Jesus apart from these stories and proves He is the true Son of God. The truth of His resurrection is what helped Christianity succeed in the face of many competitive pagan religions, even though it faced far greater persecution, and even outlived the very empire that tried to stamp it out.**

   "And Jesus Christ our Lord was shown to be the Son of God when God powerfully raised him from the dead by means of the Holy Spirit." *Romans 1:4 (NLT)*

3. **The story of the resurrection was first preached to the citizens of Jerusalem forty days after Jesus was crucified there. These were the people closest to the evidence. They had been there to call for His crucifixion, they witnessed the chaos of the missing body afterward, they could visit the empty tomb, and could talk to eyewitnesses of the risen Jesus. When the message was preached to them, they became believers in droves! If the evidence had clearly shown Jesus was still dead, Christianity never would have taken off. If they thought it was just a rehashed pagan myth, believers would not have risked imprisonment, torture, and execution by believing in a religion banned by the Roman government, while many other pagan religions were perfectly legal.**

   "Now when they heard this, they were pierced to the heart, and said to Peter and the rest of the apostles, 'Brethren, what shall we do?' ...So then, those who had received his word were baptized; and there were added that day about three thousand souls." Acts 2:37,41

"One of them, named Cleopas, answered and said to Him (Jesus), 'Are You the only one visiting Jerusalem and unaware of the things which have happened here in these days?' And He said to them, 'What things?' And they said to Him, 'The things about Jesus the Nazarene, who was a prophet mighty in deed and word in the sight of God and all the people, and how the chief priests and our rulers delivered Him to the sentence of death, and crucified Him. But we were hoping that it was He who was going to redeem Israel. Indeed, besides all this, it is the third day since these things happened. But also some women among us amazed us. When they were at the tomb early in the morning, and did not find His body, they came, saying that they had also seen a vision of angels who said that He was alive. Some of those who were with us went to the tomb and found it just exactly as the women also had said; but Him they did not see.'" *Luke 24:18-24*

"For I delivered to you as of first importance what I also received, that Christ died for our sins according to the Scriptures, and that He was buried, and that He was raised on the third day according to the Scriptures, and that He appeared to Cephas, then to the twelve. After that He appeared to more than five hundred brethren at one time, most of whom remain until now, but some have fallen asleep; then He appeared to James, then to all the apostles; and last of all, as to one untimely born, He appeared to me (Paul) also." *1 Corinthians 15:3-8*

"If Christ has not been raised, then our preaching is vain, your faith also is vain…. and if Christ has not been raised, your faith is worthless; you are still in your sins." *1 Corinthians 15:14,17*

4. **What about the similarities between the moral truths of the Bible, and the morals taught by other religions? Jesus was certainly not the first person in history who taught people to be good. Many religions have similar sounding versions of Jesus' famous "Golden Rule."**

  - Jesus: "Treat people the same way you want them to treat you." *Matthew 7:12*
  - Confucius: "What you do not wish for yourself, do not do to others." *Lunyu 12:2*
  - Buddha: "Hurt not others in ways that you yourself would find hurtful." *Udana-Varga 5:18*

5. **Christianity encourages people to be good, as do other religions. So what makes Christianity unique? Even though Jesus instructed people to be good, He also told them that they could never be good enough to get to heaven in their own power. This is a major difference between the teachings of Jesus and other religious founders. He claimed that His death on the cross is the only payment for sin that can make it possible for us to be forgiven and reach God. Trusting in Christ's payment for sin to receive the free gift of salvation is clearly not an idea borrowed from any other religion. Buddha and Confucius never claimed to be able to forgive sins.**

  "Jesus said to him, 'I am the way, and the truth, and the life; no one comes to the Father, but through Me.'" *John 14:6*

  "For there is salvation in no one else; for there is no other name under heaven that has been given among men, by which we must be saved." *Acts 4:12*

  "For there is one God, and one mediator also between God and men, the man Christ Jesus, who gave Himself as a ransom for all." *1 Timothy 2:5,6a*

  "But God demonstrates His own love for us in that while we were yet sinners Christ died for us." *Romans 5:8*

6. **Other religions basically teach that we reach God by being good. But the Bible is unique in teaching that our only hope in reaching God is by trusting in Christ, not our own righteousness. The good deeds we do can't cancel out our sins; this can only be accomplished by the payment Christ made on our behalf.**

  "For all have sinned and fall short of the glory of God." *Romans 3:23*

  "For the wages of sin is death, but the free gift of God is eternal life in Christ Jesus our Lord." *Romans 6:23*

  "And He Himself bore our sins in His body on the cross, so that we might die to sin and live to righteousness; for by His wounds you were healed." *1 Peter 2:24*

  "For God so loved the world, that He gave His only begotten Son, that whoever believes in Him shall not perish, but have everlasting life." *John 3:16*

70 Is The Bible Filled With Myths?

A giant boat filled with animals. Fire and brimstone falling from the sky. A voice from a burning bush. A sea that parts so people can walk through. A fish that swallowed a man. Walking on water. Turning water into wine. Rising from the dead. And the list goes on. Are these allegories? Metaphors? Myths? Fables? Exaggerations? Figures of speech? The Bible, like all great literature, uses many figures of speech. Sometimes a casual reading might leave the reader a bit confused whether a passage is describing something literally, or using a more poetic, symbolic description.

Jesus used fictional parables (like the Prodigal Son) to illustrate a truth, so are these sensational stories the same type of thing? Or were they historical events that happened just the way the Bible describes?

---

1. The Bible was written by about forty different authors with individual writing styles. Most of it reads as factually as a newspaper, but occasionally authors use figures of speech for effect, such as:

"Let the rivers clap their hands, let the mountains sing together for joy." *Psalm 98:8 (Here, the psalmist uses an anthropomorphism to say that nature itself reflects the glory of God.)*

"I am the door; if anyone enters through Me, he will be saved, and will go in and out and find pasture." *John 10:9 (Here, Jesus was not claiming to be a literal, wooden door, but that only through only Him can we have access to God.)*

"If your right eye makes you stumble, tear it out and throw it from you; for it is better for you to lose one of the parts of your body, than for your whole body to be thrown into hell." *Matthew 5:29 (Here, Jesus was telling His listeners to take sin seriously, and He used exaggeration to stress the importance of taking earnest measures to restructure their lifestyles to avoid the destructive consequences of sin.)*

2. Even Jesus' disciples occasionally got confused whether He was using a figure or speech or speaking plainly.

"This figure of speech Jesus spoke to them, but they did not understand what those things were which He had been saying to them." *John 10:6*

"I came forth from the Father and have come into the world; I am leaving the world again and going to the Father. His disciples said, 'Lo, now You are speaking plainly and are not using a figure of speech.'" *John 16:28,29*

3. The world's foremost authority on the Old Testament was Jesus Christ. His view of the more sensational Old Testament stories brings insight for us today. He viewed the hard-to-believe stories as historical, factual events. He considered those stories – such as Noah's ark, fire and brimstone on Sodom and Gomorrah, the burning bush, and Jonah and the whale – as being every bit as factual as the events in His own life.

"And just as it happened in the days of Noah, so it will be also in the days of the Son of Man: they were eating, they were drinking, they were marrying, they were being given in marriage, until the day that Noah entered the ark, and the flood came and destroyed them all. It was the same as happened in the days of Lot: they were eating, they were drinking, they were buying, they were selling, they were planting, they were building; but on the day that Lot went out from Sodom it rained fire and brimstone from heaven and destroyed them all. It will be just the same on the day that the Son of Man is revealed." *Luke 17:26-30*

"Then some of the scribes and Pharisees said to Him, 'Teacher, we want to see a sign from You.' But He answered and said to them, 'An evil and adulterous generation craves for a sign; and yet no sign will be given to it but the sign of Jonah the prophet; for just as Jonah was three days and three nights in the belly of the sea monster, so will the Son of Man be three days and three nights in the heart of the earth. The men of Nineveh will stand up with this generation at the judgment, and will condemn it because they repented at the preaching of Jonah; and behold, something greater than Jonah is here.'" *Matthew 12:38-41*

4. New Testament writers also considered these stories to be true, and not figures of speech or allegories.

"By faith Noah, being warned by God about things not yet seen, in reverence prepared an ark for the salvation of his household, by which he condemned the world, and became an heir of the righteousness which is according to faith. By faith they passed through the Red Sea as though they were passing through dry land; and the Egyptians, when hey attempted it, were drowned. By faith the walls of Jericho fell down after they had been encircled for seven days. By faith Rahab the harlot did not perish along with those who were disobedient, after she had welcomed the spies in peace. And what more shall I say? For time will fail me if I tell of Gideon, Barak, Samson, Jephthah, of David and Samuel and the prophets, who by faith conquered kingdoms, performed acts of righteousness, obtained promises, shut the mouths of lions, quenched the power of fire, escaped the edge of the sword, from weakness were made strong, became mighty in war, put foreign armies to flight." *Hebrews 11:7,29-34*

5. **The Bible is the story of God interacting with man. It's not far-fetched to think that when an infinite God interacts with finite man, amazing things could happen. Would it be more comforting to believe in a God who is too wimpy to do a miracle? If God didn't have infinite power, then He wouldn't be God.**

"Behold, I am the Lord, the God of all flesh; is anything too difficult for Me?" *Jeremiah 32:27*

"But He said, 'The things that are impossible with people are possible with God.'" *Luke 18:27*

6. **New Testament writers were eyewitnesses of Jesus' miracles, and had "front row seats" when He walked on water, rose from the dead, etc. They wrote about these miracles so that we could believe they really happened.**

"For we did not follow cleverly devised tales when we made known to you the power and coming of our Lord Jesus Christ, but we were eyewitnesses of His majesty." *2 Peter 1:16*

"Then He said to Thomas, 'Reach here with your finger, and see My hands; and reach here your hand and put it into My side; and do not be unbelieving, but believing.' Thomas answered and said to Him, 'My Lord and my God!' Jesus said to him, 'Because you have seen Me, have you believed? Blessed are they who did not see, and yet believed.' Therefore many other signs Jesus also performed in the presence of the disciples, which are not written in this book; but these have been written so that you may believe that Jesus is the Christ, the Son of God; and that believing you may have life in His name." *John 20:27-31*

7. **If you can't believe the Bible's more sensational stories, and you only see them as allegories or metaphors, read them anyway, then apply the truths that are taught. Once you apply the truths that are revealed, God will reveal more truth. But if you don't apply what you learn, don't expect further enlightenment to come. If the Scriptures seem impossible to believe or understand, it's probably because of something you refuse to obey.**

"He who has My commandments and keeps them is the one who loves Me; and he who loves Me will be loved by My Father, and I will love him and will disclose Myself to him." *John 14:21*

"So Jesus was saying to those Jews who had believed Him, 'If you abide in My word, then you are truly disciples of Mine; and you will know the truth, and the truth will make you free.'" *John 8:31.32*

"But people who aren't Christians can't understand these truths from God's Spirit. It all sounds foolish to them because only those who have the Spirit can understand what the Spirit means. We who have the Spirit understand these things, but others can't understand us at all." *1 Corinthians 2:14,15 (NLT)*

8. **Some of the stories in the Bible are truly amazing. But the most amazing truth the Bible teaches is the depth of God's unconditional love for us even though we are sinners. He has sent His only Son Jesus to pay the penalty for our sins so that we can begin enjoying a relationship with God that will last through all eternity.**

"Jesus said to him, 'I am the way, and the truth, and the life; no one comes to the Father, but through Me.'" *John 14:6*

"For there is one God, and one mediator also between God and men, the man Christ Jesus, who gave Himself as a ransom for all." *1 Timothy 2:5,6a*

"But God demonstrates His own love for us in that while we were yet sinners Christ died for us." *Romans 5:8*

"For the wages of sin is death, but the free gift of God is eternal life in Christ Jesus our Lord." *Romans 6:23*

"For God so loved the world, that He gave His only begotten Son, that whoever believes in Him shall not perish, but have everlasting life." *John 3:16*

71 Why Were Some Books Chosen To Be In The Bible While Others Were Excluded?

The Bible is a small library of 66 individual books – 39 in the Old Testament and 27 in the New Testament. Like any library, it has a history section (such as Genesis, Exodus, and the gospels), a legal section (Leviticus), poetry section (such as Psalms and Proverbs), a romance section (Song of Solomon), mystery section (such as Daniel, Ezekiel, and Revelation that describe future events), and even fictional sections (where Jesus used stories called "parables" to bring His truths to life). These books were written over a span of 1,500 years, by forty different authors. Some authors were from royalty (like David and Solomon), some were highly educated (like Paul), and some were working class (like Peter and James).

But in addition to these 66 books, there are many writings that were not deemed worthy to be included. Canonization is the process by which some books were included while others were not. The word "canon" means "measuring rod," so the canon is the standard that all books must meet to be included. What exactly was the criteria for determining which books would be included and which would be left out?

1. Old Testament books had to meet five tests to be considered as Scripture:

- They were written by a prophet of God.
- That prophet's authority was confirmed by an act of God.
- The prophetic writings told the truth about God in harmony with God's other prophets.
- The writings were accompanied with the power of God to change people's lives.
- The prophetic writings were accepted by the people of God as true.

Throughout the period of the writing of the Old Testament books (1,500 to 400 BC) God would declare His word through His earthly prophets, who would start off saying something like, "Thus says the Lord…" These prophets also recorded the contemporary events of their time. During this period, Israel looked to the living prophets for God's guidance in addition to writings by previous prophets. Malachi was the last prophet of the Old Testament, who wrote its final book around 400 BC. Then came 400 years of silence with no prophets declaring God's word until John the Baptist began declaring the news of Christ around 30 AD. Jesus called John the last of the line of prophets. "For all the prophets and the Law prophesied until John." (*Matthew 11:13*) Around 200 BC, with no living prophets to go to, the Hebrews assembled the books we now call the Old Testament.

2. The New Testament came about differently. In 397 AD, the Council of Carthage was held to certify which books should be included as Scripture. They asked four basic questions:

- Was the book truly written or approved by an apostle? (To qualify as an apostle, one had to be an eyewitness of the resurrected Lord and perform miracles.)
- Were its contents of a spiritual nature? (not simply having historical significance)
- Did it give evidence of being inspired by God? (evidence such as predicting future events, changing lives, etc.)
- Was it widely received by the churches?

300+ years gave ample time for the truly inspired books to "rise to the top" and others to clearly drop away. The oldest manuscript containing the entire New Testament is the Greek Codex Sinaiticus, dated appx. 350 AD, discovered in St. Catherine's monastery at Mt. Sinai in 1859. If proves the current books had been widely accepted by churches prior to the 397 Council, and the Council simply agreed upon and formalized the list once and for all.

3. There are many other writings which were rejected from the New Testament because they did not meet the previous 4 tests for authenticity. These books include:

Gospel of Thomas, Gospel of Mary, Gospel of Peter, Gospel of Judas, Mary, Magnesians, Protevangelion, Trallians, 1 Infancy, 2 Infancy, Philadelphians, Christ and Abgarus, Smyrnaeans, Letters of Herod and Pilate, Nicodemus, Polycarp, Barnabus, The Apostle's Creed, Philippians, 1 Clement, 2 Clement, Laodiceans, 1 Hermas – Visions, 2 Hermas – Commands, 3 Hermas – Similitudes, Paul and Seneca, Paul and Thecla

4. During the first and second centuries, there were many bogus books floating around claiming to have been writ-

ten by an apostle. Paul even warned his readers not to be fooled by these illigitimate writings.

"Now we request you, brethren... that you not be quickly shaken from your composure or be disturbed either by a spirit or a message or a letter as if from us, to the effect that the day of the Lord has come. Let no one in any way deceive you...." *2 Thessalonians 2:1-3a*

5. In the early years of the church, the disciples continued teaching what they had learned from Jesus. But there were other people who called themselves Christians but taught things Jesus had not taught. There were four main competing theologies, and each had their own leaders and writings:

- ORTHODOX: They followed the teachings of Jesus and the writings of His eyewitnesses/apostles. Theologically, they taught that Jesus was both fully God and fully human. This is the group who produced the writings now in our Bible.

- MARCIONISTS: They followed the teachings of Marcion rather than the apostles. Marcion (85-160) taught that Jesus was completely (but only) divine, and masqueraded as human. He only appeared to eat, bleed, suffer, and die. Marcion also taught the God of the OT was not the same god of the NT. But Marcion never met the real Jesus.

- EBIONITES: The word "ebion" meant "poor," and these people rejected material possesssions. They taught that Jesus was fully human, and only received his divine nature when God "adopted" Him at His baptism.

- GNOSTICS: also called "Separatists." They rejected the apostles' teaching. They separated Jesus into two distinct or separate beings. "Jesus" the man was completely human, and "the Christ" was completely divine. Jesus the man was temporarily indwelt by the divine Christ, enabling Him to perform miracles etc. But before His death, the divine Christ abandoned the human Jesus to face crucifixion alone. Salvation comes by gaining wisdom and enlightenment.

6. What about the Apocrypha – the collection of books placed between the Old Testament and the New Testament in Bibles used by Catholics? Why are these books not found in mainstream Bibles?

- Jesus often quoted the Old Testament, but these books were never quoted by Jesus or by the New Testament writers.

- They were written during the 400 years of silence without a prophet from God. They have historical significance, but are not considered "inspired."

- They teach things that are inconsistent with other Scriptures, such as salvation by works, the existence of purgatory, plus prayers and offerings for the dead to get them out of purgatory.

- There have been a number of authoritative testimonies from ancient times against the acceptance of these books, both from early Jewish scholars, as well as early church fathers and scholars like Athanasius and Jerome.

- The Catholic church first rejected these books, and didn't include them until the Council of Trent in 1453.

- Through the Apocrypha's teachings on purgatory, they opened the door to selling indulgences. These were payments made to the Catholic Churcn to reduce or replace one's penance, or to speed the release of departed loved ones from purgatory, or even to obtain pre-forgiveness for a sin you intend to commit. (Indulgences were one of the things Martin Luther was protesting when he started the Protestant Reformation in 1517.)

7. It's reassuring to know that the books of the New Testament have been written or approved by the people closest to Jesus Christ; people who knew Him, heard Him teach, traveled with Him, ate with Him, and saw Him resurrected. This increases the credibility and trustworthiness of the books we have. It's also reassuring that writings by people who did not know Jesus and whose teachings were vastly different from what Jesus taught have been excluded. Forged letters falsely attributed to His disciples have also been weeded out as fakes.

"For we did not follow cleverly devised tales when we made known to you the power and coming of our Lord Jesus Christ, but we were eyewitnesses of His majesty." *2 Peter 1:16*

8. The Bible is God's love letter to sinful man. It teaches we can only be reunited with God through Christ.

"For the wages of sin is death, but the free gift of God is eternal life in Christ Jesus our Lord." *Romans 6:23*

72 Should We Take The Bible Literally?

Some people disregard the Bible because it describes things that seem so hard to believe; like how God formed a man out of dirt, then there's a huge boat filled with animals, a shepherd boy who kills a giant with a pebble from a sling, a man who gets eaten by a whale, and someone who walked on water and rose from the dead. With so many sensational stories, people sometimes wonder if we should take the Bible literally. Skeptics often disregard the entire Bible because of these stories, and ignore the less sensational parts that read as plainly as the morning newspaper. Mark Twain put it this way: "It ain't those parts of the Bible that I can't understand that bother me, it is the parts that I do understand."

But should we view these stories as symbolic fables? Are they allegorical myths like Paul Bunyan, or fairy tales like Cinderella? Or do they describe actual events that happened to real people in real places throughout history? The Bible was written over 1,500 years by forty different authors. Christians believe God "inspired" these writers to communicate His truths, but they each wrote in their own unique style.

Some readers view these stories as fantasy, yet other people believe them to be completely true. The same people who consider the Bible to be a fairy tale are also likely to disregard its moral teachings and lifestyle guidelines. Does the Bible itself give us any help on whether or not it should be taken literally?

---

1. Why would God be concerned that the Scriptures be understood properly? It's because the Bible is inspired by God, and is how He reveals Himself to mankind. It also contains warnings to guard us from destructive behaviors. If we disregard His words because of a wrong interpretation, we'll miss out on what He wants us to know.

"All Scripture is inspired by God and profitable for teaching, for reproof, for correction, for training in righteousness; that the man of God may be adequate, equipped for every good work." *2 Timothy 3:16,17*

"For this reason we also constantly thank God that when you received the word of God which you heard from us, you accepted it not as the word of men, but for what it really is, the word of God, which also performs its work in you who believe." *1 Thessalonians 2:13*

"But know this first of all, that no prophecy of Scripture is a matter of one's own interpretation, for no prophecy was ever made by an act of human will, but men moved by the Holy Spirit spoke from God." *2 Peter 1:20,21*

2. In Hamlet's soliloquy, Shakespeare mentioned, "The slings and arrows of outrageous fortune." This is a figure of speech for dramatic or poetic effect, and the Bible also contains many figures of speech for the same reasons.

- "Let the rivers clap their hands, let the mountains sing together for joy." *Psalm 98:8 (Here, the psalmist is simply saying that nature itself reflects the glory of God.)*

- "I am the door; if anyone enters through Me, he will be saved, and will go in and out and find pasture." *John 10:9 (Here, Jesus was not claiming to be a literal wooden door, but that through Him we have access to God.)*

- "If your right eye makes you stumble, tear it out and throw it from you; for it is better for you to lose one of the parts of your body, than for your whole body to be thrown into hell. *Matthew 5:29 (Here, Jesus was telling His listeners to take sin seriously, and He used exaggeration to stress the importance of taking earnest measures to restructure their lifestyles to avoid the destructive consequences of sin.)*

- "Thus the heavens and the earth were completed, and all their hosts. By the seventh day God completed His work which He had done, and He rested on the seventh day from all His work which He had done." *Genesis 2:1,2 (As for the creation of the world in seven days, there is debate among Hebrew scholars whether the word "yom," which means "day," should be taken as a literal 24 hour period, or as an extended period of time. Either interpretation makes it clear that it was God who was doing the creating, and nothing came into being apart from Him.)*

3. Even Jesus' own disciples were occasionally confused whether He was using a figure or speech or speaking plainly.

"This figure of speech Jesus spoke to them, but they did not understand what those things were which He had been saying to them." *John 10:6*

"'I came forth from the Father and have come into the world; I am leaving the world again and going to the Father.' His disciples said, 'Lo, now You are speaking plainly and are not using a figure of speech.'" *John 16:28,29*

4. **The Bible is not just a collection of wise sayings. It describes real events that happened to real people in real places. Unlike stories from Greek mythology, the Bible gives names of real cities, and what ruler was in power at the time of various events. This shows that the events described are meant to be taken literally. Time and again, archeology has proven these locations and timeframes to be geographically and historically accurate. Here's an example:**

"Now in those days a decree went out from Caesar Augustus, that a census be taken of all the inhabited earth. This was the first census taken while Quirinius was governor of Syria. And everyone was on his way to register for the census, each to his own city. Joseph also went up from Galilee, from the city of Nazareth, to Judea, to the city of David which is called Bethlehem, because he was of the house and family of David, in order to register along with Mary, who was engaged to him, and was with child." *Luke 2:1-5*

(Christ's parables rarely mention character's names and never mention cities because they are clearly fictional stories meant to bring a truth to life. But stories of His miracles do mention names and places, so they should be taken literally.)

5. **Were the sensational stories from the Old Testament mere allegories or myths? Some people have said the Bible only makes sense if we don't take it literally. But the world's foremost authority on the Old Testament was Jesus Christ, and He considered those stories to be completely true. According to Jesus, the only way the Bible can make sense is if we do take it literally. He talked about those sensational stories – such as Noah's ark, fire and brimstone on Sodom and Gomorrah, the burning bush, and Jonah and the whale – as being every bit as factual as events in His own life.**

"And just as it happened in the days of Noah, so it will be also in the days of the Son of Man: they were eating, they were drinking, they were marrying, they were being given in marriage, until the day that Noah entered the ark, and the flood came and destroyed them all. It was the same as happened in the days of Lot: they were eating, they were drinking, they were buying, they were selling, they were planting, they were building; but on the day that Lot went out from Sodom it rained fire and brimstone from heaven and destroyed them all. It will be just the same on the day that the Son of Man is revealed." *Luke 17:26-30*

"Then some of the scribes and Pharisees said to Him, 'Teacher, we want to see a sign from You.' But He answered and said to them, 'An evil and adulterous generation craves for a sign; and yet no sign will be given to it but the sign of Jonah the prophet; for just as Jonah was three days and three nights in the belly of the sea monster, so will the Son of Man be three days and three nights in the heart of the earth. The men of Nineveh will stand up with this generation at the judgment, and will condemn it because they repented at the preaching of Jonah; and behold, something greater than Jonah is here." *Matthew 12:38-41*

6. **Even if you can't bring yourself to believe the Bible's more sensational stories, and only see them as allegories or metaphors, read them anyway and apply the truths that are taught. Once you apply the truths that are revealed, God will reveal more truth. But if you disregard obeying the truths you learn, don't expect further enlightenment to come. If the Scriptures seem impossible to believe or understand, it's likey because of something you refuse to obey.**

"Jesus said to the people who believed in him, 'You are truly my disciples if you keep obeying my teachings. And you will know the truth, and the truth will set you free.'" *John 8:31.32 (NLT)*

"But people who aren't Christians can't understand these truths from God's Spirit. It all sounds foolish to them because only those who have the Spirit can understand what the Spirit means. We who have the Spirit understand these things, but others can't understand us at all." *1 Corinthians 2:14,15 (NLT)*

7. **Just like Jesus, we should take the literal parts of the Bible literally, and the figurative parts figuratively. We use our common sense and language skills to shed light on difficult passages, and ask God for wisdom and understanding. God wants us to understand the Bible because it is His love letter to a fallen world. We are all separated from God because of our sin. That is why God paid for our sins by literally giving His life to demonstrate His love for us.**

"But God demonstrates His own love for us in that while we were yet sinners Christ died for us." *Romans 5:8*

"For the wages of sin is death, but the free gift of God is eternal life in Christ Jesus our Lord." *Romans 6:23*

73 Can Those Who Never Hear Of Christ Be Saved?

God's Word tells us that all who trust in Christ will be saved. But there are people in remote parts of the world who live their whole lives and never hear of Christ. Then again, there were people who never heard of Christ because they lived prior to His birth. So can those who never hear of Christ be saved? The question behind this question is: "Is God truly loving and merciful?" Some people feel God appears cruel and unmerciful by condemning people for not believing something they never had the chance to hear. Surely if God loves us, He would want everyone to be saved, and would provide a way to communicate to all people so they could decide for themselves whether or not to trust in Him.

The salvation of those who haven't heard the gospel is a deep concern for Christians. And the Scriptures tell us their salvation is also a deep concern to God as well.

---

1. God has revealed Himself to mankind through four main sources:

- Through Jesus Christ. *John 1:1-14, John 14:8,9, Colossians 1:15, Hebrews 1:1-3*
- Through the Scriptures. *Isaiah 55:10,11, 2 Timothy 3:16,17*
- Through His followers. *Matthew 28:19,20, Acts 1:8, 2 Corinthians 5:18*
- Through nature, which provides evidence of God's existence. *Psalm 8:1-9, Psalm 19:1-4, Acts 14:16,17, Romans 1:20*

2. Throughout the history of mankind, people from all over the world have had at least one of these four sources – nature – to lead them to place their trust in the Creator.

"The heavens tell of the glory of God. The skies display his marvelous craftsmanship. Day after day they continue to speak; night after night they make him known.... They speak without a sound or a word; their voice is silent in the skies; yet their message has gone out to all the earth, and their words to all the world." *Psalm 19:1,2,4a (NLT)*

"From the time the world was created, people have seen the earth and sky and all that God made. They can clearly see his invisible qualities – his eternal power and divine nature. So they have no excuse whatsoever for not knowing God." *Romans 1:20 (NLT)*

"And in the generations gone by He permitted all the nations to go their own ways; and yet He did not leave Himself without witness, in that He did good and gave you rains from heaven and fruitful seasons." *Acts 14:16,17*

"And they who dwell in the ends of the earth stand in awe of Your signs; You make the dawn and the sunset shout for joy." *Psalm 65:8*

"'Whoever will call upon the name of the Lord will be saved.' How then shall they call upon Him in whom they have not believed? And how shall they believe in Him whom they have not heard? ...But I say, surely they have never heard, have they? Indeed they have: 'Their voice has gone out into all the earth, and their words to the ends of the world.'" *Romans 10:13-14,17,18*

3. God has promised to draw men to Him, and if we seek Him, He will let us find Him. Then it's up to us to either believe in Him, ignore Him, or reject Him.

"The God who made the world and all things in it made from one, every nation of mankind to live on all the face of the earth... that they should seek God, if perhaps they might grope for Him and find Him, though He is not far from each one of us." *Acts 17:24,26,27*

"And you will seek Me and find Me, when you search for Me with all your heart." *Jeremiah 29:13*

4. Abram (later known as Abraham) is a good example of someone who never heard of Jesus Christ. He lived before the Bible was written, before Israel became a nation, and before the Law was given to the Jews. But how are we told he was saved? Not by good works, but by simply trusting in God! Most people know John 3:16 (the New Testament verse that explains the gospel in the simplest terms). But do you know the "John 3:16" of the Old Testament? It's a verse repeated in Romans, Galatians, and James to help explain the salvation process. It describes when Abram looked up at the stars and put his faith in God.

"Then the Lord brought Abram outside beneath the night sky and told him, 'Look up into the heavens and count the stars if you can. Your descendants will be like that – too many to count!' And Abram believed the Lord, and the Lord declared him righteous because of his faith." *Genesis 15:5,6 (NLT)*

"What shall we say that Abraham, our forefather, discovered in this matter? If, in fact, Abraham was justified by works, he had something to boast about – but not before God. What does the Scripture say? 'Abraham believed God, and it was credited to him as righteousness.'" *Romans 4:1-3 (NIV)*

5. **Abraham was saved by trusting God to provide salvation, rather than by trusting in his own good deeds. This is the same way we are saved today, by placing our faith in Christ who paid for our sins with His death, and who was fully God and fully man. He paid the penalty for all the sins of mankind, so that people from every tribe, tongue, people, and nation throughout history could have the opportunity to be saved, which is God's desire.**

"For You (Jesus) were slain, and purchased for God with Your blood men from every tribe and tongue and people and nation." *Revelation 5:9*

"This is good and acceptable in the sight of God our Savior, who desires all men to be saved and to come to the knowledge of the truth. For there is one God, and one mediator also between God and men, the man Christ Jesus, who gave Himself as a ransom for all, the testimony given at the proper time." *1 Timothy 2:3-6*

6. **Before Christ came, God's followers trusted in a Messiah who had not yet come to pay for their sins. Today we trust in a Messiah who has already come to pay for our sins. But we are all trusting in the same Messiah.**

"For there is salvation in no one else; for there is no other name under heaven that has been given among men, by which we must be saved." *Acts 4:12*

7. **Can we know exactly how God will judge those who were never able to hear of Christ? We do know that we will be judged by our individual response to what has been revealed to us. We will each be judged according to what we believe, what we do, what we know, and probably for what we could have known if we had sought for it; but we will not be judged for what we couldn't possibly know. Thankfully, God judges righteously and fairly.**

"Salvation and glory and power belong to our God; because His judgments are true and righteous." *Revelation 19:2*

"If you sin without knowing what you're doing, God takes that into account. But if you sin knowing full well what you're doing, that's a different story entirely." *Romans 2:12 (The Message)*

"The secret things belong to the Lord, but the things revealed belong to us and to our sons forever, that we may observe all the words of this law." *Deuteronomy 29:29*

8. **Even though someone who never hears of Christ can be saved, it does not excuse Christians from the command to spread the gospel throughout the world. God often reveals Himself to those who are seeking Him by sending His followers to them.**

"Go therefore and make disciples of all the nations, baptizing them in the name of the Father and the Son and the Holy Spirit." *Matthew 28:19*

"You shall be My witnesses both in Jerusalem, and in all Judea and Samaria, and even to the remotest part of the earth." *Acts 1:8*

9. **There are some things we cannot know for certain. But we do know for certain from Scripture that God loves us enough to pay the penalty for our sins by dying on a cross. People (such as yourself) who have heard this gospel message of God's gracious offer of forgiveness will be held accountable for your response to the truth you have been told. Today would be a great day to put your faith in Christ.**

"For God so loved the world, that He gave His only begotten Son, that whoever believes in Him shall not perish, but have everlasting life." *John 3:16*

"Jesus said to him, 'I am the way, and the truth, and the life; no one comes to the Father, but through Me.'" *John 14:6*

"But God demonstrates His own love toward us, in that while we were yet sinners, Christ died for us." *Romans 5:8*

74 If God Is Loving, Why Would He Send Someone To Hell?

The world often views Christians as the people who tell everybody they are going to hell. But we'd much rather be seen as the people who tell everybody how they can go to heaven and avoid going to hell.

Many religions believe humans have souls that live on after the body dies, and the Bible teaches this also. But many people prefer to believe hell does not exist. However, Christians believe the Bible, and references to hell are found throughout Scripture. In fact, no one spoke more about hell than Jesus Christ Himself. Perhaps one reason Jesus was willing to personally pay the price for our sins, and make it possible for us to go to heaven, was because He knew how awful hell really is.

In Matthew 25:41, Jesus referred to "the eternal fire which has been prepared for the devil and his angels." He spoke often of this place of continual fire, using the word "gehenna," which was an area outside the wall of Jerusalem where a constant fire consumed the city's garbage and the corpses of those who had no family to bury them. This description provided an extremely graphic image that was easy for people who lived in that area to understand.

Jesus also referred to hell as a place of darkness, where there would be much "weeping and gnashing of teeth." (Mathew 8:12, 22:13) This simply means that hell will be extremely lonely, as well as a place of terrible punishment and unending grief for those unfortunate enough to go there.

The thought of anyone going to hell is very disturbing, but the Bible makes it clear that hell is very real. Fortunately, the Bible also tells us how we can go to heaven and avoid going to hell.

---

1. What is hell? It is the final and eternal destination of unrighteous humans and rebellious angels.

"And all the nations will be gathered before Him (Jesus); and He will separate them from one another, as the shepherd separates the sheep from the goats; and He will put the sheep on His right, and the goats on the left. Then the King will say to those on His right, 'Come you who are blessed of My Father, inherit the kingdom prepared for you from the foundation of the world.' ...Then He will say to those on His left, 'Depart from Me, accursed ones, into the eternal fire which has been prepared for the devil and his angels.'" *Matthew 25:32,33,41*

2. Where is hell? The Bible never tells us specifically where hell is, or for that matter where heaven is. All we know for sure is that hell is a place away from the presence of God. The Bible describes hell as being "under the earth." This simply means that it is a much less desirable place to be than the earth, just as heaven is higher, or a more desirable place to be. We do know that those in hell will never be allowed into God's presence.

"At the name of Jesus ever knee should bow, of those who are in heaven, and on earth, and under the earth, and that every tongue should confess that Jesus Christ is Lord, to the glory of God the Father." *Philippians 2:10,11*

3. Why would a person's soul go to hell instead of heaven? It's because our sin separates us from God. All of us are guilty of sin, and God does not tolerate anything in His permanent presence except holiness. Because of God's perfect standards, even one sin is enough to keep us away from God's presence.

"For all have sinned and fall short of the glory of God." *Romans 3:23*

"But your iniquities have made a separation between you and your God, and your sins have hid His face from you, so that He does not hear." *Isaiah 59:2*

"Whoever keeps the whole law and yet stumbles in one point, he has become guilty of all." *James 2:10*

4. How can we become holy and therefore be allowed into God's presence? The only way is because God Himself, in the person of Jesus Christ, paid the penalty for our sins by giving His own life as our substitute.

"Jesus said to him, 'I am the way, and the truth, and the life; no one comes to the Father, but through Me.'" *John 14:6*

"For there is salvation in no one else; for there is no other name under heaven that has been given among men, by which we must be saved." *Acts 4:12*

5. **Why is Christ the only One qualified to pay for our sins? Because He is fully God and fully man, and He lived a sinless life. As the only perfect human, He is the only perfect payment for our sins because He meets God's perfect standard of absolute holiness.**

"And you know that He appeared in order to take away sins; and in Him there is no sin." *1 John 3:5*

"He (God the Father) made Him (Jesus) who knew no sin to be sin on our behalf, that we might become the righteousness of God in Him." *2 Corinthians 5:21*

"The wages of sin is death, but the free gift of God is eternal life in Christ Jesus our Lord." *Romans 6:23*

"For in Him all the fulness of Deity dwells in bodily form." *Colossians 2:9*

6. **Just as those in hell are separated from God because of sin, Jesus was temporarily separated from God the Father while on the cross. This was because He had taken on the world's sins and was no longer holy. He quoted a passage from Psalm 22 as an expression of His agony from being separated from the Father.**

"Now from the sixth hour (noon) darkness fell upon all the land until the ninth hour (3 p.m.). And about the ninth hour Jesus cried out with a loud voice saying, '...My God, My God, why have You forsaken Me?'" *Matthew 27:45,46*

7. **If God is loving, why would He send someone to hell? Actually, the decision of whether or not to go to hell is made by us, not God. He does not want anyone to go to hell. We choose hell when we choose sin over obedience, disbelief over belief, false beliefs over true beliefs, or when we pridefully choose to try to reach God by our own works rather than trusting in Christ's payment for sin. God gives us freedom of choice, but not freedom of consequences. Fortunately, God loves us so much that He has provided a way for us to escape the punishment of hell. He sent His Son Jesus who died to take our punishment and make it possible for us to go to heaven.**

"This is good and acceptable in the sight of God our Savior, who desires all men to be saved and to come to the knowledge of the truth. For there is one God, and one mediator also between God and men, the man Christ Jesus, who gave Himself as a ransom for all." *1 Timothy 2:3-6a*

"The Lord is not slow about His promise, as some count slowness, but is patient toward you, not wishing for any to perish but for all to come to repentance." *2 Peter 3:9*

"God demonstrates His own love for us in that while we were yet sinners Christ died for us." *Romans 5:8*

"For God so loved the world, that He gave His only begotten Son, that whoever believes in Him shall not perish, but have everlasting life. For God did not send the Son into the world to judge the world; but that the world should be saved through Him." *John 3:16,17*

"There is therefore now no condemnation for those who are in Christ Jesus." *Romans 8:1*

8. **We don't escape hell because we do good works. Our good works cannot blot out our sin. Salvation is a free, undeserved gift that comes only through faith in Christ.**

"For by grace you have been saved through faith; and that not from yourselves, it is the gift of God, not as a result of works, that no one should boast." *Ephesians 2:8,9*

9. **How can you escape going to hell by having Christ's payment apply to you? Simple! Confess your sins to God and trust fully in Christ's sacrificial death as the only payment your sins.**

"If we say that we have no sin, we are deceiving ourselves, and the truth is not in us. If we confess our sins, He is faithful and righteous to forgive us our sins and to cleanse us from all unrighteousness." *1 John 1:8,9*

"Therefore they said to Him, 'What shall we do, so that we may work the works of God?' Jesus answered and said to them, 'This is the work of God, that you believe in Him whom He has sent.'" *John 6:28,29*

"These things I have written to you who believe in the name of the Son of God, so that you may know that you have eternal life." *1 John 5:13*

75 Are Some Sins Too Terrible For God To Forgive?

Every human being is a sinner, and any sin is enough to separate us from our holy God. But people who have committed particularly heinous sins sometimes live in fear that their sins are beyond forgiveness. Are sins which qualify as atrocities – such as murder, torture, rape, war crimes, child abuse, adultery, and so on – so terrible that God refuses to forgive them?

1. **Even people guilty of horrible sins can be forgiven and go to heaven. Some of the most famous men in the Bible – even men God used to help write the Bible – were guilty of terrible sins, including murder.**

    - Moses killed an Egyptian guard, fled for his life, and spent the next forty years in exile.
    - David had Uriah killed (the husband of Bathsheba) so that he could marry her and cover up his adultery.
    - Paul (also known as Saul) helped lead the stoning death of the first Christian martyr, Stephen.

2. **The only way any sin is forgiven is by the payment Christ provided by dying on the cross. While on the cross, all our sins – past, present, and future – were placed onto Christ who paid the penalty our sin requires. When we confess our sins and trust in Christ, we are forgiven and made as righteous as Christ is in God's eyes.**

    "If we say we have no sin, we are only fooling ourselves and refusing to accept the truth. But if we confess our sins to him, he is faithful and just to forgive us and to cleanse us from every wrong. If we claim we have not sinned, we are calling God a liar and showing that his word has no place in our hearts. My dear children, I am writing this to you so that you will not sin. But if you do sin, there is someone to plead for you before the Father. He is Jesus Christ, the one who pleases God completely. He is the sacrifice for our sins. He takes away not only our sins but the sins of all the world." *1 John 1:8 – 2:2 (NLT)*

    "Therefore there is now no condemnation for those who are in Christ Jesus." *Romans 8:1*

3. **A sin might receive the death penalty on earth, but it can still be forgiven by God.**

    "One of the criminals who were hanged there was hurling abuse at Him, saying, 'Are You not the Christ? Save Yourself and us!' But the other answered, and rebuking him said, 'Do you not even fear God, since you are under the same sentence of condemnation? And we indeed are suffering justly, for we are receiving what we deserve for our deeds; but this man has done nothing wrong.' And he was saying, 'Jesus, remember me when You come in Your kingdom!' And He said to him, 'Truly I say to you, today you shall be with Me in Paradise.'" *Luke 23:39-43*

    "The scribes and the Pharisees brought a woman caught in adultery, and having set her in the center of the court, they said to Him, 'Teacher, this woman has been caught in adultery, in the very act. Now in the Law Moses commanded us to stone such women; what then do You say?' They were saying this, testing Him, so that they might have grounds for accusing Him. But Jesus stooped down and with His finger wrote on the ground. But when they persisted in asking Him, He straightened up, and said to them, 'He who is without sin among you, let him be the first to throw a stone at her.' Again He stooped down and wrote on the ground. When they heard it, they began to go out one by one, beginning with the older ones, and He was left alone, and the woman, where she was, in the center of the court. Straightening up, Jesus said to her, 'Woman, where are they? Did no one condemn you?' She said, 'No one, Lord.' And Jesus said, 'I do not condemn you, either. Go. From now on sin no more.'" *John 8:3-11*

4. **The only sin described in the Bible as being unforgiveable is "blasphemy against the Holy Spirit" (found in Mark 3:22-30). One of the Holy Spirit's roles is to convict us of sin and point us to our need for forgiveness through Christ. Put simply, "blasphemy against the Holy Spirit" is permanently rejecting the Holy Spirit's conviction to repent from our sins. If we never seek forgiveness of sins, or ignore Christ's sacrifice, naturally our sins go unforgiven. Anyone who seeks forgiveness through Christ is obviously not guilty of this sin.**

    And He (the Holy Spirit), when He comes, will convict the world concerning sin and righteousness and judgment; concerning sin, because they do not believe in Me; and concerning righteousness, because I go to the Father and you no longer see Me; and concerning judgment, because the ruler of this world has been judged." *John 16:8-11*

    "Dear friends, if we deliberately continue sinning after we have received a full knowledge of the truth, there is no other sacrifice that will cover these sins. There will be nothing to look forward to but the terrible expectation of

God's judgment and the raging fire that will consume his enemies. Anyone who refused to obey the law of Moses was put to death without mercy on the testimony of two or three witnesses. Think how much more terrible the punishment will be for those who have trampled on the Son of God and have treated the blood of the covenant as if it were common and unholy. Such people have insulted and enraged the Holy Spirit who brings God's mercy to his people. For we know the one who said, 'I will take vengeance. I will repay those who deserve it.' He also said, 'The Lord will judge his own people.' It is a terrible thing to fall into the hands of the living God." *Hebrews 10:26-31 (NLT)*

5. **Some people mistakenly think they aren't good enough to even become a Christian, or that they have to improve themselves before God will accept them and grant them forgiveness. But without God indwelling us, we'll never have the power to change. The power to overcome sinful habits only comes once we invite Christ into our lives.**

"I know I am rotten through and through so far as my old sinful nature is concerned. No matter which way I turn, I can't make myself do right. I want to, but I can't. When I want to do good, I don't. And when I try not to do wrong, I do it anyway. But if I am doing what I don't want to do, I am not really the one doing it; the sin within me is doing it. It seems to be a fact of life that when I want to do what is right, I inevitably do what is wrong. I love God's law with all my heart. But there is another law at work within me that is at war with my mind. This law wins the fight and makes me a slave to the sin that is still within me. Oh, what a miserable person I am! Who will free me from this life that is dominated by sin? Thank God! The answer is in Jesus Christ our Lord." *Romans 7:18-25 (NLT)*

"Therefore if anyone is in Christ, he is a new creature; the old things passed away; behold, new things have come." *2 Corinthians 5:17*

"After you have suffered for a little while, the God of all grace, who called you to His eternal glory in Christ, will Himself perfect, confirm, strengthen and establish you." *1 Peter 5:10*

"Moreover, I will give you a new heart and put a new spirit within you; and I will remove the heart of stone from your flesh and give you a heart of flesh." *Ezekiel 36:26*

6. **Knowing that God forgives us by His grace, we can also forgive ourselves. What is grace? Grace is God's undeserved gift of mercy. We can't earn it! Have you experienced God's grace and forgiveness?**

"For by grace you have been saved through faith; and that not from yourselves, it is the gift of God, not as a result of works, that no one should boast." *Ephesians 2:8,9*

"For the wages of sin is death, but the free gift of God is eternal life in Christ Jesus our Lord." *Romans 6:23*

"He saved us, not on the basis of deeds we have done in righteousness, but according to His mercy, by the washing of regeneration and renewing of the Holy Spirit, whom He poured out upon us richly through Jesus Christ our Savior." *Titus 3:5,6*

"The Lord is compassionate and gracious, slow to anger and abounding in lovingkindness. He will not always strive with us, nor will He keep His anger forever. He has not dealt with us according to our sins, nor rewarded us according to our iniquities. For as high as the heavens are above the earth, so great is His lovingkindness toward those who fear Him. As far as the east is from the west, so far has He removed our transgressions from us. Just as a father has compassion on his children, so the Lord has compassion on those who fear Him." *Psalm 103:8-13*

7. **God loves you just the way you are, and He loves you too much to let you stay just the way you are. Someone who knew the beauty of God's undeserved grace and forgiveness was John Newton, a slave trader. In 1748 he sought forgiveness, became a Christian, and wrote one of Christianity's most beautiful hymns – *Amazing Grace*.**

"I am not what I ought to be, I am not what I want to be, I am not what I hope to be in another world; but still I am not what I once used to be, and by the grace of God I am what I am." *John Newton*

"When we were utterly helpless, Christ came at just the right time and died for us sinners. Now, no one is likely to die for a good person, though someone might be willing to die for a person who is especially good. But God showed his great love for us by sending Christ to die for us while we were still sinners. And since we have been made right in God's sight by the blood of Christ, he will certainly save us from God's judgment." *Romans 5:6-9 (NLT)*

76 Do Good People Go To Hell Just Because They Don't Believe In Jesus?

Many people believe in heaven and hell. But even among those who believe that these places exist, there is great diversity of opinion on how a person ends up in either place. One of the common views concerning a person's worthiness to enter heaven is based on whether their good deeds outweigh their bad deeds. Another view is that as long as they've never committed any truly horrible crimes against their fellow man, their entrance into heaven is secure. Ask a person if he deserves to get into heaven and you'll hear comments such as: "Well, I've never killed anybody, or robbed a bank, so of course I'll get into heaven."

Sometimes people are angered to hear that someone who has committed a horrible crime like murder might be forgiven and end up in heaven, while a man like Mahatma Gandhi who did lots of good deeds might not be in heaven simply because he rejected the gospel message of Christ.

The Bible clearly explains how a person can go to heaven and avoid hell. After all, God is not in the business of sending people to hell; He's in the business of rescuing people from hell. Yet many folks, including churchgoers, are sometimes unclear on what exactly the Bible says about this very important issue. Have you ever thought about what you are trusting in to guarantee your entrance into heaven?

1. **First of all, the Bible makes it clear that God loves all humans, even the worst of sinners. And even though He gives us free will to decide for ourselves, His desire is for everyone to end up in heaven.**

   "This is good and pleases God our Savior, for he wants everyone to be saved and to understand the truth. For there is only one God and one Mediator who can reconcile God and people. He is the man Christ Jesus. He gave his life to purchase freedom for everyone." *1 Timothy 2:3-6a (NLT)*

2. **Even people guilty of horrible sins can go to heaven. Some of the most famous men in the Bible – even men God used to help write the Bible – were guilty of terrible sins, including murder.**

   • Moses killed an Egyptian guard, fled for his life, and spent the next forty years in exile.
   • David had Uriah killed (the husband of Bathsheba) so that he could marry her and cover up his adultery.
   • Paul (also known as Saul) helped lead the stoning death of the first Christian martyr, Stephen.

3. **Why would a person's soul go to hell instead of heaven? It's because our sin separates us from God. All of us are guilty of sin, and even the best people among us are not 100% innocent of sin. God does not tolerate anything in His permanent presence except complete holiness. Because of God's perfect standards, even one sin is enough to keep us away from God's presence in heaven.**

   "Indeed, there is not a righteous man on earth who continually does good and who never sins." *Ecclesiastes 7:20*

   "As it is written, 'There is none righteous, not even one.'" *Romans 3:10*

   "For all have sinned and fall short of the glory of God." *Romans 3:23*

   "But your iniquities have made a separation between you and your God, and your sins have hid His face from you, so that He does not hear." *Isaiah 59:2*

   "For all of us have become like one who is unclean, and all our righteous deeds are like a filthy garment; and all of us wither like a leaf, and our iniquities, like the wind, take us away." *Isaiah 64:6*

4. **Think of the most righteous person you know. Now think of the most evil person you know. According to the Bible, one sin is enough to put them both into the same category of being separated from God, so they are both in equal need of a Savior.**

   "Whoever keeps the whole law and yet stumbles in one point, he has become guilty of all." *James 2:10*

5. **Jesus taught that many people – even the highly religious ones – would be in for a shock when they find out that the good deeds they were trusting in won't get them into heaven.**

"Not everyone who says to Me, 'Lord, Lord,' will enter the kingdom of heaven, but he who does the will of My Father who is in heaven will enter. Many will say to Me on that day, 'Lord, Lord, did we not prophesy in Your name, and in Your name cast out demons, and in Your name perform many miracles?' And then I will declare to them, 'I never knew you; depart from Me, you who practice lawlessness.'" *Matthew 7:21-23*

6. Other religions basically teach that we reach God by being good, or by achieving enlightenment, or if we keep improving ourselves through reincarnation until we get it right. That is where Christianity is unique. The Bible teaches that we can't reach God by being good because we have to be perfectly holy to reach God – and none of us are. God has the highest possible standards for who can be allowed into heaven, and since none of us reach that perfect standard, God provided a way to make us holy and perfect. God reached down to us by coming to earth in human form as Jesus Christ, who paid the penalty for our sins by dying in our place. Our sins are placed onto Christ, and His righteousness is placed onto us.

"For God made Christ, who never sinned, to be the offering for our sin, so that we could be made right with God through Christ." *2 Corinthians 5:21 (NLT)*

"For while we were still helpless, at the right time Christ died for the ungodly. For one will hardly die for a righteous man; though perhaps for the good man someone would dare even to die. But God demonstrates His own love toward us, in that while we were yet sinners, Christ died for us. Much more then, having now been justified by His blood, we shall be saved from the wrath of God through Him." *Romans 5:6-9*

"Jesus said to him, 'I am the way, and the truth, and the life; no one comes to the Father, but through Me.'" *John 14:6*

Imagine if all the founders of all the world's religions were on the bank of a lake, and you were way offshore drowning. Mohammed, Buddha, Confucius, Joseph Smith, L. Ron Hubbard, and all the others would be shouting instructions on how you could to swim to shore and save yourself. But Jesus would be different. He would dive in, swim out to you, and offer to bring you back to shore. If you accept His offer, you would be rescued. That is what makes Jesus and His teachings unique among other religious founders. He has done the work for us!

7. According to the Bible, salvation is not something we achieve, it's something we receive.

"For the wages of sin is death, but the free gift of God is eternal life in Christ Jesus our Lord." *Romans 6:23*

"He saved us, not on the basis of deeds we have done in righteousness, but according to His mercy, by the washing of regeneration and renewing of the Holy Spirit, whom He poured out upon us richly through Jesus Christ our Savior." *Titus 3:5-6*

"For by grace you have been saved through faith; and that not from yourselves, it is the gift of God, not as a result of works, that no one should boast." *Ephesians 2:8,9*

"But to all who believed him and accepted him, he gave the right to become children of God." *John 1:12 (NLT)*

8. How can you escape going to hell by having Christ's payment apply to you? Simple! Confess your sins and invite Jesus into your life as your Savior.

"If we say that we have no sin, we are deceiving ourselves, and the truth is not in us. If we confess our sins, He is faithful and righteous to forgive us our sins and to cleanse us from all unrighteousness." *1 John 1:8,9*

"Behold, I stand at the door and knock; if any one hears My voice and opens the door, I will come in to him." *Revelation 3:20*

"Then they asked him, 'What must we do to do the works God requires?' Jesus answered, 'The work of God is this: to believe in the one he has sent.'" *John 6:28,29 (NIV)*

"'Sirs, what must I do to be saved?' And they said, 'Believe in the Lord Jesus, and you shall be saved.'" *Acts 16:30,31*

"And there is salvation in no one else; for there is no other name under heaven that has been given among men by which we must be saved." *Acts 4:12*

77 Are Good Works Necessary For Salvation?

If you were to die tonight, and you stood before the throne of God, and He asked you why He should let you into heaven, what would you say?

People often assume their entrance into heaven will be determined on the basis of how holy they've been while they were living, how many good deeds they did, or by how well they obeyed the Ten Commandments. Some people envision a system of evaluation where their good deeds are placed in one side of a scale and their bad deeds on the other side, and if the good outweighs the bad then they are allowed into heaven. The problem is, what if we do 10,000 good works in a lifetime and then find out after death that it takes 10,001 to get into heaven? How can we know with certainty that we are saved?

The Bible says a great deal about the importance of doing good works. It also explains very clearly how to be certain we are going to heaven. But surprisingly, the Bible tells us that our good works are not what get us into heaven.

1. **Many who have trusted in their good works will someday stand before the Lord and find out that their good deeds will not get them into heaven.**

   "Many will say to Me on that day, 'Lord, Lord, did we not prophesy in Your name, and in Your name cast out demons, and in Your name perform many miracles?' And then I will declare to them, 'I never knew you; depart from Me, you who practice lawlessness.'" *Matthew 7:22,23*

2. **We are commanded to do righteous deeds. But what do all our righteous deeds amount to when it relates to getting us into heaven?**

   "For all of us have become like one who is unclean, and all our righteous deeds are like a filthy garment; and all of us wither like a leaf, and our iniquities, like the wind, take us away." *Isaiah 64:6*

3. **God won't allow unholiness in heaven. How many sins does it take to be kept out of heaven? Only one.**

   "For whoever keeps the whole law and yet stumbles at one point shall be guilty of all." *James 2:10*

   "For all have sinned and fall short of the glory of God." *Romans 3:23*

4. **If all of us are sinners, then how can we obtain salvation and be allowed into heaven? Salvation is a free gift, but it's only free to us. God sent His Son Jesus to sacrifice His own sinless life as the payment for our sins.**

   "God demonstrates His own love for us in that while we were yet sinners Christ died for us." *Romans 5:8*

   "The wages of sin is death, but the free gift of God is eternal life in Christ Jesus our Lord." *Romans 6:23*

   "For God so loved the world, that He gave His only begotten Son, that whoever believes in Him shall not perish, but have everlasting life." *John 3:16*

5. **When we trust Christ as Savior, our sins are placed onto Him and His holiness is placed onto us.**

   "He (God the Father) made Him (Jesus) who knew no sin to be sin on our behalf, that we might become the righteousness of God in Him." *2 Corinthians 5:21*

6. **Obtaining salvation is not based on our good works, but only on faith in Christ.**

   "He saved us, not on the basis of deeds we have done in righteousness, but according to His mercy, by the washing of regeneration and renewing of the Holy Spirit, whom He poured out upon us richly through Jesus Christ our Savior." *Titus 3:5-6*

   "For there is one God, and one mediator also between God and men, the man Christ Jesus, who gave Himself as a ransom for all." *1 Timothy 2:5,6a*

"Jesus said to him, 'I am the way, and the truth, and the life; no one comes to the Father, but through Me.'" *John 14:6*

7. We can know for certain we are saved because our salvation depends on what Christ has already done. Knowing that our salvation comes from God's grace instead of from our good deeds brings us great peace and reassurance.

"These things I have written to you who believe in the name of the Son of God, in order that you may know that you have eternal life." *1 John 5:13*

"For this reason it is by faith, that it might be in accordance with grace, in order that the promise may be certain to all the descendants." *Romans 4:16*

8. We are not saved as a result of good works. We are saved, and good works are the result.

"For by grace you have been saved through faith; and that not from yourselves, it is the gift of God, not as a result of works, that no one should boast. For we are His workmanship, created in Christ Jesus for good works, which God prepared beforehand, that we should walk in them." *Ephesians 2:8-10*

"...our great God and Savior, Christ Jesus; who gave Himself for us, that He might redeem us from every lawless deed and purify for Himself a people for His own possession, zealous for good deeds." *Titus 2:13,14*

9. Even though good works don't save us, there are many reasons why we should do them.

- As nonbelievers observe our good works, it can lead them to want to know the Lord. *1 Peter 2:12, 1 Peter 3:15,16*
- Our good works prove to others that we are Christians. *John 13:35, 1 Timothy 4:12, James 2:18*
- Our good works bring glory to God. *1 Corinthians 10:31*
- Good works done on behalf of others is like doing them for God. *Matthew 25:34-40*
- We are commanded to do good works. *Matthew 7:12*
- Our good works bring pleasure to God. *Proverbs 12:22, Matthew 25:14-23, Hebrews 13:16*
- Our good works can help relieve the suffering of others. *2 Corinthians 1:3,4*
- Even though good works won't get us into heaven, we will be individually rewarded for our good works once we are allowed into heaven. *Matthew 19:21, Luke 14:13,14, 1 Corinthians 3:10-15*
- God has prepared our good works beforehand and expects us to do them. *Ephesians 2:10*
- Our good works help young believers grow in their faith as they observe them. *Philippians 3:17, 1 Corinthians 11:1, 1 Thessalonians 1:5-7, Hebrews 13:7*

10. We obtain salvation by confessing our sins and trusting Christ to be the only payment for our sins.

"If we say that we have no sin, we are deceiving ourselves, and the truth is not in us. If we confess our sins, He is faithful and righteous to forgive us our sins and to cleanse us from all unrighteousness. If we say that we have not sinned, we make Him a liar, and His word is not in us." *1 John 1:8-10*

"If you confess with your mouth Jesus as Lord, and believe in your heart that God raised Him from the dead, you will be saved; for with the heart a person believes, resulting in righteousness, and with the mouth he confesses, resulting in salvation." *Romans 10:9,10*

11. When the thief on the cross put his faith in Christ, he died before he was able to do good works or even be baptized. But Jesus promised he would go to heaven.

"One of the criminals who were hanged there was hurling abuse at Him, saying, 'Are You not the Christ? Save Yourself and us!' But the other answered, and rebuking him said, 'Do you not even fear God, since you are under the same sentence of condemnation? And we indeed are suffering justly, for we are receiving what we deserve for our deeds; but this man has done nothing wrong.' And he was saying, 'Jesus, remember me when You come in Your kingdom!' And He said to him, 'Truly I say to you, today you shall be with Me in Paradise.'" *Luke 23:39-43*

12. You can become a Christian right now! Simply confess your sinful nature and invite Christ into your life!

"Therefore they said to Him, 'What shall we do, so that we may work the works of God?' Jesus answered and said to them, 'This is the work of God, that you believe in Him whom He has sent.'" *John 6:28,29*

78 What Exactly Happens After We Die?

In "Hamlet," Shakespeare eloquently pondered what happens after this life ends. He described death as: "The undiscovered country, from whose bourn no traveler returns, puzzles the will, and makes us rather bear those ills we have than fly to others that we know not of."

We all must face the sobering fact that each one of us will die someday. Can we know what happens next? Many people feel that if we can't know what happens after this life, we should just worry about it when we get there. But the Bible makes it clear that the time to prepare for the next life is during this one.

1. **Our bodies wear out, but our souls will exist forever. The concept of reincarnation is not found in the Bible. It teaches that this life is the only one we have here on earth, and then we stand before God.**

   "It is appointed for men to die once, and after this comes judgment." *Hebrews 9:27*

2. **The Bible describes a future judgment where we all must stand individually before God. Those who have trusted in Christ as their Savior will be allowed into heaven. Those who have rejected Him or who have trusted in their own good deeds to get them into heaven, will not be allowed in. At that time, even Christians and non-Christians will each render account for our deeds and words, as well as the stewardship of our gifts and resources during our time on earth. You could say that Christians are forgiven, yet still accountable.**

   "For we shall all stand before the judgment seat of God. For it is written, 'As I live, says the Lord, every knee shall bow to Me, and every tongue shall give praise to God.' So then each one of us shall give account of himself to God." *Romans 14:10-12*

   "And I saw a great white throne and Him who sat upon it, from whose presence earth and heaven fled away, and no place was found for them. And I saw the dead, the great and the small, standing before the throne, and books were opened; and another book was opened, which is the book of life; and the dead were judged from the things which were written in the books, according to their deeds.... And if anyone's name was not found written in the book of life, he was thrown into the fire." *Revelation 20:11,12,15*

3. **Those who go to heaven will be given a new, resurrected body. This promise takes the sting out of death.**

   "So also is the resurrection of the dead. It is sown a perishable body, it is raised an imperishable body; it is sown in dishonor, it is raised in glory. It is sown in weakness, it is raised in power; it is sown a natural body, it is raised a spiritual body.... But when this perishable will have put on the imperishable, and this mortal will have put on immortality, then will come about the saying that is written, 'Death is swallowed up in victory. O Death, where is your victory? O Death, where is your sting?'" *1 Corinthians 15:42-44, 54*

4. **People often have the idea that we get into heaven if our good deeds outweigh the bad. But the Bible teaches that since God is so holy, even one sin is enough to keep us out of His presence. We can only be made righteous by the forgiveness that comes through Christ. Even religious people who have trusted in their good deeds instead of trusting in what Christ has already done, will be turned away.**

   "For whoever keeps the whole law and yet stumbles in one point, he has become guilty of all." *James 2:10*

   "Not everyone who says to me, 'Lord, Lord,' will enter the kingdom of heaven, but only he who does the will of my Father who is in heaven. Many will say to me on that day, 'Lord, Lord, did we not prophesy in your name, and in your name drive out demons and perform many miracles?' Then I will tell them plainly, 'I never knew you. Away from me, you evildoers!'" *Matthew 7:21-23 (NIV)*

   "This righteousness from God comes through faith in Jesus Christ to all who believe. There is no difference, for all have sinned and fall short of the glory of God, and are justified freely by his grace through the redemption that came by Christ Jesus." *Romans 3:22-24 (NIV)*

5. **God does not desire to send people to hell. He sincerely desires to rescue people from hell! That's why Jesus, who was God in the flesh, died for our sins. God set the highest price to redeem us, then paid it Himself.**

   "But God demonstrates His own love for us in that while we were yet sinners, Christ died for us. Much more then, having now been justified by His blood, we shall be saved from the wrath of God through Him." Romans 5:8,9

"This is good and acceptable in the sight of God our Savior, who desires all men to be saved and come to the knowledge of the truth. For there is one God, and one mediator between God and men, the man Christ Jesus." *1 Timothy 2:3-5*

6. In heaven, we will be rewarded for our good deeds, done with good motives here on earth, and for hardships and persecutions suffered as a result of obeying the Lord.

"And whoever… gives to one of these little ones even a cup of cold water to drink, truly I say to you he shall not lose his reward." *Matthew 10:42*

"Beware of practicing your righteousness before men to be noticed by them; otherwise you have no reward with your Father who is in heaven. When therefore you give alms, do not sound a trumpet before you, as the hypocrites do in the synagogues and in the streets, that they may be honored by men. Truly I say to you, they have their reward in full. But you, when you give alms, do not let your right hand know what your left hand is doing, that your alms may be in secret; and your Father who sees in secret will repay you." *Matthew 6:1-4*

"Blessed are you when men cast insults at you, and persecute you, and say all kinds of evil against you falsely, on account of Me. Rejoice and be glad, for your reward in heaven is great, for so they persecuted the prophets who were before you." *Matthew 5:11,12*

7. We are not saved as a result of good works. We're saved, and good works are the result. All our good deeds will be tested by God, and He will determine whether or not they deserve to be rewarded.

"For no man can lay a foundation other than the one which is laid, which is Jesus Christ. Now if any man builds upon the foundation with gold, silver, precious stones, wood, hay, straw, each man's work will become evident; for the day will show it, because it is to be revealed with fire; and the fire itself will test the quality of each man's work. If any man's work is burned up, he shall suffer loss; but he himself shall be saved, yet so as through fire." *1 Corinthians 3:11-15*

8. Those who reject God's offer of forgiveness and salvation through Christ will not be allowed into heaven. Sadly, they are sent to hell, a place of never ending suffering.

"The Son of Man will send forth His angels, and they will gather out of His kingdom all stumbling blocks, and those who commit lawlessness, and will cast them into the furnace of fire; in that place there shall be weeping and gnashing of teeth." *Matthew 13:41,42*

9. By trusting in Christ, you are destined for heaven, which gives a person great peace.

"Then I saw a new heaven and a new earth; for the first heaven and the first earth passed away, and there is no longer any sea. And I saw the holy city, new Jerusalem, coming down out of heaven from God, made ready as a bride adorned for her husband. And I heard a loud voice from the throne, saying, 'Behold, the tabernacle of God is among men, and He will dwell among them, and they shall be His people, and God Himself will be among them, and He will wipe away every tear from their eyes; and there will no longer be any death; there will no longer be any mourning, or crying, or pain; the first things have passed away.' And He who sits on the throne said, 'Behold, I am making all things new.' And He said, 'Write, for these words are faithful and true.' Then He said to me, 'It is done. I am the Alpha and the Omega, the beginning and the end. I will give to the one who thirsts from the spring of the water of life without cost. He who overcomes will inherit these things, and I will be his God and he will be My son. But for the cowardly and unbelieving and abominable and murderers and immoral persons and sorcerers and idolaters and all liars, their part will be in the lake that burns with fire and brimstone, which is the second death.'" *Revelation 21:1-8*

"Let not your heart be troubled; believe in God, believe also in Me (Jesus). In My Father's house are many dwelling places; if it were not so, I would have told you; for I go to prepare a place for you. And if I go to prepare a place for you, I will come again, and receive you to Myself; that where I am, there you may be also. And you know the way where I am going. Thomas said to Him, 'Lord, we do not know where You are going; how do we know the way?' Jesus said to him, 'I am the way, and the truth, and the life; no one comes to the Father except through Me.'" *John 14:1-6*

79 Do Children Who Die Go To Heaven?

When someone a hundred years old dies from natural causes, it's not unexpected. But when a young child dies for any reason, it's much harder for us to understand, and raises many agonizing questions.

We naturally assume that when an adult dies, their beliefs and/or actions during their lifetime will affect their ability to get into heaven. But many children die before being able to understand the concept of God, the differences in religious beliefs, or even the difference between right and wrong. The question of whether or not children go to heaven is very common, and even though the Bible doesn't give us all the details we would like on this important topic, it does give us enough information to help ease the pain. Thankfully, we can have hope and peace through the comfort of God's promises.

1. The Bible refers to any saved person as a "child of God." Jesus taught that innocent children are an excellent example – in fact the quintessential prototype – of the people who would be allowed into heaven.

"And they were bringing even their babies to Him (Jesus) so that He would touch them, but when the disciples saw it, they began rebuking them. But Jesus called for them, saying, 'Permit the children to come to Me, and do not hinder them, for the kingdom of God belongs to such as these. Truly I say to you, whoever does not receive the kingdom of God like a child will not enter it at all.'" *Luke 18:15-17*

"At that time the disciples came to Jesus and said, 'Who then is greatest in the kingdom of heaven?' And He called a child to Himself and set him before them, and said, 'Truly I say to you, unless you are converted and become like children, you will not enter the kingdom of heaven. Whoever then humbles himself as this child, he is the greatest in the kingdom of heaven.'" *Matthew 18:1-4*

2. King David had a child who died as a baby. David believed that one day they would be reunited.

"Can I bring him back again? I will go to him, but he will not return to me." *2 Samuel 12:23*

3. Apparently, when it comes to how God holds us each accountable for our sin, there is an "age of accountability." It's the time when a child begins to understand right from wrong clearly enough to make a conscious decision to choose obedience or disobedience, or to accept or reject God Himself. That specific time is probably different for every child, so it's impossible to put an exact age on it. Prior to this "age of accountability," it seems God overlooks a child's sin. Paul wrote that at an earlier but unspecified time in his own life, he was "alive" spiritually, but when he became old enough to understand God's commandments he willingly chose to sin and "died" spiritually.

"What shall we say, then? Is the law sin? Certainly not! Indeed I would not have known what sin was except through the law. For I would not have known what coveting really was if the law had not said, 'Do not covet.' But sin, seizing the opportunity afforded by the commandment, produced in me every kind of covetous desire. For apart from law, sin is dead. Once I was alive apart from law; but when the commandment came, sin sprang to life and I died. I found that the very commandment that was intended to bring life actually brought death. For sin, seizing the opportunity afforded by the commandment, deceived me, and through the commandment put me to death." *Romans 7:7-11 (NIV)*

"Therefore, just as sin entered the world through one man, and death through sin, and in this way death came to all men, because all sinned – for before the law was given, sin was in the world. But sin is not taken into account when there is no law. " *Romans 5:12,13 (NIV)*

4. God is faithful to always deal with all people through love, justice, and fairness. If anyone can be trusted to know the right thing to do with the soul of an innocent child, it is God. And He loves every child dearly.

"The Rock! His work is perfect, for all His ways are just; a God of faithfulness and without injustice, righteous and upright is He." *Deuteronomy 32:4*

"Salvation and glory and power belong to our God; because His judgments are true and righteous." *Revelation 19:2*

"And I pray that you, being rooted and established in love, may have power, together with all the saints, to grasp how wide and long and high and deep is the love of Christ, and to know this love that surpasses knowledge – that you may be filled to the measure of all the fullness of God." *Ephesians 3:17-19 (NIV)*

5. **It just doesn't seem right when a child dies; it makes us instinctively realize that the world is not a perfect place, and is far from what it should be. Why is the world filled with sadness, suffering, and death? We have suffering in the world not because God has forsaken mankind, but because mankind has forsaken God. When mankind first chose to sin, it brought the universal curse of sin upon the entire human race, which includes disease, suffering, and physical death. Even though God sometimes allows children to die, it is clearly not part of God's ideal original plan, and serves as a painful reminder to us all that we live in a world damaged by the consequences of sin.**

"So it is not the will of your Father who is in heaven that one of these little ones perish." *Matthew 18:14*

"The wages of sin is death, but the free gift of God is eternal life in Christ Jesus our Lord." *Romans 6:23*

6. **Why do children die? There is God's "perfect will," and God's "permitted will." It was not His perfect will for mankind to reject Him in the first place, but He gave us free will and permitted us to obey Him or rebel. Ultimately, as difficult as it is to comprehend the actions of an infinite, sovereign God from our limited human perspective, God's will is what is. No matter how much we analyze or discuss why a child dies, or how it could be God's will, He knows exactly how long each of us will live – even before we are born.**

"For You formed my inward parts; You wove me in my mother's womb. I will give thanks to You, for I am fearfully and wonderfully made; wonderful are Your works, and my soul knows it very well. My frame was not hidden from You, when I was made in secret, and skillfully wrought in the depths of the earth; your eyes have seen my unformed substance; and in Your book were all written the days that were ordained for me, when as yet there was not one of them." *Psalm 139:13-16*

"Oh, the depth of the riches both of the wisdom and knowledge of God! How unsearchable are His judgments and unfathomable His ways! For who has known the mind of the Lord, or who became His counselor? Or who has first given to Him that it might be paid back to him again? For from Him and through Him and to Him are all things. To Him be the glory forever. Amen." *Romans 11:33-36*

7. **Someday, the universal curse of sin will be reversed. Suffering will cease for all who accept God's gift of forgiveness. He will wipe away every tear and we will live forever in heaven enjoying perfect fellowship with God and our loved ones, never to be plagued by the curse of death again for all of eternity. This hope helps take the sting out of death.**

"But when this perishable will have put on the imperishable, and this mortal will have put on immortality, then will come about the saying that is written, 'Death is swallowed up in victory. O Death, where is your victory? O Death, where is your sting?'" *1 Corinthians 15:54-55*

"Then I saw a new heaven and a new earth; for the first heaven and the first earth passed away, and there is no longer any sea. And I saw the holy city, new Jerusalem, coming down out of heaven from God, made ready as a bride adorned for her husband. And I heard a loud voice from the throne, saying, 'Behold, the tabernacle of God is among men, and He will dwell among them, and they shall be His people, and God Himself will be among them, and He will wipe away every tear from their eyes; and there will no longer be any death; there will no longer be any mourning, or crying, or pain; the first things have passed away.'" *Revelation 21:1-4*

8. **God Himself knows the pain of losing a Son. When Jesus died on the cross it was the ultimate demonstration of how much God loves us. His death shows the cost He was willing to pay to abolish the curse of sin so we could spend eternity in heaven. It's a place of supreme joy, one of which will be our reunion with loved ones. But an even greater joy for those who have trusted Christ will be our reunion with our heavenly Father, God Himself. If you haven't trusted Christ to forgive your sins, now would be the perfect time to place your childlike faith in Him.**

"For God so loved the world that He gave His only begotten Son, that whosoever believes in Him shall not perish, but have everlasting life." *John 3:16*

"God demonstrates His own love toward us in that while we were yet sinners, Christ died for us." *Romans 5:8*

"But as many as received Him, to them He gave the right to become children of God, even to those who believe in His name." *John 1:12*

80 Why Not Worry About The Next Life Once We Get There?

Many people have a very nonchalant attitude about their transition to the next life. Maybe since the next life is so mysterious they can just, "Deal with it once they get there." This relaxed attitude was typified by Mark Twain, who said, "I do not fear death, in view of the fact that I had been dead for billions and billions of years before I was born, and had not suffered the slightest inconvenience from it." In consideration of the mystery surrounding the next life, does it make more sense to prepare for it before we die, or just deal with it when we get there?

1. **There's no debating that each of us will die someday. The debate comes over what happens after that. Is there some kind of god we answer to? The answer would certainly affect how we live this life and prepare for the next. Dostoyevsky's *The Brothers Karamazov* includes the statement: "If God did not exist, all things would be permitted." If this life is all there is, we might as well live it up here and now without concern for the next life. Even the Apostle Paul acknowledged this would be the logical conclusion – IF this life is all there is.**

   "If the dead are not raised, let us eat and drink, for tomorrow we die." *1 Corinthians 15:32*

2. **Many religions teach that we are simply re-incarnated after we die. But the Bible says we only have this one life to get ready for the next one. It gives us many clear warnings that the time to prepare for the next life is before we get there. Leaving this world unprepared for the next would be a huge mistake.**

   "And inasmuch as it is appointed for men to die once and after this comes judgment." *Hebrews 9:27*

   "Remember Him before the silver cord is broken and the golden bowl is crushed, the pitcher by the well is shattered and the wheel at the cistern is crushed; then the dust will return to the earth as it was, and the spirit will return to God who gave it." Ecclesiastes 12:6,7

3. **Uneasiness over facing the reality of death might mean you're unsure of your eternal destiny. But we all must stand before our Maker sooner or later. There's no way to escape it, so we should definitely be ready.**

   "For we shall all stand before the judgment seat of God. For it is written, 'As I live, says the Lord, every knee shall bow to Me, and every tongue shall give praise to God.' So then each one of us shall give account of himself to God." *Romans 14:10-12*

   "And I saw a great white throne and Him who sat upon it, from whose presence earth and heaven fled away, and no place was found for them. And I saw the dead, the great and the small, standing before the throne, and books were opened; and another book was opened, which is the book of life; and the dead were judged from the things which were written in the books, according to their deeds.... And if anyone's name was not found written in the book of life, he was thrown into the fire." *Revelation 20:11,12,15*

4. **Jesus told us there is a way to be at peace with dying.**

   "Let not your heart be troubled; believe in God, believe also in Me. In My Father's house are many dwelling places; if it were not so, I would have told you; for I go to prepare a place for you. And if I go to prepare a place for you, I will come again, and receive you to Myself; that where I am, there you may be also. And you know the way where I am going. Thomas said to Him, 'Lord, we do not know where You are going; how do we know the way?' Jesus said to him, 'I am the way, and the truth, and the life; no one comes to the Father except through Me.'" *John 14:1-6*

5. **If a person believes that our entrance into heaven is based on our good deeds, then that would create a very uncertain fate. What if you do 10,000 good works in your lifetime, then you die and find out the minimum quota was 10,001? But the Bible tells us that our good deeds do nothing to guarantee entrance into heaven.**

   "For all of us have become like one who is unclean, and all our righteous deeds are like a filthy garment; and all of us wither like a leaf, and our iniquities, like the wind, take us away." *Isaiah 64:6*

6. **Our entrance into heaven is based on trusting in Christ's death to pay for our sins. Knowing it is based on what Christ has already done instead of what we do, we can have peace of mind that we are going to heaven.**

"These things I have written to you who believe in the name of the Son of God, so that you may know that you have eternal life." *1 John 5:13*

"For this reason it is by faith, in order that it may be in accordance with grace, so that the promise will be guaranteed to all the descendants, not only to those who are of the Law, but also to those who are of the faith of Abraham, who is the father of us all." *Romans 4:16*

7. The Bible promises the free gift of salvation if we will accept it before we die.

"For the wages of sin is death, but the free gift of God is eternal life in Christ Jesus our Lord." *Romans 6:23*

"For by grace you have been saved through faith; and that not from yourselves, it is the gift of God, not as a result of works, that no one should boast." *Ephesians 2:8,9*

8. Our earthly bodies will perish and decay, but those who go to heaven will be given a new, resurrected body.

"There are heavenly bodies, and there are earthly bodies. But the glory of the heavenly is one, and the glory of the earthly is another.... So also is the resurrection of the dead. It is sown a perishable body, it is raised an imperishable body; it is sown in dishonor, it is raised in glory. It is sown in weakness, it is raised in power; it is sown a natural body, it is raised a spiritual body. If there is a natural body, there is also a spiritual body." *1 Corinthians 15:40,42-44*

9. God requires justice, but does not desire to send people to hell. He desires to rescue people from hell. That is why Christ, who was fully God in the flesh, came to earth and died for our sins. God set the highest possible price to pay for the penalty of our sins, then paid for it Himself.

"This is good and acceptable in the sight of God our Savior, who desires all men to be saved and to come to the knowledge of the truth. For there is one God, and one mediator also between God and men, the man Christ Jesus, who gave Himself as a ransom for all." *1 Timothy 2:3-6a*

"For God so loved the world that He gave His only begotten Son, that whoever believes in Him should not perish, but have eternal life. For God did not send the Son into the world to judge the world, but that the world should be saved through Him." *John 3:16,17*

"But God demonstrates His own love for us in that while we were yet sinners, Christ died for us. Much more then, having now been justified by His blood, we shall be saved from the wrath of God through Him. *Romans 5:8,9*

10. Those whose sins are forgiven will go to heaven and be free from all suffering forever, and they will experience uninterrupted fellowship with God and other believers for all of eternity.

"He shall wipe away every tear from their eyes; and there shall no longer be any death; there shall no longer be any mourning, or crying, or pain; the first things have passed away." *Revelation 21:4*

11. Sadly, those who decide to willfully reject God's offer of salvation through Christ will be sent to a place of never ending suffering. As for those who are aware of God's offer but simply put off deciding, this is a case where not to decide is to decide.

"The Son of Man will send forth His angels, and they will gather out of His kingdom all stumbling blocks, and those who commit lawlessness, and will cast them into the furnace of fire; in that place there shall be weeping and gnashing of teeth." *Matthew 13:41,42*

"But for the cowardly and unbelieving and abominable and murderers and immoral persons and sorcerers and idolaters and all liars, their part will be in the lake that burns with fire and brimstone, which is the second death." *Revelation 21:8*

12. If you've never prepared for the next life by asking Christ to be your Savior, now would be the perfect time.

"As God's partners, we beg you not to reject this marvelous message of God's great kindness. For God says, 'At just the right time, I heard you. On the day of salvation, I helped you.' Indeed, God is ready to help you right now. Today is the day of salvation." *2 Corinthians 6:1,2 (NLT)*

81 Are All Religions Pretty Much The Same?

Have you ever wondered how many religions there are in the entire world? And where did they all come from? Obviously, religion plays a huge role in the lives of billions of people all over the world. People throughout the centuries seem to have an innate sense of wanting to believe in some kind of supreme being (or beings) greater than themselves. Even so, religions come in all varieties. Some believe in one god; others have countless gods. Some religions believe god is good, while others (like Greek mythology) have gods who commit immoralities like rape or murder. With so many differences, it's clear that the religions of the world can't all be true.

Has mankind simply invented all the various religions throughout the centuries as a way to explain those things that are unknowable? And if this is the case, does that mean all religions are basically the same? If the religions of the world are basically the same, is it possible to combine them all together into one huge ecumenical religion? More importantly, if all religions have been created by man, does that mean God is something man has also created? Fortunately, the Bible addresses these questions, and explains why Christianity is unique among all other religions of the world.

1. First of all, we did not create God. He created us.

"Know that the Lord Himself is God; it is He who has made us, and not we ourselves; we are His people and the sheep of His pasture." *Psalm 100:3*

"In the beginning, God created the heavens and the earth." *Genesis 1:1*

2. One belief religions have in common is that a divine being (or beings) created us, and the world we see is not all there is. According to the Bible, God gave us this innate sense that there is more than we can simply see and touch.

"He made from one every nation of mankind to live on all the face of the earth... that they should seek God, if perhaps they might grope for Him and find Him, though He is not far from each one of us." *Acts 17:26,27*

"God has made everything beautiful for its own time. He has planted eternity in the human heart, but even so, people cannot see the whole scope of God's work from beginning to end." *Ecclesiastes 3:11 (NLT)*

3. Other religions teach that we reach God by being good. That is where Christianity is unique. The Bible says that we can reach God only because He reached down to us by coming to earth in the form of a man; Jesus.

"He saved us, not on the basis of deeds we have done in righteousness, but according to His mercy, by the washing of regeneration and renewing of the Holy Spirit, whom He poured out upon us richly through Jesus Christ our Savior." *Titus 3:5-6*

"For by grace you have been saved through faith; and that not from yourselves, it is the gift of God, not as a result of works, that no one should boast." *Ephesians 2:8,9*

Imagine if all the founders of all the world's religions were on the bank of a lake, and you were way offshore drowning. Mohammed, Buddha, Confucius, Joseph Smith, L. Ron Hubbard, and all the others would be shouting instructions on how you could to swim to shore and save yourself. But Jesus would be different. He would dive into the same storm-tossed, polluted sea that you're in, swim out to you, and offer to bring you back to shore. If you accept His offer, you would be rescued and live. That is what makes Jesus and His teachings unique among other religious founders. He has done the work for us!

4. Since Christianity is based on Christ, who exactly was He? The Bible tells us He was fully God and fully man. He has existed for all of eternity, He came to earth and lived a perfectly sinless life, and was therefore the only one qualified to pay the penalty for our sins as our substitute. He demonstrated His love by dying on a cross, giving His life as the punishment we deserve. He proved Himself above every other religious founder by rising from the dead.

"Christ died for our sins according to the Scriptures... He was buried... He was raised on the third day according to the Scriptures, and after that He appeared to Cephas, then to the twelve. After that He appeared to more than five hundred brethren at one time." 1 Corinthians 15:3-6

Jesus was "declared with power to be the Son of God by the resurrection from the dead." *Romans 1:4*

"For in Him (Jesus) all the fulness of Deity dwells in bodily form." *Colossians 2:9*

5. **In other religions, a teacher such as Buddha or Confucius will be followed over the centuries, and his followers will ascribe more and more authority to him, until the teacher is worshiped as a god even though he never claimed to be a god. But that is not how Christianity came to be. Jesus' birth, death, and many details from His life were predicted in the Old Testament centuries before He was even born! Specific, detailed predictions of a future individual are completely unique to Christianity.**

- He would be born from the tribe of Judah. *Genesis 49:10, Matthew 1:2, Revelation 5:5*
- He would be born in Bethlehem. *Micah 5:2, Matthew 2:1*
- He would be born of a virgin. *Isaiah 7:14, Matthew 1:18-25*
- He would work miracles. *Isaiah 61:1, Matthew 11:1-5, Luke 4:16-21*
- He would be betrayed for exactly thirty pieces of silver. *Zechariah 11:12, Matthew 26:14-16*
- Money used to betray Him would be used to buy the Potter's Field. *Zechariah 11:12,13, Matthew 27:3-10*
- His hands and feet would be pierced. *Psalm 22:16, John 19:35,37, John 20:24-28*
- He would be the divine payment for our sins by taking our sins onto Himself. *Isaiah 53:5,6, 2 Corinthians 5:21*
- People would gamble for his clothing by casting lots. *Psalm 22:18, John 19:23,24*
- He would be executed along with criminals. *Isaiah 53:9,12, Luke 23:32,33*
- He would be buried in a rich man's tomb. *Isaiah 53:9, Matthew 27:57-60*
- His body would not decay, but would be resurrected. *Psalm 16:8-11, Luke 24:1-43, Romans 1:4*

6. **Why does mankind need saving? Because we are sinners, and sin has separated us from our Creator who is holy.**

"For all have sinned and fall short of the glory of God." *Romans 3:23*

"The wages of sin is death, but the free gift of God is eternal life in Christ Jesus our Lord." *Romans 6:23*

7. **Other religions teach there are many ways to God. But Christianity is based on Jesus being the only way to reach God, therefore the Christian faith cannot be merged with other religions.**

"Jesus said to him, 'I am the way, and the truth, and the life; no one comes to the Father, but through Me.'" *John 14:6*

"For there is salvation in no one else; for there is no other name under heaven that has been given among men, by which we must be saved." *Acts 4:12*

"For there is one God, and one mediator also between God and men, the man Christ Jesus, who gave Himself as a ransom for all." *1 Timothy 2:5,6a*

8. **Most major religions of the world such as Islam, Hinduism, Confucianism, and Buddhism have one major teaching in common – they teach that God is distant and unknowable. But Christianity is unique in its teaching that God is knowable. This is why Christians see their faith not simply as a religion, but as a relationship.**

"And you will seek Me and find Me, when you search for Me with all your heart." *Jeremiah 29:13*

"As for you, my son Solomon, know the God of your father, and serve Him with a whole heart and a willing mind; for the Lord searches all hearts, and understands every intent of the thoughts. If you seek Him, He will let you find Him; but if you forsake Him, He will reject you forever." *1 Chronicles 28:9*

"Draw near to God and He will draw near to you." *James 4:8*

9. **With so many differences between Christianity and other religions, you can see why Christianity stands alone. In view of the free gift of salvation which God has provided, would you like to become a Christian?**

"For God so loved the world, that He gave His only begotten Son, that whoever believes in Him shall not perish, but have everlasting life." *John 3:16*

82 Are Human Beings Divine?

Many religions and spiritual organizations teach that all humans are divine beings. Many of these religions and organizations are based on helping humans get reacquainted with our divine nature and realize our full potential as divine beings. These groups usually have no problem agreeing that Jesus was God, because they believe we all are. Actress Shirley Maclaine has said: "The New Age is man being divine, man can become God. Man does not need a savior, he can save himself through cyclic rebirth and reincarnation." (Time magazine, December 7, 1987)

As we look honestly at the world around us, it makes us wonder how the world got to be such a mess if we are all gods. Has the human race lost touch with something along the way? If we really are gods, we need to know it, and the Bible speaks a great deal about this important subject.

1. The Bible teaches that humans are made in God's image.

"Then God said, 'Let Us make man in Our image, according to Our likeness.'" *Genesis 1:26*

2. It's important to understand what it means to be made in God's image. A statue made in someone's image will resemble some – but not all – of the original person's entire attributes. The statue might look like the person, but can't walk, talk, or think. Biblically speaking, being made in God's image means humans uniquely resemble many – but not all – of God's attributes. Some of God's traits that only humans share are:

- We have an awareness of God.
- We are "wired" to build relationships with God and others.
- We are instilled with a moral sense of right and wrong.
- We are higher-ranking and have dominion over animals and other creations.
- We have immortal souls that will exist for eternity.
- We can think, reason, and make choices rather than mere creatures of instinct.
- We are capable of love.
- We were originally created holy, and can be made holy again.

3. God's attributes that we do not share are:

- We are not all powerful.
- We are not infinitely all-knowing, or omniscient.
- We are not omnipresent.
- We have not pre-existed for all of eternity.
- We are not holy or morally perfect.
- We cannot speak things into existence out of nothing.
- We were created, but not "begotten."

4. The human race suffers not because we've forgotten we are gods, but because we've forgotten only God is God.

"Know that the Lord Himself is God; it is He who has made us, and not we ourselves; we are His people and the sheep of His pasture." *Psalm 100:3*

"Before Me there was no God formed, and there will be none after Me. I, even I, and the Lord; and there is no savior besides Me." *Isaiah 43:10,11*

"Is there any God besides Me, or is there any other Rock? I know of none." *Isaiah 44:8*

5. The desire to become a god is nothing new; the angel Lucifer (later known as Satan) tried it himself.

"For you said to yourself, 'I will ascend to heaven and set my throne above God's stars. I will preside on the mountain of the gods far away in the north. I will climb to the highest heavens and be like the Most High.' But instead, you will be brought down to the place of the dead, down to its lowest depths." *Isaiah 14:13-15 (NLT)*

6. At the heart of wanting to become like God is the rejection of His morals, the prideful refusal to worship God with

the praise He deserves, and craving that praise for ourselves. **The desire to become gods is how Satan tempted Adam and Eve to sin, and humanity has been separated from God ever since. This original sin led to the universal curse of suffering and death upon all of mankind.**

"And the serpent said to the woman, 'You shall surely not die! For God knows that in the day you eat from it your eyes will be opened, and you will be like God, knowing good and evil.'" *Genesis 3:4,5*

"Therefore, just as through one man (Adam) sin entered into the world, and death through sin, and so death spread to all men, because all sinned." *Romans 5:12*

"For all have sinned and fall short of the glory of God." *Romans 3:23*

"But your iniquities have made a separation between you and your God, and your sins have hid His face from you, so that He does not hear." *Isaiah 59:2*

7. **Even though we humans cannot become gods, God did become a man! God came to earth in human form as Jesus Christ. He was not merely in God's image; He was both fully man and fully God.**

"For in Him (Jesus) all the fulness of Deity dwells in bodily form." *Colossians 2:9*

8. **To "beget" means to reproduce something of the same nature as the parent. But the Bible says Jesus was actually begotten by God as His father and Mary as His mother, which uniquely makes Him fully divine and fully human.**

"For God so loved the world, that He gave His only begotten Son, that whoever believes in Him shall not perish, but have everlasting life." *John 3:16*

"In the beginning was the Word, and the Word was with God, and the Word was God.... He was in the beginning with God. And the Word became flesh, and dwelt among us, and we saw His glory, glory as of the only begotten from the Father, full of grace and truth." *John 1:1,14*

"By this the love of God was manifested in us, that God has sent His only begotten Son into the world so that we might live through Him." *1 John 4:9*

"This is good and acceptable in the sight of God our Savior, who desires all men to be saved and to come to the knowledge of the truth. For there is one God, and one mediator also between God and men, the man Christ Jesus, who gave Himself as a ransom for all." *1 Timothy 2:3-6a*

9. **God loves us and wants us to know Him intimately, and He sent His only begotten Son to make that possible by paying for our sins with His own sacrificial death on the cross. He demonstrated His great love for us when He took the punishment for our sins, and He offers us forgiveness by trusting in Him.**

"Jesus said to him, "I am the way, and the truth, and the life; no one comes to the Father but through Me." *John 14:6*

"But God demonstrates His own love toward us, in that while we were yet sinners, Christ died for us." *Romans 5:8*

"For there is salvation in no one else; for there is no other name under heaven that has been given among men, by which we must be saved." *Acts 4:12*

10. **Why did God come to earth as Jesus? It was because God set the highest possible standard of holiness, and when humans sinned, there was no way we could become holy again by doing good deeds or anything else. Fortunately, God loves us enough to personally pay for our sins on the cross. When we place our trust in Christ to restore our holiness, we still do not become gods, but we become holy in God's eyes and He adopts us as His beloved children.**

"But as many as received Him, to them He gave the right to become children of God, even to those who believe in His name." *John 1:12*

"For the wages of sin is death, but the free gift of God is eternal life in Christ Jesus our Lord." Romans 6:23

"Now to the King eternal, immortal, invisible, the only God, be honor and glory forever and ever. Amen." *1 Timothy 1:17*

83 Are Angels Real?

There seems to be a fascination with angels nowadays. Surprisingly, lots of people who reject many of the Bible's major teachings nevertheless believe in the existence of angels. The subject of angels is truly fascinating, and even though the Bible mentions angels almost 300 times, there are still many questions unanswered. Of the things we do know, the Bible describes four types of angels, but only mentions three angels by name; Michael, Gabriel, and Lucifer. The Bible also gives us good news and bad news regarding angels. The good news is: Yes; angels are real. The bad news is: Not all angels are good.

But who or what are angels? Why are some good and some bad, and how can we tell the difference? Plus, how do angels serve us, and how do they serve God?

---

1. Angels are spirit beings God created to praise Him, perform His will, and to serve and protect His followers.

"But angels are only servants. They are spirits sent from God to care for those who will receive salvation." *Hebrews 1:14 (NLT)*

"The angel of the Lord encamps around those who fear Him, and rescues them." *Psalm 34:7*

2. The Bible mentions four types of angels:

Archangel: Michael – He is the Chief or Prince of angels, and the highest angel administrator under their Commander-in-Chief Jesus Christ. Apparently Michael is the only Archangel, although Lucifer might have been an archangel at one time. *Jude 9, Daniel 12:1, Revelation 12:7-12, 1 Thessalonians 4:16*

Messenger Angels: Gabriel – Messenger angels are not always named, so there may be many of them. The only messenger angel specifically named in the Bible is Gabriel. He has announced events such as the birth of John the Baptist, and the birth of Christ to Mary and Joseph. Messenger angels always direct our attention to the Lord, and not to themselves. *Daniel 8:15,16, Luke 1:19,30-33, Luke 2:8-14*

Seraphim – These are a type of angel who continually praise the name and character of God in heaven. They hover above the throne of God and are said to have six wings. *Isaiah 6:1-6, Revelation 4:8*

Cherubim – They are described as being located around God's throne but not above it. They guard God and other holy places. They are said to have four wings, four faces, many eyes, and move about within gleaming "whirling wheels." *Ezekiel 10:1-22, Psalm 80:1, 99:1, Genesis 3:24, Exodus 25:18-20*

3. Apparently, children (and possibly all of us) each have an angel assigned to us beginning in infancy.

"See to it that you do not despise one of these little ones, for I say to you, that their angels in heaven continually behold the face of My Father who is in heaven." *Matthew 18:10*

4. The Bible says a lot about angels, and yet there are many common misconceptions regarding angels:

When we die, we don't become angels. Angels are not the souls of departed humans. They are a separate order of created beings, and have never been human. They may appear in human form, but they are not human themselves. *1 Corinthians 6:3, Hebrews 9:27, Ezekiel 28:13-14*

Angels are not all warm and fuzzy. Almost every account in the Bible where humans have seen angels in their heavenly form describes them as being beautiful, yet fierce and terrifying. Their first words are often, "Do not be afraid." *Luke 24:4,5, Matthew 28:1-6*

Angels also have the ability to veil their frightening appearance and appear as normal humans, or even to remain invisible. *Luke 24:4, Acts 1:10, Hebrews 13:2, 2 Kings 6:15-17*

At the final judgment day they will assist God in separating the lost from the saved. *Matthew 13:36-43*

Angels are often fierce warriors sent by God to execute judgment on earth. *2 Kings 19:35*

Angels are never to be worshiped, because worship is something reserved for God alone. *Exodus 20:1-6, Revelation 19:10, 22:8,9*

Angels are immortal, but not divine. They have been created by God, and have not pre-existed throughout eternity like God has, but they will exist for eternity into the future. *Ezekiel 28:13-15, 2 Corinthians 4:18, Revelation 5:11-14*

Not all angels are good. Fallen angels (now known as demons) may masquerade as being good, but are totally evil, deceptive, corrupt, and intent on harming us. *2 Corinthians 4:4, 11:14, Ephesians 6:10-17, 1 Peter 5:8,9*

No good angel will attempt to keep a person from believing in Jesus, but evil angels will. *1 John 4:1-3, Galatians 1:8*

Surprisingly, the Bible never mentions angels who look like the cute, chubby infants depicted in paintings. Angels are always described as male except in one rather curious passage which describes winged beings who appear female. *Zechariah 5:5-11*

5. **Like humans, angels have free will to obey or defy God. The most famous angel who rebelled against God is Lucifer. He was cast out of heaven for his prideful attempt to make himself like God. *(Isaiah 14:12-17, Ezekiel 28:12-19, Luke 10:18)* After his fall, Lucifer was referred to as the devil, or Satan. He was joined in his rebellion by a third of all the angels in heaven. *(Revelation 12:4,9)* Satan later persuaded Adam and Eve to try become like God. This is when the human race became fallen, or separated from God, when Adam and Eve first sinned by rebelling against God.**

"Satan disguises himself as an angel of light. Therefore it is not surprising if his servants also disguise themselves as servants of righteousness." *2 Corinthians 11:14,15*

"He (Satan) was a murderer from the beginning, and does not stand in the truth, because there is no truth in him. Whenever he speaks a lie, he speaks from his own nature; for he is a liar and the father of lies." *John 8:44*

"But even if we, or an angel from heaven, should preach to you a gospel contrary to what we have preached to you, he is to be accursed!" *Galatians 1:8*

6. **Satan and his fallen angels engage in spiritual warfare unseen to us. Satan wants to keep as many human souls as possible from the Lord, and he tries to afflict those who do follow the Lord. But when we rely on God's strength, He will protect us, and when He decides the time is right He will defeat Satan once and for all.**

"Put on the full armor of God, that you may be able to stand firm against the powers, against the world forces of this darkness, against the spiritual forces of wickedness in the heavenly places." *Ephesians 6:11,12*

"Now judgment is upon this world, and the ruler of this world (Satan) will be cast out." *John 12:31*

7. **God offers a precious gift to fallen humans but not to fallen angels. He offers us forgiveness through believing in His Son Jesus, who became a human so that He could pay for our sins with His sacrificial death.**

"God demonstrates His own love for us in that while we were yet sinners Christ died for us." *Romans 5:8*

8. **Some people worship angels, perhaps as a way to feel spiritual without the inconvenient lifestyle changes that come from seeking God Himself and obeying the commands in Scripture. But when the apostle John bowed to worship an angel, the angel immediately told him to stop, and to only worship God.**

"And I, John, am the one who heard and saw these things. And when I heard and saw, I fell down to worship at the feet of the angel who showed me these things. And he said to me, 'Do not do that; I am a fellow servant of yours and of your brethren the prophets and of these who heed the words of this book; worship God.'" *Revelation 22:8,9*

9. **How can you make the angels happy? They rejoice when you accept God's precious gift of forgiveness through His Son! Accept Christ as your personal Savior so you can spend eternity with God and the angels.**

"There is joy in the presence of the angels of God over one sinner who repents." *Luke 15:10*

"For God so loved the world, that He gave His only begotten Son, that whoever believes in Him shall not perish, but have everlasting life." *John 3:16*

84 Is There Really A Devil?

Many people think the devil is simply an imaginary, mythical character who merely symbolizes evil. He is often envisioned in the cartoony red suit with horns, a forked tail, and a pitchfork. But is there really a devil? And if there is a devil, how powerful is he?

In the introduction to the classic book "The Screwtape Letters" written in 1941, author C.S. Lewis offers excellent advice toward finding a proper perspective on the devil: "There are two equal and opposite errors into which our race can fall about the devils. One is to disbelieve in their existence. The other is to believe, and to feel an excessive and unhealthy interest in them. They themselves are equally pleased by both errors and hail a materialist or a magician with the same delight."

There are many misconceptions about the nature and power of the devil. The Bible makes it clear that the devil (also known as Satan) exists with as much certainty as God exists. The devil is referred to in seven Old Testament books, by every author of the New Testament, and was spoken of by Jesus. The Bible gives us a wealth of information on who Satan is, where he came from, how powerful he is, what he can do to us, and how we can be protected from him. It also describes Satan's ultimate destiny.

1. God created all the angels. One beautiful, high-ranking angel in heaven was named Lucifer, which means "Light bearer." But just like humans, angels have free will, and Lucifer became prideful and rebelled.

"You had the seal of perfection, full of wisdom and perfect in beauty. You were in Eden, the garden of God; every precious stone was your covering: the ruby, the topaz and the diamond; the beryl, the onyx and the jasper; the lapis lazuli, the turquoise and the emerald; and the gold, the workmanship of your settings and sockets, was in you. On the day that you were created they were prepared. You were the anointed cherub who covers, and I placed you there. You were on the holy mountain of God. You walked in the midst of the stones of fire. You were blameless in your ways from the day you were created until unrighteousness was found in you. By the abundance of your trade you were internally filled with violence, and you sinned; therefore I have cast you as profane from the mountain of God.... All who know you among the peoples are appalled at you." *Ezekiel 28:12b-16a,19*

2. Lucifer was cast out of heaven because he tried to make himself like God. After his fall from heaven, he was never referred to as Lucifer again. Now he's called Satan, which means "adversarsy," or the devil, which means "accuser."

"But you said in your heart, 'I will ascend to heaven; I will raise my throne above the stars of God, and I will sit on the mount of assembly in the recesses of the north. I will ascend above the heights of the clouds; I will make myself like the Most High.'" *Isaiah 14:13,14*

3. Satan apparently convinced a third of all angels to join his rebellion. These fallen angels are now called "demons." After being thrown from heaven, they came to earth.

"And his tail swept away a third of the stars of heaven and threw them to the earth. And the great dragon was thrown down, the serpent of old who is called the devil and Satan, who deceives the whole world; he was thrown down to the earth, and his angels were thrown down with him." *Revelation 12:4,9*

4. Here on earth, Satan (speaking through the form of a serpent) tempted Adam and Eve to commit the same prideful sin he had committed. He got them to doubt what God had said, and made them think they could become like God. Once sin entered the world, mankind became separated from God.

"And the serpent said to the woman, 'You shall surely not die! For God knows that in the day you eat from it your eyes will be opened, and you will be like God, knowing good and evil.'" *Genesis 3:4,5*

"Therefore, just as through one man (Adam) sin entered into the world, and death through sin, and so death spread to all men, because all sinned." *Romans 5:12*

5. Should we blame God for releasing evil into the world because He created Lucifer? The truth is, since every human has chosen to rebel against God by sinning, we are all guilty of handing our God-given dominion over to Satan, thus allowing him to cause havoc and suffering.

"For all have sinned and fall short of the glory of God." *Romans 3:23*

"And the devil said to Him (Jesus), 'I will give You all this domain and its glory; for it has been handed over to me, and I give it to whomever I wish.'" *Luke 4:6*

6. **Is Satan as powerful as God? No! God is omniscient, omnipresent, and infinitely powerful; Satan is not. The devil has temporary powers on earth, but is held in check by God who has ultimate, eternal sovereignty. What are some of the powers and tactics of Satan and the demons who serve him?**

   - They constantly try to deceive us. *John 8:44, 1 Timothy 4:1, Revelation 12:9, 20:3*
   - They blind the minds of unbelievers and interfere with the spread of the gospel. *Matthew 13:19, Luke 8:12, 2 Corinthians 4:4*
   - They hide their evil intentions and disguise themselves by doing good deeds. *2 Corinthians 11:14,15*
   - They attack God's followers through spiritual warfare. *Ephesians 6:10-18*
   - They can cause some diseases and irrational, self-destructive behavior. *Luke 13:11,17, Luke 9:37-43, Matthew 12:22*
   - They sometimes possess, or "demonize" people by dwelling within them. *Mark 5:1-13, Luke 4:35*
   - They will empower the anti-Christ who will deceive many in the end times. *2 Thessalonians 2:3-10*
   - They can predict (though not with 100% accuracy) and/or manipulate future events. *Acts 16:16-19*
   - They tempt us to sin and turn away from God. *Matthew 4:1-11, 2 Corinthians 11:3, 1 Thessalonians 3:5*

7. **Because Jesus is God, He is infinitely more powerful than Satan and will destroy him.**

   "The Son of God appeared for this purpose, that He might destroy the works of the devil." *1 John 3:8*

8. **Satan and his demons have no chance of forgiveness, and are destined to suffer eternally. But God offers a way for humans to be forgiven so we can spend eternity with Him. God sent His son Jesus to pay the penalty for our sins.**

   "And you know that He appeared in order to take away sins; and in Him there is no sin." *1 John 3:5*

   "He (God the Father) made Him (God the Son) who knew no sin to be sin on our behalf, that we might become the righteousness of God in Him." *2 Corinthians 5:21*

9. **To have victory over Satan, one must be a member of God's family, and depend on His strength. We must also avoid dabbling in any occult practices which invite demonic involvement in our lives.**

   "Submit therefore to God. Resist the devil and he will flee from you." *James 4:7*

   "But the Lord is faithful, and He will strengthen and protect you from the evil one." *2 Thessalonians 3:3*

   "In addition to all, taking up the shield of faith, with which you will be able to extinguish all the flaming missiles of the evil one." *Ephesians 6:16*

   "Greater is He who is in you than he who is in the world." *1 John 4:4*

10. **Even though Satan can offer some fun in this life, he and his followers will share a common destiny of eternal suffering. Would you rather spend eternity in hell with Satan, or in heaven with God?**

    "And all the nations will be gathered before Him (Jesus); and He will separate them from one another, as the shepherd separates the sheep from the goats; and He will put the sheep on His right, and the goats on the left. Then the King will say to those on His right, 'Come you who are blessed of My Father, inherit the kingdom prepared for you from the foundation of the world.' ...Then He will say to those on His left, 'Depart from Me, accursed ones, into the eternal fire which has been prepared for the devil and his angels.'" *Matthew 25:32,33,41*

11. **To break Satan's grip on your life, you first need to become a Christian. Simply confess your sins and ask Christ to come into your heart. Then you can access God's power to defeat satanic influence and involvement in your life.**

    "For the wages of sin is death, but the free gift of God is eternal life in Christ Jesus our Lord." *Romans 6:23*

85 Is It Right To Call Any Religion Wrong?

It's one thing to debate which note on a piano sounds the prettiest, or which color in the rainbow is the loveliest. But not everything is so subjective; we'd all have to agree that two plus two has only one absolutely true answer. But is there such a thing as "absolute truth" when it comes to religion? The thing about religion is that it's about having faith in things that are unseen, which can't always be proven or disproven, so how can a person say that one is right and one is wrong? It's understandable why many non-Christians don't like it when a Christian tells them their beliefs are wrong. Maybe it comes across as arrogant, or maybe there's just no perfect way to tell someone their religion is wrong without hurting their feelings.

We live in a postmodern world. What is Postmodernism? It is the acceptance of relativism or pluralism in relation to questions of truth. (Within Postmodernism, something true for you doesn't have to be true for someone else.) The old comparison of several blind men examining the elephant is often quoted. The man who felt only the leg believed it was like a tree, the man who felt only the tail thought it was like a snake, etc. In a nutshell, postmodern relativism maintains that it doesn't matter what you believe as long as you believe it. Christian author C.S. Lewis wrote of the danger of having no absolute standard for truth in an essay called "The Poison of Subjectivsim" in the book "Christian Reflections." He wrote that: "a belief system that depends upon one's own feelings as a standard for truth… would be like closing your eyes while driving, or blissfully ignoring the doctor's warnings."

Of course, the Bible teaches that what we believe does matter; especially on essential teachings like the divinity of Christ, His resurrection, and Jesus being the only way to heaven.

When the Roman Governor Pontius Pilate presided over Jesus' trial, he asked Jesus a simple yet profound question: "What is truth?" Some people say there is absolutely no such thing as absolute truth, which itself is a statement of absolute truth. In a similar inconsistency, some people say, "It's OK to believe what you want as long as you don't try to impose it on others," and then they try to impose that belief on others. But in matters of eternal destiny, the issues are too critical to simply avoid talking about. If a man yells to warn a woman that she is about to get hit by a bus, is that imposing his opinion on her? If one beggar tells another beggar where to find bread, has he imposed his opinion on him? If Bill believes that if his friend Joe dies without Christ then Joe will spend eternity in hell, but Bill does nothing to introduce Joe to Christ, then we have to wonder how much Bill cares about his friend Joe. When Christians share their faith, it's how we show we care.

Is Christianity – as the blossom on the stem of Judaism – really the one true faith?

---

1. **To say "a specific religion is wrong" is not completely accurate. Christians agree there are nuggets of truth to be found in the teachings of any religion, and all truth is God's truth. It is the essentials of a religion that Christians would have to disagree with, such as how a person gets to heaven, who God is, etc. Can the essentials of Christianity ever be merged with other faiths to make one universal faith? No – because of the uniqueness of Jesus.**

   "For there is one God, and one mediator also between God and men, the man Christ Jesus, who gave Himself as a ransom for all." *1 Timothy 2:5,6a*

   "Jesus said to him, 'I am the way, and the truth, and the life; no one comes to the Father, but through Me.'" *John 14:6*

   "For there is salvation in no one else; for there is no other name under heaven that has been given among men, by which we must be saved." *Acts 4:12*

2. **Even if you can't agree that Christianity is the one true faith, it's easy to agree that Christianity is different from all other religions.**

   • Christianity is more than just a collection of wise sayings to gain enlightenment.
   • Christianity teaches that God came to earth in human form, paid for our sins, and He is knowable.

- Christianity offers a way of salvation unlike other religions which teach that we work our way to Heaven.
- Christianity is not mythology. It is based on historical events that happened to actual people in real places.

3. The proof that verifies the Christian faith to be true and validates Jesus' claim to be the true Son of God is His resurrection from the dead. If the resurrection could be proven false, Christianity would be proven to be a hoax.

"And Jesus Christ our Lord was shown to be the Son of God when God powerfully raised him from the dead by means of the Holy Spirit." *Romans 1:4 (NLT)*

"Christ died for our sins according to the Scriptures... He was buried... He was raised on the third day according to the Scriptures, and after that He appeared to Cephas, then to the twelve. After that He appeared to more than five hundred brethren at one time." *1 Corinthians 15:3-6*

"If Christ has not been raised, your faith is worthless; you are still in your sins." *1 Corinthians 15:17*

"Do not be afraid; I am the first and the last, and the living One; and I was dead, and behold, I am alive forevermore, and I have the keys of death and of Hades." *Revelation 1:17,18*

4. As for proof outside of the Bible, this account of Jesus and His resurrection is included in the writings of Jewish historian Josephus Flavius from the year 93 A.D.:

"At this time (the time of Pilate) there was a wise man who was called Jesus. And his conduct was good, and he was known to be virtuous. And many people from among the Jews and the other nations became his disciples. Pilate condemned him to be crucified and to die. And those who had become his disciples did not abandon his discipleship. They reported that he had appeared to them after his crucifixion and that he was alive; accordingly, he was perhaps the Messiah concerning whom the prophets have recounted wonders." *Josephus, Antiquities*

There are ten known secular sources outside the Bible that mention Jesus within 150 years of His death. All of these writings harmonize perfectly with what the Bible tells us about Jesus. Surprisingly, over the same 150 years we have only nine mentions from secular writings of Tiberius Caesar himself – the most powerful man on earth at the time – and no serious historian doubts whether Tiberius was a real person or not.

5. One of the things that made Jesus so controversial during his public ministry was that He didn't hesitate to point out to people their misguided beliefs, and especially their hypocritical actions. For example:

"But woe to you, scribes and Pharisees, hypocrites, because you shut off the kingdom of heaven from people; for you do not enter in yourselves, nor do you allow those who are entering to go in. Woe to you, scribes and Pharisees, hypocrites, because you devour widows' houses, and for a pretense you make long prayers; therefore you will receive greater condemnation. Woe to you, scribes and Pharisees, hypocrites, because you travel around on sea and land to make one proselyte; and when he becomes one, you make him twice as much a son of hell as yourselves." *Matthew 23:13-15*

6. Jesus gave us a very simple method to determine if His teachings are true. He promised that if we obey His teachings and commands, then He will disclose more of Himself to us. You could say we don't "study our way" to closeness to God; we "obey our way" to closeness to God. If you disregard and disobey His teachings and commands, then don't expect to receive spiritual insight. Jesus promised that obedience brings clarity.

"He who has My commandments and keeps them is the one who loves Me; and he who loves Me will be loved by My Father, and I will love him and will disclose Myself to him." *John 14:21*

"If you abide in My word, then you are truly disciples of Mine; and you shall know the truth, and the truth shall make you free." *John 8:31,32*

7. Some religions teach that it takes years to reach enlightenment, but it's easy to become a Christian. It's not through doing good works, but simply by confessing your need for a Savior, and inviting Him into your heart.

"The wages of sin is death, but the free gift of God is eternal life in Christ Jesus our Lord." *Romans 6:23*

"I stand at the door and knock; if any one hears My voice and opens the door, I will come in to him." *Revelation 3:20*

86 What About Abortion?

Ever since the famous 1973 Supreme Court ruling in Roe vs. Wade, abortion has been legal in America. The court, when grappling with the question of when life begins, said this: "The judiciary, at this point in the development of man's knowledge, is not in a position to speculate as to the answer." They then decided that the answer should be left up to the mother as to whether or not the fetus developing inside her was indeed a living human being. But even though the Supreme Court made abortion legal, they did not settle the question of whether abortion is right.

Some call this the debate over when life begins. But the core of the matter hinges not so much on whether or not the developing fetus – with its functioning heart and brain – is alive; but whether or not it is a human being with all the rights and value of a human living outside the womb. As Ronald Reagan put it in 1982: "Simple morality dictates that unless and until someone can prove the unborn human is not alive, we must give it the benefit of the doubt and assume it is (alive). And, thus, it should be entitled to life, liberty and the pursuit of happiness." He also once said, "I've noticed that everyone who is for abortion is already born."

As the home of the free, the constitution considers all men to be created equal. But in our quest for unrestricted freedom, have we become biased in protecting the rights of those already born over those who have yet to be born? With today's medical advancements, premature babies born weighing less than a pound are sometimes surviving to be normal, healthy kids. Doctors take great pains to save a baby born prematurely, but are free to destroy those babies at the same stage of development still in the womb.

Many people see the right to abortion as empowering to women, but in other countries the number of female babies aborted is vastly higher than the number of males, especially in countries like China, India, Pakistan, South Korea and Taiwan where ultra-sound is available and male babies are prized.

To help shed light on this very controversial topic, it helps to look at what the Bible has to say about the value of the unborn child.

---

1. King David described the unborn child with a sense of immeasurable worth, as of one of God's greatest creations.

"For You formed my inward parts; You wove me in my mother's womb. I will give thanks to You, for I am fearfully and wonderfully made; wonderful are Your works, and my soul knows it very well. My frame was not hidden from You, when I was made in secret, and skillfully wrought in the depths of the earth; Your eyes have seen my unformed substance; and in Your book were all written the days that were ordained for me, when as yet there was not one of them." *Psalm 139:13-16*

2. Perhaps people feel justified in aborting their infants because they view the unborn child as something they have created. But what does the Bible say about who created us?

"Thus says the Lord, your Redeemer, and the one who formed you from the womb: 'I, the Lord, and the maker of all things.'" *Isaiah 44:24*

3. The Supreme Court judges decided to rule on what was legal, but they tactfully dodged deciding what was right or wrong. They decided not to decide, and let all opinions be equally valid. Ironically, it is the book of "Judges" that warns of this philosophy during a chaotic time in Israel when they had no moral compass.

"In those days there was no king in Israel; every man did what was right in his own eyes." *Judges 17:6*

4. God has given mankind free will; that is, the freedom to make our own moral decisions. He has also given us His Word to guide us in what is right and wrong. But beware; God wants us to choose what is right, and will hold us accountable for every decision we make, and for the consequences of our actions. Someday each of us will stand before God to give account of our lives and actions to Him.

"I call heaven and earth to witness against you today, that I have set before you life and death, the blessing and the curse. So choose life in order that you may live, you and your descendants." *Deuteronomy 30:19*

"For we shall all stand before the judgment-seat of God.... So then each one of us shall give account of himself to God." *Romans 14:10,12*

5. God loves all children, and He is extremely intent on punishing those who harm little children.

"See that you do not despise one of these little ones.... So it is not the will of your Father who is in heaven that one of these little ones perish." *Matthew 18:10a,14*

"It would be better to be thrown into the sea with a large millstone tied around the neck than to face the punishment in store for harming one of these little ones." *Luke 17:2 (NLT)*

6. Some say carrying a baby to full term is a big sacrifice in terms of career. But isn't that better than sacrificing the entire life of your unborn child for the sake of a career?

"I urge you therefore, brethren, by the mercies of God, to present your bodies as a living and holy sacrifice, acceptable to God, which is your spiritual service of worship." *Romans 12:1*

7. The pro-choice movement uses the slogan: "My body, my choice." Many women feel that since the decision affects their body, the decision should be hers alone. But there is more than just her body involved in the decision; there is also the body of the unborn child.

"You have been bought with a price, therefore glorify God in your body." *1 Corinthians 6:20*

"Do you not know that you are a temple of God, and the Spirit of God dwells in you? If any man destroys the temple of God, God will destroy him, for the temple of God is holy, and that is what you are." *1 Corinthians 3:16,17*

8. The timing of a pregnancy may not always be what we planned, but all children are a blessing from the Lord.

"Behold, children are a gift of the Lord, the fruit of the womb is a reward. Like arrows in the hand of a warrior, so are the children of one's youth. How blessed is the man whose quiver is full of them." *Psalm 127:3-5a*

9. Back in the time of slavery, slave owners declared it was their right to own slaves. But it was a "right" based on taking away the rights of someone else – much like the right to abortion.

"Do nothing from selfishness or empty conceit, but with humility of mind regard one another as more important than yourselves; do not merely look out for your own personal interests, but also for the interests of others." *Philippians 2:3,4*

10. Remember the Golden Rule of Matthew 7:12: "Do unto others as you would have them do unto you." If you were still a developing unborn child, would you want your mother to abort you?

"There are two victims in every abortion: a dead baby and a dead conscience." - *Mother Teresa*

11. To understand how much value God has placed on humans, both in the womb and outside the womb, remember that God loves us so much that He was willing to sacrifice His own life on a cross. This is how He paid for our sins so that we can be forgiven, made holy, and reunited with God.

"For God so loved the world, that He gave His only begotten Son, that whoever believes in Him shall not perish, but have everlasting life." *John 3:16*

"Jesus said to him, 'I am the way, and the truth, and the life; no one comes to the Father, but through Me.'" *John 14:6*

12. This is a hallmark of genuine love; when you love someone else, you make sacrifices for them. When you love only yourself, you insist others sacrifice for you. If Jesus sacrificed His life to save you, maybe you could sacrifice nine months of your life so that your child can live.

"Yes, I am the gate. Those who come in through me will be saved. Wherever they go they will find green pastures. The thief's purpose is to steal and kill and destroy. My purpose is to give life in all its fulness." *John 10:9,10 (NLT)*

87 What Does The Bible Say About Gay Marriage?

The Bible talks about marriage, divorce, love and sexuality – both heterosexual and homosexual. It was God who established the institution of marriage, and in His eyes a wedding is a sacred and joyous occasion. But the Bible never addresses the topic of two gay people marrying. Since the Bible doesn't specifically prohibit gay marriage, should that be taken as an endorsement? To arrive at a biblical perspective on gay marriage, we must look at what the Bible says about marriage, and about homosexuality in general.

Like many social and moral issues, gay marriage is very polarizing. Those who support gay marriage sometimes refer to those who oppose it as "haters" and "homophobes." Many of its supporters have argued that preventing gays from marrying is the same as discrimination based on race or gender.

Gay marriage has been the focus of courts, elections, popular opinion, and lobby groups; so it also makes sense to seek guidance from the God who has infinite wisdom, created the human race, invented marriage, and loves us dearly. Even though civil unions or other legal arrangements could likely be accommodated by a secular legal system, does the Bible's definition of marriage allow for God's blessings on two homosexuals who marry? With everything the Bible says about marriage, do the same parameters that apply for heterosexual marriage also apply for a homosexual marriage?

1. **A fire in a fireplace on a cold day is always nice. But building a fire in the middle of the living room floor could destroy the whole house. In the same way, sexual attraction and love are extremely powerful forces. If practiced within God's parameters, they can result in a new baby to start a family. But if used recklessly, can tear families apart. Sex is such a powerful force for good or harm that God gives us clear guidance on where it should be allowed or not. If God created the human race, then He knows the best way to create a relationship that's best for couples, for families, and for society. The Bible first mentions marriage during the time of Adam and Eve:**

   "For this reason a man shall leave his father and his mother, and be joined to his wife; and they shall become one flesh." *Genesis 2:24*

2. **The Bible never mentions an incident where Jesus was specifically asked His opinion on gay marriage. But He was asked about divorce, and in His answer He reiterated and confirmed the definition of marriage from Genesis 2:24 (the same verse above) where God established the institution of marriage during the time of Adam and Eve.**

   "Some Pharisees came to Jesus, testing Him and asking, 'Is it lawful for a man to divorce his wife for any reason at all?' And He answered and said, 'Have you not read that He who created them from the beginning made them male and female, and said "For this reason a man shall leave his father and mother and be joined to his wife, and the two shall become one flesh"? So they are no longer two, but one flesh. What therefore God has joined together, let no man separate.'" *Matthew 19:3-6*

3. **Some of the truths regarding God's precedent-setting definition of marriage from this passage are:**

   - God created the human race from the beginning, so it stands to reason He would know what's best for us.
   - Marriage is part of God's plan for mankind.
   - God made humans in two distinct categories – male or female.
   - Both the man and the woman would have been produced by the previous union of a man and a woman.
   - Marriage is designed to be between one man and one woman, ruling out polygamy, or other variations.
   - Marriage is intended to last a lifetime.
   - Marriage – an institution established by all-knowing God – should not be tampered with by man.

   Jesus was the most loving person who ever lived and was obviously not a "hater." But based on His clear confirmation and endorsement of the biblical model or definition of marriage, a union between two men or between two women would not really be defined as a marriage at all.

4. **Is opposing gay marriage the same as racism? No. The Bible never prohibits being black, white, hispanic, or asian, but it prohibits the practice of homosexuality; whether married or single. Whenever homosexality is mentioned – from Genesis to Revelation – there are warnings to avoid its practice and consequences. Why would God endorse homosexual mariage if He doesn't even endorse homosexuality as a lifestyle for singles?**

"For they exchanged the truth of God for a lie, and worshiped and served the creature rather than the Creator, who is blessed forever. Amen. For this reason God gave them over to degrading passions; for their women exchanged the natural function for that which is unnatural, and in the same way also the men abandoned the natural function of the woman and burned in their desire toward one another, men with men committing indecent acts and receiving in their own persons the due penalty of their error. And just as they did not see fit to acknowledge God any longer, God gave them over to a depraved mind, to do those things which are not proper." *Romans 1:25-28*

5. **Christians aren't told to be "haters" of homosexuals. We are to "hate the sin and love the sinner." We hate all sin because it harms those who practice it. Sin harms society, and it hurts the next generation who learn the same harmful patterns. By taking a stand against sin and leading people to the light, it's one way to show our love for sinners.**

"My brethren, if any among you strays from the truth and one turns him back, let him know that he who turns a sinner from the error of his way will save his soul from death and will cover a multitude of sins." *James 5:19,20*

"If someone says, 'I love God,' and hates his brother, he is a liar; for the one who does not love his brother whom he has seen, cannot love God whom he has not seen. And this commandment we have from Him, that the one who loves God should love his brother also." *1 John 4:20,21*

6. **When it comes to social and moral issues, Christians are called to uphold God's standards even if it means taking an unpopular stand and being criticized by public opinion.**

"For am I now seeking the favor of men, or of God? Or am I striving to please men? If I were still trying to please men, I would not be a bond-servant of Christ." *Galatians 1:10*

7. **God loves us the way we are, and loves us too much to let us stay the way we are. Many Christians now living for the Lord used to practice lifestyles God has warned us about. He can give His followers the strength to bring their sexual appetites within His approved parameters. When we make Christ the Lord of our lives, we submit every area to His commands; including our relationships and sexual desires. A heart not submitted to the Lordship of Christ wants to make our own rules and reject the rules God gave us for our own good. People who live a gay lifestyle should be honest enough to admit that the Bible does not condone it. When people disregard God's clear instructions in any area, they step outside God's umbrella of blessing and protection.**

"Or do you not know that the unrighteous will not inherit the kingdom of God? Do not be deceived; neither fornicators, nor idolaters, nor adulterers, nor effeminate, nor homosexuals, nor thieves, nor the covetous, nor drunkards, nor revilers, nor swindlers, will inherit the kingdom of God. Such were some of you; but you were washed, but you were sanctified, but you were justified in the name of the Lord Jesus Christ and in the Spirit of our God."
1 Corinthians 6:9-11

8. **No one has ever loved sinners more than Jesus Christ. He willingly gave His life to pay for the sins of mankind so that we can be forgiven and live forever with Him in heaven.**

"Greater love has no one than this, that one lay down his life for his friends." *John 15:13*

"But God demonstrates His own love for us in that while we were yet sinners Christ died for us." *Romans 5:8*

9. **Have you ever received Christ as your Savior and submitted every area of your life to Him as your Lord?**

"If we say that we have no sin, we are deceiving ourselves and the truth is not in us. If we confess our sins, He is faithful and righteous to forgive us our sins and to cleanse us from all unrighteousness.... The one who says, 'I have come to know Him,' and does not keep His commandments, is a liar, and the truth is not in him; but whoever keeps His word, in him the love of God has truly been perfected. " *1 John 1:8,9; 2:4-5a*

"No man can serve two masters; for either he will hate the one and love the other, or he will be to devoted to one and despise the other." *Matthew 6:24a*

"The thief comes only to steal and kill and destroy; I came that they may have life, and have it abundantly." *John 10:10*

"For the wages of sin is death, but the free gift of God is eternal life in Christ Jesus our Lord." *Romans 6:23*

88 Is The Bible Sexist Towards Women?

Take a look at this ancient quote: "Men have authority over women because God has made the one superior to the other, and because they spend their wealth to maintain them. Good women are obedient. They guard their unseen parts because God has guarded them. As for those from whom you fear disobedience, admonish them and send them to beds apart and beat them. Then if they obey you, take no further action against them." This quote typifies the general attitude toward women in ancient times; especially in the Middle East. But this quote is not taken from the Bible; it's from the Koran, written by Mohammed around 600 A.D. (See Surah 4:34.) This societal prejudice had been around centuries earlier than when Mohammed wrote it. But Jesus worked to change this negative mindset and abuse towards women.

Some women today have claimed the Bible teaches that women are second-class members of society. But compared to other faiths and cultures of the world, Christianity presents a much higher view of women. If you were to make a list of people who have most elevated the role and status of women, names would be mentioned such as Susan B. Anthony, Margaret Thatcher, Sandra Day O'Connor, Harriet Tubman, Rosa Parks, or Helen Keller. But no one has done as much to equalize the sexes as Jesus Christ.

---

1. **Some women reject Christianity because they perceive it to be a faith which teaches that all women must be subservient to all men. But this is a misconception! In God's eyes, we are all equal.**

   "For all of you who were baptized into Christ have clothed yourselves with Christ. There is neither Jew nor Greek, there is neither slave nor free man, there is neither male nor female; for you are all one in Christ Jesus." *Galatians 3:27,28*

2. **Jesus not only broke down gender barriers, but racial and social barriers as well.**

   "When a Samaritan woman came to draw water, Jesus said to her, 'Will you give me a drink?'... The Samaritan woman said to him, 'You are a Jew and I am a Samaritan woman. How can you ask me for a drink? (For Jews do not associate with Samaritans.)... Just then his disciples returned and were surprised to find him talking with a woman." *John 4:7,9,27 (NIV)*

3. **Many of Jesus' followers were women. In fact, women were honored to be the first witnesses Jesus appeared to after His resurrection, and He entrusted them to spread the news to others. (At the time, a woman's testimony was not even admissible in a court of law.) If the Bible's account of the resurrection had been a cleverly made up tale by His followers, they would not have made women the primary witnesses because of the societal prejudice against the value of a woman's opinion. Scholars see this as strong evidence that the resurrection accounts are authentic.**

   "Now after He had risen early on the first day of the week, He first appeared to Mary Magdalene.... She went and reported to those who had been with Him, while they were mourning and weeping. When they heard that He was alive and had been seen by her, they refused to believe it.... Afterward He appeared to the eleven themselves as they were reclining at the table; and He reproached them for their unbelief and hardness of heart, because they had not believed those who had seen Him after He had risen." *Mark 16:9-11,14*

   "Now they were Mary Magdalene and Joanna and Mary the mother of James; also the other women with them were telling these things to the apostles. But these words appeared to them as nonsense, and they would not believe them. But Peter got up and ran to the tomb; stooping and looking in, he saw the linen wrappings only; and he went away to his home, marveling at what had happened." *Luke 24:10-12*

4. **In ancient times, women were often treated as second-class citizens. Nevertheless, Jesus always spoke more kindly to women than the culture would have demanded. He also defended women who were oppressed by the male dominated society, as in the famous story of the woman caught in adultery.**

   "Early in the morning He came again into the temple, and all the people were coming to Him; and He sat down and began to teach them. The scribes and the Pharisees brought a woman caught in adultery, and having set her in the center of the court, they said to Him, 'Teacher, this woman has been caught in adultery, in the very act. Now in the Law Moses commanded us to stone such women; what then do You say?' They were saying this, testing Him, so that they might have grounds for accusing Him. But Jesus stooped down and with His finger wrote on the ground. But when they per-sisted in asking Him, He straightened up, and said to them, 'He who is without sin among you, let him be the first to throw a stone at her.' Again He stooped down and wrote on the ground. When they heard it, they began to go out one-by-one, beginning with the older ones, and He was left alone, and the woman, where she was, in the center of the court. Straightening up, Jesus said to her, Woman, where are they? Did no one condemn you?' She said, 'No one, Lord.' And Jesus said, 'I do not condemn you, either. Go. From now on sin no more.'" *John 8:2-11*

5. **Back in ancient times, society did not provide for widows, so they had a very difficult time supporting themselves and often had to beg. But Paul instructed the early church to provide for them.**

"The church should care for any widow who has no one else to care for her…. A widow who is put on the list for support must be a woman who is at least sixty years old and was faithful to her husband…." *1 Timothy 5:3,9 (NLT)*

6. **The backlash many people have with the perception of the Bible's view of women probably comes from teachings on the role of women in marriage. The Bible does not teach all women are to submit to all men. It says husbands and wives are equal in God's eyes, but each has a different role within marriage. Wives are taught to submit to their husbands' leadership; not because women are inferior but because without an authority structure the family will have instability and constant power struggles. Imagine a couple trying to dance with both partners trying to lead, or neither one leading – it would not be a very smooth dance. In a similar way, the Bible teaches that all three Persons of the Trinity are equal, and yet within the Trinity there is an authority structure. The same holds true in the home. But husbands are never given authority to abuse their wives or be unfair.**

"In the same way, you husbands must give honor to your wives. Treat her with understanding as you live together. She may be weaker than you are, but she is your equal partner in God's gift of new life. If you don't treat her as you should, your prayers will not be heard." *1 Peter 3:7 (NLT)*

"Husbands, love your wives, just as Christ also loved the church and gave Himself up for her." *Ephesians 5:25*

"But I want you to understand that Christ s the head of every man, and the man is the head of a woman, and God is the head of Christ." *1 Corinthians 11:3*

"Wives, be subject to your husbands, as is fitting in the Lord. Husbands, love your wives and do not be embittered against them. Children, be obedient to your parents in all things, for this is well-pleasing to the Lord. Fathers, do not exasperate your children, so that they will not lose heart." *Colossians 3:18-21*

7. **There have been misguided Christians (or people masquerading as Christians) who have deviated from what the Bible teaches regarding the equality of men and women. Perhaps someone has turned you off to Christianity because they held a distorted view of women. If you still think the Bible is sexist toward women, read the Bible for yourself and find out the truth. You might start with the Gospel of John. Don't let a previous misconception keep you from enjoying God's Word and experiencing the fulfillment of a personal relationship with God.**

"How sweet are Your words to my taste! Yes, sweeter than honey to my mouth! From Your precepts I get understanding; therefore I hate every false way. Your word is a lamp to my feet and a light to my path." *Psalm 119:103-105*

8. **There is another important area where men and women will be treated equally. And that is, when each and every one of us must stand before God to give account of our lives.**

"For we will all stand before God's judgment seat. It is written: 'As surely as I live,' says the Lord, 'every knee will bow before me; every tongue will confess to God.' So then each one of us will give an account of himself to God." *Romans 14:10-12*

9. **What ultimately matters to God even more than your gender is whether or not your sins are forgiven. Women need a Savior as much as men. God sent his only Son Jesus to take the punishment for all sin and reconcile us back to God.**

"But God demonstrates His own love toward us, in that while we were yet sinners, Christ died for us." *Romans 5:8*

"For God so loved the world that He gave his only begotten Son, that whoever believes in Him should not perish but have everlasting life." *John 3:16*

89 Is The Bible Pro-Slavery, And Therefore Pro-Racism?

Slavery was accepted in many ancient civilizations. The Bible was written during a time when slavery was common (from about 1500 B.C. to about 90 A.D.) But just because the Bible talks about slavery, doesn't mean it is in favor of it. Unfortunately, many injustices have occurred in recent centuries by people who tried to justify slavery and oppression based on isolated passages taken out of context from the Bible. Even though not every verse on the topic is a condemnation of slavery, the Bible continually stresses the equality of all people and God's compassion for the poor, helpless, and downtrodden underclass. The Bible's overall view of slavery is negative, and clearly favors freedom. Within this context, much of the Bible's anti-slavery views are implicit rather than explicit.

The Bible equips us to live in a fallen, broken world which is far from ideal. The Bible faces life as it is, giving us guidance on issues we wouldn't face in a perfect world. For example, God is not pro-divorce, but He gives us guidance on dealing with divorce because it's a reality of living in an imperfect world.

It's clear that America's founding fathers were guilty of great hypocrisy by allowing slavery on one hand, and declaring "all men are created equal" on the other. The great anti-slavery movements of the 1700's and 1800's were led by concerned Christians like William Wilberforce in England and Abraham Lincoln in America. These anti-slavery leaders were guided by a clear understanding of the truths of the Bible, and the values it teaches regarding equality.

Sweeping social changes, such as the elimination of slavery, can often take decades. For example, the importation of slaves into America was banned in 1808, but slavery itself was not abolished until 1865. Even after slavery was banned in America, the lingering effects of racism continue even today. So what exactly does the Bible say about slavery?

---

1. The Bible makes it clear that masters, slaves, and all humans are equal in God's eyes, and made in God's image. The Bible condemns the pride of thinking that one group of people is better than another group.

"For all of you who were baptized into Christ have clothed yourselves with Christ. There is neither Jew nor Greek, there is neither slave nor free man, there is neither male nor female; for you are all one in Christ Jesus." *Galatians 3:27,28*

"If I have been unfair to my male or female servants, if I have refused to hear their complaints, how could I face God? What could I say when he questioned me about it? For God created both me and my servants. He created us both." *Job 31:13-15 (NLT)*

2. The Bible is against any system where one person's rights are based on taking away someone else's rights.

"Masters, grant to your slaves justice and fairness, knowing that you too have a Master in heaven." *Colossians 4:1*

"Therefore if there is any encouragement in Christ, if there is any consolation of love, if there is any fellowship of the Spirit, if any affection and compassion, make my joy complete by being of the same mind, maintaining the same love, united in spirit, intent on one purpose. Do nothing from selfishness or empty conceit, but with humility of mind regard one another as more important than yourselves; do not merely look out for your own personal interests, but also for the interests of others." *Philippians 2:1-4*

3. The Bible encouraged slaves to obtain freedom if possible. But when it was not an option, or until the time for freedom finally came, they were encouraged to find comfort in the inner freedom that comes from knowing God.

"Are you a slave? Don't let that worry you – but if you get a chance to be free, take it. And remember, if you were a slave when the Lord called you, the Lord has now set you free from the awful power of sin. And if you were free when the Lord called you, you are now a slave of Christ. God purchased you at a high price. Don't be enslaved by the world." *1 Corinthians 7:21-23 (NLT)*

4. The Apostle Paul wrote the book of Philemon, which was one of his most intimate letters. It was a personal appeal

to a wealthy slave owner to grant freedom to his runaway slave Onesimus, and not to punish him for escaping.

"So take this as a request from your friend Paul, an old man, now in prison for the sake of Christ Jesus. My plea is that you show kindness to Onesimus. I think of him as my own son because he became a believer as a result of my ministry here in prison…. Perhaps you could think of it this way: Onesimus ran away for a little while so you could have him back forever. He is no longer just a slave; he is a beloved brother, especially to me. Now he will mean much more to you, both as a slave and as a brother in the Lord. So if you consider me your partner, give him the same welcome you would give me if I were coming." *Philemon 9,10,15-17 (NLT)*

5. **Just because the Bible doesn't ban or condemn all slavery, we shouldn't jump to the conclusion that the Bible endorses slavery. In times of desperate famine in the ancient world, people would sometimes willingly sell themselves into slavery as a last resort to simply stay alive. Even then, masters were to treat them fairly.**

"For the poor will never cease to be in the land; therefore I command you, saying, 'You shall freely open your hand to your brother, to your needy and poor in your land.' If your kinsman, a Hebrew man or woman, is sold to you, then he shall serve you six years, but in the seventh year you shall set him free. When you set him free, you shall not send him away empty-handed. You shall furnish him liberally from your flock and from your threshing floor and from your wine vat; you shall give to him as the Lord your God has blessed you. You shall remember that you were a slave in the land of Egypt, and the Lord your God redeemed you; therefore I command you this today." *Deuteronomy 15:11-15*

6. **Slavery in modern times has been more based on race than it was in ancient times. Knowing the Bible teaches all races are equal, it clearly disqualifies race as a justification to kidnap people and force them into slavery.**

"We know that the law is good if one uses it properly. We also know that law is made not for the righteous but for lawbreakers and rebels, the ungodly and sinful, the unholy and irreligious; for those who kill their fathers or mothers, for murderers, for adulterers and perverts, for slave traders and liars and perjurers – and for whatever else is contrary to the sound doctrine that conforms to the glorious gospel of the blessed God, which he entrusted to me." *1 Timothy 1:8-11 (NIV)*

7. **The Bible's way of transforming society is to first transform hearts and minds, then cultural value systems follow. Once a person is set free from the slavery to sin, they want to do what's right and don't need laws to force them to.**

"Therefore I urge you, brethren, by the mercies of God, to present your bodies a living and holy sacrifice, acceptable to God, which is your spiritual service of worship. And do not be conformed to this world, but be transformed by the renewing of your mind, so that you may prove what the will of God is, that which is good and acceptable and perfect." *Romans 12:1,2*

"You blind Pharisee, first clean the inside of the cup and of the dish, so that the outside of it may become clean also." *Matthew 23:26*

8. **Even if you've never been the property of someone else, all of us have become slaves of sin. But when we trust Jesus as our Savior and submit to His Lordship, He gives us the power to break the slavery to sin.**

"So Jesus was saying to those Jews who had believed Him, 'If you continue in My word, then you are truly disciples of Mine; and you will know the truth, and the truth will make you free.' They answered Him, 'We are Abraham's descendants and have never yet been enslaved to anyone; how is it that You say, "You will become free"?' Jesus answered them, 'Truly, truly, I say to you, everyone who commits sin is the slave of sin. The slave does not remain in the house forever; the son does remain forever. So if the Son makes you free, you will be free indeed.'" *John 8:31-36*

9. **The writers of the Bible often mentioned they were "slaves" of the Lord. This means they submitted every area of their lives to Him. Millions of believers since then have done the same, and you'll never experience the freedom, peace, joy, and contentment God has for you if you rebel against Him and live enslaved to sin.**

"But now you are free from the power of sin and have become slaves of God. Now you do those things that lead to holiness and result in eternal life. For the wages of sin is death, but the free gift of God is eternal life through Christ Jesus our Lord." *Romans 6:22,23 (NLT)*

90 Is Life Less Fun As A Christian?

People reject Christianity for all kinds of reasons. Some people don't believe God exists, some don't believe Jesus was God's Son, some prefer the beliefs of other religions. But a whole lot of people reject the idea of becoming a Christian simply because they think the non-Christian lifestyle is more fun.

Hmmm: Sex, drugs, and rock and roll; or abstinence, sobriety, and hymns?

Are Christians missing out? Yes, but only on things like syphilis, gonorrhea, AIDS, and time in prison. Does God want us to enjoy life, or is He a Cosmic Killjoy who wants us to live boring lives? Is the Christian life really as dull and boring as non-Christians think? And compared to the benefits of being a Christian, is the non-Christian lifestyle overrated?

1. **Non-Christians will always struggle to understand why Christians prefer the Christian lifestyle, and why we submit our lives to the commands and guidelines God has given us in the Bible.**

   "But people who aren't Christians can't understand these truths from God's Spirit. It all sounds foolish to them because only those who have the Spirit can understand what the Spirit means. We who have the Spirit understand these things, but others can't understand us at all." *1 Corinthians 2:14,15 (NLT)*

2. **The difference between the Christian or non-Christian lifestyle comes down pleasing God or pleasing yourself; living for the Spirit or living for the flesh; living by God's definition of right and wrong or making up your own. The fleshly lifestyle is about indulging one's physical desires and appetites on demand, but the spiritual lifestyle is about submitting to Christ as Lord over every area of your life, and only indulging in physical desires and appetites within His allowed parameters. The forces of the flesh and the spirit are in a constant battle to control our lives.**

   "For those who are according to the flesh set their minds on the things of the flesh, but those who are according to the Spirit, the things of the Spirit. For the mind set on the flesh is death, but the mind set on the Spirit is life and peace, because the mind set on the flesh is hostile toward God; for it does not subject itself to the law of God, for it is not even able to do so, and those who are in the flesh cannot please God. However, you are not in the flesh but in the Spirit, if indeed the Spirit of God dwells in you. But if anyone does not have the Spirit of Christ, he does not belong to Him." *Romans 8:5-9*

3. **Does the fleshly, non-Christian life offer thrills? Of course! It would be exhilarating to jump off the Empire State Building, but the consequences are a killer. The deeds of the flesh have one set of results, and the spiritual life submitted to God will have a completely different set of results.**

   "Now the deeds of the flesh are evident, which are: immorality, impurity, sensuality, idolatry, sorcery, enmities, strife, jealousy, outbursts of anger, disputes, dissensions, factions, envying, drunkenness, carousing, and things like these, of which I forewarn you, just as I have forewarned you, that those who practice such things will not inherit the kingdom of God. But the fruit of the Spirit is love, joy, peace, patience, kindness, goodness, faithfulness, gentleness, self-control; against such things there is no law. Now those who belong to Christ Jesus have crucified the flesh with its passions and desires. If we live by the Spirit, let us also walk by the Spirit." *Galatians 5:19-25*

4. **One of the most deceptive things about sin is that it eventually has power over you. Living for the flesh makes you a slave of sin, and only through the power of God's help can you overcome it.**

   "Jesus said to the people who believed in him, 'You are truly my disciples if you keep obeying my teachings. And you will know the truth, and the truth will set you free.' 'But we are descendants of Abraham,' they said. 'We have never been slaves to anyone on earth. What do you mean, "set free"?' Jesus replied, 'I assure you that everyone who sins is a slave of sin. A slave is not a permanent member of the family, but a son is part of the family forever. So if the Son sets you free, you will indeed be free.'" *John 8:31-36 (NLT)*

5. **Even after becoming a Christian, fleshly temptations never go completely away. There's a constant battle between the flesh and the spirit that we can only win with the power of God's help. The Apostle Paul wrote openly of this universal struggle against his old sin nature.**

   "I don't understand myself at all, for I really want to do what is right, but I don't do it. Instead, I do the very thing I hate.

I know perfectly well that what I am doing is wrong, and my bad conscience shows that I agree that the law is good. But I can't help myself, because it is sin inside me that makes me do these evil things. I know I am rotten through and through so far as my old sinful nature is concerned. No matter which way I turn, I can't make myself do right. I want to, but I can't. When I want to do good, I don't. And when I try not to do wrong, I do it anyway. But if I am doing what I don't want to do, I am not really the one doing it; the sin within me is doing it. It seems to be a fact of life that when I want to do what is right, I inevitably do what is wrong. I love God's law with all my heart. But there is another law at work within me that is at war with my mind. This law wins the fight and makes me a slave to the sin that is still within me. Oh, what a miserable person I am! Who will free me from this life that is dominated by sin? Thank God! The answer is in Jesus Christ our Lord. So you see how it is: In my mind I really want to obey God's law, but because of my sinful nature I am a slave to sin." Romans 7:15-25 *(NLT)*

6. Christians aren't perfect. When a Christian sins, we are told to confess our sins to God who forgives us.

"My dear children, I am writing this to you so that you will not sin. But if you do sin, there is someone to plead for you before the Father. He is Jesus Christ, the one who pleases God completely. He is the sacrifice for our sins. He takes away not only our sins but the sins of all the world. And how can we be sure that we belong to him? By obeying his commandments. If someone says, 'I belong to God,' but doesn't obey God's commandments, that person is a liar and does not live in the truth." *1 John 2:1-4 (NLT)*

7. Many Christians can tell you their testimony of how they used to live a fleshly lifestyle, but have now given that up to live for the Lord – and even though they are not yet perfect, they are much happier. A life devoted to glorifying God gives us joy, peace, and purpose that far outweigh the empty thrills of self-indulgent sin.

"And you were dead in your trespasses and sins, in which you formerly walked according to the course of this world, according to the prince of the power of the air, of the spirit that is now working in the sons of disobedience. Among them we too all formerly lived in the lusts of our flesh, indulging the desires of the flesh and of the mind, and were by nature children of wrath, even as the rest. But God, being rich in mercy, because of His great love with which He loved us, even when we were dead in our transgressions, made us alive together with Christ (by grace you have been saved), and raised us up with Him, and seated us with Him in the heavenly places in Christ Jesus, so that in the ages to come He might show the surpassing riches of His grace in kindness toward us in Christ Jesus. For by grace you have been saved through faith; and that not of yourselves, it is the gift of God; not as a result of works, so that no one may boast." *Ephesians 2:1-9*

"What this means is that those who become Christians become new persons. They are not the same anymore, for the old life is gone. A new life has begun!" *2 Corinthians 5:17 (NLT)*

"For whoever wishes to save his life will lose it; but whoever loses his life for My sake will find it." *Matthew 16:25*

8. God does want us to enjoy life! One of the reasons Christ came was to set us free from slavery to sin and its painful consequences to ourselves and others, so we can enjoy life to the fullest and live forever with Him.

"I am the door; if anyone enters through Me, he shall be saved, and shall go in and out, and find pasture. The thief comes only to steal, and kill, and destroy; I came that they might have life, and might have it abundantly." *John 10:9,10*

9. When you become a Christian, it doesn't make all your problems go away. But God gives us the hope and strength to cope with our problems as we trust in His love, sovereignty, wisdom, and timing.

"Trust in the Lord with all your heart and do not lean on your own understanding. In all your ways acknowledge Him, and He will make your paths straight." *Proverbs 3:5,6*

10. If you're tired of the empty thrills and painful consequences of a sinful lifestyle, you can become a Christian by confessing your sins, asking Christ into your heart, and letting Him be Lord of your life. Then your new life begins!

"For God so loved the world that He gave His only begotten Son, that whoever believes in Him shall not perish but have everlasting life." *John 3:16*

"For the wages of sin is death, but the free gift of God is eternal life in Christ Jesus our Lord." *Romans 6:23*

91 What Is The Meaning Of Life?

The meaning of life has been pondered and discussed throughout the centuries. Some of us ask ourselves this question every day of our lives. Many Americans would say the meaning of life is: "He who dies with the most toys wins." Fortunately, the Bible gives us insight into the meaning of life. Several of the Bible's writers have told us how meaning comes when we live for the Lord rather than for ourselves. The apostle Paul wrote, "For to me, to live is Christ." (Philippians 1:21)

Millions of Christians agree with Paul that Christ gives our lives meaning. But what is it about Jesus that has brought meaning, joy, and fulfillment to the lives of His followers throughout history?

1. One of the main reasons Christ came was so that we could experience life to its absolute fullest thorugh Him, and not be fooled or deceived into seeking fulfillment apart from Him.

"I am the door; if anyone enters through Me, he will be saved, and will go in and out and find pasture. The thief comes only to steal and kill and destroy; I came that they may have life, and have it abundantly. " *John 10:9,10*

"Abide in Me, and I in you. As the branch cannot bear fruit of itself, unless it abides in the vine, so neither can you, unless you abide in Me. I am the vine, you are the branches; he who abides in Me, and I in him, he bears much fruit; for apart from Me you can do nothing. If anyone does not abide in Me, he is thrown away as a branch, and dries up." *John 15:4-6a*

2. Christ presented a unique way to find purpose and meaning in life. However, His way involves self denial and humility, which is the exact opposite of how the world tells us to seek meaning and happiness.

"Then Jesus said to His disciples, 'If anyone wishes to come after Me, let him deny himself, and take up his cross, and follow Me. For whoever wishes to save his life shall lose it; but whoever loses his life for My sake shall find it. For what will a man be profited, if he gains the whole world, and forfeits his soul? Or what will a man give in exchange for his soul?'" *Matthew 16:24-26*

3. John the Baptist understood this principle of finding joy by letting Christ be more important than himself.

"And so this joy of mine is made full. He must increase, but I must decrease." *John 3:29b,30*

4. God can free us from having to live for ourselves! We gain freedom and purpose when we seek to please and glorify God rather than ourselves. As ironic as it sounds, we gain great freedom when we become servants of Christ.

"If you abide in My word, then you are truly disciples of Mine; and you shall know the truth, and the truth shall make you free.... If therefore the Son shall make you free, you shall be free indeed." *John 8:31,32,36*

5. Living for the Lord means not living for selfish pleasure, or self-serving ambition. But when we turn our lives over to Him, we don't stop enjoying life's pleasures; we actually enjoy them more once we learn not to live merely for pleasure, and we learn to enjoy pleasures the way God intended. We don't lose all ambition; we simply focus on using our gifts, talents, and accomplishments to glorify God.

"Whether, then, you eat, drink, or whatever you do, do all to the glory of God." *1 Corinthians 10:31*

6. God is our maker, and He has given each of us a craving to find meaning in Him. But so often we try to fill that craving with other things such as riches, pleasures, possessions, beauty, fame, relationships, trophies, achievements, popularity, drugs, alcohol, etc. – all of which will ultimately let us down if they are the top priority in our lives. Only God can fill the "God-shaped" space in our lives that He created for Himself.

"For whom have I in heaven but You? And besides You, I desire nothing on earth. My flesh and my heart may fail, but God is the strength of my heart and my portion forever." *Psalm 73:25,26*

"'There is no peace for the wicked.' says the Lord." *Isaiah 48:22*

"You will make known to me the path of life; in Your presence is fulness of joy; in Your right hand there are pleasures forever." *Psalm 16:11*

"For the one who sows to his own flesh shall from the flesh reap corruption, but the one who sows to the Spirit shall from the Spirit reap eternal life." *Galatians 6:8*

7. In Jesus' famous Sermon on the Mount, He gave His followers a simple explanation of priorities:

"Do not worry then, saying, 'What will we eat?' or 'What will we drink?' or 'What will wear for clothing?' For the Gentiles eagerly seek all these things; for your heavenly Father knows that you need all these things. But seek first His kingdom and His righteousness, and all these things will be added to you." *Matthew 6:31-33*

Christian author C.S. Lewis built on this truth when he wrote, "Put first things first and we get second things thrown in: put second things first and we lose both first and second things." In other words, if God is not what makes you happy, nothing else does either. If God is what makes you happy, everything else does, too. It is impossible to attain the full meaning of life apart from knowing God. Jesus Christ, who was God in the flesh, came to earth and gave His life to pay for our sins so that we can be reconciled to our Maker.

8. Christ not only gives us more enjoyment and meaning in this earthly life, He also offers us eternal life. In fact, our eternal life begins the moment we accept Him as our Savior who forgives our sins.

"And the witness is this, that God has given us eternal life, and this life is in His Son. He who has the Son has the life; he who does not have the Son of God does not have the life. These things I have written to you who believe in the name of the Son of God, in order that you may know that you have eternal life." *1 John 5:11-13*

"God demonstrates His own love for us in that while we were yet sinners Christ died for us." *Romans 5:8*

"For God so loved the world, that He gave His only begotten Son, that whoever believes in Him shall not perish, but have everlasting life." *John 3:16*

9. To start experiencing the blessings God gives to those who trust Him, ask Christ to forgive your sins, and ask Him to come in to your life and give you meaning.

"For we also once were foolish ourselves, disobedient, deceived... enslaved to various lusts and pleasures. But when the kindness of God our Savior and His love for mankind appeared, He saved us, not on the basis of deeds which we have done in righteousness, but according to His mercy." *Titus 3:3-5*

"And you were dead in your trespasses and sins, in which you formerly walked according to the course of this world, according to the prince of the power of the air, of the spirit that is now working in the sons of disobedience. Among them we too all formerly lived in the lusts of our flesh, indulging the desires of the flesh and of the mind, and were by nature children of wrath, even as the rest. But God, being rich in mercy, because of His great love with which He loved us, even when we were dead in our transgressions, made us alive together with Christ." *Ephesians 2:1-5a*

"The wages of sin is death, but the free gift of God is eternal life in Christ Jesus our Lord." *Romans 6:23*

10. It's possible to know the initial joy that comes from knowing Christ as your Savior, but the joy fades if we don't submit our lives to His Lordship. The fullest joy comes when we live for Him rather than for ourselves.

"In a similar way these are the ones on whom seed was sown on the rocky places, who, when they hear the word, immediately receive it with joy; and they have no firm root in themselves, but are only temporary; then, when affliction or persecution arises because of the word, immediately they fall away. And others are the ones on whom seed was sown among the thorns; these are the ones who have heard the word, but the worries of the world, and the deceitfulness of riches, and the desires for other things enter in and choke the word, and it becomes unfruitful. And those are the ones on whom seed was sown on the good soil; and they hear the word and accept it and bear fruit, thirty, sixty, and a hundredfold." *Mark 4:16-20*

11. When you invite God into your life, it's like flipping a switch – your unique gifts, talents, and personality come to life. Once you let Him be Lord of your life, you'll be more you than you've ever been before.

"Lord, you have brought light to my life; my God, you light up my darkness." *Psalm 18:28 (NLT)*

92 What's So Bad About Sinning If No One Gets Hurt?

Some people say that as long as no one gets hurt, then it's not a sin in the first place. People say things such as: "If it's between consenting adults, what's the harm?" Or: "If nobody gets hurt, why should that limit my freedom?" Or: "It's my body so I can do what I want." Or: "If nobody finds out, and I can get away with it, then it's OK." Then of course there's the ever-popular: "Everyone else is doing it."

The Bible teaches that many activities are wrong even though the person doing it may not see that others are being harmed whatsoever. Little white lies, cheating on tests or taxes, music pirating, insider trading, sneaking into a movie, drug or alcohol abuse, promiscuity, and countless other activities easily fall into this category of what the world sees as "sins that don't hurt anybody." But is it true that these sins don't hurt anybody? And do these sins hurt the sinner, even though they may not even realize it?

1. **Jesus Himself was once tempted to commit a sin that might not have hurt anybody else. After a very long fast, He was tempted to misuse His miraculous powers in a selfish way to satisfy His hunger by turning stones into bread. There was no one around, no one would have seen it, and no one would have known. But He chose not to sin, and He reminded Satan that God's standard is what we must follow, even when no one is watching.**

   "And the tempter came and said to Him, 'If You are the Son of God, command that these stones become bread.' But He answered and said, 'It is written, "Man shall not live on bread alone, but on every word that proceeds out of the mouth of God."'" *Matthew 4:3,4*

   "The time is coming when everything will be revealed; all that is secret will be made public. Whatever you have said in the dark will be heard in the light, and what you have whispered behind closed doors will be shouted from the housetops for all to hear!" *Luke 12:2,3 (NLT)*

2. **King David taught his son Solomon that God is always observing our actions, thoughts, and motives.**

   "As for you, my son Solomon, know the God of your father, and serve Him with a whole heart and a willing mind; for the Lord searches all hearts, and understands every intent of the thoughts. If you seek Him, He will let you find Him; but if you forsake Him, He will reject you forever." *1 Chronicles 28:9*

3. **The world's standards of right and wrong are constantly changing, depending on public opinion. But God's standard remains consistent throughout the ages.**

   "Every good thing given and every perfect gift is from above, coming down from the Father of lights, with whom there is no variation or shifting shadow." *James 1:17*

   "And do not be conformed to this world, but be transformed by the renewing of your mind, so that you may prove what the will of God is, that which is good and acceptable and perfect." *Romans 12:2*

4. **The things you do when no one is watching are the ultimate test of character. Small, private sins start your spiritual momentum going in the wrong direction. Little compromises turn into big compromises. Little choices are excellent indicators of character, and are good indicators of how we will decide major choices.**

   "He who is faithful in a very little thing is faithful also in much; and he who is unrighteous in a very little thing is unrighteous also in much." *Luke 16:10*

5. **Knowing the right thing to do but not doing it, is wrong in God's eyes, even if no one else is watching.**

   "Therefore, to one who knows the right thing to do and does not do it, to him it is sin." *James 4:17*

6. **Every time you choose to sin and ignore the inner conviction of your conscience, it dulls your conscience for the next moral decision. When we listen to our conscience, it helps fine-tune it for the next moral decision. Our moral choices will either create a positive spiral of consequences, or a negative spiral of consequences.**

   "Cling tightly to your faith in Christ, and always keep your conscience clear. For some people have deliberately violated their consciences; as a result, their faith has been shipwrecked." *1 Timothy 1:19 (NLT)*

"Trust in the Lord with all your heart and do not lean on your own understanding. In all your ways acknowledge Him, and He will make your paths straight. Do not be wise in your own eyes; fear the Lord and turn away from evil. It will be healing to your body and refreshment to your bones." *Proverbs 3:5-8*

7. God's love for us is unconditional. But closeness and intimacy with God are conditional on our obedience to His commands. When we choose obedience, our relationship with God deepens and becomes more intimate, but when we disobey He becomes more distant. You could say we "obey our way" to closeness to God.

"He who has My commandments and keeps them is the one who loves Me; and he who loves Me will be loved by My Father, and I will love him and will disclose Myself to him." *John 14:21*

8. Unwanted pregnancies and incurable diseases aren't the only reason to avoid promiscuity. It also creates deeply ingrained behavior patterns of giving in to all sexual desires. These patterns are difficult to unlearn once a person tries to be faithful in a monogamous relationship. Many marriages and families are destroyed because of behavior patterns learned before the relationship even started. Being able to control sexual desire is a hallmark of a faithful partner; allowing sexual desire to control you is a hallmark of an unfaithful partner.

"But each one is tempted when he is carried away and enticed by his own lust. Then when lust has conceived, it gives birth to sin; and when sin is accomplished, it brings forth death. Do not be deceived, my beloved brethren." *James 1:14-16*

"Flee immorality. Every other sin that a man commits is outside the body, but the immoral man sins against his own body. Or do you not know that your body is a temple of the Holy Spirit who is in you, whom you have from God, and that you are not your own? For you have been bought with a price: therefore glorify God in your body." *1 Corinthians 6:18-20*

9. Sin can be fun and exciting at the moment, but afterwards it yields painful consequences.

"Bread obtained by falsehood is sweet to a man, but afterward his mouth will be filled with gravel." *Proverbs 20:17*

"The woman named Folly is loud and brash. She is ignorant and doesn't even know it. She sits in her doorway on the heights overlooking the city. She calls out to men going by who are minding their own business. 'Come home with me,' she urges the simple. To those without good judgment, she says, 'Stolen water is refreshing; food eaten in secret tastes the best!' But the men don't realize that her former guests are now in the grave." *Proverbs 9:13-18 (NLT)*

10. God loves us just the way we are, and He loves us too much to let us stay just the way we are. Sin enslaves us, but letting Jesus be Lord of your life sets us free from the slavery to sin, and gives us power to resist temptation.

"For speaking out arrogant words of vanity they entice by fleshly desires, by sensuality, those who barely escape from the ones who live in error, promising them freedom while they themselves are slaves of corruption; for by what a man is overcome, by this he is enslaved." *2 Peter 2:18,19*

"It was for freedom that Christ set us free; therefore keep standing firm and do not be subject again to a yoke of slavery." *Galatians 5:1*

11. All disobedience short-changes us from God's fullest blessings. Sin brings death, but Christ took the death penalty our sin deserves so that we can become alive spiritually and be with God forever in heaven. To receive the forgiveness Christ offers, confess your sins and ask Christ into your heart as your Savior and Lord.

"The wages of sin is death, but the free gift of God is eternal life in Christ Jesus our Lord." *Romans 6:23*

"If we say we have no sin, we are only fooling ourselves and refusing to accept the truth. But if we confess our sins to him, he is faithful and just to forgive us and to cleanse us from every wrong. If we claim we have not sinned, we are calling God a liar and showing that his word has no place in our hearts." *1 John 1:8-10 (NLT)*

"I am the door; if anyone enters through Me, he will be saved, and will go in and out and find pasture. The thief comes only to steal and kill and destroy; I came that they may have life, and have it abundantly." *John 10:9,10*

93 What About People Who Have No Interest In Spiritual Things?

Everybody has certain things they are interested in, and certain things they're not interested in. You might be passionate about sports cars, fly fishing, and jazz, but have no interest in weaving, square dancing, or skeet shooting. To be more specific, when it comes to spiritual things, some people love to read, study, and discuss spiritual matters, but lots of people just aren't interested in spiritual things. To describe this type of mindset, someone coined the term "apatheists." Maybe apatheists grew up in a family that never talked about spiritual things. Or maybe they've been turned off by churches in the past. Maybe some hypocrite made them think spirituality was phony. Or maybe spiritual people came across as unintelligent or gullible. Or maybe they feel that if they can't see it, touch it, or smell it, then it's probably not real. Another possible reason why apatheists might close their eyes to spiritual things is because they are afraid of what they might find – sort of like a person who won't see a doctor for fear of getting bad news. But whatever the reason is for not caring about spiritual things, many people will testify that there are many blessings to be had by being a seeker of God and His spiritual truths.

1. God loves us, He is knowable, and if we seek Him wholeheartedly, He will let us find Him.

"And you will seek Me and find Me, when you search for Me with all your heart." *Jeremiah 29:13*

"The God who made the world and all things in it... made from one, every nation of mankind to live on all the face of the earth... that they should seek God, if perhaps they might grope for Him and find Him, though He is not far from each one of us." *Acts 17:24,26,27*

"Draw near to God and He will draw near to you." *James 4:8*

"Shout joyfully to the Lord, all the earth. Serve the Lord with gladness; come before Him with joyful singing. Know that the Lord Himself is God; it is He who has made us, and not we ourselves; we are His people and the sheep of His pasture. Enter His gates with thanksgiving and His courts with praise. Give thanks to Him, bless His name. For the Lord is good; His lovingkindness is everlasting and His faithfulness to all generations." *Psalm 100:1-5*

2. Not only are we told to seek God, but God is seeking us, so that we can form a closer relationship with Him.

"For the eyes of the Lord move to and fro throughout the earth that He may strongly support those whose heart is completely His." *2 Chronicles 16:9*

"True worshipers shall worship the Father in spirit and truth; for such people the Father seeks to be His worshipers." *John 4:23*

"For the Son of Man (Jesus) has come to seek and save that which was lost." *Luke 19:10*

3. We can't experience life to the fullest without a relationship with God.

"I am the door; if anyone enters through Me, he shall be saved, and shall go in and out, and find pasture. The thief comes only to steal, and kill, and destroy; I came that they might have life, and might have it abundantly." *John 10:9,10*

"Then Jesus again spoke to them, saying, 'I am the Light of the world; he who follows Me will not walk in the darkness, but will have the Light of life.'" *John 8:12*

4. Jesus reached out to people, but not all people responded. He talked about those who were disinterested, unresponsive, hard-hearted, apathetic, and overly critical. Because of these traits, they missed who He was.

"'How shall I describe this generation?' Jesus asked. 'With what will I compare them? They are like a group of children playing a game in the public square. They complain to their friends, "We played wedding songs, and you weren't happy, so we played funeral songs, but you weren't sad." For John the Baptist didn't drink wine and he often fasted, and you say, "He's demon possessed." And I, the Son of Man, feast and drink, and you say, "He's a glutton and a drunkard, and a friend of the worst sort of sinners!" But wisdom is shown to be right by the lives of those who follow it.'" *Luke 7:31-35 (NLT)*

"For the hearts of these people are hardened, and their ears cannot hear, and they have closed their eyes – so their eyes cannot see, and their ears cannot hear, and their hearts cannot understand, and they cannot turn to me and let me heal them." *Matthew 13:15 (NLT)*

5. Jesus said Christians who are apathetic and disinterested in knowing Him are distasteful to Him.

"I know your deeds, that you are neither cold nor hot; I wish that you were cold or hot. So because you are lukewarm, and neither hot nor cold, I will spit you out of My mouth." *Revelation 3:15,16*

6. What makes us disinterested in the things of God? All humans have sinned, and our sinful nature makes us want to avoid God and live by our own rules instead of His. Sin also makes us avoid exposure to the light of God's truths.

"The Lord has looked down from heaven upon the sons of men, to see if there are any who understand, who seek after God. They have all turned aside; together they have become corrupt; there is no one who does good, not even one." *Psalm 14:1-3*

"The heart is more deceitful than all else and is desperately sick; who can understand it? I, the Lord, search the heart, I test the mind, even to give to each man according to his ways, according to the results of his deeds." *Jeremiah 17:9,10*

7. It takes effort and discipline to grow spiritually. Many people might be disciplined in other areas, but they are spiritual sluggards. They can have spiritual nourishment at their fingertips (available in the Bible, Christian books, or churches) but be too lethargic to make an effort to grow spiritually.

"Some people are so lazy that they won't even lift a finger to feed themselves." *Proverbs 19:24 (NLT)*

"The soul of the sluggard craves and gets nothing, but the soul of the diligent is made fat." *Proverbs 13:4*

8. God has provided a way for us to have access to Him and know Him, through His Son Jesus Christ.

"Jesus said to him, 'I am the way, and the truth, and the life; no one comes to the Father, but through Me.'" *John 14:6*

"For there is one God, and one mediator also between God and men, the man Christ Jesus, who gave Himself as a ransom for all." *1 Timothy 2:5,6a*

9. Our sinful nature tends to keep us from seeking God. But God is willing to forgive all our sins thanks to the payment Jesus made on the cross. He gave His life to take the punishment for our sins.

"For God so loved the world, that He gave His only begotten Son, that whoever believes in Him shall not perish, but have everlasting life. For God did not send the Son into the world to judge the world; but that the world should be saved through Him." *John 3:16,17*

"For the wages of sin is death, but the free gift of God is eternal life in Christ Jesus our Lord." *Romans 6:23*

"But God demonstrates His own love for us in that while we were yet sinners Christ died for us." *Romans 5:8*

10. By confessing your sins and inviting Christ into your life, your new life as a Christian will begin.

"This is the message we have heard from Him and announce to you, that God is Light, and in Him there is no darkness at all. If we say that we have fellowship with Him and yet walk in the darkness, we lie and do not practice the truth; but if we walk in the Light as He Himself is in the Light, we have fellowship with one another, and the blood of Jesus His Son cleanses us from all sin. If we say that we have no sin, we are deceiving ourselves and the truth is not in us. If we confess our sins, He is faithful and righteous to forgive us our sins and to cleanse us from all unrighteousness. If we say that we have not sinned, we make Him a liar and His word is not in us." *1 John 1:5-9*

"Come to Me, all who are weary and heavy-laden, and I will give you rest. Take My yoke upon you and learn from Me, for I am gentle and humble in heart, and you will find rest for your souls." *Matthew 11:28,29*

94 If Church Has Turned You Off, Why Take A Second Look?

Go to any church long enough and eventually someone will annoy you. Someone will disappoint you. Someone may even hurt you. It won't take long to realize that not every churchgoer is a saint. Perhaps this has happened to you at some point in your life. Maybe you crossed paths with people who were mean or hurtful. Maybe you were the victim of someone who was rude, gossipy, condescending, controlling, dishonest, immoral, legalistic, deceptive, abusive, or worse. Maybe the hurtful person was a layperson, or even a nun, priest, pastor, or staff member you trusted. Maybe you reached out for help, but your situation was swept under the rug by people living in denial and afraid to deal with the real problem.

If you've been hurt by someone in your church, it can rock the very core of your faith. Many people who have been hurt by Christians decide that "organized religion" is not for them. So they wash their hands of the whole thing and never go back. It can often lead to years of pain and bitterness. In spite of previous pain and letdowns, there are lots of reasons to look beyond the so-called Christians and take a second look at a relationship directly with Jesus Christ.

1. Jesus had many confrontations with religious leaders who were not living in a way that pleased God. He never minced words when He told them how their hypocrisy dishonored God and drove people away.

"But woe to you, scribes and Pharisees, hypocrites, because you shut off the kingdom of heaven from people; for you do not enter in yourselves, nor do you allow those who are entering to go in. Woe to you, scribes and Pharisees, hypocrites, because you devour widows' houses, and for a pretense you make long prayers; therefore you will receive greater condemnation. Woe to you, scribes and Pharisees, hypocrites, because you travel around on sea and land to make one proselyte; and when he becomes one, you make him twice as much a son of hell as yourselves." *Matthew 23:13-15*

2. In Jesus' time, there were people who were misusing their position in His temple for monetary profit, and He chased them out!

"In the temple area he saw merchants selling cattle, sheep, and doves for sacrifices; and he saw money changers behind their counters. Jesus made a whip from some ropes and chased them all out of the temple. He drove out the sheep and oxen, scattered the money changers' coins over the floor, and turned over their tables. Then, going over to the people who sold doves, he told them, 'Get these things out of here. Don't turn my Father's house into a marketplace!'" *John 2:14-16 (NLT)*

3. Many people who claim to follow Christ yet do not live by His teachings may not be Christians at all. They are masquerading as Christians. Jesus warned us about these phonies, and said their deeds would expose them as fakes.

"Beware of the false prophets, who come to you in sheep's clothing, but inwardly are ravenous wolves. You will know them by their fruits. Grapes are not gathered from thorn bushes nor figs from thistles, are they? So every good tree bears good fruit, but the bad tree bears bad fruit. A good tree cannot produce bad fruit, nor can a bad tree produce good fruit. Every tree that does not bear good fruit is cut down and thrown into the fire. So then, you will know them by their fruits. Not everyone who says to Me, 'Lord, Lord,' will enter the kingdom of heaven, but he who does the will of My Father who is in heaven will enter." *Matthew 7:15-21*

4. The Apostle Paul gave strict instructions not to tolerate hypocrisy and gross misbehavior within the church.

"I wrote you in my letter not to associate with immoral people; I did not at all mean with the immoral people of this world, or with the covetous and swindlers, or with idolaters; for then you would have to go out of the world. But actually, I wrote to you not to associate with any so-called brother if he should be an immoral person, or covetous, or an idolater, or a reviler, or a drunkard, or a swindler – not to even eat with such a one." *1 Corinthians 5:9-11*

"Now I urge you, brethren, keep an eye on those who cause dissensions and hindrances contrary to the teaching which you learned, and turn away from them. For such men are slaves, not of our Lord Christ, but of their own appetites; and by their smooth and flattering speech they deceive the hearts of the unsuspecting." *Romans 16:17,18*

5. **All people are sinners. Even people who are genuine followers of Christ and who are trying to please Him can still have blind spots. We're all at various places in our spiritual maturity.**

"Indeed, there is not a righteous man on earth who continually does good and who never sins." *Ecclesiastes 7:20*

6. **When other Chrsistians let you down, it's crucial to remember that we place our faith in Christ, not other Christians.**

"For there is salvation in no one else; for there is no other name under heaven that has been given among men, by which we must be saved." *Acts 4:12*

"For there is one God, and one mediator also between God and men, the man Christ Jesus, who gave Himself as a ransom for all." *1 Timothy 2:5,6a*

7. **God holds hypocrites accountable for their actions. Someday God will personally evaluate the lives and actions of hypocrites, as well as every human who has ever lived – including you.**

"So then each one of us shall give account of himself to God." *Romans 14:12*

"And I saw a great white throne and Him who sat upon it, from whose presence earth and heaven fled away, and no place was found for them. And I saw the dead, the great and the small, standing before the throne, and books were opened; and another book was opened, which is the book of life; and the dead were judged from the things which were written in the book of life, according to their deeds. And if anyone's name was not found written in the book of life, he was thrown into the lake of fire." *Revelation 20:11,12,15*

8. **So often, we feel justice is done when a guilty person is punished for their evil deeds. But we forget that, even though hypocrites are guilty of their sin, all of us are also guilty of our own sin and will be held accountable. One of the hallmarks of a hypocrite is to focus on the sins of others and ignore their own. But sin is what causes each of us to be separated from God, both now and after we die.**

"For all have sinned and fall short of the glory of God." *Romans 3:23*

"But your iniquities have made a separation between you and your God, and your sins have hid His face from you, so that He does not hear." *Isaiah 59:2*

9. **Fortunately, because of God's great love for us, He sent His sinless Son Jesus to pay the price for all the sins of mankind so that we can escape the punishment of being separated from God.**

"God demonstrates His own love for us in that while we were yet sinners Christ died for us." *Romans 5:8*

"For God so loved the world, that He gave His only begotten Son, that whoever believes in Him shall not perish, but have everlasting life." *John 3:16*

"The wages of sin is death, but the free gift of God is eternal life in Christ Jesus our Lord." *Romans 6:23*

10. **It's usually easy to see when someone else is guilty of sin, but it can be more difficult to see our own. In order to receive forgiveness for our sins, we must confess to God that we are sinners. If we refuse to admit that each of us have sin in our lives, then that makes us hypocrites ourselves.**

"If we say that we have no sin, we are deceiving ourselves, and the truth is not in us. If we confess our sin, He is faithful and righteous to forgive us our sins and to cleanse us from all unrighteousness. If we say that we have not sinned, we make Him a liar, and His word is not in us." *1 John 1:8-10*

11. **According to the Bible, Jesus is the only way for sinful man to be reconciled to God who is holy. Confess your sin to Him today and invite Him into your life. He's definitely worth a second look!**

"Jesus said to him, 'I am the way, and the truth, and the life ; no one comes to the Father but through Me.'" *John 14:6*

"Behold, I stand at the door and knock; if any one hears My voice and opens the door, I will come into Him." *Revelation 3:20*

95 With So Many Hypocrites, Why Become A Christian?

When you look at the church, the people you notice most are often the hypocrites. Everyone knows a spiteful churchgoer, unfaithful preacher, or greedy televangelist. If Christians are so far from perfect, why become one? As Voltaire put it: "If Christians want us to believe in a Redeemer, let them act redeemed."

One man who is now a devoted Christian, never liked churchgoers while he was growing up. One day as a kid, while living next to a family of churchgoers, his football went over the fence. The little girl who lived there immediately ran out into the yard and popped his ball with an ice pick. He automatically assumed all churchgoers were just as spiteful. So often, the people who live the teachings of Christ don't get noticed as much as hypocrites, or at least don't get as much publicity as an unfaithful televangelist. Hypocrisy is hated by people outside the church, but it was hated more by Jesus Himself. Hypocritical followers were harming His message! Many of His sermons dealt with hypocrisy.

"Hypocrite" was the Greek word for "mask wearer." Actors in Greek theatre were called hypocrites because they wore masks to represent the various characters they portrayed. This is a perfect way to understand what a hypocrite is; someone masquerading as someone he is not. When evaluating the Christian faith, try to look beyond the hypocrites who claim to follow Christ. Instead, look closely at Christ Himself and the large number of fully devoted followers whose lives have been changed by genuinely following His teachings. And next time you get mad because someone acts like a hypocrite, examine yourself and look for any of your own shortcomings. It's always easier to focus on someone else's sins rather than your own.

1. Jesus forcefully denounced many different forms of hypocrisy; such as:

- Hypocrites who perform religious acts simply to be noticed by others. *Matthew 6:1-18, 23:5-7*
- Hypocrites who denounce the sins of others while ignoring blatant sins of their own. *Matthew 7:5*
- Hypocrites who prevent others from finding the Kingdom of God. *Matthew 23:13*
- Hypocrites who devour the finances of poor widows. *Matthew 23:14*
- Hypocrites who do not "practice what they preach." *Matthew 23:13*
- Hypocrites who expect more godly behavior from others than they expect from themselves. *Matthew 23:4*
- Hypocrites who corrupt the faith of young believers. *Matthew 23:15*
- Hypocrites who swear false oaths they don't intend to keep. *Matthew 23:16*
- Hypocrites who perform religious duties yet ignore basic virtues like justice and mercy. *Matthew 23:23*
- Hypocrites who practice legalism. *Luke 13:15*
- Hypocrites who appear righteous on the outside yet are evil on the inside. *Matthew 23:25-28*
- Hypocrites who claim to follow God yet disregard obeying Him. *Matthew 23:29-36*

2. The apostle Paul detested hypocrisy, and told people within the church to avoid hypocritical and immoral persons who claim to be Christians. Paul did not want Christ's reputation damaged by hypocrites.

"I wrote you in my letter not to associate with immoral people; I did not at all mean with the immoral people of this world, or with the covetous and swindlers, or with idolaters; for then you would have to go out of the world. But actually, I wrote to you not to associate with any so-called brother if he should be an immoral person, or covetous, or an idolater, or a reviler, or a drunkard, or a swindler – not to even eat with such a one."
1 Corinthians 5:9-11

"Now I urge you, brethren, keep an eye on those who cause dissensions and hindrances contrary to the teaching which you learned, and turn away from them. For such men are slaves, not of our Lord Christ, but of their own appetites; and by their smooth and flattering speech they deceive the hearts of the unsuspecting." *Romans 16:17,18*

3. Many of the people who claim to be Christians, yet do not live by His teachings, may not be Christians at all. Jesus warned us to look out for these fake Christians who mislead others and misrepresent His teachings.

"Beware of the false prophets, who come to you in sheep's clothing, but inwardly are ravenous wolves. You will know them by their fruits. Grapes are not gathered from thorn bushes nor figs from thistles, are they? So every good tree bears good fruit, but the bad tree bears bad fruit. A good tree cannot produce bad fruit, nor can a bad tree produce good fruit. Every tree that does not bear good fruit is cut down and thrown into the fire. So then, you will know them by their fruits. Not everyone who says to Me, 'Lord, Lord,' will enter the kingdom of heaven, but he who does the will of My Father who is in heaven will enter." *Matthew 7:15-21*

4. God will personally evaluate the actions of hypocrites, as well as every other human – including you.

"So then each one of us shall give account of himself to God." *Romans 14:12*

"For the Son of Man (Jesus) is going to come in the glory of His Father with His angels, and will then recompense every man according to his deeds." *Matthew 16:27*

"And I saw a great white throne and Him who sat upon it, from whose presence earth and heaven fled away, and no place was found for them. And I saw the dead, the great and the small, standing before the throne, and books were opened; and another book was opened, which is the book of life; and the dead were judged from the things which were written in the book of life, according to their deeds.... And if anyone's name was not found written in the book of life, he was thrown into the lake of fire." *Revelation 20:11,12,15*

5. So often, we feel justice is done when a guilty person is punished for their evil deeds. But we forget that even though hypocrites are guilty of their sin, all of us are also guilty of our own sin and will be held accountable. One of the hallmarks of a hypocrite is to focus on the sins of others and ignore their own.

"For all have sinned and fall short of the glory of God." *Romans 3:23*

"But your iniquities have made a separation between you and your God, and your sins have hid His face from you, so that He does not hear." *Isaiah 59:2*

6. Just because you may be good most of the time, it only takes one sin to separate you from God.

"Whoever keeps the whole law and yet stumbles in one point, he has become guilty of all." *James 2:10*

"Indeed, there is not a righteous man on earth who continually does good and who never sins." *Ecclesiastes 7:20*

7. Fortunately, because of God's great love for us, He sent His sinless Son Jesus to pay the price for all the sins of mankind so that we can escape the punishment of being separated from God.

"God demonstrates His own love for us in that while we were yet sinners Christ died for us." *Romans 5:8*

"The wages of sin is death, but the free gift of God is eternal life in Christ Jesus our Lord." *Romans 6:23*

"For God so loved the world, that He gave His only begotten Son, that whoever believes in Him shall not perish, but have everlasting life." *John 3:16*

8. It's often easy to see someone else's sin, such as hypocrisy or whatever. But it can be more difficult to see our own sin and admit that we are sinners. To receive forgiveness for our sins, we must confess them to God. If we refuse to admit that each of us have sin in our lives, then that makes us hypocrites ourselves.

"If we say that we have no sin, we are deceiving ourselves, and the truth is not in us. If we confess our sin, He is faithful and righteous to forgive us our sins and to cleanse us from all unrighteousness. If we say that we have not sinned, we make Him a liar, and His word is not in us." *1 John 1:8-10*

"I acknowledged my sin to You, and my iniquity I did not hide; I said 'I will confess my transgressions to the Lord;' and You forgave the guilt of my sin." *Psalm 32:5*

9. According to the Bible, Jesus is the only way for sinful man to be reconciled to God who is holy. You can confess your sinfulness to Him today and invite Christ into your life.

"Jesus said to him, 'I am the way, and the truth, and the life; no one comes to the Father, but through Me.'" *John 14:6*

"I stand at the door and knock; if any one hears My voice and opens the door, I will come into Him." *Revelation 3:20*

96 Is Organized Religion Necessary For Spiritual Growth?

Lots of people who are spiritually-minded feel they can grow closer to God on their own than by getting involved in any kind of church or group setting. They feel like they just don't get much out of worshiping in a church setting; and depending on the health and maturity of the church they are describing, they could be right.

A person's spirituality can be a very personal thing, and the definition of "spirituality" can vary from person to person. To some people, it might mean doing yoga, chanting, observing a sunset, or calling a psychic hotline. To others it might mean being alone in the great outdoors. Within a Christian context, it would likely include the practices of prayer, Bible intake, and personal worship. Spending time alone with God is important for spiritual growth, but is this all we need? Did Jesus and the New Testament teach that the isolationist trend of "Just-Jesus-and-me" is the best way to grow closer to God – without involvement in a church community? Is that how God designed us, or do we need each other to grow spiritually?

1. **The Bible stresses the importance of individual time spent directly with God without interference or distractions from anyone else. Jesus often slipped away to have private fellowship with God the Father.**

   "In the early morning, while it was still dark, Jesus got up, left the house, and went away to a secluded place, and was praying there. Simon and his companions searched for Him; they found Him, and said to Him, 'Everyone is looking for You.'" *Mark 1:35-37*

   "It was at this time that He went off to the mountain to pray, and He spent the whole night in prayer to God." *Luke 6:12*

2. **Even though we are to spend time individually with God, and we can't develop a close relationship with Him with out it, the Bible also stresses the importance of staying connected with others.**

   "Let us consider how to stimulate one another to love and good deeds, not forsaking our own assembling together, as is the habit of some, but encouraging one another; and all the more as you see the day drawing near." *Hebrews 10:24,25*

   "He who separates himself seeks his own desire, he quarrels against all sound wisdom." *Proverbs 18:1*

3. **The Bible clearly presents the idea of balance for our spiritual lives. Spending time alone with God is critical to growing spiritually, but so is fellowship with other like-minded believers. It's like which wing of a bird is more important; the left or the right? If you grew up in a church setting which gave you bad memories, it might have turned you off to getting involved in organized religion ever again. Maybe the word "religion" brings up the idea of legalism, control, or hypocrisy. But to understand our need for "organized religion," it helps to understand the true definition of the word "religion." The "lig" is a latin word meaning "connect." It's the same root word found in the word "ligament." The "re" at the beginning makes the true meaning "re-connect." So when we assemble with other believers, we are reconnecting with like-minded people who share similar values and beliefs, which strengthens our faith. True religion is also how we reconnect with God Himself.**

   "Those who believed what Peter said were baptized and added to the church – about three thousand in all. They joined with the other believers and devoted themselves to the apostles' teaching and fellowship, sharing in the Lord's Supper and in prayer." *Acts 2:41,42 (NLT)*

4. **How does fellowship with other believers strengthen our faith? At the moment of conversion, God gives every Christian at least one spiritual gift for the specific purpose of helping others and building each other up. Paul wrote extensively about spiritual gifts within the church in 1 Corinthians 12 – 14. He compared the church to a human body, where every part plays a vital role in the overall heatlh of the body.**

   "Now concerning spiritual gifts, brethren, I do not want you to be unaware.... Now there are varieties of gifts, but the same Spirit. And there are varieties of ministries, and the same Lord. There are varieties of effects, but the same God who works all things in all persons. But to each one is given the manifestation of the Spirit for the common good.... For even as the body is one and yet has many members, and all the members of the body, though they are many, are one body, so also is Christ. For by one Spirit we were all baptized into one body, whether Jews or Greeks, whether slaves or free, and we were all made to drink of one Spirit. For the body is not one member, but many. If the foot says, 'Because I am not a hand, I am not a part of the body,' it is not for this reason any the less a part of the body. And if the ear says, 'Because I am not an eye, I am not a part of the body,' it is not for this reason any the less a part of the body. If the whole body were an eye, where would the hearing be? If the whole were hearing, where would the sense of smell be? But now God has placed the members, each one of them, in the body, just as He desired.... And if one member suffers, all the members suffer with it; if one member is honored, all the members rejoice with it. Now you are Christ's body, and individually members of it." *1 Corinthians 12:1,4-7,12-18,26-27*

5. **If you are a Christian, God has invested a lot in you. If you refuse to get involved in a church, then you are not exercising your spiritual gift as God intended. As a result, other believers will suffer because of your refusal to get involved and use your gift. You will also be stunted spiritually because you are not benefitting from the gifts of other believers. Imagine if your eye, hand, or lung decided it didn't want to be part of your body. Not only would your body suffer, but that part would wither and die because it's not getting nourished by the rest of the body.**

"God has given gifts to each of you from his great variety of spiritual gifts. Manage them well so that God's generosity can flow through you." *1 Peter 4:10 (NLT)*

6. **A healthy, biblical church is like a spiritual ecosystem where every member contributes in a meaningful way. Any living organism taken from its ecosystem quickly dies of starvation or suffocation. On the other hand, a church that is unhealthy, immature, and toxic is more like an "ego-system," where people with selfish motives clammor to rise to power or reach the inner circle with little regard for serving the spiritual needs of others. People in unhealthy churches often attend with a "what can I get out of it" mindset rather than a "what can I contribute" mindset. And as a result of the spiritually toxic environment, spiritual growth is virtually snuffed out.**

"Bear one another's burdens, and thereby fulfill the law of Christ." *Galatians 6:2*

"And now, a word to you who are elders in the churches. I, too, am an elder and a witness to the sufferings of Christ. And I, too, will share his glory and his honor when he returns. As a fellow elder, this is my appeal to you: Care for the flock of God entrusted to you. Watch over it willingly, not grudgingly – not for what you will get out of it, but because you are eager to serve God. Don't lord it over the people assigned to your care, but lead them by your good example." *1 Peter 5:1-3 (NLT)*

7. **Some people are turned off by the idea of any kind of authority over them, especially in their spiritual life. But church leaders who are serving God well are there for your benefit, and can greatly enhance your spiritual growth.**

"Therefore encourage one another and build up one another, just as you also are doing. But we request of you, brethren, that you appreciate those who diligently labor among you, and have charge over you in the Lord and give you instruction, and that you esteem them very highly in love because of their work. Live in peace with one another. We urge you, brethren, admonish the unruly, encourage the fainthearted, help the weak, be patient with everyone. See that no one repays another with evil for evil, but always seek after that which is good for one another and for all people." *1 Thessalonians 5:11-15*

8. **It's entirely possible to be spiritual but not a Christian. Many non-Christians enjoy thinking about spiritual issues, but the Bible teaches that being spiritual is not what will get us to heaven. A person may be spiritual, but we're also sinners, and sin separates us from our holy God. Jesus, God's fully divine Son, died to pay the penalty for our sin so that we can be forgiven. To accept His payment for your sins, confess your sins to God and ask Christ into your life. Then find a godly church where they teach God's Word; get plugged in, start growing, and start using your gifts.**

"For the wages of sin is death, but the free gift of God is eternal life in Christ Jesus our Lord." *Romans 6:23*

"But God demonstrates His own love toward us, in that while we were yet sinners, Christ died for us." *Romans 5:8*

"If we confess our sins, He is faithful and righteous to forgive us our sins and to cleanse us from all unrighteousness." *1 John 1:9*

"For God so loved the world, that He gave His only begotten Son, that whoever believes in Him shall not perish, but have eternal life." *John 3:16*

97 Is Christianity Outdated For Today's Modern World?

Many non-Christians think it is unrealistic to expect people today to live by a faith which is thousands of years old. Should modern people still live by Jesus' teachings? Should we let our values and lifestyles be shaped by a book written centuries ago? Is Christianity just a nostalgic fantasy?

After all these centuries, has anything been discovered that renders the Bible obsolete? Or has anything better come along from the fields of philosophy, theology, politics, ethics, or psychology that offers deeper insight into the human condition than the Bible? Famous non-Christians throughout the ages, such as Marx, Lenin, Hitler, or Voltaire, have confidently declared that Christianity should be discarded as an obsolete belief system, only to have their own philosophies discarded as flawed and obsolete a few decades later – while Christianity continues to thrive.

Since the Bible was written, fashions have changed, borders have changed, and philosophies have come and gone. Methods of communication, travel, entertainment, business, and warfare have changed. Advancements in science and medicine have been discovered. But have people changed? Has the human heart changed? Do people today have the same spiritual needs and struggles that every generation has had throughout the centuries? Do the Bible's moral guidelines still apply today? And would the world be a better place if people's morals were still shaped by the Bible?

1. As humans we must realize that the passing of time is not the same with God as it is with us. He is eternal and transcends time. Centuries come and go, and things change here on earth, but God does not change.

"For I, the Lord, do not change." *Malachi 3:6*

"Jesus Christ is the same yesterday, today, yes and forever." *Hebrews 13:8*

"Before the mountains were born or You gave birth to the earth and the world, even from everlasting to everlasting, You are God. For a thousand years in Your sight are like yesterday when it passes by, or as a watch in the night." *Psalm 90:2,4*

"We look not at the things which are seen, but at the things which are not seen; for the things which are seen are temporal, but the things which are not seen are eternal." *2 Corinthians 4:18*

2. God still loves people today just as much as He loved the people back in ancient times.

"For God so loved the world, that He gave His only begotten Son, that whoever believes in Him shall not perish, but have everlasting life." *John 3:16*

"But You, O Lord, are a God merciful and gracious, slow to anger and abundant in lovingkindness and truth." *Psalm 86:15*

3. Something all humans have in common is that we are all sinners, and sin separates us from our holy God.

"For all have sinned and fall short of the glory of God." *Romans 3:23*

"But your iniquities have made a separation between you and your God, and your sins have hid His face from you, so that He does not hear." *Isaiah 59:2*

"The heart is more deceitful than all else and is desperately sick; who can understand it? I, the Lord, search the heart, I test the mind, even to give to each man according to his ways, according to the results of his deeds." *Jeremiah 17:9,10*

4. One more thing we have in common with people throughout the ages is our universal need for a Savior. Only Jesus is qualified to provide forgiveness so that we can be reconciled to God.

"Wretched man that I am! Who will set me free from the body of this death? Thanks be to God through Jesus Christ our Lord!" *Romans 7:24,25*

"And we have beheld and bear witness that the Father has sent the Son to be the Savior of the world." *1 John 4:14*

5. Jesus was crucified centuries ago, but His death paid for the sins of all people throughout the ages!

"We have been made holy through the sacrifice of the body of Jesus Christ once for all... But He having offered one sacrifice for sins for all time, sat down at the right hand of God. For by one offering He has perfected for all time those who are sanctified." *Hebrews 10:10,12,14 (NIV)*

"For Christ also died for sins once for all, the just for the unjust, so that He might bring us to God, having been put to death in the flesh, but made alive in the spirit." *1 Peter 3:18*

6. The Bible contains incredible insights into the human condition. The wisdom, truths, and principles written in the Bible are just as true and alive today as when the ink was still wet. Philosophies, religions, and nations fade away, but God's Word will never fade away.

"All flesh is grass, and all its loveliness is like the flower of the field.... The grass withers, the flower fades, but the word of our God stands forever." *Isaiah 40:6b,8*

"For the word of God is full of living power. It is sharper than the sharpest knife, cutting deep into our innermost thoughts and desires. It exposes us for what we really are." *Hebrews 4:12 (NLT)*

"If you abide in My word, then you are truly disciples of Mine; and you shall know the truth, and the truth shall make you free." *John 8:31,32*

7. The fact that Christianity has been around so long should not be considered a drawback or weakness. Christianity's longevity simply proves that it has stood the test of time, it continues to meet real needs, and has withstood all the efforts of its critics to destroy it. Christianity may have started centuries ago, but it has been thriving ever since.

"This same Good News that came to you is going out all over the world. It is changing lives everywhere, just as it changed yours that very first day you heard and understood the truth about God's great kindness to sinners." *Colossians 1:6 (NLT)*

"Heaven and earth will pass away, but My words will not pass away." *Matthew 24:35*

8. Modern science, philosophy, and psychology have offered many theories and assumptions regarding humanity and the origin of the universe, but have yet to disprove any part of the Bible.

"There is no wisdom and no understanding and no counsel against the Lord." *Proverbs 21:30*

"Let God be found true though every man be found a liar." *Romans 3:4*

9. Many non-Christians today embrace some of the Bible's teachings on topics like the Golden Rule, yet they reject the Bible's restrictions on certain lifestyles and sexual behavior. But just think how the world would be different if everyone lived by the lifestyle guidelines taught in the Bible:

- There would be no more crime, rape, incest, murder, or stealing.
- There would be no unwanted and unloved children in the world.
- There would be far fewer divorces and broken homes.
- There would be no more abuse or molestation of children.
- There would be far less sexually transmitted diseases; possibly even none.

10. God's offer to forgive us through Christ and have a personal relationship with Him is as true today as it ever was!

"But God demonstrates His own love toward us, in that while we were yet sinners, Christ died for us." *Romans 5:8*

"Jesus said to him, 'I am the way, and the truth, and the life; no one comes to the Father, but through Me.'" *John 14:6*

"The wages of sin is death, but the free gift of God is eternal life in Christ Jesus our Lord." *Romans 6:23*

98 Has Christianity Done More Harm Than Good?

People who have professed to be Christians and claim to represent Christ have done some cruel things to people inside the church and outside. True followers of Christ should indeed stand against these injustices and not sweep them under the rug.

But do critics of the faith look only at these mistakes? Do they refuse to recognize the good things Christianity brings to the world, and try to sweep those under the rug? Some vocal critics of the faith seem to do just that. For example:

- *Voltaire: "Christianity is the most ridiculous, the most absurd and bloody religion that has ever infected the world… Every sensible man, every honorable man, must hold the Christian sect in horror."*
- *Oscar Wilde: "When I think of all the harm the Bible has done, I despair on ever writing anything to equal it."*
- *Bertrand Russell: "I say quite deliberately that the Christian religion, as organized in its churches, has been and still is the principal enemy of moral progress in the world."*

On the other hand, it would be disingenuous of critics to say that Christians have brought no positive impact to the world whatsoever. Many of Christianity's critics ignore the contributions of Christians like anti-Nazi fighters Dietrich Bonhoeffer and Corrie Ten Boom; anti-slavery abolitionists like Wilbur Wilberforce and Harriet Tubman; scientists like Sir Isaac Newton and Galileo; relief workers like Mother Teresa and Henri Nouwen; artists like Bach and Rembrandt, or writers like Dostoevsky and T.S. Eliot. Countless churches give financial support for orphanages, hospitals, and colleges. Many impactful charities like the Red Cross, Salvation Army, Feed the Children, Habitat for Humanity, Samaritan's Purse, and World Vision have a deeply rooted Christian heritage.

As we weigh the good that Christianity brings to the world compared to the bad things done in the name of Christianity, what is the final verdict? Has Christianity ultimately done more harm than good?

---

1. **As Christians, we are called to be salt and light in a dark and suffering world. By helping to relieve suffering and improve society, we bring glory to God.**

   "You are the salt of the earth; but if the salt has become tasteless, how can it be made salty again? It is no longer good for anything, except to be thrown out and trampled under foot by men. You are the light of the world. A city set on a hill cannot be hidden; nor does anyone light a lamp and put it under a basket, but on the lampstand, and it gives light to all who are in the house. Let your light shine before men in such a way that they may see your good works, and glorify your Father who is in heaven." *Matthew 5:13-16*

2. **If people claiming to be Christians live in such a way that they deny the very teachings they claim to be following, the result is to bring shame and dishonor onto God Himself. Instead of being the "salt of the earth," people claiming to be Christians – but who don't act in love – can be more like "salt in the wound."**

   "Well then, if you teach others, why don't you teach yourself? You tell others not to steal, but do you steal? You say it is wrong to commit adultery, but do you do it? You condemn idolatry, but do you steal from pagan temples? You are so proud of knowing the law, but you dishonor God by breaking it. No wonder the Scriptures say, 'The world blasphemes the name of God because of you.'" *Romans 2: 21-24 (NLT)*

3. **It could be that those who claim to follow Christ, yet deny Him by their actions, aren't Christians at all but merely masquerading as His followers. Jesus taught us to look at their deeds rather than their words, and if their deeds do not conform to His teachings, we should not be fooled into assuming they are Christians.**

   "Beware of the false prophets, who come to you in sheep's clothing, but inwardly are ravenous wolves. You will know them by their fruits. Grapes are not gathered from thorn bushes nor figs from thistles, are they? So every good tree bears good fruit, but the bad tree bears bad fruit. A good tree cannot produce bad fruit, nor can a bad tree produce good fruit. Every tree that does not bear good fruit is cut down and thrown into the fire. So then, you will know them by their fruits. Not everyone who says to Me, 'Lord, Lord,' will enter the kingdom of heaven, but he who does the will of My Father who is in heaven will enter." *Matthew 7:15-21*

4. **Sadly, there are extremist elements in every religion, including Christianity. We are commanded to stand firmly against financial impropriety, physical or sexual abuses, and hypocritical inconsistencies by people claiming to be Christians. The Apostle Paul warned his readers to be on the lookout for those who pose as followers of Christ but are really the exact opposite. Paul told us to expose them for what they are.**

"For this you know with certainty, that no immoral or impure person or covetous man, who is an idolater, has an inheritance in the kingdom of Christ and God. Let no one deceive you with empty words, for because of these things the wrath of God comes upon the sons of disobedience. Therefore do not be partakers with them; for you were formerly darkness, but now you are Light in the Lord; walk as children of Light (for the fruit of the Light consists in all goodness and righteousness and truth), trying to learn what is pleasing to the Lord. Do not participate in the unfruitful deeds of darkness, but instead even expose them; for it is disgraceful even to speak of the things which are done by them in secret. But all things become visible when they are exposed by the light, for everything that becomes visible is light." *Ephesians 5:11-13*

5. **We shouldn't condemn practicing medicine just because there have been some cruel doctors. We shouldn't disband all police forces because of an occasional corrupt policeman. Similarly, it's not the practice of Christianity that has been harmful; it's the malpractice of it. When we stray from how Christians are commanded to live, we start behaving like the world we're supposed to be making better.**

"The one who says, 'I have come to know Him,' and does not keep His commandments, is a liar, and the truth is not in him; but whoever keeps His word, in him the love of God has truly been perfected. By this we know that we are in Him: the one who says he abides in Him ought himself to walk in the same manner as He walked." *1 John 2:4-6*

6. **The truth is, mankind is desperately fallen and is capable of using any excuse to secure power over others – whether that excuse involves religion or not. Atheist regimes in Russia, North Korea, China, and Cambodia brought horrible violence to their own people. Before these, the French Revolution did the same, even though it was based on "human reason." Hitler loathed Christianity because it showed compassion for the weak. When a philosophy attempts to ignore God's biblical parameters for human behavior, the results can be disastrous. Throughout history, people continue to prove we are all sinners and therefore we all need a Savior.**

"But your iniquities have made a separation between you and your God, and your sins have hid His face from you, so that He does not hear." *Isaiah 59:2*

"For all have sinned and fall short of the glory of God." *Romans 3:23*

"The heart is more deceitful than all else and is desperately sick; who can understand it? I, the Lord, search the heart, I test the mind, even to give to each man according to his ways, according to the results of his deeds." *Jeremiah 17:9,10*

7. **Sometimes people pretending to be Christians commit terrible sins. But as history has clearly shown, even actual Christians can get it wrong. And when we do get it wrong, we should confess it and learn from the mistake. But just because Christians are far from perfect, the whole Christian faith should not be written off as worthless. Our faith is not based on how perfect we are; it's based on Jesus Christ – fully God and fully man – who paid the price for the sin in all of us. Only through Him can we find forgiveness. If you're a non-Christian, you'll get a much clearer picture of who Christ is by looking directly at Him and His teachings.**

"The Son reflects God's own glory, and everything about him represents God exactly." *Hebrews 1:3a (NLT)*

"Jesus said to him, 'I am the way, and the truth, and the life; no one comes to the Father, but through Me.'" *John 14:6*

"This is good and acceptable in the sight of God our Savior, who desires all men to be saved and to come to the knowledge of the truth. For there is one God, and one mediator also between God and men, the man Christ Jesus, who gave Himself as a ransom for all." *1 Timothy 2:3-6a*

"For the wages of sin is death, but the free gift of God is eternal life in Christ Jesus our Lord." *Romans 6:23*

99 Are All Christians Supposed To Speak In Tongues?

One of the things that many non-Christians find most puzzling about Christianity is that some churches and Christian groups engage in the mysterious practice of speaking in tongues. It's an issue that makes many non-Christians uneasy about joining the faith, or even examining the claims of Christ. But not all churches or Christian groups engage in this practice. Quite honestly, disagreements over this controversial practice are not uncommon, and have caused some divisions within the faith. Some churches teach that speaking in tongues is the proof of a true Christian, but most churches maintain that speaking in tongues is not something every Christian should expect to be able to do. What exactly is the history and purpose of speaking in tongues?

1. **Speaking in tongues is one of many "spiritual gifts." God gives each believer at least one spiritual gift at the moment of conversion, and we are told to develop and exercise our gifts to help others. Paul wrote extensively about spiritual gifts in 1 Corinthians 12 – 14, and also in Romans 12 and Ephesians 4. Some of the gifts mentioned are: Encouragement, giving, leadership, mercy, prophecy, serving, teaching, administration, faith, healing, miracles, tongues, interpreting tongues, discernment, knowledge, wisdom, hospitality, evangelism, and others.**

   "Now there are different kinds of spiritual gifts, but it is the same Holy Spirit who is the source of them all. There are different kinds of service in the church, but it is the same Lord we are serving. There are different ways God works in our lives, but it is the same God who does the work through all of us. A spiritual gift is given to each of us as a means of helping the entire church." *1 Corinthians 12:4-7 (NLT)*

2. **The purpose of all the gifts is to help us (as fallen, imperfect people) build up others by helping them grow closer of God, and to help relieve the sufferings that come from living in a cursed, fallen world. No believer has all the gifts, and the Bible never promises the gift of tongues to every believer. Every gift is given for the benefit of others, and the gifts help keep us connected as the body of Christ because we all need the benefits of gifts that we don't have. Paul compares the church to the human body, where every member depends on each other.**

   "For even as the body is one and yet has many members, and all the members of the body, though they are many, are one body, so also is Christ. For by one Spirit we were all baptized into one body, whether Jews or Greeks, whether slaves or free, and we were all made to drink of one Spirit. For the body is not one member, but many." *1 Corinthians 12:12-14*

3. **Of all the spiritual gifts listed, nobody argues that gifts like mercy, teaching, and serving are still around today. Most of the controversy surrounds the more miraculous sign gifts such as healing, speaking in tongues, interpreting tongues, and predicting future events with absolute certainty. As you read the entire Bible, the presence of miraculous signs were really the exception to the rule, and only appear in brief spurts throughout the Bible. Miraculous signs were given by God to authenticate a new message and the messenger.**

   "Then Moses said, 'What if they will not believe me or listen to what I say? For they may say, "The Lord has not appeared to you."' The Lord said to him, 'What is that in your hand?' And he said, 'A staff.' Then He said, 'Throw it on the ground.' So he threw it on the ground, and it became a serpent; and Moses fled from it. But the Lord said to Moses, 'Stretch out your hand and grasp it by its tail' – so he stretched out his hand and caught it, and it became a staff in his hand – 'that they may believe that the Lord, the God of their fathers, the God of Abraham, the God of Isaac, and the God of Jacob, has appeared to you.'" *Exodus 4:1-5*

4. **The gift of tongues first showed up at Jerusalem's Feast of Pentecost, 40 days after Christ's resurrection. Christians were suddenly able to miraculously share the gospel in languages previously unknown to the speaker, yet understood by people visiting from foreign lands. It marked the official launch of the Church Age.**

   "When the day of Pentecost had come, they were all together in one place. And suddenly there came from heaven a noise like a violent rushing wind, and it filled the whole house where they were sitting. And there appeared to them tongues as of fire distributing themselves, and they rested on each one of them. And they were all filled with the Holy Spirit and began to speak with other tongues, as the Spirit was giving them utterance. Now there were Jews living in Jerusalem, devout men from every nation under heaven. And when this sound occurred, the crowd came together, and were bewildered because each one of them was hearing them speak in his own language. They were amazed and astonished, saying, 'Why, are not all these who are speaking Galileans? And how is it that we each hear them in our own language to which we were born? Parthians and Medes and Elamites, and residents of Mesopotamia, Judea and Cappadocia, Pontus and Asia, Phrygia and Pamphylia, Egypt and the districts of Libya around Cyrene, and visitors from Rome, both Jews and proselytes, Cretans and Arabs – we hear them in our own tongues speaking of the mighty deeds of God.'" *Acts 2:1-11*

5. The gift of tongues was an evangelism tool to share the gospel with unbelievers in their native language.

"So then, tongues are for a sign, not to those who believe, but to unbelievers." *1 Corinthians 14:22*

Perhaps the ultimate test for anyone who claims to have the genuine, biblical gift of tongues would be to have the person parachute into an unreached people group in Borneo or New Guinea and strike up a conversation about Jesus. If the people understand the words that come out of your mouth then you have the genuine gift of tongues. If the natives can't understand your words, then it's impossible to say for sure what your gift of tongues really is. It could just be gibberish.

6. Sadly, this miraculous gift degenerated into a spiritual status symbol among the first-century church in Corinth. They abused the gift of tongues to impress people and exalt themselves rather than building up others. Paul reprimanded them for using this gift to selfishly build up themselves instead of others.

"The one who speaks in a tongue builds up himself, but the one who prophesies builds up the church." *1 Corinthians 14:4 (ESV)*

The modern concept of tongues being a "prayer language" understood only by God is clearly not the same as the gift of tongues in the New Testament, where it is described as recognizable languages for the specific purpose of witnessing to unbelievers in their native language. If the gift of tongues is given to be a prayer language that only benefits the speaker, then it would be the only spiritual gift on the entire list that doesn't serve the purpose of building up others – which is the very reason we have spiritual gifts. Imagine if someone were to say, "I have the gift of serving, but I only use it to serve myself." Or, "I have the gift of teaching, but I only use it to teach myself." That would be the exact opposite purpose of what a spiritual gift is for.

7. Should we encourage or discourage the use of tongues in churches today? As we read 1 Corinthians 12 – 14, Paul discouraged the use of tongues for anything other than its original purpose as an evangelism tool. When misused it tends to become divisive, and actually turns off visiting non-Christians – which is the exact opposite purpose for this gift. (This same result occurred in the case of the Corinthians.) It's safe to say that Paul never forbid the use of tongues, he simply forbid the misuse of tongues.

"Even so, if unbelievers or people who don't understand these things come into your meeting and hear everyone talking in an unknown language, they will think you are crazy. " *1 Corinthians 14:23 (NLT)*

8. The original purpose of the gift of tongues was to share the good news of the gospel – that Christ has paid the penalty for our sins, and by placing our faith in Him we can be forgiven and receive the free gift of eternal life.

"For God so loved the world, that He gave His only begotten Son, that whoever believes in Him shall not perish, but have everlasting life." *John 3:16*

9. When Christ returns, all Christians will be transformed (1 John 3:2). We'll be spiritually holy and physically healthy. From then on – throughout all eternity in heaven – no one will be sick so we won't need doctors, hospitals, or anyone with the gift of healing. Everyone will be saved so we won't need the gift of evangelism or the gift of tongues, which is an evangelism tool. No one will be suffering so we won't need the gift of mercy. No one will be hungry or in need, so we won't need the gift of giving. Everyone will know God so we won't need anyone teaching how to know Him. (Also see Jeremiah 31:34.) As odd as it sounds, there won't even be any churches or temples in heaven (Revelation 21:22) because the Lord is the temple. While living here in an imperfect world with the consequences of sin all around us, the perfection of heaven is difficult to imagine; but that's what we have to look forward to, thanks to God's love. And as Paul mentioned in 1 Corinthians 13:8, even though all the gifts will cease, "love never fails."

"But God demonstrates His own love for us in that while we were yet sinners Christ died for us." *Romans 5:8*

"For the wages of sin is death, but the free gift of God is eternal life in Christ Jesus our Lord." *Romans 6:23*

100 Why Do Christians Proselytize So Much?

Non-Christians are often puzzled by the fact that many Christians actively share their faith and try to persuade people of other religions and philosophies to become Christians. Many other belief systems place little or no emphasis on persuading others. Some people feel that a person's religious beliefs should remain personal, and trying to influence someone to join a different faith is simply being pushy. What is it about Christianity that makes Christians want to keep sharing their faith with outsiders, even at the risk of ruffling a few feathers? And sometimes, even at great personal risk to their own lives?

1. If you find an amazing restaurant, movie, book, vacation destination, or a great sale, it's natural to share the news with your friends. Now imagine if you had fantastic news to share that had completely changed your life.

"The one who existed from the beginning is the one we have heard and seen. We saw him with our own eyes and touched him with our own hands. He is Jesus Christ, the Word of life. This one who is life from God was shown to us, and we have seen him. And now we testify and announce to you that he is the one who is eternal life. He was with the Father, and then he was shown to us. We are telling you about what we ourselves have actually seen and heard, so that you may have fellowship with us. And our fellowship is with the Father and with his Son, Jesus Christ." *1 John 1:1-3 (NLT)*

2. If you were a starving beggar, and you found a huge supply of bread, it would be selfish not to tell other beggars about it. Christians look at sharing the gospel like one beggar telling another beggar where to find bread.

"'For the bread of God is that which comes down out of heaven, and gives life to the world.' Then they said to Him, 'Lord, always give us this bread.' Jesus said to them, 'I am the bread of life; he who comes to Me will not hunger, and he who believes in Me will never thirst.... For this is the will of My Father, that everyone who beholds the Son and believes in Him will have eternal life, and I Myself will raise him up on the last day.'" *John 6:33-35,40*

3. If you saw a man about to get hit by a bus but you didn't warn him, you wouldn't be very caring. Sometimes, Christians are seen as telling everybody they're going to hell. But God is not in the business of sending people to hell; He's in the business of rescuing people from hell. Christians believe that those who do not know Christ will spend eternity away from God, and we care enough to tell people that God provides a way to avoid this fate.

"I am the door; if anyone enters through Me, he will be saved, and will go in and out and find pasture. The thief comes only to steal and kill and destroy; I came that they may have life, and have it abundantly." *John 10:9,10*

"For God so loved the world, that He gave His only begotten Son, that whoever believes in Him shall not perish, but have eternal life. For God did not send the Son into the world to judge the world, but that the world might be saved through Him." *John 3:16,17*

"And the testimony is this, that God has given us eternal life, and this life is in His Son. He who has the Son has the life; he who does not have the Son of God does not have the life. These things I have written to you who believe in the name of the Son of God, so that you may know that you have eternal life." *1 John 5:11-13*

4. Hopefully, when Christians share the gospel we will be motivated by love. Unfortunately, there will be times when someone shares the gospel with improper motives which can turn people away. It's a case of the right action with the wrong motive. But the gospel is so life-changing that a bad gospel presentation can still have a positive result.

"If I speak with the tongues of men and of angels, but do not have love, I have become a noisy gong or a clanging cymbal. If I have the gift of prophecy, and know all mysteries and all knowledge; and if I have all faith, so as to remove mountains, but do not have love, I am nothing. And if I give all my possessions to feed the poor, and if I surrender my body to be burned, but do not have love, it profits me nothing." *1 Corinthians 13:1-3*

"Some, to be sure, are preaching Christ even from envy and strife, but some also from good will; the latter do it out of love, knowing that I am appointed for the defense of the gospel; the former proclaim Christ out of selfish ambition rather than from pure motives, thinking to cause me distress in my imprisonment. What then? Only that in every way, whether in pretense or in truth, Christ is proclaimed; and in this I rejoice. Yes, and I will rejoice." *Philippians 1:15-18*

5. **Unfortunately, zealous Christians sometimes resort to kooky, less-than-dignified ways to share the gospel. Bizarre witnessing techniques often turn unbelievers away and do more harm than good. It's a case of the right motive but the wrong action. The Bible instructs us not to lose our dignity in the process of sharing our faith.**

"In all things show yourself to be an example of good deeds, with purity in doctrine, dignified, sound in speech which is beyond reproach, so that the opponent will be put to shame, having nothing bad to say about us." *Titus 2:7,8*

6. **Jesus warned that not everyone who claims to be a Christian is genuine. People who claim to be Christians but misrepresent His teachings by their hateful deeds probably aren't Christians at all.**

"A good tree can't produce bad fruit, and a bad tree can't produce good fruit. So every tree that does not produce good fruit is chopped down and thrown into the fire. Yes, the way to identify a tree or a person is by the kind of fruit that is produced. Not all people who sound religious are really godly." *Matthew 7:18-21b (NLT)*

7. **Sometimes Christians share our faith using religious phrases like "born again," "washed in the blood," or "at the foot of Calvary," which may not communicate with people who didn't grow up in the church. Fortunately, as we get better at sharing our faith, we learn how to communicate with people from all different types of backgrounds.**

"Let your conversation be gracious and effective so that you will have the right answer for everyone." *Colossians 4:6 (NLT)*

8. **As Christians, we're commanded to spread the good news of the gospel throughout the world. People come to God through Christ, and they usually come to Christ through us. As Christ's followers, every believer has the privilege and responsibility of representing Christ to the world as His ambassador.**

"Therefore if anyone is in Christ, he is a new creature; the old things passed away; behold, new things have come. Now all these things are from God, who reconciled us to Himself through Christ and gave us the ministry of reconciliation, namely, that God was in Christ reconciling the world to Himself, not counting their trespasses against them, and He has committed to us the word of reconciliation. Therefore, we are ambassadors for Christ, as though God were making an appeal through us; we beg you on behalf of Christ, be reconciled to God." *2 Corinthians 5:17-20*

"Go therefore and make disciples of all the nations, baptizing them in the name of the Father and the Son and the Holy Spirit, teaching them to observe all that I commanded you; and lo, I am with you always, even to the end of the age." *Matthew 28:19,20*

9. **Early church founders zealously shared their faith in the resurrected Lord Jesus Christ amidst terrible persecution. Even today, believers in certain countries of the world can be imprisoned or executed for sharing their faith. But they look beyond present distresses and persecutions to their future rewards in Heaven.**

"And as God's grace brings more and more people to Christ, there will be great thanksgiving, and God will receive more and more glory. That is why we never give up. Though our bodies are dying, our spirits are being renewed every day. For our present troubles are quite small and won't last very long. Yet they produce for us an immeasurably great glory that will last forever! So we don't look at the troubles we can see right now; rather, we look forward to what we have not yet seen. For the troubles we see will soon be over, but the joys to come will last forever." *2 Corinthians 4:15b-18 (NLT)*

10. **Other religions are basically ways to improve ourselves, do good deeds, gain enlightenment, and work our way to heaven. This is where Christianity is unique. We get to heaven not based on what we do, but on what Christ has already done. We don't climb up to God – He has reached down to us!**

"Jesus said to him, 'I am the way, and the truth, and the life; no one comes to the Father, but through Me.'" *John 14:6*

"But God demonstrates His own love toward us, in that while we were yet sinners, Christ died for us." *Romans 5:8*

11. **The only way to fully understand why Christians love to share our faith is to begin your own relationship with Christ. Then you can experience the joy of personally knowing God and sharing Him with others.**

"But to all who believed him and accepted him, he gave the right to become children of God." *John 1:12 (NLT)*

"For the wages of sin is death, but the free gift of God is eternal life in Christ Jesus our Lord." Romans 6:23

101 How Old Is The Earth?

Does the Bible tell us the exact age of the earth and the universe? Many people have tried to answer this question. Bishop James Ussher (1581-1656) was an Archbishop of the Church of Ireland who is famous for his attempt to calculate the age of the earth. By studying secular history and genealogies written in the Bible, he concluded the earth came into existence on October 22, 4004 BC.

Did Bishop Ussher get it right? For centuries, the Christian world accepted Bishop Ussher's age of the earth, but today it has fallen out of favor among Bible-believing Christians; even among those who advocate a "young earth" position. We must remember that biblical genealogies that list "who was the son of whom," the phrase "son of" can either mean the "direct son of someone," or it can sometimes mean "descendant of." For example, Jesus was called the "Son of David," and the Jews were called "Sons of Abraham." These genealogies are meant to show the line of descent, and may contain large gaps, so it's not realistically possible to reach an accurate date of the earth's creation based on these genealogies.

If all forms of life on earth descended from a common ancestor by way of evolution through natural selection, then an ancient earth would certainly be required to accommodate the gradual, transitional changes of descent with modification. On the other hand, if God created the earth with its plants and animals fully formed, then a young earth could be an option.

Many people make fun of Christians who view the earth as being young. The underlying assumption is that if the Bible says the earth is young, but science tells us it's old, then science has disproven the Bible. And if the Bible is wrong on one point, why should we trust anything else it says? It may come as a surprise to people who haven't read the Bible that it never gives an exact date of when the earth was made. And you'll find sincere Christians – many with scientific backgrounds – who have arrived at very different conclusions on this question. Some view the earth as billions of years old, and some view the earth as only thousands of years old. In all fairness, if a person asks when the earth was made, doesn't it also make sense to ask who made it? Could nothing have created everything?

And is the issue of a young earth or old earth critical to the Bible's overall message?

---

1. **From a biblical, theological standpoint, the question of whether the earth is billion of years old or only thousands of years old hinges on the definition of the Hebrew word "yom," which means "day." Is the Genesis 7-day creation account to be understood as literal 24-hour days, or more metaphorically as indefinite periods of time? Many Hebrew scholars have debated this, and there is some hermeneutical justification for either position. If God has unlimited power, He could have created the universe in 7 days, or 7 seconds, or 7 triillion years. And He certainly could have told us its exact age if He had wanted us to know.**

   "The secret things belong to the Lord, but the things revealed belong to us and to our sons forever, that we may observe all the words of this law." *Deuteronomy 29:29*

2. **Not only does the Bible avoid giving us a crystal clear date for the age of the earth, but nature is full of surprises, and puzzling scientific observations must be sorted out. For example:**

   • Light from distant stars would take millions of years to get to earth, leading us to conclude the universe is old.

   • Dinosaur bones of T-Rex and others are occasionally found that still have soft, pliable tissues inside, suggesting the earth might not be as old as some think.

   • The fossil record contains many "polystrate fossils" which are usually vertical, fossilized tree trunks. They can span several layers of rock that have been estimated to be millions of years apart. But how is this possible unless the rock layers were laid down much quicker than previously thought?

3. **There is something to remember that can quickly complicate our efforts to ascertain the age of the earth. We must remember that if God really is all powerful so that He can, for example, create light, then He's probably also powerful enough to create light already arriving from a star millions of light-years away the instant the star came into existence. If God is all powerful, He could have created the universe fully formed with the appearance of age. For**

two biblical examples: Adam and Eve were created as fully formed adults with no childhood; on the day they were created they would have appeared older than they really were. And at the first public miracle of Jesus, He turned water into fine wine that obviously had the appearance of age even though it was only seconds old.

"And He said to them, 'Draw some out now and take it to the headwaiter. So they took it to him. When the headwaiter tasted the water which had become wine, and did not know where it came from (but the servants who had drawn the water knew), the headwaiter called the bridegroom, and said to him, 'Every man serves the good wine first, and when the people have drunk freely, then he serves the poorer wine; but you have kept the good wine until now.' This beginning of His signs Jesus did in Cana of Galilee, and manifested His glory, and His disciples believed in Him." *John 2:8-11*

4. **Even though the Bible does not tell us the exact age of the earth, it tells us the age of God – sort of. It says He has pre-existed throughout all of eternity, with no beginning. He will also exist through eternity into the future.**

"Before the mountains were born or You gave birth to the earth and the world, even from everlasting to everlasting, You are God." *Psalm 90:2*

"For a child will be born to us, a son will be given to us; and the government will rest on His shoulders; and His name will be called Wonderful Counselor, Mighty God, Eternal Father, Prince of Peace." *Isaiah 9:6*

"But as for you, Bethlehem Ephrathah, too little to be among the clans of Judah, from you One will go forth for Me to be ruler in Israel. His goings forth are from long ago, from the days of eternity." *Micah 5:2*

5. **It's one thing to examine what the Bible says about this world. But in fairness we should also closely examine what the Bible says about the next world.**

"If I (Jesus) told you earthly things and you do not believe, how will you believe if I tell you heavenly things?" *John 3:12*

6. **According to the Bible, after we die we will all stand before the Maker of the earth. The good news is that while you're standing there you can ask God exactly how old the earth is. The bad news that He will ask you to give an account of your life, deeds, and beliefs during your time here on the earth that He made.**

"For we shall all stand before the judgment seat of God. For it is written, 'As I live, says the Lord, every knee shall bow to Me, and every tongue shall give praise to God.' So then each one of us shall give account of himself to God." *Romans 14:10-12*

"And I saw a great white throne and Him who sat upon it, from whose presence earth and heaven fled away, and no place was found for them. And I saw the dead, the great and the small, standing before the throne, and books were opened; and another book was opened, which is the book of life; and the dead were judged from the things which were written in the books, according to their deeds.... And if anyone's name was not found written in the book of life, he was thrown into the fire." *Revelation 20:11,12,15*

7. **Our salvation doesn't depend on what we believe about the age of the earth. It depends on what we believe about the God who created the earth. According to the Bible, God sent His Son Jesus who lived a perfectly sinless life, and died to take the punishment for the world's sin. Only by trusting in His payment for sin can we have forgiveness and spend eternity with God. From Genesis to Revelation, this is the central teaching of the Bible. The Bible may not be specific on the age of the earth, but it is crystal clear about God's infinite love and how we can receive salvation.**

"Jesus said to him, 'I am the way, and the truth, and the life; no one comes to the Father, but through Me.'" *John 14:6*

"For there is one God, and one mediator also between God and men, the man Christ Jesus, who gave Himself as a ransom for all." *1 Timothy 2:5,6a*

"For God so loved the world, that He gave His only begotten Son, that whoever believes in Him shall not perish, but have everlasting life." *John 3:16*

"For the wages of sin is death, but the free gift of God is eternal life in Christ Jesus our Lord." *Romans 6:23*

"But God demonstrates His own love for us in that while we were yet sinners Christ died for us." *Romans 5:8*

102 Is Christianity Anti-Science?

In 1633, Galileo (who was a Christian) proclaimed his discovery that the earth revolved around the sun, and not vise versa. He was then imprisoned by the Catholic Church for heresy, because his statement was thought to go against Psalm 104:5: "Who laid the foundations of the earth, that it should not be removed forever." The Catholic Church persecuted Galileo not simply because they didn't understand science, but because they didn't understand that all truth is God's truth. Even to this day, this sad event has given Christianity a reputation as being anti-science, and continues to be brought up by critics of the faith.

If we're going to trust what the Bible says about the next world, we should certainly be able to trust its descriptions of this world. However, the Bible is not a science textbook; but neither are the works of Shakespeare, Twain, Hemmingway, etc., and no one would suggest disposing of those writings. When the Bible touches on issues of science, it talks about them in very broad strokes. While the natural sciences tend to focus on the relationship between man and animals, the Bible focuses on the relationship between man and God. Should the teachings and life lessons of the Bible be disregarded simply because it is not a science textbook? And are Christianity's critics accurate in proclaiming Christianity to be anti-science?

1. Many famous scientists in history have been Christians, and have made major contributions in many fields.

- Nicholas Copernicus (1473-1543) First astronomer to propose planets revolve around the sun.
- Sir Francis Bacon (1561-1627) Established scientific method through experimentation and inductive reasoning.
- Johannes Kepler (1571-1630) Established laws of planetary motion.
- Blaise Pascal (1623-1662) Mathematician, physicist, inventor, writer, and theologian.
- Sir Isaac Newton (1642-1727) Chemist and mathematician.
- William Thomson Kelvin (1824-1907) Laid the foundation for modern physics.
- Louis Pasteur (1822-1895) Chemist and microbiologist.
- George Washington Carver (1864-1943) Botanist, educator, inventor.

2. In spite of the contributions of scientists who are Christians, Christianity is still perceived as anti-science by many critics. They're particularly critical of the Bible's claim that a supernatural God created the universe. Many atheist scientists believe that when anything supernatural is brought into science, it automatically "pollutes" the science, which is the study of the material universe consisting of atoms and molecules. As atheist scientist Carl Sagan put it, the natural, material world is: "all that is, or ever was, or ever will be." Sagan has also said:

"Our planet is a lonely speck in the great enveloping cosmic dark. In our obscurity, in all this vastness, there is no hint that help will come from elsewhere to save us from ourselves."

3. One of the fundamental laws of physics is the law of "Conservation of Matter." It states: "Matter can neither be created nor destroyed." Many atheists see the existence of matter as a "given," and have no way to prove how matter originally came into existence, nor can they create new matter out of nothing in a laboratory. But the Bible offers an explanation in its very first verse – which immediately puts the Bible at odds with atheist scientists.

"In the beginning God created the heavens and the earth." *Genesis 1:1*

4. People often criticize Christianity based on the issue of intelligent design (creationism) or evolution. Did God create animals and plants fully formed, or did they evolve over time from a common ancestor with no involvement from a supernatural being? Fortunately, the earth itself contains a record of life in the fossil record. Over and over again, we see species appear in the fossil record fully formed, without evidence of countless transitional forms before or after. Evolution doesn't simply require a missing link; it requires a missing chain. Even Darwin admitted this was a major argument against his theory of evolution in *The Origin of Species*:

"The number of intermediate varieties which have formerly existed on Earth must be truly enormous. Why then is not every geological formation and every stratum full of such intermediate links? Geology assuredly does not reveal any such finely graduated organic chain; and this, perhaps, is the most obvious and gravest objection which can be urged against my theory."

"If numerous species belonging to the same genera or families, have really started into life all at once, the fact would be fatal to the theory of descent with slow modification through natural selection."

5. **Atheist scientists mock and persecute scientists who see evidence of God's handiwork in the details of the universe. However, atheist scientists aren't doing this because they don't understand the Bible, but because they don't understand science – which should follow the evidence objectively, wherever it leads, with no preconceived agenda. Richard Dawkins, a thought leader among atheist scientists, wrote an essay called, *Why I Won't Debate Creationists:***

"Winning is not what the creationists realistically aspire to. For them, it is sufficient that the debate happens at all. They need the publicity. We don't. To the gullible public which is their natural constituency, it is enough that their man is seen sharing a platform with a real scientist…. Inevitably, when you turn down the invitation you will be accused of cowardice, or of inability to defend your own beliefs. But that is better than supplying the creationists with what they crave: the oxygen of respectability in the world of real science."

Does this sound like a scientific mind willing to follow the evidence wherever it leads? Even non-Christian scientists are sometimes hesitant to go public with findings if their evidence disrupts conventional opinion on evolutionary thought, because they are afraid of jeopardizing grant money or being lumped in with creationists. Also, because of a hyper-sensitivity to the idea of separation of church and state, many public schools and universities won't teach intelligent design along with evolution for fear of lawsuits they can't afford.

6. **Harvard genetics professor Richard Lewontin has made the secular agenda of scientific investigation quite clear:**

"Our willingness to accept scientific claims that are against common sense is the key to an understanding of the real struggle between science and the supernatural. We take the side of science in spite of the patent absurdity of some of its constructs… in spite of the tolerance of the scientific community for unsubstantiated just-so stories, because we have a prior commitment, a commitment to materialism. It is not that the methods and institutions of science somehow compel us to accept a material explanation of the phenomenal world, but, on the contrary, that we are forced by our a priori adherence to material causes to create an apparatus of investigation and a set of concepts that produce material explanations, no matter how counterintuitive, no matter how mystifying to the uninitiated. Moreover, that materialism is absolute, for we cannot allow a Divine Foot in the door." (Richard Lewontin, *Billions and Billions of Demons*, New York Review of Books, January 4, 1997)

7. **We don't stop using our brains once we become Christians. Just the opposite! God encourages us to use our minds!**

"And you shall love the Lord your God with all your heart, and with all your soul, and with all your mind, and with all your strength." *Mark 12:30*

8. **The book of Proverbs stresses the importance of gaining wisdom and knowledge. But the book also contains one very important verse that is sort of a "disclaimer" to the rest of the book. It reminds us not to put our ultimate, complete trust in our own human wisdom, but to trust God who knows infinitely more than we do.**

"Trust in the Lord with all your heart and do not lean on your own understanding. In all your ways acknowledge Him, and He will make your paths straight." *Proverbs 3:5,6*

9. **So if the Bible is not a science textbook, then what is it? It's been called "God's love letter to man," as well as, "The ultimate textbook on human nature." It shows that man, despite our intellectual achievements, is still not morally perfect. We are still prideful, depraved, and separated from God because of our sin. Fortunately, God has provided a way for us to be reconciled to Him – through trusting in His only begotten Son, Jesus, who paid our penalty for sin.**

"For the wages of sin is death, but the free gift of God is eternal life in Christ Jesus our Lord." *Romans 6:23*

10. **We can't prove forgiveness and redemption in a test tube, but there are millions of "living test tubes" walking around who are more than happy to tell you the miraculous difference Christ has made in their lives.**

"Therefore if anyone is in Christ, he is a new creature; the old things passed away; behold, new things have come." *2 Corinthians 5:17*

103 Is There A Biblical Perspective On Stem Cell Research?

Shortly after your conception, you were a collection of stem cells. The stem cells of a human embryo are truly amazing because of their capacity to differentiate into specialized cell types, with the potential to develop into just about any type of tissue; such as an organ, an eye, skin, bone, etc. Because these cells have the ability to be shaped into specific tissues, they are considered as a way to help ailing adults. They have the potential to cure diseases, reverse brain or spinal cord injuries, grow bone marrow, re-grow organs, and even reverse baldness. If these cells can do so much to help adults, then why is there any debate over whether it's right or wrong?

The Bible would not raise any ethical red flags over harvesting stem cells from umbilical cords or a placenta. But the question is whether it is right to terminate the life of an unborn child so that his or her stem cells can be harvested to improve the health of an adult. Modern science has made it possible to do amazing things; but just because we can do something, does that mean we should do it? Considering that the Bible was written centuries before the invention of the microscope, much less before stem cell research, can its teachings on humanity, ethics, and morality still apply today?

1. **The human stem cell is amazing because the human embryo is amazing. Every child – in fact every cell – reveals God's handiwork. When King David described the unborn child in the womb, he gave it a sense of immeasurable worth as of one of God's greatest creations.**

   "You made all the delicate, inner parts of my body and knit me together in my mother's womb. Thank you for making me so wonderfully complex! Your workmanship is marvelous – and how well I know it. You watched me as I was being formed in utter seclusion, as I was woven together in the dark of the womb. You saw me before I was born. Every day of my life was recorded in your book. Every moment was laid out before a single day had passed. *Psalm 139:13-16 (NLV)*

2. **Perhaps people feel justified in ending the life of an unborn child because they feel the child is something we have created. But the Bible says God created us, and we are in His image.**

   "Thus says the Lord, your Redeemer, and the one who formed you from the womb: 'I, the Lord, am the maker of all things, stretching out the heavens by Myself and spreading out the earth all alone.'" *Isaiah 44:24*

   "Know that the Lord Himself is God; it is He who has made us, and not we ourselves; we are His people and the sheep of His pasture." *Psalm 100:3*

   "God created man in His own image, in the image of God He created him; male and female He created them." *Genesis 1:27*

   If all humans are equal, then the idea that a child could be sacrificed to improve the health of an adult would be just as unethical as killing an adult to improve the health of a child.

3. **In view of the precious value of every child, the Bible gives extremely stern warnings against harming them.**

   "See that you do not despise one of these little ones, for I say to you that their angels in heaven continually see the face of My Father who is in heaven.... So it is not the will of your Father who is in heaven that one of these little ones perish." *Matthew 18:10,14*

4. **Thinking that the strong should be allowed to take unfair advantage of the weak is the exact opposite of biblical love and responsibility. Showing compassion for the weak is one of the ways to show our love for God.**

   "Then the King will say to those on His right, 'Come, you who are blessed of My Father, inherit the kingdom prepared for you from the foundation of the world. For I was hungry, and you gave Me something to eat; I was thirsty, and you gave Me something to drink; I was a stranger, and you invited Me in; naked, and you clothed Me; I was sick, and you visited Me; I was in prison, and you came to Me.' Then the righteous will answer Him, 'Lord, when did we see You hungry, and feed You, or thirsty, and give You something to drink? And when did we see You a stranger, and invite You in, or naked, and clothe You? When did we see You sick, or in prison, and come to You?'

The King will answer and say to them, 'Truly I say to you, to the extent that you did it to one of these brothers of Mine, even the least of them, you did it to Me.'" *Matthew 25:34-40*

5. If you could be helped by the money, car, or possessions of someone else, does that give you the right to take his life to get those things? If you needed a new kidney, it would clearly be murder to kill your neighbor to take hers. So should we have the right to kill an unborn child and harvest her stem cells to grow a new kidney?

"Do nothing from selfishness or empty conceit, but with humility of mind regard one another as more important than yourselves; do not merely look out for your own personal interests, but also for the interests of others." *Philippians 2:3,4*

6. Stem cells from an unborn child might cure an adult's blindness, but would that justify taking the life of a child who will never see, walk, or laugh? Would you want someone ending your life to harvest your cells?

"In everything, therefore, treat people the same way you want them to treat you." *Matthew 7:12a*

7. Depriving a person of a cure is sad, but depriving a person of life would be evil. God values every life.

"The thief comes only to steal and kill and destroy; I came that they may have life, and have it abundantly." *John 10:10*

"I call heaven and earth to witness against you today, that I have set before you life and death, the blessing and the curse. So choose life in order that you may live, you and your descendants." *Deuteronomy 30:19*

8. Killing an innocent person (even for a good cause like curing blindness) is still murder. The Bible calls murder a sin; and sin separates us from God.

"But your iniquities have made a separation between you and your God, and your sins have hid His face from you, so that He does not hear." *Isaiah 59:2*

9. When we submit fully to God as the author of life, He can give us the power and contentment to live with a less than ideal physical situation until we get to heaven where we receive new bodies that never wear out.

"Because of the surpassing greatness of the revelations, for this reason, to keep me from exalting myself, there was given me a thorn in the flesh, a messenger of Satan to torment me – to keep me from exalting myself! Concerning this I implored the Lord three times that it might leave me. And He has said to me, 'My grace is sufficient for you, for power is perfected in weakness.' Most gladly, therefore, I will rather boast about my weaknesses, so that the power of Christ may dwell in me. Therefore I am well content with weaknesses, with insults, with distresses, with persecutions, with difficulties, for Christ's sake; for when I am weak, then I am strong." *2 Corinthians 12:7-10*

"So also is the resurrection of the dead. It is sown a perishable body, it is raised an imperishable body; it is sown in dishonor, it is raised in glory; it is sown in weakness, it is raised in power; it is sown a natural body, it is raised a spiritual body. If there is a natural body, there is also a spiritual body." *1 Corinthians 15:42-44*

10. All of us are constantly aging and headed for the ultimate inevitability of death. In this life we all groan from the pains of our aging bodies. But God gives us hope that in the next life there will be no suffering.

"'He shall wipe away every tear from their eyes; and there shall no longer by any death; there shall no longer be any mourning, or crying, or pain; the first things have passed away.' And He who sits on the throne said, 'Behold, I am making all things new.'" *Revelation 21:4,5*

11. To understand God's love – for humans in the womb and out – remember that He loves us so much that Christ was willing to gives His life for us and be crucified on a cross. This is how He paid for our sins to reunite us with God.

"For God so loved the world, that He gave His only begotten Son, that whoever believes in Him shall not perish, but have everlasting life." *John 3:16*

"God demonstrates His own love for us in that while we were yet sinners Christ died for us." *Romans 5:8*

"The wages of sin is death, but the free gift of God is eternal life in Christ Jesus our Lord." *Romans 6:23*

Section Three

❧

Topical Scripture File

Christ Is The Only Way To God

"I am the door; if anyone enters through Me, he shall be saved, and shall go in and out, and find pasture. The thief comes only to steal, and kill, and destroy; I came that they might have life, and might have it abundantly." *John 10:9,10*

"Jesus said to him, 'I am the way, and the truth, and the life; no one comes to the Father, but through Me.'" *John 14:6*

"For there is salvation in no one else; for there is no other name under heaven that has been given among men, by which we must be saved." *Acts 4:12*

"For there is one God, and one mediator also between God and men, the man Christ Jesus, who gave Himself as a ransom for all." *1 Timothy 2:5,6a*

Confession And Forgiveness

"I acknowledged my sin to You, and my iniquity I did not hide; I said, 'I will confess my transgressions to the Lord'; and You forgave the guilt of my sin." *Psalm 32:5*

"Though your sins are as scarlet, they will be white as snow." *Isaiah 1:18*

"But He was pierced through for our transgressions, He was crushed for our iniquities; the chastening for our well-being fell upon Him, and by His scourging we are healed. All of us like sheep have gone astray, each of us has turned to his own way; but the Lord has caused the iniquity of us all to fall on Him." *Isaiah 53:5,6*

"If we say that we have no sin, we are deceiving ourselves, and the truth is not in us. If we confess our sins, He is faithful and righteous to forgive us our sins and to cleanse us from all unrighteousness. If we say that we have not sinned, we make Him a liar, and His word is not in us." *1 John 1:8-10*

"O God, it is You who knows my folly, and my wrongs are not hidden from You." *Psalm 69:5*

"For as high as the heavens are above the earth, so great is His lovingkindness toward those who fear Him. As far as the east is from the west, so far has He removed our transgressions from us." *Psalm 103:11,12*

"'They will not teach again, each man his neighbor and each man his brother, saying, 'Know the Lord,' for they will all know Me, from the least of them to the greatest of them,' declares the Lord, 'for I will forgive their iniquity, and their sin I will remember no more.'" *Jeremiah 31:34*

Deity Of Christ

"In the beginning was the Word, and the Word was with God, and the Word was God.... And the Word became flesh, and dwelt among us, and we beheld His glory, glory as of the only begotten from the Father, full of grace and truth.... For the law was given through Moses; grace and truth were realized through Jesus Christ." *John 1:1,14,17*

"For this cause the Jews were seeking all the more to kill Him, because not only was He breaking the Sabbath, but also was calling God His own Father, making Himself equal with God." *John 5:18*

"The Jews answered Him, 'For a good work we do not stone You, but for blasphemy; and because You, being a man, make Yourself out to be God.'" *John 10:33*

"And they came, bringing to Him a paralytic, carried by four men. Jesus seeing their faith said to the paralytic, 'My son, your sins are forgiven.' But there were some of the scribes sitting there and reasoning in their hearts, 'Why does this man speak that way? He is blaspheming; who can forgive sins but God alone?'" *Mark 2:3,5-7*

"For in Him all the fulness of Deity dwells in bodily form." *Colossians 2:9*

"For the grace of God has appeared, bringing salvation to all men, instructing us to deny ungodliness and worldly desires and to live sensibly, righteously and godly in the present age, looking for the blessed hope and the appearing of the glory of our great God and Savior, Christ Jesus; who gave Himself for us, that He might redeem us from every lawless deed and purify for Himself a people for His own possession, zealous for good deeds."
Titus 2:11-14 (Also see *Titus 1:1-5*)

"'I am the Alpha and the Omega,' says the Lord God, 'who is and who was and who is to come, the Almighty.' ...And when I saw Him, I fell at His feet as a dead man. And He laid His right hand upon me, saying, 'Do not be afraid; I am the first and the last, and the living One; and I was dead, and behold, I am alive forevermore, and I have the keys of death and of Hades.'" *Revelation 1:8,17,18*

"For a child will be born to us, a son will be given to us; and the government will rest on His shoulders. And His name will be called Wonderful Counselor, Mighty God, Eternal Father, Prince of Peace." *Isaiah 9:6*

False Messiahs And Teachers

"See to it that no one mislead you. For many will come in My name, saying, 'I am the Christ,' and will mislead many.... And many false prophets will arise, and will mislead many.... Then if any one says to you, 'Behold, here is the Christ,' or 'There He is,' do not believe him. For false Christs and false prophets will arise and will show great signs and wonders, so as to mislead, if possible, even the elect. Behold, I have told you in advance."
Matthew 24:4,5,11,23-25.

"Beware of the false prophets, who come to you in sheep's clothing, but inwardly are ravenous wolves. Not everyone who says to Me, 'Lord, Lord,' will enter the kingdom of heaven; but he who does the will of My Father, who is in heaven. Many will say to Me on that day, 'Lord, Lord did we not prophesy in Your name, and in Your name cast out demons, and in Your name perform many miracles?' And then I will declare to them, 'I never knew you; depart from Me, you who practice lawlessness.'" *Matthew 7:15,21-23*

"But even if we, or an angel from heaven, should preach to you a gospel contrary to what we have preached to you, he is to be accursed ! As we have said before, so I say again now, if any man is preaching to you a gospel contrary to what you received, he is to be accursed!" *Galatians 1:8,9*

God Is The Only God

"Who is like You among the gods, O Lord? Who is like You, majestic in holiness, awesome in praises, working wonders? *Exodus 15:11*

"Know therefore today, and take it to your heart, that the Lord, He is God in heaven above and on the earth below; there is no other." *Deuteronomy 4:39*

"Before Me there was no God formed, and there will be none after Me. I, even I, and the Lord; and there is no savior besides Me." *Isaiah 43:10,11*

"Is there any God besides Me, or is there any other Rock? I know of none." *Isaiah 44:8*

"Know that the Lord Himself is God; it is He who has made us, and not we ourselves; we are His people and the sheep of His pasture." *Psalm 100:3*

"Now to the King eternal, immortal, invisible, the only God, be honor and glory forever and ever. Amen."
1 Timothy 1:17

Inviting Christ Into Your Life

"But as many as received Him, to them He gave the right to become children of God, even to those who believe in His name." *John 1:12*

"For God so loved the world, that He gave His only begotten Son, that whoever believes in Him shall not perish, but have everlasting life. For God did not send the Son into the world to judge the world; but that the world should be saved through Him." *John 3:16,17*

"If you confess with your mouth Jesus as Lord, and believe in your heart that God raised Him from the dead, you will be saved." *Romans 10:9*

"Behold, I stand at the door and knock; if any one hears My voice and opens the door, I will come in to him, and will dine with him, and he with Me." *Revelation 3:20*

Judgment

"For we shall all stand before the judgment-seat of God... So then each one of us shall give account of himself to God." *Romans 14:10,12*

"But because of your stubbornness and unrepentant heart you are storing up wrath for yourself in the day of wrath and revelation of the righteous judgment of God, who will render to every man according to his deeds." *Romans 2:5,6*

"But when the Son of Man comes in His glory, and all the angels with Him, then He will sit on His glorious throne. All the nations will be gathered before Him; and He will separate them from one another, as the shepherd separates the sheep from the goats; and He will put the sheep on His right, and the goats on the left. Then the King will say to those on His right, 'Come, you who are blessed of My Father, inherit the kingdom prepared for you from the foundation of the world. For I was hungry, and you gave Me something to eat; I was thirsty, and you gave Me something to drink; I was a stranger, and you invited Me in; naked, and you clothed Me; I was sick, and you visited Me; I was in prison, and you came to Me.' Then the righteous will answer Him, 'Lord, when did we see You hungry, and feed You, or thirsty, and give You something to drink? And when did we see You a stranger, and invite You in, or naked, and clothe You? When did we see You sick, or in prison, and come to You?' The King will answer and say to them, 'Truly I say to you, to the extent that you did it to one of these brothers of Mine, even the least of them, you did it to Me.' Then He will also say to those on His left, 'Depart from Me, accursed ones, into the eternal fire which has been prepared for the devil and his angels; for I was hungry, and you gave Me nothing to eat; I was thirsty, and you gave Me nothing to drink; I was a stranger, and you did not invite Me in; naked, and you did not clothe Me; sick, and in prison, and you did not visit Me.' Then they themselves also will answer, 'Lord, when did we see You hungry, or thirsty, or a stranger, or naked, or sick, or in prison, and did not take care of You?' Then He will answer them, 'Truly I say to you, to the extent that you did not do it to one of the least of these, you did not do it to Me.' These will go away into eternal punishment, but the righteous into eternal life." *Matthew 25:31-46*

"Then I saw a great white throne and Him who sat upon it, from whose presence earth and heaven fled away, and no place was found for them. And I saw the dead, the great and the small, standing before the throne, and books were opened; and another book was opened, which is the book of life; and the dead were judged from the things which were written in the books, according to their deeds. And the sea gave up the dead which were in it, and death and Hades gave up the dead which were in them; and they were judged, every one of them according to their deeds. Then death and Hades were thrown into the lake of fire. This is the second death, the lake of fire. And if anyone's name was not found written in the book of life, he was thrown into the lake of fire." *Revelation 20:11-15*

"Not everyone who says to Me, 'Lord, Lord,' will enter the kingdom of heaven, but he who does the will of My Father who is in heaven will enter. Many will say to Me on that day, 'Lord, Lord, did we not prophesy in Your name, and in Your name cast out demons, and in Your name perform many miracles?' And then I will declare to them, 'I never knew you; Depart from you, you who practice lawlessness.'" *Matthew 7:21-23*

"For we know Him who said, 'Vengeance is Mine, I will repay.' And again, 'The Lord will judge His people.' It is a terrifying thing to fall into the hands of the living God." *Hebrews 10:30,31*

"It is appointed for men to die once, and after this comes judgment." *Hebrews 9:27*

Rapture, Second Coming

"For the Lord Himself will descend from heaven with a shout, with the voice of the archangel, and with the trumpet of God, and the dead in Christ shall rise first. Then we who are alive and remain shall be caught up together with them in the clouds to meet the Lord in the air, and thus we shall always be with the Lord."
1 Thessalonians 4:16,17

"Now we request you, brethren, with regard to the coming of our Lord Jesus Christ, and our gathering together to Him, that you may not be quickly shaken from your composure or be disturbed either by a spirit or a message or a letter as if from us, to the effect that the day of the Lord has come. Let no one in any way deceive you."
2 Thessalonians 2:1-3

"Beloved, now we are children of God, and it has not appeared as yet what we shall be. We know that, when He appears, we shall be like Him, because we shall see Him just as He is. And everyone who has this hope fixed on Him purifies Himself just as He is pure." *1 John 3:2,3*

"Behold, He is coming with the clouds, and every eye will see Him, even those who pierced Him; and all the tribes of the earth will mourn over Him." *Revelation 1:7*

"And after He had said these things, He was lifted up while they were looking on, and a cloud received Him out of their sight. And as they were gazing intently into the sky while He was going, behold, two men in white clothing stood beside them. They also said, 'Men of Galilee, why do you stand looking into the sky? This Jesus, who has been taken up from you into heaven, will come in just the same way as you have watched Him go into heaven.'"
Acts 1:9-11

Reincarnation

"Remember Him before the silver cord is broken and the golden bowl is crushed, the pitcher by the well is shattered and the wheel at the cistern is crushed; then the dust will return to the earth as it was, and the spirit will return to God who gave it." *Ecclesiastes 12:6,7*

"It is appointed for men to die once, and after this comes judgment." *Hebrews 9:27*

Resurrection

"See My hands and My feet, that it is I Myself; touch Me and see, for a spirit does not have flesh and bones as you see that I have. And they gave Him a piece of broiled fish; and He took it and ate it in their sight." *Luke 24:39,42,43*

"I am the good shepherd, and I know My own, and My own know Me... and I lay down My life for the sheep. No one has taken it away from Me, but I lay it down on My own initiative. I have authority to lay it down, and I have authority to take it up again. This commandment I received from My Father." *John 10:14,15,18*

"And I, if I be lifted up from the earth, will draw all men to Myself." *John 12:32*

"Jesus Christ our Lord was shown to be the Son of God when God powerfully raised him from the dead by means of the Holy Spirit." *Romans 1:4 (NLV)*

"For just as Jonah was three days and three nights in the belly of the sea monster, so will the Son of Man be three days and three nights in the heart of the earth." *Matthew 12:40*

"Christ died for our sins according to the Scriptures... He was buried... He was raised on the third day according to the Scriptures, and after that He appeared to Cephas, then to the twelve. After that He appeared to more than five hundred brethren at one time." *1 Corinthians 15:3-6*

"If Christ has not been raised, your faith is worthless; you are still in your sins." *1 Corinthians 15:17*

"Do not be afraid; I am the first and the last, and the living One; and I was dead, and behold, I am alive forever-more, and I have the keys of death and of Hades." *Revelation 1:17,18*

Salvation By Faith Alone

"Then they asked Him, 'What must we do to do the works God requires?' Jesus answered, 'The work of God is this: to believe in the One He has sent.'" *John 6:28,29*

"Of Him all the prophets bear witness that through His name every one who believes in Him has received forgiveness of sins." *Acts 10:43*

"'Sirs, what must I do to be saved?' And they said, 'Believe in the Lord Jesus, and you shall be saved.'" *Acts 16:30,31*

"For this reason it is by faith, that it might be in accordance with grace, in order that the promise may be certain to all the descendants." *Romans 4:16*

"For the wages of sin is death, but the free gift of God is eternal life in Christ Jesus our Lord." *Romans 6:23*

"If you confess with your mouth Jesus as Lord, and believe in your heart that God raised Him from the dead, you shall be saved." *Romans 10:9*

"For by grace you have been saved through faith; and that not from yourselves, it is the gift of God, not as a result of works, that no one should boast." *Ephesians 2:8,9*

"He saved us, not on the basis of deeds we have done in righteousness, but according to His mercy, by the washing of regeneration and renewing of the Holy Spirit, whom He poured out upon us richly through Jesus Christ our Savior." *Titus 3:5,6*

"These things I have written to you who believe in the name of the Son of God, in order that you may know that you have eternal life." *1 John 5:13*

Salvation Through Christ

"For the Son of Man (Jesus) did not come to be served, but to serve, and to give His life as a ransom for many." *Matthew 20:28*

"For the Son of Man has come to seek and save that which was lost." *Luke 19:10*

"But as many as received Him, to them He gave the right to become children of God, even to those who believe in His name." *John 1:12*

"John saw Jesus coming toward him and said, 'Look, the Lamb of God who takes away the sin of the world!'" *John1:29*

"For God so loved the world, that He gave His only begotten Son, that whoever believes in Him shall not perish, but have everlasting life. For God did not send the Son into the world to judge the world; but that the world should be saved through Him." *John 3:16,17*

"This is My commandment, that you love one another, just as I have loved you. Greater love has no one than this, that one lay down his life for his friends." *John 15:12,13*

"For the wages of sin is death, but the free gift of God is eternal life in Christ Jesus our Lord." *Romans 6:23*

"But God demonstrates His own love for us in that while we were yet sinners Christ died for us." *Romans 5:8*

"Therefore if any man is in Christ; he is a new creature; the old things passed away; behold, new things have come." *2 Corinthians 5:17*

"God was in Christ reconciling the world to Himself, not counting their trespasses against them." *2 Corinthians 5:19*

"He made Him who knew no sin to be sin on our behalf, that we might become the righteousness of God in Him." *2 Corinthians 5:21*

"But now in Christ Jesus you who formerly were far off have been brought near by the blood of Christ... for through Him we both have our access in one Spirit to the Father." *Ephesians 2:13,18*

"For Christ also died for sins once for all, the just for the unjust, in order that He might bring us to God, having been put to death in the flesh, but made alive in the spirit." *1 Peter 3:17*

"And we have beheld and bear witness that the Father has sent the Son to be the Savior of the world." *1 John 4:14*

"And the witness is this, that God has given us eternal life, and this life is in His Son. He who has the Son has the life; he who does not have the Son of God does not have the life." *1 John 5:11,12*

"And you know that He appeared in order to take away sins; and in Him there is no sin." *1 John 3:5*

"For we do not have a high priest who cannot sympathize with our weaknesses, but one who has been tempted in all things as we are, yet without sin." *Hebrews 4:15*

"...knowing that you were not redeemed with perishable things like silver or gold from your futile way of life inherited from your forefathers, but with precious blood, as of a lamb unblemished and spotless, the blood of Christ." *1 Peter 1:18,19*

"And they sang a new song, saying, 'Worthy are You to take the book and to break its seals; for You were slain, and purchased for God with Your blood men from every tribe and tongue and people and nation.'" *Revelation 5:9*

Satan

"How you have fallen from heaven, O star of the morning, son of the dawn! You have been cut down to the earth, you who have weakened the nations! But you said in your heart, 'I will ascend to heaven; I will raise my throne above the stars of God, and I will sit on the mount of assembly In the recesses of the north. I will ascend above the heights of the clouds; I will make myself like the Most High.' Nevertheless you will be thrust down to Sheol, to the recesses of the pit." *Isaiah 14:12-15*

"You had the seal of perfection, full of wisdom and perfect in beauty. You were in Eden, the garden of God; every precious stone was your covering: the ruby, the topaz and the diamond; the beryl, the onyx and the jasper; the lapis lazuli, the turquoise and the emerald; and the gold, the workmanship of your settings and sockets, was in you. On the day that you were created they were prepared. You were the anointed cherub who covers, and I placed you there. You were on the holy mountain of God; you walked in the midst of the stones of fire. You were blameless in your ways from the day you were created until unrighteousness was found in you." *Ezekiel 28:12b-15*

"You are of your father the devil, and you want to do the desires of your father. He was a murderer from the beginning, and does not stand in the truth, because there is no truth in him. Whenever he speaks a lie, he speaks from his own nature; for he is a liar, and the father of lies. But because I speak the truth, you do not believe Me." *John 8:44,45*

"The god of this world has blinded the minds of the unbelieving, that they might not see the light of the glory of Christ, who is the image of God." *2 Corinthians 4:4*

"For even Satan disguises himself as an angel of light. Therefore it is not surprising if his servants also disguise themselves as servants of righteousness." *2 Corinthians 11:14,15*

"Little Children, let no one deceive you; the one who practices righteousness is righteous, just as He is righteous; the one who practices sin is of the devil; for the devil has sinned from the beginning. The son of God appeared for this purpose, that He might destroy the works of the devil." *1 John 3:7,8*

"Then that lawless one will be revealed whom the Lord will slay with the breath of His mouth and bring to an end by the appearance of His coming; that is, the one whose coming is in accord with the activity of Satan, with all power and signs and false wonders, and with all the deception of wickedness for those who perish, because they did not receive the love of the truth so as to be saved." *2 Thessalonians 2:8-10*

"And the devil who deceived them was thrown into the lake of fire and brimstone, where the beast and the false prophet are also; and they will be tormented day and night forever and ever." *Revelation 20:10*

Seeking God

"If you seek Him, He will let you find Him; but if you forsake Him, He will reject you forever." *1 Chronicles 28:9*

"For the eyes of the Lord move to and fro throughout the earth that He may strongly support those whose heart is completely His." *2 Chronicles 16:9*

"The Lord has looked down from heaven upon the sons of men, to see if there are any who understand, who seek after God. They have all turned aside; together they have become corrupt; there is no one who does good, not even one." *Psalm 14:1-3*

"And you will seek Me and find Me, when you search for Me with all your heart." *Jeremiah 29:13*

"The God who made the world and all things in it… made from one, every nation of mankind to live on all the face of the earth… that they should seek God, if perhaps they might grope for Him and find Him, though He is not far from each one of us." *Acts 17:24,26,27*

"Draw near to God and He will draw near to you." *James 4:8*

"True worshipers shall worship the Father in spirit and truth; for such people the Father seeks to be His worshipers." *John 4:23*

Sin

"For all of us have become like one who is unclean, and all our righteous deeds are like a filthy garment; and all of us wither like a leaf, and our iniquities, like the wind, take us away." *Isaiah 64:6*

"But your iniquities have made a separation between you and your God, and your sins have hid His face from you, so that He does not hear." *Isaiah 59:2*

"For all have sinned and fall short of the glory of God." *Romans 3:23*

"The wages of sin is death, but the free gift of God is eternal life in Christ Jesus our Lord." *Romans 6:23*

"For whoever keeps the whole law and yet stumbles at one point shall be guilty of all." *James 2:10*

"For I know that nothing good dwells in me, that is, in my flesh; for the wishing is present in me, but the doing of the good is not." *Romans 7:18*

"The Lord has looked down from heaven upon the sons of men, to see if there are any who understand, who seek after God. They have all turned aside; together they have become corrupt; there is no one who does good, not even one." *Psalm 14:1-3*

"The heart is more deceitful than all else and is desperately sick; who can understand it? I, the Lord, search the heart, I test the mind, even to give to each man according to his ways, according to the results of his deeds." *Jeremiah 17:9,10*

"If we say that we have no sin, we are deceiving ourselves and the truth is not in us. If we confess our sins, He is faithful and righteous to forgive us our sins and to cleanse us from all unrighteousness. If we say that we have not sinned, we make Him a liar and His word is not in us." *1 John 1:8-10*

The Trinity

"Then God said, 'Let Us make man in Our image, according to Our likeness.'" *Genesis 1:26*

"Then I heard the voice of the Lord, saying, 'Whom shall I send, and who will go for Us?' Then I said, "Here am I. Send me!" *Isaiah 6:8*

"Go therefore and make disciples of all the nations, baptizing them in the name of the Father and the Son and the Holy Spirit." *Matthew 28:19*

"And after being baptized, Jesus went up immediately from the water; and behold, the heavens were opened, and He saw the Spirit of God descending as a dove, and coming upon Him; and behold, a voice out of the heavens, saying, 'This is My beloved Son, in whom I am well pleased.'" *Matthew 3:16,17*

"But Peter said, 'Ananias, why has Satan filled your heart to lie to the Holy Spirit and to keep back some of the price of the land? While it remained unsold, did it not remain your own? And after it was sold, was it not under your control? Why is it that you have conceived this deed in your heart? You have not lied to men but to God.'" *Acts 5:3,4*

"The grace of the Lord Jesus Christ, and the love of God, and the fellowship of the Holy Spirit, be with you all." *2 Corinthians 13:14*

"Then he showed me a river of the water of life, clear as crystal, coming from the throne of God and of the Lamb.... The Spirit and the bride say, 'Come.' And let the one who hears say, 'Come.' And let the one who is thirsty come; let the one who wishes take the water of life without cost" *Revelation 22:1,17*

Trustworthiness Of Scripture

"Heaven and earth will pass away, but My words will not pass away." *Matthew 24:35*

"All Scripture is inspired by God and profitable for teaching, for reproof, for correction, for training in righteousness; that the man of God may be adequate, equipped for every good work." *2 Timothy 3:16,17*

"For the word of God is living and active and sharper than any two-edged sword, and piercing as far as the division of soul and spirit, of both joints and marrow, and able to judge the thoughts and intentions of the heart." *Hebrews 4:12*

"If you abide in My word, then you are truly disciples of Mine; and you shall know the truth, and the truth shall make you free." *John 8:31,32*

"The secret things belong to the Lord, but the things revealed belong to us and to our sons forever, that we may observe all the words of this law." *Deuteronomy 29:29*

"For as the rain and snow come down from heaven, and do not return there without watering the earth, and making it bear and sprout, and furnishing seed to the sower and bread to the eater; so shall My word be which goes forth from My mouth; it shall not return to Me empty, without accomplishing what I desire, and without succeeding in the matter for which I sent it." *Isaiah 55:10,11*

"If any man is willing to do His will, he shall know of the teaching, whether it is of God, or whether I speak from Myself." *John 7:17*

"'For My hand made all these things, thus all these things came into being,' declares the Lord. 'But to this one I will look, to him who is humble and contrite of spirit, and who trembles at My word.'" *Isaiah 66:2*

"This book of the law shall not depart from your mouth, but you shall meditate on it day and night, so that you may be careful to do according to all that is written in it; for then you will make your way prosperous, and then you will have success." *Joshua 1:8*

"How blessed is the man who does not walk in the counsel of the wicked, nor stand in the path of sinners, nor sit in the seat of scoffers! But his delight is in the law of the Lord, and in His law he meditates day and night. He will be like a tree firmly planted by streams of water, which yields its fruit in its season and its leaf does not wither; and in whatever he does, he prospers." *Psalm 1:1-3*

CPSIA information can be obtained at www.ICGtesting.com
Printed in the USA
LVOW02s1622180913

353045LV00003B/282/P